kick-starter.com

The definitive European Internet start-up guide

edited by

Stephen Harpin

with expert participation:

Andersen Consulting
John Walter Thompson
Korn/Ferry and
Clifford Chance

MACMILLAN
Business

First published in Great Britain 2000 by
MACMILLAN PRESS LTD
Houndmills, Basingstoke, Hampshire RG21 6XS
and London
Companies and representatives throughout the world

A catalogue record for this book is available from the British Library.

ISBN 0–333–94582–4

 First published in the United States of America 2000 by
ST. MARTIN'S PRESS, INC.,
Scholarly and Reference Division,
175 Fifth Avenue, New York, N.Y. 10010

ISBN 0–333–94916–1

Library of Congress Cataloging-in-Publication Data is available

This book is printed on paper suitable for recycling and made from fully managed and sustained forest sources.

10 9 8 7 6 5 4 3 2 1
09 08 07 06 05 04 03 02 01 00

Editing and origination by
Aardvark Editorial, Mendham, Suffolk

Printed and bound in Great Britain by
Creative Print & Design (Wales), Ebbw Vale

CONTENTS

LIST OF FIGURES

List of Figures

ACKNOWLEDGEMENTS

This publication set out to collate the leading eCommerce experts' points of view from some of the world's leading firms active in the eCommerce industry. As a consequence, 15 authors have contributed from five different firms. I would like to thank them all for their efforts in pulling this publication together.

The authors would like to thank many people who provided point expertise and assistance. These include Josh Sokolof and Ben Burnsdall for their mCommerce expert input, Julian Day for his legal research, Alex McKie from @jwt for his eMarketing experience, and Siew Pheng Tan, Andrew Harkness and Paul Gerber who helped David Lane fulfil his promise. Paul Nunes would like to send special thanks to Jane Linder and Ajit Kambil of the AC Institute for Strategic Change for their insightful contributions on new business models and Ceri Carlill would like to thank Anne, Alexander and Oliver for their expert opinions.

My thanks go to Donna Gildea and Eamonn Toland from Andersen Consulting for their support in setting up the kick-starter.com web site and Michael J. Gannaway for his positive encouragement and entrepreneurial spirit. Stephen Rutt at the publishers and Linda Norris from Aardvark Editorial deserve special thanks for publishing the book in treble quick time.

This book is a collection of experiences, made possible by my colleagues at Andersen Consulting and my clients. Thanks to my friends David Russell, Simon Eaves and Adam Meredith-Jones for the many evenings and weekends we spent together developing our ideas, and Richard John and Stephen Carter who guided us with wise counsel and deep insight.

Finally, but most importantly, thanks to Nix for putting up with and without me.

Andersen Consulting is an $8.3 billion global management and technology consulting organisation whose mission is to help its clients create their future. The organisation works with clients from a wide range of industries to link their people, processes and technologies to their strategies. Andersen Consulting has approximately 70,000 people in 48 countries. In 1999, it was rated by IDC as the world's largest eCommerce consultancy. Andersen Consulting provides a full service to and has equity stakes in many Internet start ups. Andersen Consulting's authors include:

Stephen Harpin works within Andersen Consulting Strategic Services, specialising in eCommerce. He has worked with the boards of the world's leading companies and start-up entrepreneurs to set up European B2C and B2B Internet businesses and incubators. Most recently he also set up the UK Andersen Consulting Dot-com launch centre with specific responsibility for business development. Stephen spends much of his time speaking on corporate entrepreneurialism and coaching entrepreneurs. Prior to his consultancy career, Stephen progressed a brand management career in SmithKline Beecham and Procter & Gamble and was a seaman officer in the Royal Navy. He lives in Gloucestershire with his wife Nikki where they are restoring their Georgian pile. Email: Stephen@kick-starter.com

Paul Nunes is a research fellow in Andersen Consulting's Institute for Strategic Change, where his research has focused on the new and shifting roles of intermediaries in electronic channels, new IT-enabled business models and market mechanisms, and the particular challenges large organisations face in confronting electronic commerce. His frameworks have been used extensively in Andersen Consulting's strategy work, and have been recognised with two internal thought leadership awards. Paul is the author of numerous articles on eCommerce, which have been published in the *Harvard Business Review*, the *International Journal of Electronic*

Commerce, Computerworld, Andersen Consulting's client focused publication *Outlook,* and *Wired* magazine. He regularly presents at related industry conferences, and has guest lectured at the Harvard Business School. Paul holds an MBA from Northwestern's Kellogg Graduate School of Management.

Ceri Carlill is an associate partner with Andersen Consulting. He is based at the Andersen Consulting European technology headquarters in Sophia Antipolis, France, where he is a member of the emerging applications specialty team responsible for eCommerce activities. The group specialises in the planning, design and implementation of business solutions involving new and emerging technologies. Ceri has worked in Europe, North America and Australia on eCommerce developments for clients in industries including government, communications, financial services and retail.

David Lane is an associate partner in Andersen Consulting's eBusiness practice focused on the media and entertainment industry. David specialises in the development and launch of both pure dot.com and click-and-mortar.com businesses. His career spans both consulting and industry roles. While in the retail industry, David had experience running retail, rental and mail order fulfilment operations. Recently, David has been working on the development of a major pan-European enterprise for online order taking linked to physical and electronic fulfilment which is due to launch in late-2000. David has also pioneered several European initiatives to develop direct-to-consumer business models and pan-industry cooperation around shared eCommerce infrastructure.

Daniel J. Deganutti is an associate partner with Andersen Consulting. He is based at the Andersen Consulting European technology headquarters in Sophia Antipolis, France, where he leads the European security specialties team. This group specialises in the planning, design, and implementation of secure business solutions. Daniel has worked extensively throughout North America and Europe, focusing primarily on solutions for the financial services industry.

Paul Eijkemans works for Andersen Consulting in the Netherlands. He focuses on wireless technologies and mobile commerce. Before joining AC he managed his own eCommerce company and did various Internet projects in areas such as eFood, ticket-reservation systems and entertainment. In Southeast Asia he conducted research on the broadband network Singapore ONE and the use of information technology in the port of Singapore. In South America he did research on the position of Chile's national

IT and communications sector. In the past he contributed to several publications on information technology. Paul holds a master degree in information management/economics from Rotterdam University.

Rahul Bhandari is a member of the Andersen Consulting alliances and ventures team where he leads the selection of B2B eCommerce investment portfolio companies. Most recently he also set up the Andersen Consulting Dot-com launch centres with responsibility for business development and alliances. As a research fellow at the Institute for Strategic Change, an Andersen Consulting strategy think tank, Rahul developed frameworks to enable dot-coms to roll out across global boundaries. A sought after speaker, panelist, investor and executive coach for start-up ventures, Rahul serves on the board of Internet start-ups, organisations supporting entrepreneurship, and non-profit organisations. Rahul has a decade of senior executive and management experience in the telecommunications (INTELSAT), emerging technologies (Oracle Corporation), professional services (Dyncorp) and publishing industries (Thomson International). Rahul is a graduate of the Harvard, Stanford and Georgetown Business Schools. He has a BA in computer science and business from Northwestern College and holds five Oracle Master level certifications. He lives in San Francisco and Washington, DC. Email: rahul@webnokar.com

Eduardo Krumholz has been a leader in both the theoretical and applied fields of the technology arena for the last twelve years. Eduardo began his career as a professor for telecommunications and computer programming at the Universidad Anahuac in Mexico City. As a senior manager at Andersen Consulting, he assisted clients in the energy, utilities and telecommunications industries to create and implement technical capabilities including ERP, CRM, eCommerce applications, IP/data service offerings and system architectures. He has also worked closely with Andersen Ventures, a recently formed Andersen subsidiary that focuses on venture capital investment in the Internet technology arena and start-ups.

J. Walter Thompson is the world's leading communications agency employing almost 10,000 people in 248 offices across 89 countries. Working with a broad spectrum of clients they provide communication strategy and implementation to some of the world's most famous brands. They are in business to create enduring brands and their investment in knowledge and training ensures that the people they employ are the best in the business. Their client list includes a wide variety of eCommerce business, including start-ups. JWT authors include:

Kate Eden read English literature at Cambridge, before starting a career in marketing at the brand consultancy Interbrand (now Interbrand Newell and Sorrell). Here, she worked on a variety of projects, ranging from brand-name development and brand valuation to corporate identity and packaging design. Key clients included Lego, Glaxo, Ford and Bass. She later joined DMB&B as a planner, where she worked across a number of P&G accounts, including Always, Clearasil, and Crest, and also on the Chanel and House of Fraser accounts. Since joining JWT in 1996, Kate has worked on Kellogg's, Merrill Lynch, Rimmel, Boots, and Nestlé Rowntree. Kate enjoys playing the viola, singing, and going on long country walks, although rarely at the same time.

Marco Rimini left Oxford University with a degree in philosophy, politics and economics and embarked upon a career in advertising at Ted Bates, which he joined as an account planner. He later moved to Still Price before emerging, while still in his twenties, at Euro RSCG as the head of planning. During this time he worked for a variety of different clients, including Peugeot, Lloyds TSB, Daewoo, and MIM Britannia. In a bid to discover his roots, he spent a year in Milan and picked up an MBA along the way. On his return to London he decided to try his hand in the booming world of media planning and buying. He joined CIA Media Network, first as deputy MD, and then as vice chairman. Marco joined JWT in 1998 to become their first director of strategy and development. This means that Marco is responsible for organising and developing the knowledge areas of JWT (IT, planning, and information), and advising on the strategic development of both JWT and their clients. Marco's claim to fame is that he taught the playwright Patrick Marber how to play poker while at university. Should you be reading this, Patrick, Marco would like the money that you owe him as soon as possible.

Clifford Chance LLP is one of the largest law firms in the world with over 3,000 legal advisers. It is ranked joint number one IT and telecommunications law firm in the 1998 *Legal 500* and 1998 Chambers' surveys of law firms and in the German and French 1998 *Legal 500* survey. Clifford Chance can provide Internet start-ups with high quality legal advice. Clifford Chance authors include:

David Griffiths is a partner in the media, computer and communications group of international law firm Clifford Chance. His practice encompasses a broad range of eCommerce, information technology and online services industry work including data protection, encryption export regulation,

regulation of digital signatures and certification services, software and hardware distribution arrangements, development and licensing agreements and outsourcing. He speaks regularly at conferences on information technology issues. He was coordinating editor of *Law and Regulation in European Multimedia* (FT Telecoms & Media Publishing, 1994–1995) and is co-author of *Restraint of Trade and Business Secrets: Law and Practice* (3rd edn, FT Law & Tax 1996).

Kirsty Foy is an assistant in the media, computer and communications group of Clifford Chance and works on a broad range of eCommerce, information technology and online services industry matters. She is qualified as a solicitor in England and Wales and in British Columbia, Canada and, before joining Clifford Chance in 1997, worked for a multimedia software developer and a leading Canadian law firm.

Toby Hornett is an assistant in the media, computer and communications group of Clifford Chance. He has a Master of Arts degree (with honours) in French and Business Studies from Edinburgh University and qualified as a solicitor in August 1999. He carries out a broad range of commercial, eCommerce, information technology and media work.

Korn/Ferry International is the world's largest executive search firm and, with 1,650 search professionals based in 71 offices across 40 countries, has the broadest global presence in the executive search industry. Korn/Ferry's clients range from the world's largest and most prestigious public and private companies, middle-market and emerging growth companies such as Internet start-ups. A specialist team focusing on eCommerce and mCommerce combines Korn/Ferry's industry expertise with Internet-based experience across Europe, providing venture capitalists, incubators, entrepreneurs and bricks and mortar companies with leadership capital solutions for eSpace. The company's primary services – executive recruitment, advertised recruitment and Internet-based recruitment – are offered exclusively on a retained basis. In 1998, Korn/Ferry set up Futurestep.com through a strategic alliance between Korn/Ferry International and *The Wall Street Journal*. Futurestep combines the speed and reach of the Internet with Korn/Ferry's executive search expertise and proprietary candidate assessment software to fill positions for clients at the middle management, emerging leadership level. Korn/Ferry authors include:

Joyce Renney took the position of director of marketing at Korn/Ferry International in 1996 to head up the firm's marketing strategy in Europe and Asia/Pacific. Based in London, she also has specific responsibility for specialist client services, including Korn/Ferry's marketing strategy for eCommerce and mCommerce across Europe. Prior to joining Korn/Ferry, Joyce was head of international public relations at CNN, responsible for Europe, Middle East, Africa and South Asia. She previously worked in marketing and public relations for consumer goods, notably Krug and Rothschild wines, following a career in publishing, during which she was the youngest-ever commissioning editor at Euromoney Publications. Outside work, her passion is music - she combined her early career with performing as a pianist, after studying at the Guildhall School of Music. Joyce holds an MA in law and history from Trinity College, Cambridge University.

Metin Mitchell is managing vice president of Korn/Ferry's eBusiness practice in Europe, based in the firm's London office. He leads a pan-European team that serves clients across a range of industries to help them realise their eCommerce and mCommerce strategic objectives. In his eight years with Korn/Ferry, he has worked with leading financial institutions, as well as established organisations going on-line, start-ups and Internet-focused venture capital funds. His outside interests are centred on the life, history and culture of the French Pyrenees. Metin Mitchell has an under-graduate degree in French and history and a post-graduate degree in business studies from the London School of Economics.

And finally...

David Russell is an Internet entrepreneur and finance professional who has provided financial advice to Internet start-ups. He is currently a managing consultant with the information, communications and entertainment practice of PricewaterhouseCoopers and specialises in the telecommunications area. Previously he was head of finance for two GEC-Marconi subsidiaries. He is a qualified and prize-winning chartered accountant. Email: darussell10@hotmail.com

CHAPTER 1

Introduction: A Kick-starter

Stephen Harpin
ANDERSEN CONSULTING STRATEGIC SERVICES

'Actions speak louder than words'

The Internet is growing at eSpeed (fast!), driven by the wonderfully compelling customer and business value, an emerging supportive environment and a dramatically improving technological infrastructure. On the whole, European businesses have been slow to embrace the Internet opportunity but are waking up – fast. Those businesses that don't wake up will soon lose share and, more importantly, customers to US businesses, their competitors and a set of entrepreneurs that got ahead of the wave. That wave is always about to break, so European entrepreneurs must move very very quickly to capitalise on this opportunity before US firms arrive, or the local off-line players wake up. If you're an entrepreneur this book will help you kick-start your plans. Good luck!

Internet growth is at eSpeed

Suffice to say that Internet traffic is doubling every 100 days. Whereas it took only five years for 50m US users to be online, it took nearly three times as long to rack up 50m telephone users.[1] Every fundamental Internet growth curve is a hockey stick. It doesn't matter if we are talking about customers online, buying or conversion; the trend is the same. The Internet revolution is happening fast. The drivers of this exponential growth are fuelled by four mutually reinforcing factors (see Figure 1.1). If you understand these factors, you may find the way to get ahead of the game.

Compelling customer value

As obvious as it sounds, make sure your start-up is more compelling to customers than the competitors. Consider new business models that will

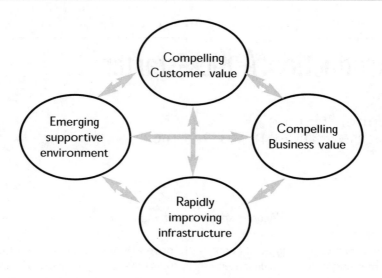

Figure 1.1   Factors driving the eCommerce revolution

make it more convenient, a richer shopping experience, sell at lower or tailored prices, tailor products to meet individuals' needs, integrate commerce with content, have a deeper or broader range and develop a motivated community. As sites become more compelling, customers will be driven online to realise these benefits. Don't carve out a small share of the market value – create new market value by doing something different. The opportunities are limited only by entrepreneurs' ability to deliver the unthinkable and undeliverable. What will really drive your customer value to new levels?

- *Convenience* For 'time poor' people the Web is a convenient means of shopping. This convenience can revolutionise the 10% of the world's population who are disabled. It is no wonder that they represent one of the most eEnabled groups. What do your customers find inconvenient? How will you help them find the Holy Grail?

- *Shopping experience* This can be so superior versus traditional direct retailing. Catalogues can not rotate or zoom in on the product (for example IPIX.com), you can't see the product in situ or in 3D (for example Goodhome.com), you can't try it on (for example Landsend.com) or see if it fits (for example the Nordstromshoes.com Fit Advisor) and a catalogue can't suggest which product you should be buying (for example Amazon.com). It is no wonder that the average German AOL customer uses the net approximately 50% more than they spend reading magazines. How is your shopping experience going to be competitive versus the on- and offline equivalents?

■ *Price* 80% of eCustomers who have made purchases online were motivated by low prices.[2] As the early European eCommerce retailers battle to acquire customers faster than each other, this is likely to continue for some time. The increasing availability of 'perfect' pricing information in market forums and the increase in shopping robot sophistication will drive prices lower. Aggregated purchasing models (for example letsbuyit.com) and auction sites (for example QXL.com) may increase downward pressure. The Internet is also enabling dramatic decreases in price as a new second hand market emerges (for example eBay.com). The Internet can drive sales of distressed and low-turnover inventory at higher prices than would normally be possible. In addition, a more granular understanding of individual customers will enable tailored pricing. What is your pricing policy? Is it tailored to the individual? Are discounts across the board or on specific products? Is your service so superior you can charge more?

■ *Tailored offerings* Visit Barbie.com to understand how products and services can be tailored to the individual. At this wonderful site you can design your own Barbie, give it a name and get it shipped to your daughter. Ask yourself who you will tailor offerings to give outstanding satisfaction and loyal site evangelists – the true goal (see Figure 1.2)?

■ *Integrated offerings* Many successful sites will integrate both content and commerce. Magazines are bought for content, but have consistently failed to integrate any selling. So when you see the perfect room in your home magazine, you can't recreate it, because you don't know where you can buy all the products – until now. Visit Goodhome.com for a good example of how the two can be integrated. Which off-line magazines are there that are similar to your business idea? How important is

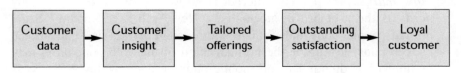

Figure 1.2   Building customer loyalty

content? Where will you get it? How can you merchandise your selling within the content?

■ *Breadth and depth of product offering* Be more competitive than bricks and mortar retailers. They are constrained in their range by the need to have high sales densities in stores. As Internet retailers are unencumbered by stores, you can have a broader and deeper offering. Wal-Mart has six times as many products for sale on its Internet site than in its stores. Although you should bear in mind that you will only achieve buying scale on best selling items, and your business model shouldn't be so complex that you can't roll it out into other European countries. If your product range is so broad that it involves lots of suppliers, you may start sacrificing customer service in your early growth years.

■ *Interactive communities* FirstTuesday.com, TheChemistry.com and e-start.com are rich communities for eEntrepreneurs. iVillage.com and Women.com female communities are some of the most visited on the Web. These communities represent the stickiest sites on the Web where customers continually return to their 'friends' for advice and interaction. Elements of community range from bulletin boards to chat rooms, expert advisors online to offline events, and greenhouses to share business plans to email clubs. How important is a community in your site? What will you do to create one?

Customer value is driving people online

Customers are adopting the Internet at an unprecedented rate driving the Internet to mass market status and opening dramatic opportunities for entrepreneurs to meet granular customer segment needs. Some businesses have chosen to wait for their customers to move online in bigger numbers so they can realise profits faster. Don't wait or you will be beaten to the opportunities. Laggards will struggle to make any profits at all, and they will be top of the 70% of start-ups that are forecast to wither away in the inevitable industry shake out.

■ *Mass market medium* The Internet is no longer the preserve of techy nerds as the user profile normalises. New Web users in the US are normal people, split male/female with average wages and educational backgrounds. In Europe the normalisation of the Web population may be quicker as digital TV and mobile phone usage enables Web access for all. It is reasonable to assume that like the telephone, radio and tele-

vision nobody will want to be without it. Before I receive complaints –
I aspire to techy nerd status and the wealth they have generated for all.

- *Opportunities to meet granular customer segment needs* It used to be
  tough to have a beekeeping shop that could afford to offer advice and
  hold an inventory of beekeeping products because the population of
  keepers is so small and dispersed. After all, there are only 450,000
  beekeepers across the whole of Europe. The Internet has enabled entrepreneurs to access small segments of customers with the required scale
  to make some money. 'The beekeeping ring' is not one site, but a
  network of sites enabling people to meet their specific beekeeping
  needs. They can buy and sell products, chat, diagnose diseases and even
  buy a few more bees. How granular will your customer segments be?
  Will their needs be met within one site or a network of sites?

Compelling business value

The Internet has the potential to revolutionise European businesses. Like
all revolutions most won't change, but it is clear that participation is no
longer an option. At some point in time all firms will join in, or be downrated by the financial institutions, although the speed with which that will
happen depends on the nature of the business. An entrepreneur that can get
ahead of these firms is a likely purchase as they try to catch up before they
are downrated. If you are setting up a business venture, where is the value?
How much is there? How much will go online? Will you be number one or
two? You may find compelling business value in:

- *Increasing sales and profit* Amazon.com 1999 revenues of $1.6bn are
  still increasing at 300% per year (fuelled by a cash rich business model
  with inventory turns over five times faster than bricks and mortar
  competitors). This growth will fuel forecast profit within 2000. Dell is
  generating in excess of $18.5bn sales in 2000, growing at 40% per
  year with net income of $1.3bn with an eEnabled supply chain.
  Internet retailing can and will be a very profitable business for the
  market leaders. Goldman Sachs judge that Internet businesses will
  have a long term incremental pre-tax profit advantage over bricks and
  mortar stores of 1% point. Judge your long-term success by your
  ability to deliver sustainable profits and shareholder value. The two are
  inextricably linked, even if the markets are being patient in their desire
  to make the association.

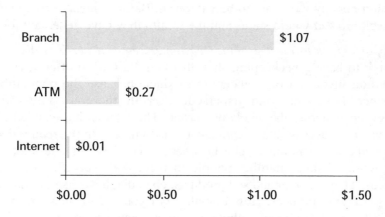

Figure 1.3   Banking transactional costs
Source: Andersen Consulting Analysis

■ *Decreasing transaction costs* The magnitude of improvement is high (see Figure 1.3). Consider the decrease in transactional costs available in the banking industry where a single Internet transaction can cost as little as one cent. The UK Internet bank egg.co.uk reports costs per Internet customer to be a quarter of a telephone customer and a tenth of those who shop through a branch network. Lower cost transactions are only significant when you have enough scale to get above the fixed costs of setting up the business. Barclays, the UK bricks and mortar bank, expects little saving until 10% of its customer base is online. This reduction in transactional and customer costs has the potential to enable first movers to find superior competitive advantage. How will your business decrease transactional costs? How big do you need to be to realise competitive advantage? How will you use this advantage?

■ *Decreasing procurement costs* Forrester and IDC corporation are forecasting that business-to-business (B2B) transactions will be 9% of business sales in 2003, growing at a compound annual growth rate of nearly 92–99%. This may seem pessimistic when British Telecommunications estimate that the Internet will reduce the average procurement cost from £50 to £5.[3] Hardly surprising then that Cisco is using the Internet to introduce internal catalogues, where individuals can buy direct from suppliers at the corporate rate. These purchases are routed electronically for approval and out to the supplier. As catalogue content management is standardised and the benefits are clarified with proven examples, eProcurements will increase in importance. The end point in this development is the fully integrated supply chain throughout the industry. How will your business procure from suppliers? Can it afford to implement leading edge Commerce One and Ariba systems at launch? When is the right time to introduce these systems?

- *More efficient markets* Visit market makers like e-steel.com, buildonline.co.uk and Chemdex.com. These sites bring together buyers and sellers into their site and enable the two to trade cost effectively . In return they take a small percentage of the transaction. If you are looking for big ideas, find a fragmented and relationship-based market and set one of these up. The opportunity is as huge as the market. Can your business idea fit into a market-making role?

- *More visible value* In the old world, those who relied on imperfect information to make money may lose out to those who provide more perfect information. These people fit into two camps. The first was the buyer's 'agent' who, like the insurance broker, helped people navigate through the information to find the best deal for them. The offline buyer's agent will lose out to the online buyer's agent that enables the customer to navigate through the information themselves. The second is the business which relied on imperfect information to boost profits. There was probably always a better deal for the customer, but they weren't likely to find it. With the emergence of shopping robots (for example Valuemad.co.uk, mysimon.com, askjeeves.com) customers are more likely to find that deal. How will your business deliver visible value?

- *Helping store-based retailers survive* Retailing is a high fixed-cost business where small changes in volume sold can have a serious impact on the profit. Andersen Consulting research indicates that 12% of electrical goods will be sold online by 2003, forcing a few electrical store closures. However, 88% of people prefer to shop in stores. Stores own the customer masses today and in the foreseeable future. In fact, stores can use the Internet to dramatically add value to their customers. Gap has introduced Web seats in its stores to enable an increase in product range and breadth. Computer retailers are considering removing in-store inventory by linking up networks to shell computers. Complex sales can be better handled by introducing Customer Assisted Selling Processes, where the assistant is prompted by a computer to help detail all the information required by the customer. Sophisticated customer relationship management (CRM) processes can be introduced across channels with Siebel type systems. The store has a rosy future *because of* the Internet. How will your business use stores?

Rapidly improving infrastructure

Technology is improving dramatically. It is becoming faster and cheaper. Exciting new applications are emerging and in particular there are some pockets of excellence available within Europe that could be a kick-start to entrepreneurs.

The price-performance of enabling technologies is doubling every 18 months. 28.8 kbps modems will be replaced by larger modems, ISDN lines ADSL/IXL technology or cable modems. European telecommunications deregulation has driven down the cost of transmitting voice and from ten times US prices in 1995 to three times in 1998, and recent events are increasing this trend. In parallel with this, new more advanced technology is emerging. Essential transaction enablers such as smart cards, transaction servers and encryption technology are but a few.

There are some pockets of excellence within Europe; it is behind the game, but it has some strategic assets that entrepreneurs may be able to exploit to create wealth. Ask yourself how you can utilise the following assets:

- *Minitel:* Minitel accounted for twice the amount of eCommerce traffic within Europe until 1997. Prior to 1997 the French eCommerce market was bigger than the US market. What is so exciting is that it proves that customers will go online when there are cheap access, secure transactions, attractive offers and ease of use. Minitel is now outdated technology that will migrate to the Internet.

- *Mobile telephony:* The convergence of mobile phones and computing devices offers eCommerce on the move. Specifically, digital phones equipped with smart cards can provide a gateway to the Internet and portals provided by entrepreneurs and phone companies alike. Phones operating on the Global System for Mobile Communication (GSM) standard can be used in every European country making this a potential killer application. Read Chapter 7 to understand the opportunities for your business.

- *Digital TV:* Europe has the potential to take the lead in digital television for eCommercial purposes. Digital TV can broadcast electronic information from the Internet to an individual's TV set. Providing the set or set top box is connected to a phone line, orders and other information can easily be sent back to service providers. As European ownership of home computers is significantly lower than US levels, there is a greater opportunity to develop digital TV. Anecdotal UK evidence suggests that product sales through digital TV have exceeded retailers' expectations.

■ *Smart cards:* Europe leads the world in the production and use of smart-cards. Smartcards facilitate the development of eCommerce, and the wider eEconomy, providing tools for identification and security, which are themselves areas of European technical leadership. Smartcards are already in widespread use in Europe for purchase of items such as electricity, telephone calls, car parking space and as loyalty cards.

■ *Language telephony:* Europe has a lead in voice recognition and translation software. These applications could radically ramp up the potential for European eCommerce. Future biometric voice identification is not only easier than pin codes and passwords but also more secure. Voice recognition removes a further barrier to European adoption of mobile eCommerce, since it is removes the need for a keyboard. Automatic translation will increase the scale economies of European businesses.

Emerging supportive environment

European funding groups are moving fast to fund the best ideas, driven by the extraordinary market capitalisation of Internet/eCommerce new entrants. The money is out there, for the right teams and ideas. Governments seem to be moving in the right direction, even if this is a little slower than eSpeed.

Money is becoming increasingly available

US Internet-related investments increased nearly six-fold from $3.4bn in 1998 to $19.9bn in 1999, accounting for 56% of total investments. Average funding, at $11.1m, was double that of 1998. Compare this to all European technology investments which accounted for only 28% of the total European investments in 1998. This figure has grown by 75% since 1997, and is ramping up big time. Encouragingly, the amount of capital committed to European early-stage (seed and start-up) deals more than doubled in 1998. European figures are ramping up dramatically – there is money around for the right ideas and teams. Check out the European Venture Capital Association (EVCA.com) Web site to see if the year 2000 figures are out yet. Bear in mind – there is a load of dumb money for dumb ideas but most plans still don't get funded!

Entrepreneurial environments are emerging, but have a way to go

A new entrepreneurial environment is developing across Europe, driven by the Internet phenomena. It started within the entrepreneurial/Internet clubs and has swept out into the consultancies and on into business. Europe has a long way to go to catch up with the US entrepreneurial spirit where rewards are greater for the winners and the losers aren't horsewhipped:

- *Rewards need to be greater for the winners:* If you are a young European millionaire you will be deeply admired by those who aspire but you won't reach the hero status given to the US winners. If you are French, your stock options will be taxed at 80%. If it is social acceptance or money that drives you, the rewards are greater in the US than in Europe. This is changing fast and shouldn't frighten you into inactivity. If you fail in eCommerce your entrepreneurial and functional skills will be in great demand. If you have the emotional resilience – go for it!

- *Losers should not be horsewhipped:* At a recent dinner of eCommerce gurus, the US millionaire suggested that filing for bankruptcy was an effective 'financial planning tool'. The UK millionaire advised that bankruptcy was a social stigma that could threaten your ability to get another job. Indeed, it is impossible to drive a London taxi as a bankrupt. You may want to weigh this up – for a nano-second or two. Entrepreneurs tend not to plan for failure but it is important to manage your downside. In the current skills shortage, people who have failed in their eEndeavours will be warmly welcomed into the very best firms. Those firms who don't want to employ 'those who tried' are so arrogant and shortsighted that they will probably end up having their own downside to manage.

- *Enlightened governments will see further than the end of their noses:* Governments have a duty to improve the delivery of their citizen services, make operations more efficient, boost competitiveness and create wealth. eCommerce does all of these elements and more. All governments have the power to unleash entrepreneurs from the shackles their predecessors have imposed. But don't wait for government action – get on with your plans and get round the hurdles. Despite my soap box moaning, everything seems to be moving in the right direction. If you do speak to your elected representative, you may want to mention:

- *Put government money where the growth is:* Many European governments have a rather peculiar tendency to invest in subsidising loss-making industries, rather than investing in the growth areas. Frustrating, but tough! Use your vote and get on with it.

- *Best people deliver jobs for local people:* Mobility of labour from outside the EU is positively discouraged in some European countries. A German company can't hire a non-EU national without proving it can't find a German or other EU citizen qualified for the job. Specialists from some countries, such as China or India, often can't get work permits at all. It is legal for a German company to transfer a foreign manager to Germany if it already employs him abroad, but such transfers require a work permit which labour officials may refuse to issue. This is incredibly shortsighted when there aren't enough people with technology skills locally and the best people will often come from the US, Russia, China and India. Entrepreneurs can't staff ideas with 100% green beans and they haven't the time or money to start training people in the start-up days. If entrepreneurs lose, so do economies, so do local people.

- *Low-cost access – fast:* Many of the giant telephone monopolies in Europe are being dismantled too slowly, with former state-run companies in Germany, France and Italy still using their traditional ties to governments to block competitors or any further deregulation. Recently, UK Chancellor of the Exchequer, Gordon Brown has brought pressure to bear on the telecom companies and the industry regulator, Oftel, to introduce competition faster, bringing about big cuts in prices. This may soon be replicated across Europe.

European businesses have been slow to embrace the Internet opportunity, but are waking up

Wake up Europe and smell the American coffee! The US has an undisputed lead in eCommerce and is coming here fast (see Figure 1.4). European businesses have had the opportunity to see such phenomenal US growth but many have failed to act fast enough to seize it themselves. Learn from this. The intellectual satisfaction of having an idea first is exceptionally shallow when you read of the bold and brave who did it first, even if they failed.

There is a damaging misconception that this lack of action can be traced solely to an inferior European infrastructure or a lack of customers online and buying. Sadly, the single greatest difference between US and UK Internet businesses is the lack of quality transactional sites. It is a supply side issue more than a demand side issue. Those that wait for more customers online or increased computing power before they develop their business will see the supply side issue solved by the US competition or entrepreneurial start-ups. Ironically, for most managers or entrepreneurs, setting up a transactional site is the only factor they can influence.

There are some strong indications that Europe is smelling the coffee. An Andersen Consulting survey has tracked the changing attitudes of European businessmen. Based on interviews with European business managers, the study, eEurope Takes Off, shows bricks and mortar firms beginning to 'get the e-thing'– a worrying trend for the entrepreneur trying to beat them to the action. Although many see tremendous ePotential, not all are eImplementing:

- In 1999 almost two-thirds of respondents (64%) saw an eCommerce offering as a real competitive advantage in their marketplace today, compared to 51% in 1998, with those expressing a strong belief rising from 23% to 33%.

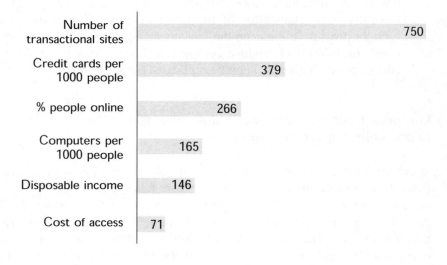

Figure 1.4   Europe versus the US
(US statistics indexed on EU = 100)

Source: Andersen Consulting analysis

An increased number of Europeans agreed strongly that they have plans for future use of eCommerce – up to 44% from 31% in 1998.

However, nearly two-thirds have not even started to apply eCommerce to procurement, logistics, finance, and product development functions.

The message is clear – if the bricks and mortar firm is your competition of the future, you have a race on your hands. Take heart from the venture capitalist principle that they 'invest in people that are doing, not people that are going to do'. So do. If you are fast enough, these firms could be looking for your skills and may provide a suitable partner.

Established European business will lose share and customers to US sites if they do not act

European firms that don't grasp the opportunity will lose sales and customers to US Internet businesses entering Europe. A Boston Consulting Group report found that a fifth of the Western European online retailing market was dominated by US businesses. In today's market, sales losses may be small as the total eCommerce sales are a small percentage of most markets. However, a small percentage decline in sales numbers can have a dramatic effect on the profitability of businesses with high fixed costs. Failing to react to the market shifts now will store problems up for later.

Losing customers is the greater issue. Procter and Gamble used to argue that it cost six times as much to win a lapsed customer back than to have kept them in the first place. In the Internet-enabled world, it may cost significantly more. This reflects the increasing returns to scale that will enable the best sites to scale fast and lock in the best customers.

This dynamic is the function of three key virtuous circles (see Figure 1.5):

Community size drives community value: As the e-start.com Internet entrepreneurial community grows, the value that entrepreneurs realise will increase dramatically. Visit e-Start, tour their site and imagine the virtuous circle of community growth – value growth – that would occur throughout their site. As the 'ask an expert' section answers entrepreneurs' questions the richness of the archive will drive more visits and questions. As the human resource centre successfully places people in jobs, more of the hunters and hunted will be drawn. As the offline courses and conferences result in higher attendance, there will be more events and more segmented events, driving greater and greater value.

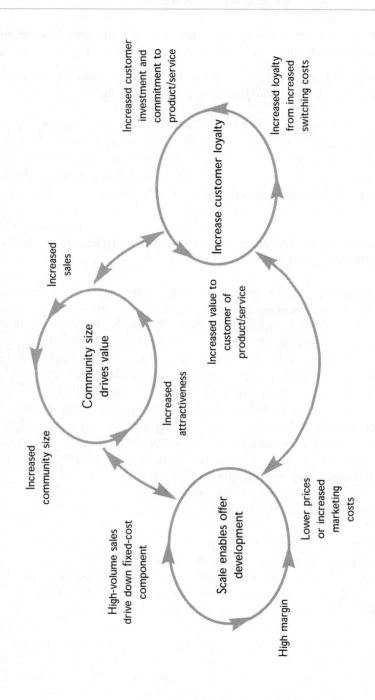

Figure 1.5 Three observable drivers of increasing scale and profitability

Source: Adapted from 'Increasing returns and the new world of business', W. Brian Arthur, *Harvard Business Review*, January, 1996

▪ *Scale enables incremental offer development:* Visit geocities.yahoo.com and you can set up a Web site for free, but to set up a European scalable Internet-based business that can dominate its market could cost well in excess of €50m. Much of the technology, staffing and marketing costs will be fixed. As a major Web business's sales increase, the fixed cost component per unit sold will decrease. This incremental margin can then be reinvested in lower prices or incremental marketing to drive sales further and beat your competition. This emphasises the need to scale fast.

Boston Consulting Group estimate that 93% of European retailers who have set up Internet businesses have restricted them to their home country. This is an enormous lost opportunity in a business environment where you can scale a business across major European countries within six months. If you are an entrepreneur you need to build scale fast to compete with domestic businesses. The fastest way is probably across geography.

▪ *Customer loyalty can be increased as the Internet enables tailored experiences:* The best sites have the capability to learn about their customers. As they do, they will tailor the shopping experience which may increase the level of satisfaction and consequently customer loyalty. Customer learning will be pieced together from many different sources. Most sites will attach cookies to visitors to understand how often they visit. As customers surf through Web sites, their route 'down the spine' will be tracked. They may be asked a 'quick quiz' question to detail their beliefs. On some sites customers will happily register to gain access to a restricted area or to buy a product, detailing their personal information. Leading sites will collate this information to rapidly improve the customer shopping experience next time they visit. BroadVision.com, BlueMartini.com, and other one-to-one technologies will enable business to recommend products that 'people like you like'. Sites can tailor the merchandising of their products to the individual customer. Many portals (for example my.yahoo.com) will let the customer tailor the site to better meet their needs. They can then reduce repetitive tasks such as form filling, by recording your details (for example amazon.com, 1-click purchasing). All of these applications are designed to collate customer knowledge and use it to increase customer satisfaction. This satisfaction will rapidly build loyalty and the cost to the customer if they choose to move to the competitor who has little information available. This can be summarised in the rather insightful 'the more you give (whether you know it or not) the more you get' model (see Figure 1.6).

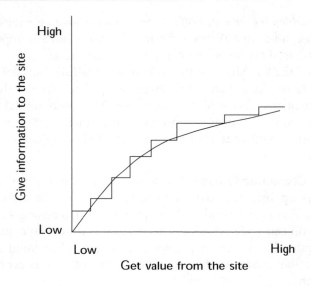

Figure 1.6   The 'give and get' model

European entrepreneurs must move quickly to capitalise on this opportunity

The market valuations of Internet business are very heavily weighted towards the big brands within any particular market. The big three investment questions any entrepreneur should use to test their plans are all related to scale:

Q1:   How big is the market?
Q2:   What percentage is likely to go online?
Q3:   Will the business plan make you one of the top few players?

If a business is in the top few brands in its market, then it is more likely to be locked into a virtuous circle of scale and profitability. It also follows that businesses are much more likely to dominate their markets quicker if they are first to arrive. Consequently, executional speed is one of the defining strategies for success. Business methodologies with logical phases of design–plan–build–prototype–test–roll out are being rapidly replaced with short sprints of do–learn–do more–learn more. Speed will define the winners and the losers:

■ *Lock in customers with speed:* First to market has the opportunity to lock in customers sooner than the competition. With customers come scale and profitability. With the prospect of these elements comes financial help to start the business. As a start-up it may be difficult to raise the funding for the expensive one-to-one technology required to truly build loyalty, but this merely emphasises the speed required to prove the customer appeal of the concept and expand the offer. There is a fine balance to be struck between speed and customer service. A fast uncompetitive offer will lock your potential customers out quicker. When IPC, a UK magazine publisher, launched BEME.com, a late entry into the intensely competitive UK female portal market, they did it with a blaze of publicity including a high profile sponsorship of the Ally McBeal TV programme. The launch directed people to a graphically advanced site under development with very little authoritative content, no active community and a promise of 'commerce soon'.

■ *Affordable brand building is fast brand building:* The later a business is launched, the more it will cost to establish a brand with appropriate values. The first mover can freely advertise, taking 100% share of voice within its market and build considerable and broad appeal for its services. The second mover, spending a similar amount will only have 50% share of voice and will be communicating a differentiated and potentially more niche position. Compounding this situation is the dramatic growth of dot.com advertising. The AOL European dot-com commercial in 1998 was a novelty that aroused interest in the whole 'Internet thing'. Those days are going fast. For a bit of perspective, on a recent trip to the US I found that $7/8$ths of all TV advertising was dot.com related; there was advertising on the airport runway and on 38 billboards between the airport and my hotel, one mile away. This is an expensive place to be noticed; soon Europe may be the same.

■ *Fast firms can tie up the strategic assets:* A strategic asset may include customers, relationships with content providers, suppliers of product and the rights to differentiated technology. If start-ups can acquire them early and limit the ability of latecomers to replicate their business models, then they will increase their chances of success. When a UK Internet start-up exchanges equity with Freeserve, the UK's leading portal, it is acquiring an exclusive right to a prime position that will help them acquire their 1.5m online customers. If may be difficult for any late entrant to acquire such important assets and beat the start-up to the number one local position, and subsequent European roll out, an initial public offering and category domination.

- *Early to market, early to exit:* Investors prefer to invest in the first movers because they are more likely to be successful. Consequently the exit strategy will have greater clarity. The most common European exit strategies for investors are likely to include a trade purchase, perhaps by a local offline laggard wanting to speed up its progress, a US business expanding across Europe or an Initial Public Offering. All of these exit strategies are more likely to be available to the early mover who will be well positioned by the time the option arrives.

- *Speed breeds enthusiasm, slow movers breed doubt:* As entrepreneurs start to set up their businesses, they need to demonstrate speed and delivery. Every deal will take longer than expected and all potential partners will have ample time to watch the business plans progress. Venture capitalists often like to watch the entrepreneur develop plans to see if they have the capability to close deals. If potential partners see speed, they will develop a fear of being left behind, and great confidence in the entrepreneur's ability to make everything happen. Conversely, if they realise that they have the ability to slow the development of the business with protracted negotiations and don't see other activity being closed, they may walk away. This may include the entrepreneur's team who will seek the next great opportunity that may happen. This is not uncommon in Silicon Valley where the average employee moves job every 2 years.

If you are an entrepreneur this book may help you kick-start your plans

The Internet has sparked a latent entrepreneurial spirit in the hearts and souls of European entrepreneurs in bricks and mortar firms and garage start-ups alike. As a 'dot.com consultant', I have been privileged enough to work with these entrepreneurs. I have helped them generate their ideas, qualify them, write business plans, raise money and bring them to market. I have found start-up entrepreneurs to be a wonderfully eclectic bunch of individuals with a very few, but very important, set of common traits. They all believe passionately in their vision *and* have the ability to drive the vision to the market. They have the ability to learn from their many, many mistakes and buckets of emotional resilience to keep picking themselves up and drive their plans on… and on… and on…

   If you plan to be one of these entrepreneurs, you may feel insecure without the depth and breadth of knowledge to get through every step and over every hurdle by yourself. If you are just starting to formulate your embryonic ideas and craft plans to deliver them, you are probably looking for advice and sounding boards. Almost certainly, you will have found it tough to get a holistic view of your plans, especially when you don't have the money to recruit a team or to pay consultancy fees. It is imperative to get the best advice early in your thinking to differentiate your business plan and increase your chances of success. Atlas Venture is a well respected Internet venture capitalist. Their London office alone will get over 9,000 business plans a year to review. In their last $400m fund they invested in only 26 European companies over 11 months. If your business plan is flawed in any way, you won't get to see the venture capitalist. If you haven't thought through all the issues, you may find that nobody will be willing to fund the plans. I have found no holistic source of early advice for you. There is a gap in the market waiting to be filled.

This book hopes to fill that gap. It has brought together some of the finest Internet industry experts to help you develop more credible ideas and write more effective plans. Individually, these experts have some of the deepest knowledge of this fast-moving market available. Collectively, they hope to offer you a holistic kick-start to your entrepreneurial endeavours.

If you are an entrepreneur with a vision, move fast to deliver it. You are the difference between success and failure. When a venture capitalist funds your business, they are betting on you. Your employees and partners will always look to you for leadership, now and for years to come. Being founder is very special, everyone will know that, only you will feel it. No book will ever change this, but let me know if it helped you get there.

This is a living book. If you want to write a chapter for the next edition, share some comments or to work for or with Andersen Consulting, email me: Stephen@Kick-starter.com.

Notes

1. Morgan Stanley, *The Internet Advertising Report,* 1998
2. Low cost online creates rapid-response pricing mandate, *Jupiter report,* July 1998
3. *Financial Times,* Monday 21 February 2000

CHAPTER 2

Creating a Unique Internet Business

Paul Nunes
ANDERSEN CONSULTING INSTITUTE FOR STRATEGIC CHANGE

In 1849, someone who wasn't looking for gold found it near Sutters Mill, in California. It was easy to find – in fact, he tripped over a big nugget. The hopeful hordes who poured into California from the East expected it would be almost that easy for them too. Equipped with simple tools, and no knowledge of mining or geology, they planned to scoop gold nuggets out of the streams or lift gold dust by the spadeful from the soft and giving California landscape. Some very smart people went broke in the gold rush. Mark Twain was one of them. He wrote a hilarious book about his experiences as a '49er.

It's a pity Mark Twain wasn't alive to see the Internet. On the other hand, the straight facts of Internet business designs are sometimes so hilarious it's hard to imagine what a comic genius could add to them. Anyone who doubts that the Internet business is a sort of contemporary gold rush need only take a look at the following example of a business plan for a children's learning site called InteliChild that appeared in January 2000[1]:

> Our business model is based on the sale of our products over the site. Because the site is also intended to create brand equity and awareness, we are building for high traffic. Our model requires giving users an excellent free experience and to develop trust to increase sell-through. We plan to lose money for the first three years while we build traffic and develop our position for the long term.

The best that can be said for this plan is that it's no worse than a lot of others. Spurred by stories of apparently effortless success, the hordes are converging on cyberspace as they once converged on California: equipped with simple tools, little knowledge, and high hopes.

This chapter aims to change that, first by dashing the high hopes.

Contrary to popular misconception, the Internet is an extraordinarily tough place to do business. It's very hard to make money in eCommerce. Even the stock market is beginning to mark down the shares of Internet stocks in the light of new data about the behaviour of online customers that seems to prove that the money raised on Initial Public Offerings is all the money that many Internet business ideas will ever produce.

Yet while it is hard to make money in eBusiness, it is also impossible for businesses to ignore the Internet. By changing the menu of choices available to customers (whether business or consumer sector), the Internet is changing the way all business must work. For many managers, the question is not whether they should be in eBusiness but rather how they can best adapt their business for survival in a new regime that the Internet brought to their industry while they were busy with other things.

Every business, online or off, must be an Internet business these days, to the extent that it must factor the Internet's presence into every business plan. Building a successful Internet business means building a business that can survive and prosper in the age of the Internet.

This chapter will help readers to do that.

It begins with a discussion on how the Internet has changed the menu of choices available to customers, and provides real examples of businesses that found new ways to use the Internet to create value for their customers. Then it analyses their successes in terms of four distinct channel strategies, each requiring different organisational and resource commitments.

Once the basics of customer value creation and channel strategy are clear, we move on to the design of Internet business models. New research and fresh data have debunked some of the truisms of the Internet, and any business model that ignores these findings will probably fail – so the chapter of course includes them.

Creating value

Value creation begins with understanding the customer and what the customer wants. There are five basic areas (see Figure 2.1) in which innovators can add value for customers.[2]

1. *Buying:* Buying includes a whole set of activities or relationships. Buyers must first define their needs, assess various suppliers, and place-orders. Afterward, they must pay for and take delivery of the product orservice bought. Customers take risks and spend both time and money in the process of buying.

2. *Using:* Having bought the product or service, customers must use it. Using also requires some expenditure of time and/or money. For example, it may be necessary to read manuals or take specialised training, or purchase additional hardware. Therefore use involves risk, the risk that the investment of time and money will not produce the benefits the customer expects.

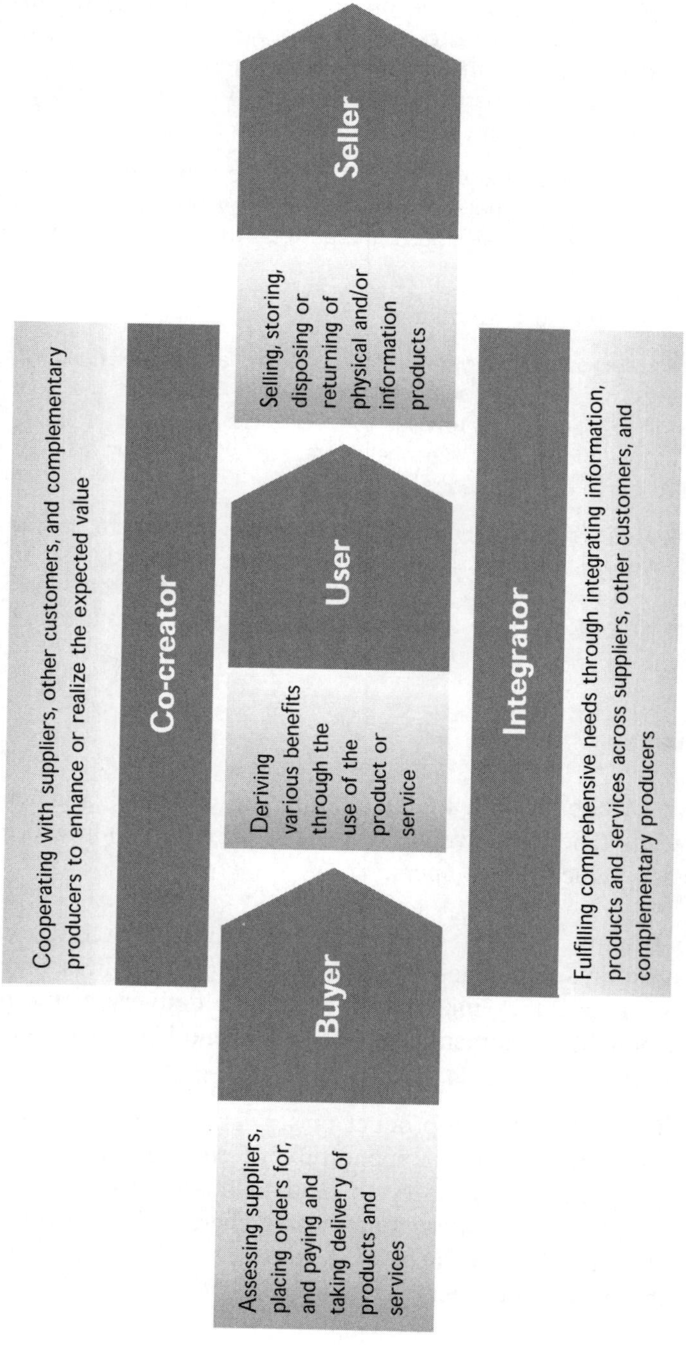

Figure 2.1 Customer interactions

Buyer

Assessing suppliers, placing orders for, and paying and taking delivery of products and services

Co-creator

Cooperating with suppliers, other customers, and complementary producers to enhance or realize the expected value

User

Deriving various benefits through the use of the product or service

Seller

Selling, storing, disposing or returning of physical and/or information products

Integrator

Fulfilling comprehensive needs through integrating information, products and services across suppliers, other customers, and complementary producers

3. *Selling/transferring:* Customers may buy in order to resell or for their own use. Information and know-how can be stored, transferred to others, or resold. Physical products may be used up, discarded, or recycled.

4. *Co-creating:* Customers cooperate to create or enhance the product or service.

5. *Integrating:* Customers combine information, products and services from various suppliers and even other customers in order to fulfill a range of needs.

Buying and using

Until the Internet came along, most companies focused on two core customer needs: buying and using. The Internet has made it possible to do a much better job of helping customers to buy and use products. Dell, for example, combined standardised components with direct sales, phone-based and online ordering and product support, to set a new standard in its industry. Dell does 30% of its business on the Web. Its 'Premier Pages' offer customised, account-specific information to streamline the buying process for corporate customers.

Toyota has also used the Internet to make buying more comfortable, convenient and customised. Toyota's customers will soon be able to shop for a car online by specifying the car they are interested in and receiving in return a listing of all matching vehicles in stock at dealers nationwide. Toyota customers will be able to buy in several ways. Those who are completely comfortable with online business will have the opportunity to complete their vehicle purchase via the Internet. Others may choose what part of the buying process they want to do via online access and what part they still prefer to use a dealer for.

eToys.com, Drugstore.com and Priceline.com have all tapped the power of the Internet to offer consumers more or better buying opportunities. Hewlett Packard puts EXPRESS terminals in convenience stores to sell printer cartridges and other supplies. Barpoint.com allows mobile users to type or scan product barcodes into a handheld device and get in return comparison prices from online sources, contact information, and links to purchase the item from eCommerce vendors.

In the B2B sector, Altra Energy built a large and successful electronic energy trading platform. General Electric established a trading post network for intra-company purchases from external suppliers. Chemdex built a virtual warehouse for the global life-science market. Each of these companies redefined 'buying' in its industry. Boeing sells two-thirds of its spare parts online (a $3bn business).

But buying is just the beginning. eCommerce provides powerful tools to improve the way customers use products and services. Online updates of software and customer service support are common examples. 3Com, for instance, provides a self-service database of technical information to enable customers to diagnose problems or upgrade their data networks, while Double Click, an Internet advertising business, enhances the use of their services by compiling case studies and posting thoughts on successful Web marketing and advertising strategies.

In the travel industry, Biztravel.com plans meetings, tracks frequent-flier award points and miles, and offers an online travel magazine full of travel tips and entertaining stories. Biztravel.com upgrades its site every six weeks with new, first-class applications and programs that make it hard for members not to use the service. Among the recent offerings are: 'BizA-lert' sends messages of gate information, updates on delays or cancellations to members' pagers; 'CalendarDirect' downloads travel itineraries to members' Palm Pilots or other calendar programs.

The home improvement vendor Home Depot creates value for users of its Web site by giving step-by-step instructions for over a hundred home improvement projects – and recommends the tools required to complete them.

Although many success stories came out of the effort to improve how customers buy and use products, competitors are converging on that end of the customer-value spectrum. It is important, therefore, to find new ways to create value. Some early entrants have shown how value can be added by helping customers sell/transfer, co-create, and integrate.

Selling/transferring

There is an old joke about the sign in the window of a small shop: 'We buy junk, sell antiques.' What has the Internet done to that store? After posting positive earnings for three years – quite a claim to distinction among Internet businesses – online-auctioneer eBay.com achieved a market capitalisation of more than $19bn by the spring of 2000.

Thousands of similar sites had sprung up on the Internet, selling everything from used sports equipment to farm equipment. Neoforma.com extended the concept to the resale of medical equipment and almost everything else related to healthcare. Auctioning of such devices as CAT scanners and X-ray machines changes not only the used equipment market but also the outlook for new product sales in this industry. For a fee, Neoforma will also handle liquidations, even to the point of selling off an entire hospital full of equipment.

Returnexchange.com has found its niche in helping companies to recover residual value from returned products. By offering its business customers a channel through which they can resell returned merchandise, it hopes to become the king of used goods recovery. That is potentially quite a lucrative kingdom – Forrester Research predicts US companies will have to deal with $11bn in returns by 2002.

The popularity of online resale sites has incidentally created entirely new business opportunities. Consider iEscrow, a company that makes money by reducing customer risk in these resale markets. Buyers send funds to iEscrow, which then instructs the seller to send the goods to the buyer. Once the buyer approves the merchandise, iEscrow releases the funds to the seller.

Co-creating

The Internet not only makes it possible for customers to find what they want – it even lets customers create what they want. Fiat tested new design concepts with more than 3,000 customers online. The effort generated ideas that Fiat used to improve its product line. Numerous loyal users and programmers created and continually refined the Linux operating system, thereby enabling companies like Red Hat Software to derive commercial benefits. The Zagat Survey, now online, is a popular restaurant guide whose business model consists simply of scoring restaurants according to reviews by Zagat's own customers.

Online communities are another example of the customers co-creating the value. Dobedo has captured over 200,000 dedicated teenage followers by sending the them the first chapter of Dobedo's story and encouraging them to continue the story online. Because the teenagers create the content themselves, it always remains current.

Meanwhile, other businesses enable customers to co-create individually. Getty Images' Art.com lets customers match posters or prints with mats and frames of their choice. iPrint, an online self-service print shop, claims to have achieved a 25–50% saving on printing costs for consumers, by allowing them to design and order their own products. Seven Cycles, a small, premium priced, custom-build bicycle manufacturer, enables its wired and quality-conscious customers to select materials and recommend design configurations.

Integrating

Integrating customer value creation culminates in weaving together a variety of products, services, and information to build an 'Intentions Value Network'. For example, Microsoft's HomeAdvisor integrates content and services from American Finance & Investment, Principle Residential, RE/Max, SchoolMatch, and RentNet to offer customers who intend to move to a new community everything they need. Essential.com offers one-stop shopping for all the essential services needed to run a home or business. Planet Rx, a Web site for health and well-being, SkyMall, a provider of one-stop access to Web travel sources, and Garden.com, a vendor of high-quality garden supplies and advice, all subscribe to a similar, integrating model.

We have now addressed the five key interactions through which businesses create value for customers: buying, using, transferring/selling, co-creating and integrating. A focus on these interactions is the first step to creating a differentiated, value-creating Internet business. An examination of any industry will reveal imperfections in how customers are served during each interaction. These imperfections are business opportunities. Capitalising on these opportunities, however, requires a thorough understanding of how the Internet is changing channels to the customer.

Reinventing channels[3]

Electronic commerce is creating new intermediaries and making the dominant channels of the past obsolete. From the medieval guilds to the New York Stock Exchange, the survival and prosperity of intermediaries has depended on control of information. In an era where the Internet has made information all but uncontrollable, creative destruction is inevitable.

For example, the old-fashioned travel agent prospered because he or she had information that customers could not easily find themselves. But travellers no longer need an agent to find cheap airline tickets and vacation packages or to book trips. They can get this information easily, online, from such vendors as Travelocity, Preview Travel, and Microsoft's Expedia. And the service that costs a travel agent $40, on average, costs electronic commerce less than a dollar, on average. The I-Way also lets car buyers take a detour around traditional auto dealerships. Pete Ellis, CEO of Auto-by-Tel, is a former auto dealer whose network of 16 dealerships was forced into bankruptcy in 1994. Sweet revenge – Auto-by-Tel is one of the pioneers of the new online auto distribution channel, along with Microsoft's CarPoint, AutoWeb.com and OneSwoop.com.

These services pre-empt the prime time sales show put on by old-fashioned dealers – the time during which sales people sized up customers and decided (among other things) just how much margin they could be talked into paying and how many pricey extras could be loaded into the deal before the bewildered customer drove that lemon off the lot. Customers don't have to sit still for the old high-pressure job anymore. Now, the online services let them evaluate and price cars in the privacy of their homes. The services do refer customers to dealers – but only to handle the final paperwork and take delivery of the car. The selling is all but over by then.

These online auto sites helped an estimated four million people in the US select and buy a car last year.[4] That translates to a market share of 25% of all cars sold there. Incidentally, they aren't satisfied with just selling cars. They have also branched out into insurance and servicing support, creating powerful new intermediaries that cross the range of automobile related offerings.

Similar things are happening in the business to business sector. Most chemical companies were caught flat-footed as the Internet disrupted channel relationships that had been in place for over 80 years. Such new electronic channels as Chemdex, ChemConnect, Polymerland, and Chem-Match have reduced the buyer costs associated with procurement by 5–10%, realised purchase prices by 20–30%, and even significantly reduced the cost of delivery. Electronic markets not only cut costs, they also make supply and demand more transparent, allowing suppliers to manage inventories more efficiently. But this increased transparency comes at a cost of control, as the new online markets shift information and power from the supplier to the customer.

The old channel logic

The traditional channel roles of the wholesaler/distributor and retailer were typically organised on the following assumptions:

- Shopping convenience requires a physical retail outlet or sales agent as close to the customer as possible
- Shopping variety is best created by bringing diverse products and services physically together at retail outlets (note the emergence and success of category killers such as Toys R Us)

- Waiting times from purchase to use are best reduced by local stock-piling of goods (for example the creation of retail store inventory)
- Customer service and promotion information are best provided by a local sales or service force
- Manufacturers cannot efficiently provide small lot sizes desired by customers.

Given these assumptions, and the (then) high cost of direct communications between the supplier and the customer, the wholesaler/distributor and retailer channels did add value. Wholesalers/distributors and retailers created tremendous efficiencies by breaking bulk in each stage of the distribution channel and leveraging different scale and scope efficiencies.

For example, wholesalers and retailers realised economies of scope from aggregating and servicing multiple products, creating efficiencies and benefits both for upstream suppliers and for downstream customers. They also realised economies of scale and scope in storage and distribution, thereby creating channel value.

But that was then.

The new channel logic

Two major trends have made the old channel logic obsolete. The first is the trend to greater product customisation. The second is the trend to cheaper, faster means of communication and transportation.

The trend towards customisation means that traditional channels hinder rather than help the customer. There are in general two ways to customise a product. The first is to produce a standard product, then take it apart, then customise it, then put it back together again. The second way is to build the custom features into the product from the very start. The second way is generally cheaper and more efficient than the first. But it requires direct communication between producer and consumers. Traditional wholesalers and retailers just get in the way.

Meanwhile, cheaper communication and transportation makes it economical for customers and producers to talk directly with each other. Toll-free phone numbers, 24/7 call centres, overnight delivery services like UPS, Fed-Ex, DHL, and of course the Internet have made the need for local inventory stockpiles very questionable. Table 2.1 illustrates how assumptions about the provision of value to the customer are being transformed.

Table 2.1   The transformation of assumptions about
the provisions of value to the customer

Buyer values	Old channel logic	The new channel opportunity
Convenience of access	Locate close to the customer	Provide 24/7 access anywhere, anytime through the Internet
Varied product assortment	Large retail stores (category killers)	eCategory killers – with hyperlinks to varied offers and infinitely configurable shelf space
Short wait times	Provide retail outlets and up-stream warehouses with sufficient inventory stockpiles to fulfill customer needs	Trade-off speed for cost and efforts ■ Use quick shipment through third-party logistics ■ Use electronic networks to deliver digital products instantaneously ■ Leverage better forecasting and improved supply chains to deliver quickly to customers from central-ised warehouses
Product knowledge	Have sales people provide most product knowledge to users	Have customers pull relevant inform-ation, or push product knowledge to customers online
Product size/ replenishment	Limited variety	Provide product in the size and quantity desired by the customer through continuous replenishment

Source: Andersen Consulting 1999

As information-processing costs fall, the trends toward product customi-sation and cheaper communications are driving value from intermediaries who focus on managing the flow of goods toward 'infomediaries' who manage the flow of information.[5]

The emerging channel model

But what exactly do these new infomediaries look like?

Our research suggests the emergence of a new channel model built around six distinct intermediary roles: buyer agent, seller agent, market maker, context provider, payment enabler, and fulfilment enabler. We expect channel infomediaries to increasingly specialise in these roles, with each category creating its own distinctive value in the channel, and each role characterised by its own revenue model. See Figure 2.2 for example.

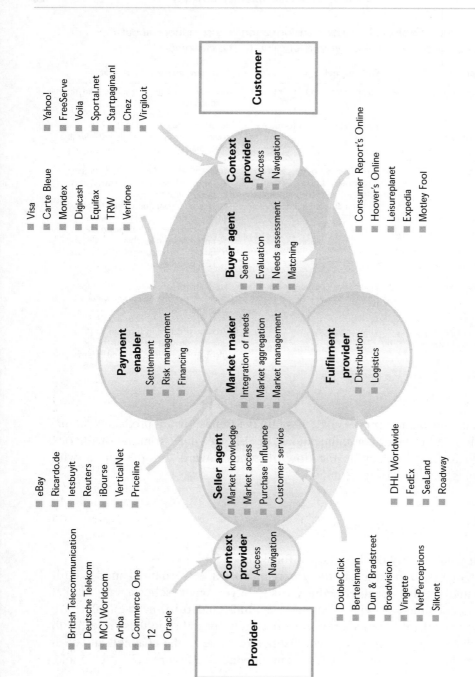

Figure 2.2   eCommerce-enabled electronic channel system model

Let's examine these roles and consider the conditions under which specialised 'infomediaries' prosper.

Buyer agents

Buyer agents create value in four important ways: they help customers assess their needs; they identify suitable offers to fulfil needs; they compare and evaluate offers; and they match a particular offering with the customer in an attempt to get the 'best deal' for the customer. In sum, these activities create greater convenience and better choices for buyers in the purchase process.

Previously, many buyer-agency roles were undertaken by the customer or seller. Electronic commerce is increasing the value of independent buyer agents by expanding access to buyers and sellers, and by making the role economically viable. Buyer agents create value by reducing the search effort for a product that will meet the customer's needs at an attractive price. The value of buyer agency grows with the number and complexity of available choices.

Thus intelligent software agents, or 'bots', create value by searching for product information and bargains and by checking inventories to determine which products are available. Users enter descriptions of items they want to buy and let the bot do the shopping. Bots reduce the selection and delay risks for the customer, and save time. Examples include Jango on Excite Shopping, Junglee on Yahoo! Shopping, mySimon, Comparenet, and Bidder's Edge.

In the automobile industry discussion above, we mentioned Auto-by-Tel, CarPoint, and OneSwoop. These sites provide detailed information on cars, and help consumers to comparison shop (an activity anathema to traditional dealers) and they help lower costs by engaging dealers in a bidding war for the customer's business. These services all add considerable value for online customers.

Of course, while the buyer agents help customers to shop, they also gather information about the customers themselves. Some do this directly, through online surveys (see www.epinion.com and www.bizrate.com); others indirectly, by observing buying behaviour, mining the data, and making inferences about preferences. The higher the volume of transactions and the number of participants, the easier it is for companies like Amazon.com to make useful recommendations to customers (the 'collaborative filtering' technology is more likely to surface real similarities in preferences across participants).

LetsBuyIt.com is a new firm that takes buyer agency even further to help customers get the best deal. Through its concept of 'co-buying,' it allows consumers to pool their purchasing power and negotiate with suppliers from a position of relative strength. Such services shift power from the supplier to the consumer. Incidentally, most of the early online buyer agents have had an advertising-based revenue model. But, as the buyer-agency business moves more in the direction of aggregating buyer power and negotiating prices, we expect the revenue model will include a brokerage fee. Moreover, it seems that online consumers are often indifferent about saving money,[6] so we expect buyer agents to focus mainly on supporting the purchase of high-value and high-involvement goods.

Seller agents

The greatest opportunity yet to be fully exploited online may lie in the area of providing value to sellers. Seller agents focus on helping producers present themselves to customers and to the marketplace. They do this by helping producers gain knowledge of and access to the market, influencing customer purchasing and providing customer service.

The need for specialised seller agency is growing for two reasons. First, lower transaction costs drive producers to concentrate on design and production, and to outsource online sales and service. Second, the Internet has introduced new customers and new marketplaces to every industry. So seller agents can rapidly achieve scale by serving large numbers of producers, and increase their offering levels in an area that now requires specialised skills.

Doubleclick, one of the most successful Internet seller agents, identifies likely viewers of online advertisements and targets messages to those viewers as they browse. ADSmart, another seller agent, designs online promotions and delivers the technologies customers need to manage the buying and selling of Internet advertising. In the pharmaceuticals industry, Professional Detailing leverages the power of the Internet to represent drug companies that wish to outsource their dedicated sales force. Maintaining this capability in-house is difficult for all but the largest pharmaceutical companies. Professional Detailing employs over 900 sales representatives who are shared by its clients, including six of the top ten pharmaceutical companies.

Similarly, INSWeb has created the online equivalent of the independent sales agent in the insurance industry by creating a site the informs users of the offerings of many insurance companies. Such online seller agents allow their clients to focus on the core competencies of developing winning products to fulfil customer needs, rather than the vagaries of eBusiness.

Success for new seller agents relies on a number of important factors, including: (1) unique customer knowledge or relationships, otherwise unavailable to the seller, which can support sales (DoubleClick, for example, has detailed data on Web-user behaviours and online demographics), and (2) enough knowledge of the producer's product and business to effectively represent them.

Adding value to the sales process requires doing more for the producer than the producer can do alone. Although the Internet has reduced barriers to entry, economies of scale and preferential access to market makers are still important to sellers, and to the success of seller agents.

Market makers

A third intermediary role is that of market maker. Net-enabled market makers have arisen in almost every industry segment, including electronics components, financial markets, seafood, utilities, telecommunications bandwidth, airline tickets, and even flea markets. Some have been wildly successful. OnSale grew from $140,000 to $89m in sales in its first three years of business and now sells over $200m annually. The market capitalisation of eBay, at $20bn, is more than double that of leading US bricks and mortar retailer Federated Stores, owner of well-known chains like Bloomingdale's and Macy's.

There are two kinds of market maker: vertical market makers that focus on selling to a particular industry, and horizontal market makers that focus on a particular function or product type across industries. Stock market investors seem to think that both approaches can be rewarding; they've put high multiples on Internet market makers in both categories. Vertical market makers include eSteel, Chemdex, PaperExchange.com, and VerticalNet.com. Horizontal market makers include Ariba in procurement, CommerceOne in maintenance, repair and operation (MRO) and Adauction in media buying.

These market makers use a variety of market-clearing mechanisms: English auctions, reverse auctions, Dutch auctions, real-time trading, electronic Requests For Quotations (RFQs), and more. Some innovate by introducing previously understood mechanisms into new markets. For example, iBeauty gives its online customers the ability to receive shipments of their favourite cosmetics and fragrances on a customer-defined schedule, introducing continuous replenishment to the online health and beauty market.

Some market makers offer 'all in one' markets that use several market mechanisms to satisfy a range of customer needs. Egghead.com is one of the few retailers to shift successfully from bricks and mortar to online selling. Its 'Shop Three Times Smarter' program combines online super-stores with auctions and liquidation selling to offer three ways to shop. Similarly, Amazon.com offers customers the alternative of buying from the company store or bidding in an online auction.

Multi-mechanism, all-in-one markets can help a business capture or keep customers who cross traditional market segments, for example consumers who buy airline tickets both for business and for leisure travel, or business customers who at one time need the original product and at another time the replacement parts.[7]

Success for new market makers depends on:

- Liquidity – failure to quickly achieve a critical mass of users leads to market failure

- The ability to create greater value for buyers, sellers, and intermediaries. Most market makers add value by allowing these market participants to determine a market clearing price through an auction instead of through direct negotiations

- The ability to create all-in-one markets that combine multiple transactions on the same platform.

Context providers

Context providers create value for customers by simplifying access, providing information, and creating online spaces where customers can gather, interact, and conduct commerce. Many of the portals, such as Yahoo, America Online, and MSN, create Internet malls that fill many of the needs served by physical malls – except, of course, that of allowing early morning exercisers a place to power walk.

Disney established its Go network in December 1998 as a portal for the delivery of content from Disney's media channels: ABC News, ESPN, Family.com, and Mr. Showbiz. At its launch it became the fourth most-visited portal on the Web. Like owners of physical malls, the context providers depend on the volume of traffic to their sites. They often earn revenues from the rental of choice 'marketspace' and from advertising – both of which are dependent on consumer attention and interest.

Payment enablers

Forty years ago, even before mainframe computers, payment-support
activities moved to speciality providers through the introduction of credit
cards. Companies like American Express and bank consortia like Visa and
Mastercard made payment and financial risk management an independently branded activity that today spans almost every industry and every
geographic location. Later, these organisations and fledgling independents
began to offer corporate procurement cards.

The Internet has created new possibilities. Most ventures in the online
payment field have focused on four technology sets for conducting transactions over the Internet: credit cards, digital cash, sales aggregation, and
smart cards. Traditional players dominate the online credit card business,
but digital cash has seen a number of determined – albeit struggling – new
entrants, including CyberCash, First Virtual, and DigiCash.

Qpass, Intercoin, and Clickshare have entered the aggregator space;
they make it possible for many online charges to show up as a single
charge on the customer's credit card.

The fourth technology set, 'smart cards', allows users to cross between
the virtual and physical worlds by loading cash balances onto chips
imbedded in what looks like a credit card. Mondex has been a leader in
this technology, which has been tested in the United Kingdom, but
consumer acceptance has been slow.

As electronic commerce continues to grow, the payment specialists
must rapidly grow their network memberships to drive efficient scale, or
risk being overrun by larger players. This market will probably support
only a few vendors. The big winner will be able to manage online bill
presentation and payment, an area of cross-channel value destined to
belong to the first mover to capture commanding market share.

Fulfilment providers

Fulfilment involves both distribution (the transfer and storage of goods)
and the management of information. FedEx, UPS, Roadway, Ryder,
SeaLand, CSX and the Postal Services are among the leading providers of
fulfilment services. The Internet has reduced costs and made it possible for
these companies to offer more options. For example, online technology
has helped Ryder and CSX, and their customers, to achieve flexible scale
through less-than-load shipping, that is the ability to ship in increments
that are smaller than a full truck, train car or container ship. Consequently,

between 1991 and 1995 the proportion of Fortune 500 manufacturing companies making use of third-party logistics increased from 37% to 60%. Sales at FedEx have grown from $5.17bn in 1989 to $13.25bn in 1998, a compound average growth rate (CAGR) of 11.03%.

Yet even these market leaders in fulfilment must continue to innovate to prevent new entrants from poaching customers. For example, Pandesic, a joint venture of Intel and SAP, offers a turnkey electronic commerce package that covers all the activities between the storefront and invoicing, including inventory management, warehousing, shipping, and returns. Pandesic and similar fourth-party logistics (4PL) services offer complete logistics outsourcing to clients through a single interface. Two detailed studies, one for a petrochemical company and another for a pharmaceutical firm, found cost savings of 26% and 39% from the use of these services.

Channel strategy as Internet strategy

Beyond choosing a role in the new channel system, companies must still identify how they will compete and on what resources and capabilities, that is, they must formulate a strategy. Our research suggests that companies may choose from a set of four distinct strategic options when they make the transition from traditional to Internet channels. They may compete, control, combine, or coordinate (see Figure 2.3).

Compete

In this strategy, companies choose to compete in a particular intermediary role. For example, PriceScan has concentrated on delivering objective price information across online and offline markets. Leveraging its core competence at gathering and disseminating pricing information, PriceScan has diversified its services across multiple industries. Another example is Priceline, a new specialist in the market making role that is leveraging its patent on a reverse-auction like process to compete in market making across airline tickets, automobiles, loans and even groceries.

Payment enablers such as Amex, Visa, and Mastercard, and fulfilment providers such as FedEx, UPS, and the Postal Service also compete through specialisation. It is important to note that each specialist competitor must cling to its core competence and forsake all others. Growth comes not from offering many services but from offering the core service in many industries and sectors, as PriceScan and Priceline have

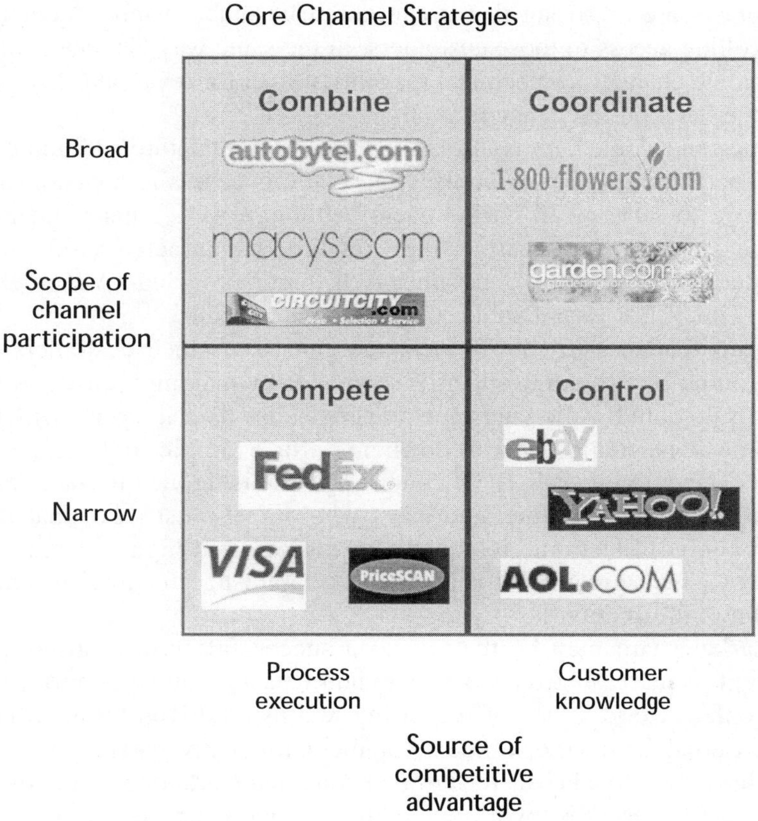

Core Channel Strategies

Figure 2.3   Internet channel strategies

done, and from continuous improvement in processes and technology that help leaders maintain market share.

Control

Instead of offering a core competence in many industries, some infomediaries attempt to control the flow of resources in a single industry by focusing on the role that provides the greatest amount of leverage over relationships in the channel – what might be called the linchpin role.

For example, eBay dominates in customer-to-customer commerce not because its technology is unique but because its relationships with customers are so strong that it can dominate other channel members by controlling access to those customers. In the same way Chemdex controls the online channel for chemical reagents, eSteel for rebar and sheet metal, and the Seafood Exchange for fish.

Once an infomediary controls a channel, it can capture additional value from partnerships. For example, AOL controls access to a customer base of close to 10% of all online users. Although AOL's main business is online access, a single partnership with Tel Save garnered $100m of new revenue. Other revenue generating AOL partners include ABC, the New York Times, BarnesandNoble.com, and Amazon.com.

Firms that seek to control a channel must keep their customers in the fold, either by providing superior service or by making it costly to leave. Portals do both by allowing users to personalise their interface with information of particular interest to them – for example, portfolio performance, news, and weather. Of course, personalising the interface requires some investment of time, and users who defect must leave that investment behind. Electronic retailers have also created high switching costs (and provided greater convenience) by capturing customer billing and shipping information.

Market share may be the key to a successful control strategy. The concept of increasing returns is common to many online control players. The online world's 'law of increasing returns' is driven by both internal and external factors (network externalities). Internally, most online companies have high fixed costs for infrastructure and marketing, but a low variable cost to serve. Network externalities come from new users creating value for subsequent new users. For example, a large customer base makes buyer agents more valuable to new customers.

But increasing returns can fail, and control can be elusive. An 80%-plus market share was not enough to save Netscape, a company that for a time seem ready to break the hegemony of Microsoft. Nets.Inc. also seemed to have the right talent, funding, and position, but this early business-to-business market maker ran out of steam shortly after its founding. Even AOL's continued dominance is uncertain in the face of competing technologies like cable-modem Internet player Excite@Home, browser-maker Microsoft, and Web portals like Yahoo!

Combine

In the past, high transaction costs made it economical to combine different channel roles within a single organisation. Although transaction costs have fallen, there are still some economic incentives to combine roles. Even Amazon.com benefits by combining buyer agency with a certain amount of market making and fulfilment capability. Although thwarted in its attempt to buy distributor Ingram, Amazon has recently invested in physical warehouses to reduce the delivery time of its books to certain areas of the US.

And some traditional retailers have leveraged their existing model quite fluidly into the Internet space. The British supermarket Tesco moved quickly into online selling, and now has over 80,000 registered users for its direct shopping model. It has even become an Internet Service Provider (ISP), offering Internet access to its customers.

Another motivation to combine roles is to exploit cross-subsidies for competitive advantage. Cross-subsidies enable companies to give away the value in one activity in order to secure greater margins or value in another activity. Cross-subsidies occur in most industries and often make customers feel (rightly) they have got something for nothing. While less effective in the new economy, cross subsidies remain a part of online selling. For example, the electronics market maker NECX.com provides free buyer agency by showing customers the best prices available from its competitors – even when competitors' prices are better than their own – in the belief that customers will in the end prefer NECX's total package.

All this suggests the need to give serious consideration to combining as a strategy, even in a world that is allegedly being torn apart by eCommerce.

Coordinate

A coordination strategy creates a one-stop shopping experience – facilitating the creation of customer solutions without the need to own resources. Coordination is a particularly strong strategy in three situations: (1) there are many undifferentiated infomediary competitors, (2) inter-firm cooperation is low, and (3) variety is required in the channel. Catalogue retailers have understood this strategy for years. They added value by creating options, allowing customers to specify a preferred shipper and form of shipment (that is, next-day air, surface, and so on) and a preferred payment provider. Nowadays, in addition to payment and shipping, online customers can choose the context in which they wish to participate, the company that will inform their purchase decision, and the market in which their transaction should occur.

1-800-Flowers has leveraged information technology to become the service of choice for long-distance flower and gift delivery. It has succeeded by creating a network of over 2,500 allied independent agents, market makers, and fulfilment providers. Garden.com applies the same strategy to link over 40 grower/suppliers, and a large number of fulfilment and payment partners, to their online base of customers.

Another approach to coordinating the channel is to assign roles to specific sole-source providers, as IBM's eChemicals does. This newly formed channel uses select specialised partners in each role: Yellow Freight is the partnering fulfilment provider, SunTrust Banks Inc. is the payment enabler, and eChemicals itself is the market maker and coordinater. By leveraging its strong brand and information-management capabilities across channel roles, IBM is able to garner a larger share of the channel rents than if it were simply to compete in a particular role.

Successful coordination typically requires a direct interface to the customer and the capacity to integrate multiple specialised providers dynamically. The latter requires efficient information-management capabilities to exist or be built across channel roles.

Compete, control, combine, or coordinate – how to leverage an electronic channel system

Electronic channel systems are in their infancy, and companies in many industries are successfully undertaking each of the above strategies.

For example, consider the changing nature of the car dealership. Traditional auto dealers combine multiple channel roles under the same roof. They inform, they sell, they finance, and they deliver. But the Internet has allowed new infomediaries to emerge.

For example, Edmund's competes in the buyer-agency role by providing pricing, feature, and other information to the customer. This infomediary's core competence is in the processes of accumulating, organising, and publishing data about cars. Edmund's influences buyer decisions and negotiations with dealers, although it is not involved in the transaction.

In contrast, Auto-by-Tel illustrates the control strategy. Auto-by-Tel has expanded from providing basic information to delivering qualified customer leads to partner dealerships under exclusive contract. This attempt to control the flow of information between dealers and customers provides greater revenue opportunities than just publishing information. Its exclusive contracts create barriers to entry for prospective competitors.

CarsDirect illustrates the strategy of coordinating multiple specialists and roles. CarsDirect actually sells cars online, but relies on its relationships and partnerships, not an asset base, to perform the actual sourcing, delivery, and payment support of the transaction.

As specialised infomediaries emerge, we expect smart firms will increasingly want to provide a total solution by dynamically coordinating the most desirable infomediaries to solve a customer's problem. Process-execution advantages diminish over time due to the technology improvements available to all competitors. In contrast, the relational assets of the 'infomediary' are harder to copy and thus provide the greater competitive advantage. Thus, firms will migrate to control and coordination strategies by investing in relationships, information and good will to control/dominate channels.

This migration is beginning to occur in the auto industry. All major car companies host Web sites. This is a first step. Some major players are positioning themselves to take ownership of infomediaries (that is, Ford and Carpoint) which have access to customer queries about cars across multiple vendors. We believe that manufacturers will increasingly invest in customer insight to execute a control or coordination strategy in their channels.

Creating a business model

The myths of easy Internet success have a hard core of truth. It should be clear from the foregoing discussion that there are many ways to do business in the wired new world. But no one should consider launching an Internet business without first thinking through the issues of value proposition and channel strategy discussed above.

For example, E-bay's founder hadn't intended to create a dominant Internet business when he started the company. He merely wanted to trade Pez candy dispensers with like-minded collectors. Word about his site got around, collectors of other items found it, posted messages about items they were interested in, and soon made E-Bay the most successful auction site on the Web.

The story is true – a true myth, if you will. It has inspired a superstition that Internet business success often depends on acting without careful forethought.

But that isn't the right conclusion to draw from the E-Bay story. It doesn't matter that E-Bay was the accidental product of spontaneous generation. E-Bay could not have built and sustained its competitive position without meticulous thinking about customer value and channel strategy. And when that kind of thinking is absent from Internet ventures, they fail – as E-Bay's many would-be competitors have failed.

Two particularly dangerous superstitions about cyberspace business involve advertising revenues and online customer spending.

The notion that new Internet businesses will be able to earn substantial advertising revenues is, in general, wrong. Lycos, Yahoo! and other portal companies have made lucrative, high-profile marketing deals; Buy.com and OnSale sell to customers at cost, and rely on advertising revenues to generate profit. But these early successes are unlikely to be duplicated. There are several reasons why.

First, advertising rates are dropping quickly. AdKnowledge, a Palo Alto firm specialising in Web-based advertising, reports that online advertising fell 6% last year – for the second year in a row (see Figure 2.4). The

Figure 2.4   Online banner advertising costs (CPM)

Source: AdKnowledge.com website

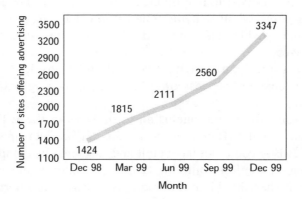

Figure 2.5   Sites offering advertising

Source: AdKnowledge.com website

problem: more sites are competing for attention and ad dollars (see Figure 2.5), so online advertising is becoming a buyer's market. It turns out that two-thirds of all online advertising dollars go to just nine Web sites, leaving only one-third of the reported billions in spending for the remaining thousands of sites.

Lucrative multi-year agreements of the past can no longer be relied on either. A survey of executives of companies with long-term online advertising deals found only 5% of respondents 'highly likely' to renew their existing agreements, because more than two-thirds of these executives reported that their costly online advertising deals had produced disappointing sales results.[8]

The progress of technology also threatens advertising revenues. As access speeds and bandwidth grow, consumers click through screens faster, and spend less time looking at ads. Worse – from an advertiser's perspective – those consumers who really dislike ads can now block them altogether, using software from such vendors as Privnet to prevent browsers from downloading advertisements.

Another superstition is the belief that the ease of doing business on the Internet will prompt customers to spend more. This logic has driven the stock market valuations of many Internet companies. But a recent Deutsche Bank study found that most online spending merely replaces offline spending.[9] In no category did overall spending increase. Thus, the Internet does not expand the market pie – it merely introduces more competition for the pieces. This conclusion was reinforced by another recent study that found the lifetime value of online customers could be predicted with the same models used by offline retailers.[10]

So, while the Internet is driving innovation, it is not repealing the basic law that success in business requires careful planning and sound operating and strategic business models.

An operating business model is the organisation's essential logic for consistently achieving its principal objectives.[11] The business model of a profit-oriented enterprise explains how it consistently makes money. These should not be confused with *components* of business models (see Table 2.2). Since organisations compete for customers and resources, a good business model highlights the distinctive activities and approaches that enable the firm to attract investors, employees and customers in order to deliver products and services profitably.

Consider the operating business model of SupplyGenie.com, a business-to-business office products site:

1. SupplyGenie.com sells office products at dealer cost over the Internet.

Table 2.2   Components of a business model

They say 'business model' but they mean:	For example:	As in:
Pricing model	■ Cost plus ■ CPM (cost per thousand)	'Free is almost a default business model on the Web.' *Fortune*, March 1999.
Revenue model	■ Advertising or broadcast model ■ Subscription or cable model ■ Fee-for-service	'The solution for many established companies and startups [to their difficulty of finding good business models], has been to apply traditional business models such as advertising, subscription services and retail sales to the Web...' *Webmaster Magazine*, October 1999.
Channel model	■ Bricks 'n' mortar ■ Clicks 'n' mortar ■ Direct-to-customer	'Disintermediation is already taking a hit on the busines-to-consumer front, where new business models, such as cobranding and digital channel management – as opposed to channel cannibalization – are beginning to take hold.' *Computerworld*, December 1999.
Commerce process model	■ Auction ■ Reverse auction ■ Community	'Ancient history may perhaps be a good place to find a new business model. Traditional auctions have been held since the time of Babylon. Requirements? A community of interested buyers and sellers, agreed rules of conduct, a time and place. Auctions are a time-honoured method of getting the best price for goods.' PriceWaterhouseCoopers, August 1999.
Internet-enabled commerce relationship	■ Market-maker ■ Aggregator ■ Virtual supply alliance ■ Value network	'The real key to competing in the New Economy is in business model innovation. Based on the Internet, fundamentally new models of the firm and its interaction with external entities have emerged...' *Business 2.0*, November 1999.
Organisational form	■ Stand-alone business unit ■ Integrated Internet capability	'The eCommerce Steering Committee considered the following electronic commerce business models: skunkworks, standing steering committee, eCommerce executive VP, new business unit, spin off, and outsourcing.' *Big 5 Consultant*, December 1999.
Value proposition	■ Less value and very low cost ■ More value at the same cost ■ Much more value at greater cost	'There are two basic business models. Companies either compete on price, or they compete on quality.' *Oil and Gas Industry Analyst*, January 2000.

2. The opportunity to buy at dealer cost attracts small and mid-sized firms accustomed to paying 25% to 40% markups.
3. Good service (including wide selection, next day delivery, and phone centre support) keeps customers coming back.
4. This builds volume.
5. High volume enables SupplyGenie to negotiate purchase discounts with wholesale suppliers.
6. These discounts, and a lean cost structure, provide SupplyGenie's profit margin, allowing it to attract investors.
7. Growth and the promise of an initial public offering (IPO) help the company attract top talent, and continue to improve service and performance.

This operating business model shows what SupplyGenie must do consistently and uniformly in order to succeed (see Figure 2.6). By contrast, its strategic model shows how it must change. Business models do suffer a sort of time decay. That is, their value declines as their distinctiveness erodes. In the Internet this happens quickly, because competitors are quick

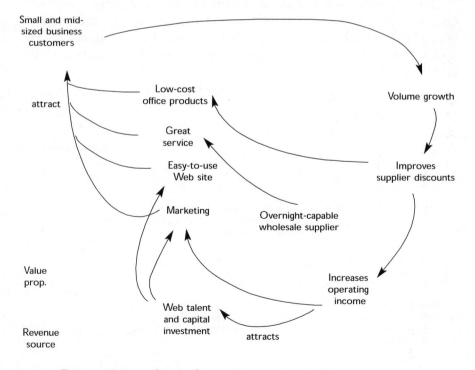

Figure 2.6   SupplyGenie.com operating business model

to imitate any successful innovation. How does SupplyGenie leverage its most important assets, capabilities, relationships, and knowledge to achieve an advantage over time? Here, briefly, is the strategic model:

1. SupplyGenie.com's operating model gives it an important asset: a base of satisfied small and mid-sized business customers.
2. SupplyGenie leverages this asset by expanding its offerings to these customers to include other convenience goods and services at excellent prices – such as office furniture, payroll services, insurance, and temporary help.
3. The broader product/service line increases SupplyGenie's value for convenience- and cost-oriented customers
4. Which improves customer retention and account size, and…
5. … shuts out competitors.
6. Increased sales enable SupplyGenie to continue to expand its product line, customer service, and marketing reach
7. Which fuels growth and increases profitability.

Thus, developing a sustainable Internet business requires a thorough understanding of customer value, channel strategy, and business modelling. These elements are the foundation of a sound operating model. The operating model, in turn, is the foundation of the strategic change model (see Figure 2.7).

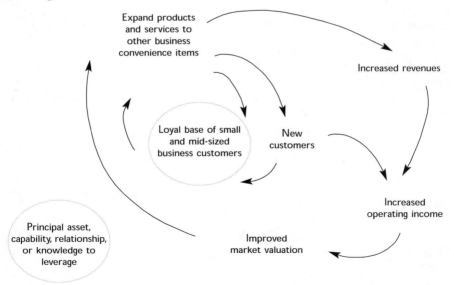

Figure 2.7   SupplyGenie.com strategic change model

The first steps toward building an operating model for Internet business are:

1. Identify all sources of revenue.
2. Select a clear value proposition.
3. Decide on channel strategy – how to deliver value profitably and consistently.

The assets, capabilities and relationships of the enterprise should come together in the kind of 'round' logic illustrated by SupplyGenie's operating model. The strategic change model builds on the operating model by identifying:

- the most important asset used to create new sources of value
- the supporting assets
- new revenue sources, value proposition(s) and/or cost structure(s) that can be created by leveraging these assets, and what is required to profitably create these new opportunities.

Clarifying a company's operating and strategic business models will not only sharpen the business focus and enhance its competitiveness, but also position the firm for inevitable change. Investors typically require this level of clarity in a business model before committing capital. Is it too rigorous to demand such discipline in the rapidly-moving environment of the Internet? Cyberspace is changing quickly, but future uncertainty does not excuse present poor planning.

Notes

1. From the sample business plan of InteliChild, January 2000, at www.bplans.com
2. Excerpted and adapted from Ajit Kambil, Erik Esilius, 'Value Innovation in the eEconomy', Andersen Consulting Organization and Change Strategy *Forum* article, November 1999
3. Excerpted and adapted from Nunes, P., Kambil, A., and Wilson, D., 'How will you go to Market in the eEconomy', Andersen Consulting working paper, November 1999
4. According to a 1998 J. D. Power and Associates survey
5. Hagel, John and Sanger, Marc (1998) 'Net Worth' coined the term 'infomediaries'. Sarkar, Mitra Barun, Brian Butler, and Charles Steinfield (1995), 'Intermediaries and Cybermediaries: A Continuing Role for Mediating Players in the Electronic Marketplace', *Journal of Computer Mediated Communication*, Special Issue on Electronic Commerce (online issue 3, vol. I, no. 3) use the term cybermediaries in the same way to illustrate emerging electronic channel participants
6. See Brynjolfsson, E., Smith, M. D., (1999) 'Frictionless Commerce? A Comparison of Internet and Conventional Retailers', Sloan School working paper, for an analysis of consumer willingness to pay higher prices at particular online and offline retailers

7. See Nunes, P., Kambil, A., and Wilson, D., 'The All-in-One Market', *Harvard Business Review* May/June 2000 and Kambil, A., Nunes, P., and Wilson, D., 'Transforming the Marketspace with All-in-One Markets', *International Journal of Electronic Commerce*, Vol.3, No. 4, Summer 1999, for a detailed discussion of these Internet enabled markets

8. Jupiter Communications study, 1999

9. See Deutsche Bank Report, 'Bricksandmortar.com; Retailing Meets the Internet', August 1999 available online

10. Working Paper #99-023 – 'Forecasting Repeat Sales at CDNow: A Case Study' by Professor Peter S. Fader and Bruce G.S. Hardie, Wharton School of Business, 1999

11. Excerpted and adapted from Jane Linder and Susan Cantrall, 'So What *Is* a Business Model Anyway?', working paper of the Andersen Consulting Institute for Strategic Change, 6 January 2000

CHAPTER 3

Finding an Attractive Market

Stephen Harpin
ANDERSEN CONSULTING STRATEGIC SERVICES

Most people setting up in businesses start in familiar geographic and product markets, where the team has what we call 'domain expertise'. Investors will look closely at this factor, because it defines the ability of the team to identify the right suppliers and buyers and bring the two together. This ability to make it happen will be the defining success factor. However, familiarity with an individual launch market is not enough; the 'end game' also needs to be attractive. This will probably entail expansion into other geographic markets. Therefore, the key questions to be addressed before embarking on any venture are:

▦ Which geographic markets are attractive?

▦ How appealing will the business concept be in these markets?

▦ What are the strategic options to enter them?

This chapter explores these three questions. First, it defines the relative attractiveness of the various European markets. It then defines the broad elements of an attractive Internet concept and illustrates how these elements may vary across markets. Finally it looks at the strategic options to be considered when entering these markets. By the end of this chapter you should be able to confirm the attractiveness of a concept within the chosen markets and to define your market entry strategies.

Attractive geographies

While the European market is very attractive because of its size, it is highly fragmented and can not be treated as a homogenous whole. To give a sense of the extent of European fragmentation, consider these facts:

▦ *Political* – Europe now contains 46 sovereign states

▦ *Linguistic* – Europe's communities speak scores of mutually unintelligible languages. Italy alone contains 12 minority language groups

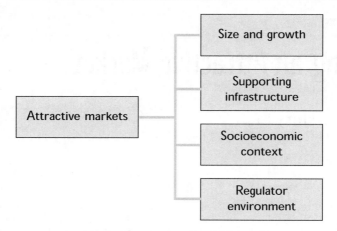

Figure 3.1   Attractive markets

- *Economic* – Europe's nations vary widely in their per capita incomes, ranging from Luxembourg, which has the highest per capita GDP in the world at $40,000, to Poland with a per capita GDP of just $2,809

- *Cultural* – Of the eight major business cultures in the world, five can be found in Europe: Anglo-Saxon, Latin European, Germanic, Near Eastern and Nordic.

Anyone setting up a European Internet business will need to navigate carefully through this fragmentation to identify the most attractive markets (see Figure 3.1). Attractive markets are big, with high online growth rates. They have a rapidly developing and supportive infrastructure, a positive socio-economic context and a positive regulatory environment. Of course, not all markets that seem attractive will be relevant to every business concept, but taking a quick view on which markets are attractive will enable you to focus more intensive concept research in the right areas.

Size and growth

The overriding driver of attractiveness is size and Europe is big. Key considerations are not just the size of the population, but also the extent to which that population is getting online and buying from the Internet.

Size of the population

The top 15 European countries contain 373m people, over 100m more than the US. Over 80% of this population can be found in just five countries: the UK, Germany, France, Italy and Spain (see Figure 3.2). By conquering these countries a European business can start to achieve the scale needed to compete with the US. This need for European scale is even more acute for an Internet start-up, as the Internet still only represents less than 1% of European retail purchasing. Those that only play on their home ground will be unable to compete with local and European 'bricks/clicks and mortar' retail players with access to the other 99% of the market. Equally, it is difficult to imagine a local Internet start-up competing successfully with European and global Internet players. For many local businesses, success for entrepreneurs will come from joint ventures with or even selling out to those who will compete across many geographic markets. But you can't

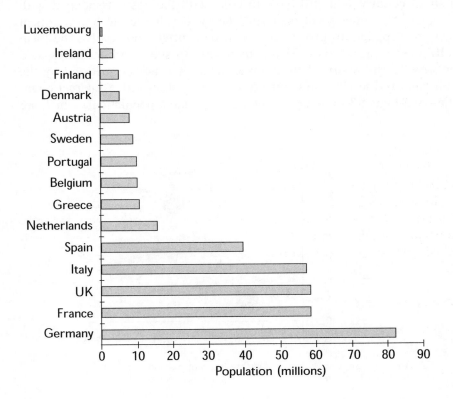

Figure 3.2   Population by European countries

Source: Economist World pocket book 2000

rely on the sale option: people only buy attractive businesses and attractive Internet businesses are scaling fast, often geographically. The message is simple: if you plan to stay at home, go home.

Size of the online opportunity

Some of the countries with the highest online penetration are still not the most attractive to Internet businesses because they are so small. Scandinavian countries may have been enthusiastic early adopters of the new technology and have generated many new ideas, but the biggest opportunities are now in the UK, Germany and France. Although Finland has the highest percentage of its population online, its small population of only 5m makes it unattractive for most businesses. The costs and complexities of entering new geographic markets are relatively fixed. An Internet business entering a small country will still have to cope with the costs associated with changing the language of their site, they will still need to find a critical mass of suppliers to give authority to their offer, and resolve the local fulfilment issues. It is difficult, therefore, to see small countries as a priority, as the return of these investments will not be justified by the opportunity. The UK and Germany are the most attractive Internet countries (see Figure 3.3), with a combination of large populations, which are

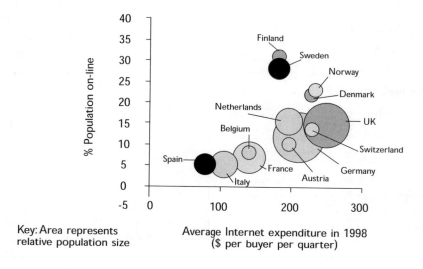

Key: Area represents relative population size

Average Internet expenditure in 1998 ($ per buyer per quarter)

Figure 3.3   Western European Internet market attractiveness

increasingly getting moving online and spending significant amounts of money there. For most business, capturing the UK, France and Germany equals European domination.

Online growth rates

Most analysts judge the European Internet markets to be 18–24 months behind the US, but beginning to catch up. The pace of change in Europe may have been accelerated by the AOL/Time Warner merger in January 2000 which showed the potential for American firms to dominate eCommerce in Europe. To illustrate the size of these mega deals, the combined value of both companies is roughly equal to 30% of the gross national product of Spain. However, there are indications that Europe is catching up with the US. European retailers doubled their online revenue in 1999, outpacing growth in the US market of approximately 150%. The gap between US innovation and European imitation is also rapidly diminishing. European consumers going online for the first time have far more sophisticated content and services available to them than US consumers did only a few years ago. Numerous Europeans have English language proficiency and visit US sites, so that European sites are now benchmarked against current US sites. Some innovations are even appearing earlier in Europe than they are in the US. Businesses can no longer rely on a two-year gap before the US competition arrives, nor can they start Internet businesses with poor sites in the same way that the original US pioneers did. Today's customers expect more and successful businesses will need to raise the money to deliver it. It is also fair to assume that any 'white space' in an online market will have many businesses charging towards it: in this environment, the growth of online competition is even more important than the growth rate of online users.

Supportive infrastructure

Telecom issues in Europe are impacted by the decisions of regulators operating at a number of levels: global, European, country by country and intra-country (see Table 3.1). In principle the regulators support competition, but in practice they frequently block real changes and shield the market position of incumbent state monopolies. The EC also legislates to increase competition, but while this is working in some countries, such as the UK, it still allows particular countries to maintain local monopolies for

Table 3.1   Infrastructure parameters

	Telecom liberalisation (Score 0–100)	Fixed phone lines (% Penetration)	Mobile phones (% Penetration)	Computer power per capita (MIPS per 1000 people)	Telephone costs (US$)
Germany	43	51	15	24212	1.19
France	51	58	15	24446	0.91
UK	61	49	18	29567	1
Benelux	28	53	20	28158	1.47
Sweden	53	71	48	36947	1.39
Spain	34	39	15	13288	1.83
Italy	26	44	22	15563	1.55
Greece	13	51	10	6829	1.56
Ireland*	48	39	15	27458	1.3

Information Sources

Telecom liberalisation: Euro Telecoms – Key Trends Gartner Group 1998. Based on Gartner's analysis across five dimensions: regulation, licensing, interconnect, portability and pro-competitiveness. *Figures for Ireland adjusted to show recent liberalisation.

Fixed phone lines: UK, France, Germany, Sweden, Benelux – FT Telecoms7 Industry Issues 1998; Spain, Italy, Greece, Ireland – The World Competitiveness Yearbook 1998, figures based on 1997 data.

Mobile phones: UK, France, Germany, Sweden, Benelux – FT Telecoms7 Industry Issues 1998; Spain, Italy, Greece, Ireland figures estimated from 1996 data which was doubled to achieve final figure.

Computer power per capita: The World Competitiveness Yearbook 1998, figures based on 1997 data.

Telephone costs: The World Competitiveness Yearbook 1998, figures based on 1997 data.

the time being, as in Belgium and Portugal. However, as the wave of deregulation spreads across Europe there is a real opportunity for consumers to benefit from consequent downward pressure on tariffs. On an optimistic note, it is possible that all major European countries' telecoms industries will be liberalised by 2001.

Attractive socioeconomic environment

Europe is a wonderful mix of countries with not only diverse cultures but very different stages of development. That is what makes it such an exciting place to live in or visit. For an Internet business, an understanding of this diversity can make the difference between success and failure. Although the attractiveness of markets will also vary according to the business concept, in general terms they can be measured by:

  ▪ *Income:* GDP per head ranges from \$21,213 in Germany to \$11,423 in Greece. Generally, the higher the income the more attractive the country

Table 3.2 Socioeconomic parameters

	GDP PPP per capita (US$) 1996	GDP per head (US$) 1997	Higher level education (% of 20–24 years) 1993	PC penetration (per 1000) 1997	National culture index 1997	Internet penetration (% total population) 1998/99	% Population under 15 1996
Germany	21213	25363	35.6	231	6.31	8.7	16.4
France	21650	23691	49.5	234	5.95	5.2	19.9
UK	20013	21952	37.4	283	7.07	16	19.2
Benelux	21278	23482	41	275	8.38	7.54	18.25
Sweden	19595	25559	38.3	353	7.37	33	18.5
Spain	15495	13282	41.1	127	7.3	6.6	17.7
Italy	20205	19821	37.3	158	6.83	4.14	15.5
Greece	12506	11423	25	73	7.59	1	17.6
Ireland	18818	19079	34.2	263	8.18	11	25.9

Information source: The World Competitiveness Yearbook 1998
Internet penetration information source: Nua

- *Higher education:* The percentage of 20 to 24 year olds in third level education ranges from 49.5% in France to 25% in Greece. The higher the educational level the faster the Internet uptake tends to be.

- *PC penetration:* PCs per 1,000 people range from 353 in Sweden to 25 in Greece. If Greece represents an opportunity then significant offline activity may be required to enable enough people to experience the offer.

- *Influence vs insularity:* According to the World Competitiveness Yearbook, the degree to which individual countries are open to external influences ranges from a low of 5.9 in France to a high of 11 in Ireland. If you want to sell in France, then use the French language and localise the content.

- *Credit/debit cards per head:* Europe is at a significant disadvantage here compared to the USA where there are many more credit and debit cards available in the market (see Figure 3.4). In addition this factor varies widely between European countries. Firms wishing to do business in Europe will have to enable payment by debit card as well as by credit card. Where even these payment methods are not common place, businesses will have to use more traditional forms of payment such as invoicing or introduce new forms of ePayment such as digicash.

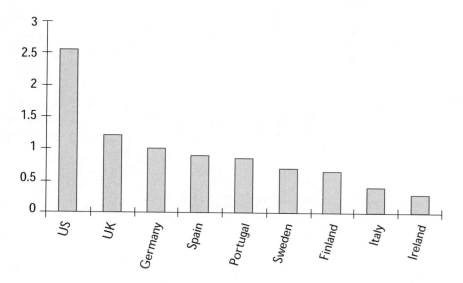

Figure 3.4   Number of credit/debit cards per head (1998)

Source: Boston Consulting Group

Attractive regulatory environment

At the time of writing the European Commission had five key eCommerce-orientated directives under consideration. These covered topics ranging from copyright, data protection, distance selling and electronic signatures, as well as the European commerce directive itself. There is considerable doubt about the implications of this legislation, particularly the extent to which it will fuel or constrain eCommerce. However, in all my discussions with entrepreneurs, none has suggested that they weren't going to start their business simply because the regulatory environment wasn't quite right. It's entrepreneurs that make businesses successful and while governments can help or hinder you shouldn't wait for them to act before making your mind up. Perhaps the most useful regulatory knowledge you require is that sellers must pay taxes in the country they are based in. This factor alone may determine your decision on where to locate your business.

Appealing concepts within the markets

Having defined a shortlist of attractive markets, you will need to assess the extent to which your business concept will appeal to them. Your concept's appeal will depend on the attractiveness of the target audience, the existing product market and the intensity of competition. Each of these elements will vary both by European country and by concept. However, at the end you should feel comfortable in justifying your choice of which markets to enter. This choice will be a function of three key elements:

- How attractive is your target audience and how will this vary by country?
- How attractive is your product market and how will this vary by country?
- What is the level of competitive intensity by country?

How attractive is your target audience and how will this vary by country?

When businesses segment their markets and decide which segments to target, they evaluate the attractiveness and accessibility of each individual segment. In the fast moving Internet world the attractiveness and accessibility of target audiences will change dramatically over time and by

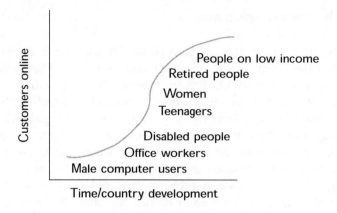

Figure 3.5   Internet adopter development

country. The early adopters in all global Internet markets have been young male computer users, but over time the online population is becoming more representative (see Figure 3.5). However, if you accept that the speed at which scale is achieved will separate the winners from the losers, you may not be able to wait until your target audience is fully online before you can introduce your business.

The appeal of any particular concept will be defined by customer attributes, values and behaviour. Customer attributes (such as wealth, disability, age and sex) drive their values (such as convenience, price, or choice)

Table 3.3   Illustrative attributes, values and behaviours for a home decoration site

Target audience attributes	Key values	Behaviours
High income	Convenience: short of time	Employs interior designers and contractors to complete the work
Female	Quality: high income	
Aged 20–40	Choice: large house with many rooms	Buys high value items
House worth > 300,000 Ecus	Information: wants to match the wallpaper and furniture to the house	High average spend
Married		Uses the Internet to research off-line purchases
Working/housewife with children		Visits on average four interior design shops to find the right look
Online		Buys eight home magazines a year for inspiration
		Buys ten samples to every purchase

which in turn drive their behaviour (buying online or directly). To illustrate this relationship, think about this example of an impoverished widow in her late sixties. Her attributes are 'poor', 'retired', 'widow', 'aged 65+'. Because she is poor, she may value price above all else, because she is housebound she values convenience and social contact. This in turn explains her behaviour – spending significant amounts of time on the Internet surfing for the best deal on the thirdage.com community site. Internet business will derive the most benefit from discovering their customers' values, and matching these with their Web sites and merchandising principles. Attributes are commonplace, behaviour can be tracked, but matching your offering to their values is the glue that will make your customers stick by you. Achieving this is further complicated by the fact that customer attributes and consequently values and behaviour will also vary by country. Table 3.4 illustrates how you can draft out what your customer attributes, values and consequent behaviour may be.

Now you can consider the implications of these values and behaviours for an Internet offering targeting this segment. This particular concept is very appealing to the online target audience because it can satisfy the customer's deeply held values.

Having completed this table for your business, you can then try to research the extent to which the target segment is found across Europe in your previously chosen attractive markets. There are three key questions to research:

▪ *Attributes:* Is there a large number of people with these attributes across different geographies? If so can they be reached cost effectively? This will determine the topline European opportunity.

Table 3.4   Customer value delivery

Value	Illustrative motivating eCommerce application
Convenience	Sell integrated room solutions rather than just products
	Sell samples that are collated together
	Offer 'white gloves' service delivery to install products
	Offer decoration solutions including the contractors to put up the wallpaper
Quality	Sell high value branded products
	Superior guarantees
Choice	A broad product range and architecture covering all major rooms and styles
Information	Have a content rich site, perhaps by integrating magazine articles
	Group merchandise by house style
	Include expert advice from interior designers

▪ *Values:* Does the target audience value the same things? This will determine the extent to which any business proposition will be appealing.

▪ *Behaviours:* Do they behave in the same way? This will determine how people satisfy their values today and the extent to which a new Internet offer is competitive. Without deep market knowledge, it is difficult to identify if an Internet offer is appealing enough to change customer purchasing behaviour. For example if a business sells E1000 sofas, and people in Greece do not buy them, the offer will need to be tailored. This is discussed further in the section on replicability below.

How attractive is your product market and how will this vary by country?

The business opportunity will differ dramatically by product market. In any Internet business case there are two key drivers of product market attractiveness. The first is the size of the market; the second is the percentage of customers moving online. These figures vary significantly by product market: during Christmas 1999 only 0.8% of European retail sales were via the Internet. But in some product areas Internet share is far higher: 15% of retail stockbroking and 5% of book sales in Europe now take place over the net. Travel, computer hardware, books and financial brokerage alone account for three-quarters of the European online market. In addition, in some categories the Internet will be used as an essential source of information before a traditional purchase, or for aftersales support and advice. Take airline tickets (see Figure 3.6): although 18% of UK online buyers had actually bought airline tickets through the Internet, 51% of them had used it to research their choice. Participation in the eWorld is thus not an option but a necessity for airlines and travel agents.

The product market opportunity also varies enormously by country. For example, by 2003 over 15% of the UK and German populace will be buying online, while Spain will still be below the critical threshold with only 4% of its population buying online. Generally speaking, the attractiveness of entering a new category depends on the level of competitive development in any particular country.

Now we need to assess the attributes of a product category that make it 'Internet friendly'. There is no black and white answer to this; rather there are a number of attributes which each contribute to product market attractiveness (see Figure 3.7). By the end of this section you should be able to evaluate the extent to which product markets are attractive.

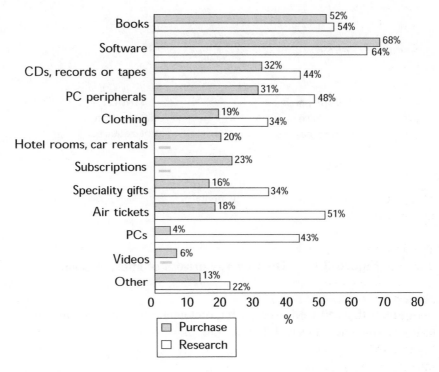

Figure 3.6   Purchase vs research of product categories

Source: Jupiter UK online projections, April 1999

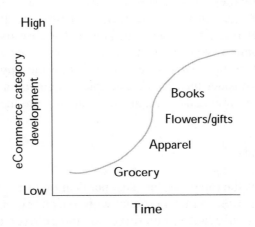

Figure 3.7   Category attractiveness

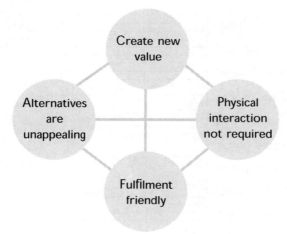

Figure 3.8   The four key drivers of Internet selling

Products that sell well over the Internet generally have a combination of four key characteristics (see Figure 3.8).

Create new value

The best ideas are those created by the Internet itself. These ideas create new value in the market, rather than just carving out a piece of the old market value as it goes online. Customers will find the experience so different to any off-line equivalent that they will realise true value and return again and again. If your products or services have these characteristics then they will be very successful. To illustrate the opportunities to create new value, consider these three examples: aggregation of information, product customisation and dynamically changing product selections.

Aggregation of information

The Internet enables the rapid and low cost publication of content or information. This information can be a product within itself, or an added value service, giving a significant competitive advantage over offline sales where the information may not be available. Not only is this information becoming accessible online, but shopping robot technology helps customers search through it to find information that is relevant to them. The implications of the publication and collation of information are immense:

- Hard to find products in fragmented markets represent an online opportunity. If you are looking for a Georgian armchair you could spend months touring antique shops to find the right one. Now you can visit Southeby.Amazon.com or icollector.com who are integrating many antique dealers' stocks in one place.

- Firms earning high margins because the customer does not have perfect information will see their margins decline. Oneswoop.com, the online European car dealer is helping customers find the best European price for their car, matching the buyers and sellers in an Internet-enabled open environment.

- Intermediaries are at risk. With shopping robot technology, customers can find the best product to meet their needs themselves, reducing the need for intermediaries – is this the end of the financial services salesman?

- Information rich products will sell more online. If you compare looker/buyer ratios of 'researched technical products' such as computer equipment, they tend to be 33% higher than average looker/buyer ratios. An information rich online service will always win over an underinformed shop assistant who doesn't understand the complex products.

- Category-led businesses may differentiate themselves by becoming service- rather than product-based retailers online, integrating information or content with the commerce element to produce a differentiated site. The proliferation of wedding sites across Europe illustrates this concept well. These sites are based on the desire to have a wonderful wedding rather than 'selling categories'. For example, if you plan to get married, then you may need to:
  - Make sure you are marrying the right person!
  - Prepare for the wedding day
  - Manage the wedding list
  - Get married – the day itself
  - Start a new life with someone (preferably the one you have married).

Creating a community around the site can also add interactive information. This could include interactive ideas such as:

- Chat rooms, enabling brides-to-be to talk to each other
- Expert advisors: enabling people to talk to 'gurus': priests, travel organisers, wedding organisers, caterers
- Bulletin Boards: Static advice from customer to customer, products for sale
- Customer reviews and suggestions: Lists of customer suggestions ranging from product reviews to choice of hymns
- Customer Web pages: a convenient location for all the details that your guests will want to know: locations, dress codes, wedding lists.

A wedding site that integrates all of the content, commerce and community may look like Table 3.5. If you can't find one, feel free to launch it. If you have a different idea, try to ramp up the content and community aspects to increase your own competitive edge.

Introduce customisation

Internet businesses that customise products have the opportunity to add dramatic value to their products. You could, for example, visit Barbie.com and design your own Barbie doll with its own name, hair and eye colour. Retailers who stock products in stores can not produce customised products as efficiently as a high volume, online, back-end make-to-order operation. If Barbie.com doesn't impress you, try buying a configure-to-order computer from Dell.com or your own selection of music on a custom made CD from CDNOW.com.

Dynamically change product selections

If the products businesses sell are currently sold from catalogues, there is a good reason to believe that they will sell over the Internet. However, catalogue selling has its limitations: with product lead times of over four months customers can be left disappointed when lines sell out. If the products don't sell, the retailer is left with excess inventory. Internet retailing has a number of distinct advantages for customers and businesses alike. The customer can be assured that products are in stock if the business has a near real-time inventory and merchandising system. The business can tailor prices to reflect inventory positions and maximise margins. Thus we have seen the emergence of new second-hand markets, and distressed inventory markets with 'when it's gone its gone' offers.

Table 3.5   Illustrative wedding site

	Central content pillars				
	Be sure I'm marrying the right person	**Have a hassle free preparation**	**Manage the wedding list**	**Have happiest day of my life**	**Start a perfect life together**
Content	■ Compatibility tests ■ What to look for in relationships with potential ■ Self-improvement tips ■ Star signs	■ Wedding etiquette ■ Setting a budget ■ Where to marry ■ Who to invite ■ Type of reception ■ How to buy a dress ■ Legal advice ■ Guest home page	■ Gift ideas ■ Product catalogues ■ Product details and prices ■ Status of products on wedding list	■ Schedule for wedding day ■ Example speeches ■ Ideas for finishing touches	■ Honeymoon ideas ■ How to buy a house ■ Considerations when starting a family ■ How to manage joint finances
Commerce	■ Dating agencies ■ Self-improvement courses/materials ■ Trial holidays	■ On-line purchase of products/services/books/magazines ■ Planning software ■ Invitation/stationery service ■ Link to Yellow Pages	■ On-line purchase of gifts ■ Product customisation ■ Gift wrapping/delivery	■ On-line purchase of luxury/finishing touch products ■ Customisation of products	■ On-line honeymoon booking ■ Links to property sites/estate agents ■ Links to banks ■ On-line purchase of books/magazines
Interact/Community	■ Forum detailing how people met/could meet ■ E-mail for advice on compatibility	■ Home page for wedding guests ■ Requests for special services ■ Forum for problems encountered	■ On-line wedding list ■ Forum for present ideas and gifts hard to find	■ Forum for worried brides/grooms	■ Forum of ideas for honemoons ■ Forum for setting up new life together

Physical interaction is not required

Products that do not require physical interaction between the customer and product are very suitable for Internet selling. Otherwise purchase over the Internet is a risk for the customer, who will only discover if the product is really suitable on delivery. If you need to try on (clothing), smell (perfumes), taste (food), or see (wallpaper and paint shades) the product before you can assess its quality, then buying over the Internet is a risk. People may be happy to do this, but expect product returns to be very high and the costs can be crippling. For perspective, the UK catalogue business generally offers a 14-day return policy and records return rates of over 30% on clothing and footwear. Footwear especially can easily exceed 50% return rates. Alternatively if the product is a generic commodity, it will sell well through the Internet. While the extent to which people need to interact with products is dependent on the customer as much as the nature of the product, there are some factors that can be applied to mitigate customer risks (see Figure 3.9).

- Trusted products/brands. Businesses that sell well-known brands such as Chanel No 5 will achieve higher looker/buyer ratios than those whose products are unknown. Businesses such as Drugstore.com and Tescodi-rect.co.uk are relying on repeat purchases, where the consumers have purchased the products before and trust is not a major issue.

  Oneswoop.com is an Internet-based European car trading service that is minimising the customer's perception of risk by associating itself with valuable brands. Thus it has registered the site with Verisign to assure customers that the site is safe, offers financial services from Marks and Spencer and insurance from 15 branded firms. It is also backed by well known equity firms and Andersen Consulting, the world's largest management consultancy.

- Low risk trial packages. Another way of reducing risk is by offering samples first. Furniture. com's fabric sampling service is an essential element in achieving customer satisfaction and minimising returns of bulky and expensive sofas.

- Guarantees. Returns policies are effective guarantees for people who purchase direct and are a requirement in most European countries.

- Technology applications. There are now a number of technology and design applications which try to mimic the physical experience for the customer. Ipix.com's 360-degree viewing technology enables a prospec-

Physical interaction desired
- try on/touch
- taste
- smell
- see

Risk mitigation factors
- trusted products/brands
- low risk trial packages
- guarantees reassurance/
  quality checked
- technology applications

Figure 3.9   Mitigating customers' buying risk

tive buyer to view a house almost as if they were there. Snowdrops.com, a Swedish beauty site, enables customers to scan in a photograph and experiment with different hair colorants and lipsticks. Landsend.com enables a customer to create a computer image with their own body measurements to see what different clothing combinations could look like. Goodhome.com's iDecorate enables a customer to see what their room would look like with different decorative styles and furniture. All of these applications decrease the need to see and touch the products before purchase.

The product is fulfilment friendly

If the products or services can't be cost effectively delivered when customers want them, then they are not suitable for Internet selling (see Table 3.6). Let's take each of these elements in turn to explore what this means for the Internet business.

- *Delivered when customers want them.* If the product can be delivered against expectations, then it is suitable for Internet selling. Expectations are generally set by the offline equivalents. Consequently, it is difficult to imagine MacDonalds Corp selling hamburgers over the Internet, as hunger strikes quicker than hamburger delivery vans can travel. However, if it takes six weeks to deliver furniture offline, an Internet business that delivers in four may be an attractive proposition. Indeed, because it is easier to update your online catalogue, inventory can be better managed and the opportunity to deliver against your promise is greater. Businesses need to establish how quickly customers require the product, and how the Internet can be used to speed up delivery and manage stocks better.

Table 3.6   Attributes of fulfilment friendly and unfriendly products

Fulfilment friendly	Fulfilment unfriendly
Fit through the letterbox	Bulky 2-man delivery
Robust	Fragile
Light	Heavy
Single product	Collation required
Non-perishable	Perishable
Delivery cost low percentage of order value	Delivery cost high percentage of order value
Steady demand – low stock required	Variable demand – high stocks required
Sell and make to order	Sell from stock

If the product can be delivered immediately, it is a very attractive Internet proposition. A new set of eProducts have been developed that can be downloaded to satisfy immediate demand in a way that was never possible before. Check out the MP3 downloads of music as an example. Another is the development of Qpass.com as an Internet payment mechanism which enables individuals to download varied digital products ranging from news to software immediately and pay for them with one click of the mouse.

Online casinos have proven particularly popular, particularly as your money doesn't have to navigate through the credit card payments system for up to a week. Those seeking instant gratification can now sign up to TheGoldCasino.com where they use eGold to bet with. Here you can buy eGold, bet with it, win some more and then use your winnings to go to other eGold affiliated sites and buy a holiday to celebrate your new found wealth.

■ *Delivered cost effectively.* Fulfilment costs can account for up to 20% of gross revenues for many Internet businesses, although this is dependent on a number of factors. This section details the extent to which different products are cost effective to deliver. It is important to remember that the overall delivery cost is only relevant when considered as a percentage of profit. For example, upholstered furniture may be difficult to deliver because of its size and weight, and it may even have a high level of returns, but the margins and prices are high.

Alternatives are unappealing

The appeal of any Internet business is directly linked to the appeal of the next best alternative. In the case of retail Internet businesses this is shopping offline. There are a number of Internet businesses that would have an incremental chance of success because either the customer or the business finds the offline alternative unappealing. Specifically:

- *Stores with broad appeal but small geographic coverage.* Hamleys claims to be 'the finest toy store in the world'. They are certainly one of the best known and have a wonderful selection of over 40,000 toys. Until Hamleys.com came along, the only alternative for most shoppers was to go to its Regent Street flagship store. If you live in Glasgow or Spain this alternative is an unattractive prospect. For companies like Hamleys, eCommerce represents a significant untapped opportunity.

- *Ranges with low sales density and high inventory costs.* JCPenny.com has an Internet offer for special-sized women including plus, tall and petite sizes on its Web site. In addition to these ranges they have also launched a separate just4meplus.com site specialising in larger female sizes. These products are targeted at niche segments and unlikely to achieve the sales density in stores to justify the cost of the selling space. Furniture.com offers a significantly greater range of furniture products than bricks and mortar stores. This is cost effective, as Internet retailers like furniture.com do not need to hold inventory in stores to illustrate their product ranges. With both of these examples, a single distribution point and an Internet site create a highly cost effective channel.

- *Boring shopping.* Let's face it, shopping for grocery items is boring for most people. The first Internet retailer to make this process easy and simple gets my order.

What is the level of competitive intensity by country?

When entrepreneurs have evaluated the most attractive geographic and product markets and identified the attractive customers within them, they will need to find competitive advantage. The biggest and best ideas will be in the 'white space', an area that is not occupied by a credible player in the market. The key questions to be answered are:

- Who are the competitive candidates online?
- Which of these candidates are credible?
- Who is likely to compete in the future – whether on- or offline?
- How are you differentiated, in a sustainable way, from these players?

Who are the competitive candidates online? The starting point for any competitive review will be an Internet search for potential competitors. If you want to set up a wedding business visit some of the key search engines and type in wedding. You will find many competitors:

Key word search results for wedding

Key word	Euroferret.com	Go.com	Lycos
Wedding	176,132	627,867	163,126

Don't despair, 99% of these sites will not be credible sites. A further – and fast – review of these sites will be required to establish those that are.

Offline candidates are potential competition and also a potential exit strategy for investors, as they may want to buy the site. Consider very carefully how you will compete against the offline players. Often there is an opportunity to offer better prices. This alone can be a competitive edge for Internet players as the established businesses find it difficult to undermine their store-based pricing policy. Try not to rely on this unless you can build enough scale to be the 'category killer', or your margins will be low.

Which of these candidates are credible? Spend a couple of hours checking the major offerings by searching the portal sites to see which firms they have linked into their sites. If you find a potential competitor, search the industry publications (for example redherring.com, wired.com) to see how much money they have raised. These publications will usually discuss other competitors to the site you have found. This 'big site down' approach will lead you to the major players.

As soon as you have defined the likely sources of product supply, call those key suppliers and find out if they have any Internet offerings. Most suppliers will usually be happy to disclose this information. Assuming that there are competitors out there, start-ups will need to prove that they can effectively beat them in the market. A start-up competitive checklist should include a comparison of:

- Target audience – Is it different?
- Content – Is it motivating? Is it branded? Is it relevant?
- Commerce – Is it making money in the same markets? Does their product and service offering have superior brands, or depth and breadth of range? Are their products cheaper, or is there a broader price architecture?
- Community – Is there a 'sticky' community? What elements of community are offered? (For example chat rooms, bulletin boards, high levels of personalisation?)

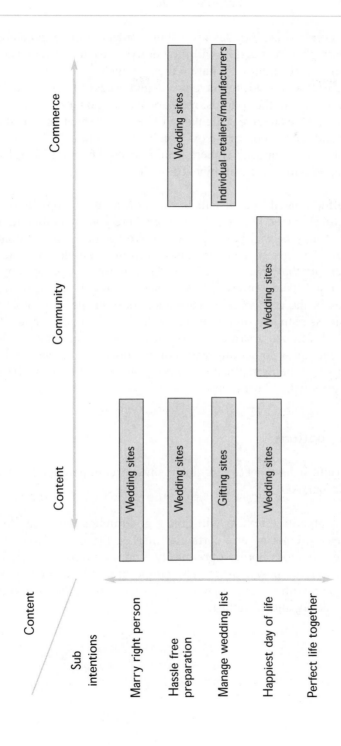

Figure 3.10 I-Wed.com target space competitive summary

- Customer service – Do they take telephone orders, is there a customer service offering? How quickly will they deliver products and services? What is their returns policy? What do they charge?
- Access to customers – Does it have privileged access to customers such as partnerships with other portals, retailers and magazines?
- Buying scale – Does it have scale that will be used to beat you? Is it part of a bricks and mortar enterprise or an industry grouping?
- Funding – Is it well funded? Is there venture capital backing? Is it likely to get more, perhaps via an imminent flotation?

Are you differentiated in a sustainable way? Map the competitive sites against your offering (see Figure 3.10) to see where you are competitive in each country. It may be that you are competitive because you are content rich, or perhaps because of your breadth of offering. The key to Internet success is to ensure that your competitive edge can not be replicated by the competition. Established Internet businesses can react very quickly to minor changes in the competitive landscape, consequently a competitive edge in a business plan may not be there by the time you get to market.

If you have developed a strategic asset or perhaps a partnership with a major player who adds something your competition can't, always ask for exclusivity to stop it being replicated. Nobody will invest in ideas that can be copied by established businesses.

Market entry options

> Strike the right balance between globalism and commercialism. (Steve Case, Chairman, AOL)

An effective competitive review will give a good indication of the likelihood of success in entering any particular market. Once you have established that there is cross border opportunity, you now have to decide the best way to enter the new market. The single greatest consideration is whether to launch with a local, regional, or global offer. Whatever you do you should think big and scale fast.

Launching with a local, regional or global offer

There are three options open to any business. They can create a worldwide offer with no localisation, go for a regional launch, or introduce separate local offers.

There is no right or wrong answer here: the decision will rest on a balance of factors: can you globalise your offer and achieve economies of scale, but at the same time localise enough of it to satisfy customers? Consider QXL.com, a leading European auction site, founded in 1997. QXL now operates in seven countries and its sites have more than 20m page views in a month, giving it a very broad European reach. QXL ran a parallel process, rapidly launching a focused core offer across Europe, while deepening the depth and breadth of its offer in each of the seven countries.

A phased launch with a core offer also makes the scaling process easier:

- *Phased (but fast) launch across countries or regions:* Attractive markets are those where you can rapidly scale your business. Perhaps the most famous attempt to take on the whole world at once is Boo.com, which was launched simultaneously across the US and Europe. Not everyone is that brave or stupid but even local launch business plans should demonstrate European potential – think big, even if you start small. Thinking

Table 3.7   Launching with a local, regional or global offer

Launch Method	Pros	Cons
Pan European Launch	■ Economies of scale ■ Easier to manage ■ Cheaper, since multiple language versions can be avoided	■ Unattractive to customer due to lack of customization ■ Difficult to administer and be locally responsive
Region Launch	■ Leverages common language and other sources of homogeneity across countries ■ Economies of scale relative to country approach	■ Will still need country specific content ■ Need to provide local content and merchants
Country Launch	■ Locally oriented management will ensure content is most relevant to countries	■ Smaller countries, such as Austria likely to be ignored despite favourable demographics ■ Economically inefficient

Figure 3.11   Illustrative European regions

big requires a European rollout plan, European finances and a competitive review across the whole of Europe, not just the local market. This analysis will lead you to a deep understanding of a relevant core offer that can both satisfy customers and be replicated across regions or countries easily. If you decide to phase the launch by region you can group countries together by language and cultural similarities (see Figure 3.11).

■ *Core offer development:* the most attractive markets are those that will enable you to rapidly roll out your core offer. Most Internet offers start with an initial core offer that rapidly becomes deeper and broader (see Figure 3.12). This core offer will be delivered to market in the fastest time possible to 'claim the space' and build business momentum. The first question any prospective partner will ask is 'do you have a Web site set up?' Having your site up and running will give partners the confidence that you can achieve your business goals. It will also give potential competitors an indication of the speed you are moving at and potentially warn them off. Also, if your business exit strategy is dependent on a trade purchase, then they are more likely to find you if you have a Web site up and running. Any core offer must satisfy these criteria.

- *Customer satisfaction:* Always launch with an offer that will satisfy your customers. The key to success here is to understand your target customer and what their reasons for visiting your site are. At Goodhome.com, a US site selling furniture, decoration products and housewares, people visited the site for its 'home solutions'. The initial core offer was a restricted range of five different room styles shown in pictures similar to those in magazines. This meant that most site visitors would find at least one style they liked. The visiting customer could easily grasp the site's unique concept, that enabled them to buy everything they saw in the photograph. Goodhome.com also signposted future on-site developments by demonstrating the 3D functionality that the site would shortly offer. This market-based approach contrasts to the familiar 'under construction' pasted over most new sites.

- *Authority in what you do:* Businesses increase customer satisfaction if their core offer has retail 'authority'. Authority is what you stand for and is probably the reason why people will visit you versus the competition. Amazon has authority in books, Dell in computers, and lastminute.com in weekend breaks. If you ever have a choice of developing depth or breadth in your offer, go for depth first. Depth builds authority and customer satisfaction. It is unwise to launch a shallow core offer in the rush to expand geographically. A shallow offer will disappoint your customers who will be lost to the competition. Many Internet businesses will lay claim to their space with a big PR campaign, but only open the site when they are ready to create a positive customer experience. Oneswoop.com, the European car trading business, launched a new PR campaign with each round of funding. By building a network of major established businesses and raising an enormous amount of money, Oneswoop.com gave people a reason to believe the business would be successful. Those who were inspired by the PR campaign to visit the site found a 'holding' site, which explained the concept, detailed the partnerships in place and enabled customers to register. Those who registered were updated with steady progress enabling the business to build a relationship with them. Only when a positive customer experience was assured was the site opened for business.

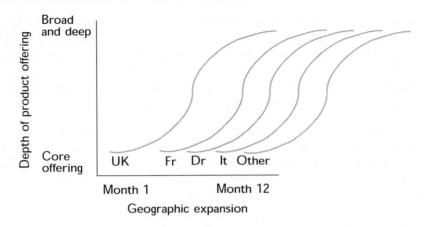

Figure 3.12   European launch countries

- *Replicability:* The core offer should embrace a simple enough business model to enable fast replication in different countries. When letsbuyit.com first rolled out across Europe it began with a restricted number of suppliers of standard European products that could be delivered direct to customers. This enabled the firm to claim the space in a number of countries at the same time as it was developing deeper and broader localised offers. By contrast, a business plan which promises to cut out the inventory costs of retailers by, for example, doing deals with 150 suppliers may not be replicable. It is a very high-risk strategy to try to replicate complex core offers across geography in the exponential growth stages of an immature Internet business. The result is likely to be poor customer service and ultimate failure.

There are always some elements of a plan that may not be totally replicable. These may include local access to the Internet, local news offerings where they relate to cultural tastes and local fulfilment centres. Local management will usually be required to help navigate through alliances and legal issues.

Think big, start small, scale fast

The idea is to get into a market first, not when it matures. (Matei Mihalca, Internet analyst with Merrill Lynch)

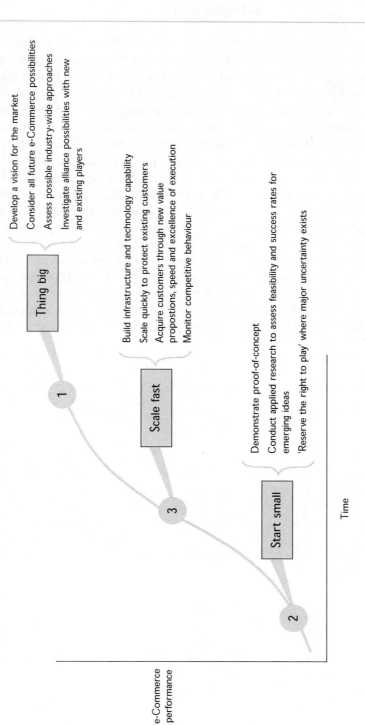

Figure 3.13 Three steps to scale an Internet business
Source: Andersen Consulting

The degree of market attractiveness and hence likely success will also depend on the size of the opportunity. Scalability is the overwhelming driver of attractiveness. Consequently, all start-up firms should have a big vision and rapidly move towards it (see Figure 3.13). You may start small to prove success in your home markets, but make sure you don't lose your first mover advantage to achieve European scale. If your business model relies on attracting advertising to the site, the importance of size is even more acute. Take PlanetMedica.com, a health portal launched simultaneously in the UK, Germany and France. Without this geographic scale it could never achieve enough 'eyeballs' to drive advertising revenues. Also consider Letsbuyit.com, a site which aggregates customer purchasing power to enable consumers to buy everyday products at a cheaper price. Letsbuyit.com's first site was launched in Sweden in April 1999. Within ten months of launch it had entered 13 other European countries. It is difficult to imagine a similar idea now being able to achieve similar funding and being successful. Remember that market valuations go to the number one or two in the category – you cannot afford to hang around if that leaves you in the number three or four position so scale fast, very fast.

CHAPTER 4

Marketing and Communications Development

Marco Rimini and Kate Eden, J WALTER THOMPSON

For many internet businesses the differentiating factor will be the ability to attract and retain customers. This chapter will help you do this. It is equally valid for Internet start-ups, and for established brands that are seeking to add an Internet strand to their existing business offering. It assumes an audience which is not necessarily expert in marketing and communications. If you are already an old hand at these, you might find some useful reminders, but the chances are that much will already be familiar to you.

Introduction: the Internet brand landscape

Developing a communications strategy and plan

So you've got your business idea, the technology is being tested, the funding is on the way, but you still need a marketing and communications strategy to complete your business plan and move into action. Where do you start? What do you need to do?

Co-creating

Is marketing an Internet brand the same as a brand from the offline world?

Yes and no. Many of the questions and disciplines remain the same, but the priorities are slightly different.

'Strategy needs to be created from the future backward, not the present forwards' (Gary Hamel, business guru and co-author of *Competing for the Future*, 1994). Because many of the Internet companies are start-ups, they are less weighted by the past and can therefore avoid the old structures and invent a better solution. Although the dot.com brands have a greater freedom to re-invent the established rules, the rush of new companies means that those looking for long term business success may find they need an even deeper understanding of their potential customers, their needs and motivations, than was the case for traditional brands.

Probably the greatest difference introduced by online businesses is the amount of time taken to move from brief to finished ad. Conventionally, the process might take months of research, analysis, honing, refinement and deep thinking. With the dot.coms, the timing is more likely to be in days, rather than weeks or months. In itself this is transforming the traditional communications companies, who are having to re-think how they do business.

These time pressures demand a new way of working. No longer the old fashioned silos of responsibility. Such a compression of usual timetables requires a more co-operative approach; clients and their agency/business partners need to work together to 'co-create'. More fun for everyone, but it also requires a high degree of discipline in terms of who can approve ideas. (The outside architecture of the Millennium Dome was signed-off by one person; its interior was decided by a committee of public servants and politicians – decide for yourself.)

There may not be enough time to implement all of the different elements of the process in depth, but the questions and issues remain the same. This chapter seeks to provide straightforward help and support as to how to develop a powerful and effective communications plan and execution. For those who do not have time to get any further than this page, go straight to the end of the chapter, where you will find a 10-minute strategy plan.

Dare to dream

Companies operating on the Internet are driven by energy and a 'can do' mentality. They are reintroducing the entrepreneurial spirit of small business into many larger corporations which, until recently, had managed to insulate themselves from this momentum. So dare to dream, and dream big. One of the most exciting aspects of the Internet is that all sorts of opportunities are now possible. In the past, they would have been unimaginable. The technology is creating new possibilities to connect with other people.

There is, however, a balance of the dream: dream your dream to the limits; and at the same time be very down-to-earth when it comes to implementation. One of the crucial objectives is not only getting people to the site, but making sure they come back again and again. The key task is to be clear about your goals and your brand vision, understanding as much as possible about your potential customers and how you can encourage them to spend the maximum amount of time and money with you.

If you only have time and energy to ask one question, make it – 'why will anyone come to me; what do I have to offer?' And keep asking it of yourself every day.

Pace of change

There is a tendency with all technology to overestimate the speed at which change will occur and to underestimate its ultimate impact. And so it is with the Internet. As recently as 1995, many commentators assumed that this particular technology would never really catch on. Now the assumption is that every single aspect of life will be 'e-driven', leading to the end of shopping, the end of paper, and the end of the office. Probably not. For instance, the much predicted 'paperless office' looks ever less likely for all but the profoundly orderly (or memory-gifted). In the 1940s the introduction of vitamin tablets predicted the end of food. Perfect nutrition with a single tablet. But of course food has only a little to do with nutrition and a lot to do with sociability, nurturing, gratification and entertainment. The recently announced nutrition chip might well take notice.

This is a cautionary tale: think carefully about what your brand is really delivering to people. Understanding this can dramatically increase your chances of success. Many of the current business plans for Internet start-ups seem to by-pass any notion of their ultimate benefit to the consumer; the assumption is simply that people will flock there in their millions.

In contrast, the Internet's much-hyped ability to transcend geographical boundaries, gathering the world's farthest-flung consumers into a single network, is already a proven reality. This, of course, raises its own cultural challenges, which must be addressed throughout the communications development.

Managing the corporate memory

How will you keep the relationship going? How will you keep talking and listening to your customers? If effective communications are a way of beginning a conversation, how will you then keep the initial conversation going and take it to new levels? This is particularly important for Internet companies, as the Internet facilitates ongoing conversation between provider and customer. People expect companies to understand the interactive basis of the net world and not just to treat it as yet another 'passively consumed' medium.

The customer relationship may come into difficulties very early in the process. This is evidenced by the many companies which manage their shipping through semi-personalised emails. The customer makes a purchase, and an email whizzes back to them, confirming that their order has been received and will soon be despatched. But then a further email arrives, announcing that their purchase is not available in the colour they want. So they email the company back, requesting the product in blue. And the customer hears... Often nothing at all. Because the person who apparently signed the customer's email doesn't actually receive any replies. So rather than deepening the relationship, you leave your customer stranded in cyberspace. If the customer could find a phone number for the company, then they could pursue the request further, but even if there is a number, it is more than likely to leave the customer in 'voice-mail hell'.

Customer service is not an optional extra for an Internet company; it is the core business. Get this wrong, and problems will happen very fast. As many Internet companies found this last Christmas when, having taken the orders, they found they could not deliver. For other companies, the Christmas delivery deadlines were only met because all available employees – from the managing director to the security guard (plus their families!) – spent the last few days before Christmas working like Santa's elves in the packing factory. A powerful testimony to their belief in the centrality of customer service to their business.

Online relationships develop in much the same way as those in real life. They take time and effort. They go through different stages, each of which is fragile, precious and in need of constant care and attention:

- Introduction
- Acquaintance
- Rapport
- Bonding/trust.

Much of this relationship management will depend on how you develop your systems within the company. Data is vital – but try to think of it not just as 'data' or numbers, but rather as an invaluable memory of your customer. Strong relationships depend on the other person remembering who you are and what has happened in your life. Rarely the case with marketing relationships. So don't think of after-sales and databases as rather boring technical add-ons; they are your brand's memory. And memory is what makes us human.

Avoid the 'wild and wacky' trap

In the race for success, understanding the role of communications and how to spend budgets most effectively will become key. At the moment, many Internet start-ups focus only on building awareness. This is certainly a vital first stage: if no-one knows you are there, or cannot remember your site address correctly, it will be very difficult to succeed. However, long term success will rely on people returning; and for this you need to go beyond awareness and to start building rapport.

As we have already acknowledged, time pressures are great – but even if you only have ten minutes to think about what you are doing, you need to spend that time thinking about where you want to be in the long term, and not just next week. If you know where you are going, it is much easier to develop communications which not only work today, but are also building towards tomorrow's success. More cost-effective, and an accelerator to business growth.

The biggest trap to fall into is what seems to have become the 'generic net ad' – a wild and wacky visual (designed to upset a significant proportion of the population), weird graphics (borrowed from men's mags or *Wired*), a funny monosyllabic name, and there you go. Well indeed there you may go, but for how long? Nothing wrong in a snappy name, of course, but better if it also says something more substantive about you and what you have to offer. These are today's mistakes, best avoided – doubtless new ones will come along tomorrow.

The five difficult questions

The planning cycle is a simple set of questions, which may be difficult to answer – but keep going and your communications plan will be much the richer for it. And keep asking yourself these questions once your brand is up and running; it will help ensure that your ongoing business development is informed by sound strategic thinking.

The need to keep questioning and evaluating what you are doing becomes even more important in the net world, as things are evolving very quickly. Much may change: what looks like a good answer today, may not

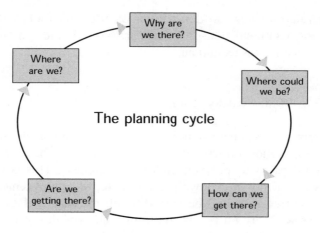

Figure 4.1   The planning cycle

be so next year. The questions, however, will stay the same. They are known, collectively, as 'The Planning Cycle' (see Figure 4.1) and – since their development in the late 1960s – have provided an invaluable strategic framework across the communications industry and beyond.

Where are we?

What assets do you currently have? Are you an established brand or company, looking to the net to develop your existing business? Or are you a completely new brand? In either case, look at what you already have, not only in terms of tangible assets on your business plan, but also your intangible assets. For those established brands which already trade across several geographical boundaries, this audit can be particularly extensive.

This audit is likely to comprise elements such as:

- The name
- The look/design
- The products you offer
- The service you deliver
- Your personality
- Your reputation
- Every point of communication and contact.

If you're an established brand, you're likely to pay a lot of attention to your above-the-line advertising (partly because it is so expensive), but in doing so you may overlook many other elements of your communication mix. If at all possible, look at everything you send to your customers. What do your invoices look like? Do they reflect the brand personality and positioning? Virgin is a brand which is not only distinctive, but projects itself with impressive coherence: whereas most airlines' on-board shopping magazines look very similar and bear titles such as *In-flight Shopping*, Virgin's is labelled *Retail Therapy* and flagged 'go on, you know you need it'. A perfect understanding of the customer's in-flight boredom, and of Virgin's capacity to overcome this state of mind.

Why are we there?

What has happened to put you in this position? What lessons can you learn from the past?

This stage will be very different if you are an established brand moving online – think very carefully about what you have done so far:

- What is your real goal in going online – to develop a new distribution channel, to target a new audience, or to evolve the brand image? Or all of these?
- How have your communications helped to create the brand?
- What worked well? What worked less well?
- What elements of your current brand and its personality are strong?
- Do you want to preserve these qualities and attributes for the brand online?
- Or do you want to evolve your brand/personality?
- Is it about resolving the brand's mid-life crisis?

For start-ups, meanwhile, the key question remains: why has your business plan developed the way it has? What factors have driven you so far?

Where could we be?

Where do you want to go? How will you know when you have achieved your goals? And how will that feel?

Decide what you really want and also how you will know when this has happened. This is important for the bad days as well as the good days. On the bad days, it is reassuring to be able to explain to yourself why you are working 16 hours a day with little immediate sight of profit and lots of people watching. And on a good day, you need to be able to spot that it *is* a good day. Too often it is easier to define what you don't want, rather than be clear about what you do want. This means you will be very good at knowing when life is a bitch, but may miss the days when your cup is actually more than half-full.

Having clear goals and targets is also very important for the organisation itself; often each of the founding partners has slightly different goals. It is vital, therefore, to understand these individual goals, to decide how each person will judge their own success, and for everyone to agree the overall balance of objectives. Communications within the company can be as important as those targeted at customers. This is particularly true when there is a strong service element to the brand (as there always is for an Internet company). The old models of authority in industrial society have disappeared: you can't tell colleagues what to do; you have to inspire them to want to be part of what you are doing.

One of the most telling quotes describing 'Generation X' attitudes to employment is: 'why go on strike when you can destroy the company through surly service?' It may be very difficult to know how good your service is. It relies on trust: trust between you and the others within the company, and trust between the company and its customers, demonstrated in how you treat them. Companies need to think carefully about their sales and return policies. Many of the complaints about home shopping relate to a delivery (or often, a non-delivery). Demanding proof from your customer may make sense for the logistics department, but it also reflects a fatal lack of trust in your customers.

Trust is a quality which is vitally important in the networked world, but unfortunately one that is in increasingly short supply. Trust has become more personal, more specific and more volatile. People expect to be kept informed: consumers are no longer prepared to sit and be a passive audience; they want to be involved, and one of the most powerful aspects of the net is its ability to give these people a voice.

How can we get there?

- What are the products that will help you achieve your goals?
- What are the services you will offer?
- How will communications help?
- What role do you expect them to play?
- What are the key messages?

If you are going to achieve your goals, you have to maintain the flexibility to learn from what you are doing. Keep true to the overall strategy, but be prepared to change specific tactics if things are not going the way you would like them to. Do not keep changing the strategy itself; it confuses people and wastes money.

Are we getting there?

This question may seem like a luxury ('If things are going well, why worry? Let's just keep doing what we've already been doing'). In fact, keeping a constant check on how you are performing is vital.

The important element of this stage is to decide what information you will need to assess your success. There can be a tendency to do the same as everyone has always done – carry out a regular survey and ask the questions which are already asked by your competitors. But if the Internet is a new medium, creating a new model and a new way of working, why would you want to stick with the same old approach to evaluation?

Make the evaluation process part of your business; involve your customers in your success. Don't just send out the usual questionnaires; instead, run discussion groups and forums, asking people what they would like you to be doing next – and listen to what they have to say. You don't have to follow their advice, but you do have to acknowledge their ideas and thank them.

Summary

So, now that we've looked at the planning cycle, let's see what specific tools and techniques we have at our disposal to take us from start-to-finish, and back again.

TTB overview

The tools and techniques which follow in the subsequent sections are based upon a practice known as Thompson Total Branding (TTB) (see Figure 4.2). This is the route map and tool box used across the J Walter Thompson (JWT) network. However, each of the agencies that you work with will have their own equivalent techniques for ensuring that each stage of the Planning Cycle is implemented to full effect. The various TTB

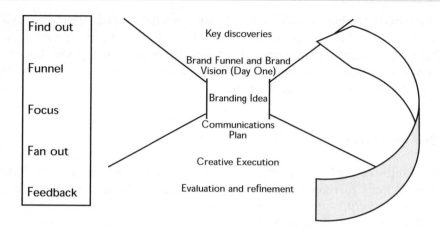

Figure 4.2   The TTB overview

processes described in the following sections should therefore be treated as an overall guide to the types of exercises which your own agencies will choose to cover.

TTB involves six sequential stages. Based upon the Planning Cycle, it starts with a broad-based survey of the opportunities and issues (Key Discoveries), then uses these to inform the development of the brand positioning (the Brand Funnel & Brand Vision, developed at the Day One session). This positioning is subsequently expressed in a Branding Idea; and this, in turn, helps guide the development of the communications plan and creative executions. Finally, the campaign's in-market performance is evaluated, these findings being used to help refine the campaign's subsequent development.

No matter how strong your time pressures, each of these six steps is necessary to the development of an effective communications program. To by-pass any individual step would be fatal, and an extra week invested at this stage of the process could pay huge dividends in terms of your eventual business performance.

It nevertheless holds true that many of the time pressures of Internet business development simply cannot be ignored. Please bear in mind, therefore, that although the process described in the following sections may seem overly time-consuming, each of these six steps can be significantly fast-tracked and streamlined.

Key discoveries – what have you got to work with?

Finding out more – the accelerators and brakes to making your vision happen

The first stage of the TTB process is to look at what surrounds you, trying to understand what is happening in the world, and what opportunities and insights it offers you. These opportunities and insights are known as Key Discoveries, and divide into the following five groups:

- Category discoveries
- Consumer discoveries
- Brand discoveries
- Communications discoveries
- Client discoveries.

As the name suggests, each of the Key Discoveries should be:

- *Key:* Cut through the data overload by identifying the handful of crucial factors which will have a significant impact on your business. Distinguish the 'need to know' single sheet of A4 from the 'nice to know' filing cabinet.

- A *discovery:* Try to approach the issues in a new, provocative way. Identify the words you use the most often in describing your business opportunity – and then ban them! Think lateral, fresh, and innovative.

The richness and quality of the Key Discoveries will affect every subsequent stage of communication development. They should therefore be as innovative and insightful as possible. This, in turn, demands that they are approached with just as much energy, passion and creativity as the development of the campaign idea itself. 'Creativity' is emphatically *not* the unique property of the advertising agency; it is a state of mind and a working practice which should be felt and applied by all participants throughout all stages of the process. If you assume that 'creativity' only kicks in when the agency's creative team begin to consider how they can bring your brand proposition to life, then you are truly missing one of the biggest tricks in the business.

Category discoveries

The first question is 'what category are you in?' Although this may seem obvious, the Internet is, in fact, blurring many of the traditional marketing definitions. The traditional view of one's category was 'people who make the same sort of products'. But this may not be how people are comparing your brand; they may see you primarily as a dot.com company, and therefore the bedfellow of other dot.coms, regardless of your actual product.

It's also worth remembering that every brand – regardless of category – has to compete for the time, money and energy of an increasingly discerning audience. Why would anyone want to attend to your advertising, when they could be talking with their kids, their friends? Or getting more sleep, going to the pub, writing their own winning Internet business strategy… ?

You may have to look at yourself as belonging to a number of different categories:

- *Manufacturing category:* The companies who make the same sorts of products as you do

- *Service category:* The companies who offer the same sort of service

- *Dot.com category:* Are you seen as competing with amazon and last-minute, even if you're selling organic wine?

- *Needs category:* What are people looking for when they buy from you? You might think you're selling organic wine, but your customers may put you in their 'health food' category, their 'cranks' category, their 'recovery' category, their 'deserved indulgence' category, or their 'green creds' category.

Think about the variety of categories to which you belong almost as membership of various clubs; and look at the 'rules' of those clubs. It may be that the different forms of category involve conflicting criteria.

The benefits of this exercise are:

- Understanding the competition and where the future pressures may come from
- Understanding the conventions of different categories
- Understanding the key trends and drivers of change which you may be able to exploit for your brand.

Ask yourself:

- Where do you fit in?
- Do you want to fit in, or do you want to break the rules?
- Which are the categories that feel more comfortable? What can you learn from them?
- Who are your category heroes and role models? What makes them special to you?
- What are the driving forces for each of the categories?
- What are the future trends?
- What can you do to make the most of these changes?
- Do your systems and plans have sufficient flexibility and scalability? Will they be able to meet demand and growth?

Consumer discoveries

This is the most important area to spend time thinking about. If you only have the time and resources to give serious consideration to one of the Key Discoveries, make it this one.

First, a word of caution. Although the term 'consumer' is much used these days, few people define themselves as 'consumers'. Consuming is something people do; it is not a part of their identity. 'Consumer' remains the most useful collective term, so we'll stick with it, but remember that consumers are real people with lots of relationships, an increasing list of things they think they should be doing, a complex lifestyle, and more and more people trying to talk to them, when all they want to do is have a few moments to themselves.

Be courteous in everything you do. Remember that the balance of power between brands and consumers is changing, and that by setting up an Internet company, you are one of the drivers of change. People know that their ability to shop gives them real power. There is over-supply: those companies who deliver real benefits to people will do well; and those who do not really think of their customers will not survive for very long. So keep asking yourself 'why should anyone want to spend their hard-earned time, money and energy on what I have to sell?' Because your potential customers will be asking this of themselves every time your name registers on their crowded radar.

As we have already seen, the existing models of consumer behaviour do not necessarily embrace the particular characteristics of the Web. You therefore need to remain aware that your hypotheses may be wrong.

Rather than insisting on a fixed model of either business or consumer behaviour, you may instead benefit from working to a broad hypothesis, which you continually test and refine in the light of your experiences. Take nothing for granted, question everything and keep looking and listening.

One of your most effective forms of research may be direct experience. Business books can be helpful, but sometimes the real world is even better. So, break out of your office and observe your target audience in their own environment, listening to how they talk about things. Carry out more formal research by all means, but also get out there and observe it all for yourself, first hand. The insights gained could well lead to your strongest competitive advantage.

Ask yourself:

- What are these people doing, thinking, feeling? You will need to understand as much as possible about your potential customers. Not only who they are and what they're looking for, but also the nature of their motivations. What are the underlying trends which your brand might be able to fulfil?

- What are the opportunities to make contact with him/her? When should you make the first move?

- Do you understand their moods and need states? For instance, the telephone company may want to do some research to find out about its customers, but calling people at home after a long day at work can easily feel like an intrusion or nuisance call.

- How can your brand use this insight to its advantage? Knowing what the consumer is missing may create even greater business opportunities. Why, for instance, does Starbucks not provide plugs for people to recharge their mobile phones? Why doesn't the phone company sometimes call up simply to chat, but also be prepared to withdraw immediately if people prefer to be left alone? Why do they always phone simply to sell their latest scheme?

- (If, as is likely, your business plans are international): are there any cultural factors which affect the values, attitudes and behaviour of your different consumer nationalities? Or do they share the same basic consumer need? And can this consumer need be satisfied in the same way across the different territories, or should your business plan accommodate different modes of communication and operation within each market?

Triggers for purchase

What are the triggers for products and services like yours? The more you understand about the triggers for purchase, the greater your chance of developing a communications plan and message which tap into these needs, ensuring that you are doing the right things at the right time.

Lastminute.com is an interesting example of a company whose name is easily remembered and which taps into the consumer's moment of need – you know exactly when to go there, the name alone providing many clues as to what to expect. This psychology is also exploited in the brand's above-the-line advertising. Immediately prior to the recent Valentine's Day, for instance, a poster campaign served to disparage the conventional gifts (such as a bunch of flowers from the garage), and recommend Lastminute.com as the means to a much more interesting solution.

The basic triggers for purchase tend to fall into four broad categories:

- *Routine:* The sort of things people buy every day or every week and don't even really think about any more.

- *Impulse:* The things you see and 'have to have'. At its most extreme this may be the most resistant category for Internet purchase, unless there emerges a radical new form of delivery which can get chocolate to your door within two minutes.

- *Solution:* To a problem. Suddenly those unpleasant stains appear and where do you find something to get rid of them? The stakes are often high where a specific solution is needed, and delivery in all its forms is important.

- *Lifestyle*: 'For the way you live your life today'. The products and services that say more about you (and that's why you choose them). Luxury cars are a great example: most buyers say that factors such as comfort and engineering are what drove their choice. Dig deeper, however, and (male) Jaguar drivers often talk about the first time they took their father out for a drive in their new Jag and the resulting sense of achievement (move over Sigmund).

Ask yourself:

- What kind of purchase is it? Does it fall into any of the above distinctions, or are there different drivers?

The buying process

People's buying behaviour can seem rather irrational. But that very 'strangeness' may represent a huge market opportunity for your Internet business.

As an example, take retailing. With the advent of the Internet, it is quite possible that the respective processes of 'shopping' and 'buying' may become separated. Consumers will continue to visit the real-life store to look and touch, to meet with friends and to socialise. However, having made full use of the retailer's expensive real estate, these same consumers may then return home to their PC, to trawl the world for the cheapest prices on the objects which earlier caught their eye. Much of the discussion about net shopping assumes that the real-life store/virtual store experience will be an 'either/or'; in reality, it may be an 'and/and'. People will sometimes use the net and will sometimes go to the store – and it is as likely to depend on their mood as any rational decision.

The consumer's relationship system – exploring how your customers relate to you

Are your customers relating to you at all? Are you relating with them? Or are you on the verge of a stand-off? Endless books have been written about customer relationship management (CRM), but you may find it more worthwhile to spend a few moments thinking about it as a human being, and to forget the jargon. Think, also, about what you are saying about yourself: 'viral marketing' is one of the current buzzwords, but do you really want your brand to be regarded as a virus? Just be sure you mean what you say.

Deepening the relationship

How are Internet relationships developed? In much the same way as in real life. People need to know who you are and what to expect of you (a process which kicks off from the moment you're introduced). In fact, the person's direct experience becomes even more important when buying online, as many of the physical cues for reassurance are lacking. Relationships are built up over time; they depend on shared values, shared experiences and shared memories.

Because the Internet is new and not yet taken for granted, the purchase is always a conscious 'experience'. This means that the service and relationship elements of the deal are particularly important. Your direct dealings with the customer are always your most powerful form of communication. Thus, weak service systems (for example a stroppy representative at the call centre) can easily invalidate the perceived benefits which your advertising campaign had worked to hard to build. Your recovery systems need to be watertight in order to offset any negative experience with a more positive one. If you don't understand that your customers are in charge, you may find yourself losing those customers fast. Even worse, they may decide to take their revenge by bad mouthing you.

Ideally, you will be able to manage your customer relationships so that they deepen throughout the following four stages:

Introduction: awareness/acquisition

▪ When and where are the relevant times and places that people will come into contact with your brand? Will they recognise you? Do you need to create some form of introduction reminder – for example point-of-sale materials which link to the advertising style or idea? Does the packaging link to the brand personality and look?

▪ You need to be remembered – but how do you want to be remembered? At the moment, many online brands seem to think that wearing bright colours and 'shouting' at people is the best way. But although this strategy may indeed be effective in terms of pure awareness, will people ever want to spend time with you as a brand?

▪ Think about your personality – if your brand were a person, how would he/she behave when introduced to someone? Does your name give people clues as to what to expect? For instance, www.askjeeves.com (a search engine) creates vivid associations of what to expect through its logo (see Figure 4.3).

Trying out: experiencing/on trial

▪ The initial experience of your brand is critically important. You need to be able to deliver the promise. If something goes wrong, your recovery systems need to be in place. And if things go badly wrong, go back to older technology and try to talk with the person direct. Ideally, the

Figure 4.3   Logo for www.askjeeves.com

founder does the calling: Richard Branson still gets on the phone to customers who have had problems – and this personal involvement makes an immense difference to people.

Using and appreciating: experiencing the brand more often

▪ This is all about deepening the relationship, being a brand that is valued by people. Think carefully about cross-selling and incentives. Additional revenue may be all you want, but what is the benefit to your customer? Should they be grateful to you, or should you be grateful to them? We rarely hear much about a company's gratitude; maybe it would make a difference.

▪ The idea that 'the customer is king' is often replayed, but most customers feel that they're only treated as kings when they're spending like kings. They would like to be treated as the master, with the brand as servant – but rarely find this to be the case. Even with service brands such as hotels, people complain that they are not recognised, even when they regularly stay at the same venue. On every visit, they have to fill out the same old forms. Loyalty cards may help some of this, but to be recognised for yourself remains the most powerful way of making someone feel good. The need for acknowledgement is increasing in a world where life is more transitory and many of the traditional relation-ships are breaking down.

Loyalty: becoming a repeat purchaser

- Loyal customers are the core for most successful businesses. Pareto's Law still holds: 20% of your customers will account for 80% of your sales. But how can you identify and look after those customers? And how will that make other customers feel? Wanting to move closer? Or excluded/less favoured?

- Remember that loyalty always belongs to the customer and not to the brand. Customers can withdraw their loyalty whenever they like; and many of the recent studies show that loyalty, like trust, is becoming more fragile. This is in part due to manufacturers' complacent assump-tions that their products are 'good enough', and that their customers' loyalty can therefore be guaranteed.

- The Internet is driving the need to rethink how marketing and commu-nications operate. A more conversational and co-operative style of working is now possible; and it is via the Internet that many of the old expectations are being turned on their head. You can relate to your customers in many different ways – just make sure you have decided what you are doing and that everything your brand does fits with the overall personality and vision.

Brand discoveries

Interrogate your brand until it confesses its entire characteristics: good, bad and ugly. A time-honoured way to achieve this is to undertake a form of analysis known as SWOT (Strengths, Weaknesses, Opportunities, Threats):

Strengths

Perhaps the secret of this tool's enduring appeal is that it starts with the good news (that is, the brand's strengths)! Remember, however, that to qualify as a 'strength' the factor has to make a genuine and positive differ-ence to the consumer.

- What are your brand's differential advantages versus the competition?

- Are these advantages functional or emotional? Or both?

- Are they genuine strengths or merely 'hygiene factors'? For instance, the fact that your planned site is easy to navigate, entertaining and true to your brand character is not necessarily a strength; it is merely the minimum requirement set by your potential customers.

- Can these advantages be emulated by your competitors?

- If so, how long will this take? What advantages – if any – will you be left with? How will this affect your brand's performance, both in the immediate term and in the longer term?

- If your search fails to reveal any advantages, then clearly it's time for a serious re-think. At the very least, you can console yourself with the thought that you have saved yourself a serious amount of time, effort and money in taking this particular proposition any further.

Weaknesses

Every brand has an Achilles heel; it doesn't necessarily mean that the brand is a no-hoper; merely that it needs to be managed with these limitations in mind.

- What are your brand's liabilities/shortcomings?

- How did they develop?

- Are these disadvantages functional or emotional? Or both?

- Can they be overcome and if so, how?

- If they cannot be overcome, what impact are they likely to have on your brand's performance, both in the immediate term and in the longer term?

Opportunities

This is the section where you get to 'dream big' for your brand. As the brand's proud parent, guardian and fairy godmother, you are likely to get carried away by your offspring's seemingly endless possibilities ('organic wine today; organic bath salts/newspapers/private jets tomorrow'). The trick, therefore, is to temper your dreams with a huge dose of realism: keep your head in the clouds but your feet planted firmly on the ground.

- How will your brand be able to grow – and keep on growing?

- Can it create new audiences/distribution channels/product offerings/ strategic alliances?

- What 'outside' factors (for example economic trends, political climates, technological innovations) are likely to have a positive effect upon your brand? How can you use these to maximum advantage?

Threats

Not a pleasant task for anyone with a nervous disposition. This is where you force yourself to confront a whole raft of 'nightmare scenarios', any one of which could spell curtains for your brand, your business, your mortgage, your early retirement plans… So why put yourself through this agony? Because 'forewarned is forearmed'; it may help you to prevent the very disaster you fear, or at the very least, minimise the damage.

- What factors are likely to damage your brand?

- Internal factors, for example lack of funding, or core members of the team defecting to the opposition

- Competitive brand factors, for example new brand launches

- Category factors, for example City scepticism

- 'Outside' factors, for example unsympathetic economic trends or hostile political climates.

If you are a new start-up, this exercise will be particularly tricky. So play the 'brand fantasy' game. Dream your dreams and write them down. Then be realistic, identifying the potential weaknesses and threats which your dreams may face. Positive thinking is absolutely vital, but it must of course by tempered by a huge dose of reality. Many Internet start-ups seem to assume that they own a unique position in the world. Unfortunately, this is the wrong way to think: your reason for being is entirely defined by your customers; put yourself at the centre of the universe, and you may face a rude awakening.

In thinking about the future, remember that you have to plan for multiple futures. The only safe prediction of the future is that it is uncertain. The most difficult changes to spot will relate to those factors which you take for granted, and have thus become invisible to you. So think the unthinkable, and see where that gets you. If nothing else, it may create some new ideas for the next stage of your business development.

By the end of this exercise, you should have a pretty good picture of your brand's potential.

Communications discoveries

Spend some time looking at what other relevant brands are doing. Look at your competitors in all the different categories in which you might be competing. Look in particular at the most popular and successful communications – why are they working? What do they tap into, to elicit such a response? What would feel right for your brand?

The Internet has finally completed the destruction of the boundaries between 'above-the-line' disciplines (that is TV, press, radio, posters) and 'below-the-line' activity (for example direct mail, sponsorship, field marketing and sales promotion). So think of all communications activity as holistic, and look at as many different communications as possible, interrogating this evidence from every angle: the intended message, the design, the logos, the colour schemes, and how all of these are perceived by their target audience.

Your communications audit should look at:

- Current activity: who is doing what?

- External influences: can you spot the movies, the art, the music and so on which are being alluded to?

- Semiotic analysis: what are the signs and symbols of the category? You can change the rules, but try to understand what the established conventions are. And remember that since many of the 'rules' are implicit rather than explicit, it is easy to break the rules without realising. Airlines aiming at business customers tend to show those customers only within the plane and office; showing them in a pleasant outdoor surrounding implies that travellers are not working hard enough and that flying business class is an indulgence rather than a serious business decision.

As a general rule, put yourself in the consumer's shoes:

- Read those magazines that you might not normally read, but which are read by your target audience. Look at the editorial as well as the ads: which of these have the most engaging images?

- Watch the same TV programmes as your target audience. Try and see the world through their eyes.

- Do you know what music they are listening to? Spend some time listening to their charts and looking at who is being talked about/ written about.

- Participate in the more 'underground' forms of communication: the chat rooms, the forums, the newsgroups. Don't just listen to what is being said; be prepared to take part.

Finally, remember to consider any international implications:

- How do the international brands manage their communications? Is their approach monolithic (one campaign across all markets), or highly specified (a different campaign for each individual market), or somewhere in-between (for example one campaign for Europe, another campaign for North America)? What do you believe has led to this approach? Is it, for instance, driven by the genuine needs and possibilities of the company's consumer base? Could it also be driven by the company's budget constraints, and/or their overall management philosophy?

- If your own business plan involves communicating across a number of different markets, you need to decide which of the above three routes would be best for you, and why. Providing your target market is sufficiently homogenous across the different markets, then a cross-border campaign is generally preferred. This type of campaign not only minimises production costs and helps unite all members of your organisation into the same team, but also ensures that your internationally-travelled customers experience your brand in the same way wherever they happen to be.

- However, this type of campaign requires rigorous and constant policing in order to ensure that any necessary adaptations for local markets (from the translation of a poster headline, to the coverage of body parts in the Middle East) remain true to the campaign's overall spirit. If each individual country is given open licence to adapt the campaign as they please, then your intended monolithic campaign will soon fragment beyond recognition. This is not, of course, because your colleagues are deliberately attempting to destroy your campaign; it is simply because any single message can be interpreted in any number of seemingly legitimate ways.

Client discoveries

This area is entirely distinct from 'brand discoveries'; it focuses on those aspects of the client's own culture which will affect how the brand and its communications are developed and managed. These aspects could include:

- Specific individuals: experience, expertise, priorities, approaches

- Team structure: is it hierarchical or 'flat'?

- Resources: are budgets already available within the company, or do they have to be raised through third parties?

- History/profile: is the client already known to consumers/the city/decision-makers? What opinion do these audiences have of 'the force behind the brand'?

- Philosophy/culture: is there a predefined attitude/'way of doing things', or is each individual left to evolve their own system? This can be a particularly thorny issue where internationally based companies are concerned!

- Working practices: what sort of relationships and etiquette exist within the company? Does the company recognise that the former modes of command and control are less appropriate to the networked world? Are they achieving the more relevant working practices of co-operation and co-creation?

Clearly, this exercise requires clients to expose some rather 'personal' characteristics to their agency partners, and therefore requires that a large degree of trust and mutual respect has already been built up among the team. But it's obviously easier for everyone if these cultural issues are acknowledged before the process of communications development begins in earnest. (For what it's worth, the agencies should be equally willing to take the client through any relevant aspects of their own culture, as this can have just as profound an impact on the process and end result.)

Defining and refining your brand positioning

Having spent some time trying to find out as much as you can about your customers and your competition, you now need to try and organise and convert this information into a practical, actionable template for your brand. Remember that the twin principles of 'creativity' and 'co-creation' are as vital to this stage as any other.

Brand Funnel – capturing the key elements of your brand offer

The JWT Brand Funnel is designed to help ensure that your brand positioning is as strong and differentiated as possible. In common with various other positioning tools, it starts with the brand's physical qualities, and gradually progresses to the brand's more emotive/personality-driven aspects.

There are, in fact, six different levels (see Figure 4.4).

However, in strong contrast to other positioning tools, the JWT Brand Funnel requires that the list of attributes be limited to three, and that each successive layer be directly related to the one before, thus ensuring a maximum of three entries at each level. It also requires that the Brand Vision be limited to two words – ideally, creating a combination which is inherently provocative.

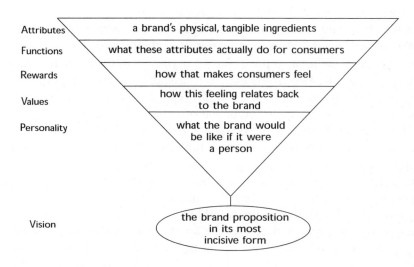

Figure 4.4 The JWT Brand Funnel

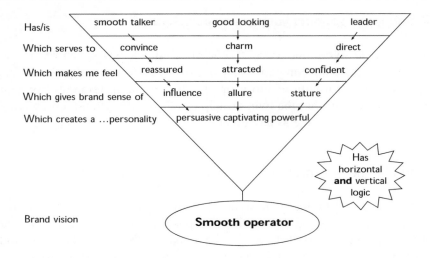

Has/is	smooth talker	good looking	leader
Which serves to	convince	charm	direct
Which makes me feel	reassured	attracted	confident
Which gives brand sense of	influence	allure	stature
Which creates a ...personality	persuasive captivating powerful		

Has horizontal **and** vertical logic

Brand vision

Smooth operator

Figure 4.5   The JWT Brand Funnel applied to Bill Clinton

In order to preserve client confidentiality, the example given in Figure 4.5 relates to the 'brand' known as Bill Clinton.

Brand vision – your brand offer (in two words)

This process is about defining your dream and then working out the map that will help you successfully to navigate your chosen path. The significance of the Brand Vision is immense; it is the most distilled version of your message, acting as a prism for what you want to say about yourself. Although it is only two words long, it is arguably the most important thing you will write throughout the entire process. It will represent the distillation and direction for the development of all communications.

Defining the essence of the brand and expressing it in just two words is the product of rigorous and inspired thinking. The Brand Vision can take various forms, but it always explains the relationship between the brand's offering and the consumer's desires. And it is often most successful when it puts two apparently conflicting thoughts together.

Developing the Brand Vision should be a collective process: it is a vital stage of development and acts as the spark between the 'information in' and 'ideas out'. Without a clear (and collectively agreed) Brand Vision, your chances of success are drastically reduced. The Brand Vision should not only make rational sense, but should also feel instinctively right to the team.

To work effectively, the Brand Vision needs to:

▪ Encapsulate how your brand is positioned versus the competition
▪ Capture the emotional relationship as well as the rational one, making it richer and more comprehensive
▪ Be agreed with all the key members of your team
▪ Say something distinctive about you – blandness will not help.

A strong Brand Vision has many benefits; it:

▪ Provides greater focus
▪ Allows you to concentrate on key tasks
▪ Helps you identify issues which you can safely ignore
▪ Increases the chances of developing a compelling creative idea
▪ Thus increasing the chances of your message being noticed and remembered
▪ Gives everyone in the company an expression which helps them to navigate the future
▪ Makes it easier to assess and evaluate potential sponsors and brands with whom there may be synergy
▪ Makes it easier to develop an integrated communications programme.

The Day One – unleashing the dynamic force of 'co-creation'

If you were working directly with JWT, this process of developing/ defining the Brand Funnel and Brand Vision would take place in a 'Day One' session (so-called because it manages to compress the usually protracted process of brand positioning development into a single day). At a Day One session, all participants work together towards an agreed Brand Funnel and Brand Vision.

Crucially, the participants should comprise not just the client and their agency partners (for example advertising, media, PR, design), but also any colleagues from related functions (such as production, distribution or consumer research) who can contribute a relevant additional perspective. By involving all key decision-makers in the Day One process, a sense of collective momentum is also generated which can then be sustained throughout all subsequent stages (from the communications planning to the creative development and beyond).

Equally important is that the Day One should be held off-site (away from all those emails and emergency meetings). It should take place in an environment which stimulates fresh thinking and brings the consumer to life (for example for a kids' entertainment site, the day might be held in a multiplex entertainment centre).

The final 'rule' of the Day One is that all participants should spend the entire day in the consumer's shoes – to the extent that they try to articulate all comments in the consumer's 'first person' voice. To help facilitate this process, the participants are surrounded by a rich variety of stimuli. For example, if we were dealing with an eTrading brand, this stimulus might comprise the financial press, clips from Nicola Horlick's various TV appearances and representations of the purchases which the aspirant eTraders are hoping to buy with their profits.

Bringing your Brand Vision to life – the branding idea

Only by the discovery of a big idea around which every promotion effort can be made to circle can you gain real distinction for your product… It should be expressed in the package, the container, and every physical accompaniment of the product. Every detail of the printed message and of its form should be fitted to its telling. (James Webb Young, 1916)

If the Brand Vision is the internal expression of what your brand should stand for, the Branding Idea is its external manifestation. It is the enduring, ownable expression that gives your brand fame, meaning and distinctiveness. And it stems directly from the brand positioning, as articulated by the Brand Funnel and the Brand Vision.

A successful Branding Idea is a multi-faceted expression that tells the brand's story to all its audiences so well, so powerfully, that nobody else can ever attempt to do it in the same way. An enduring Branding Idea does this by generating Brand Properties that provide a powerful way to identify the brand. And because the Branding Idea transcends any specific creative execution or media channel, it also helps the team to avoid making premature media assumptions (for example 'We've got to have a TV ad') and concentrate, instead, on finding the core creative property which will bring the brand alive for the consumer.

With more and more brands out there, more and more competition for people's attention, and more and more countries added to the business's field of operation, it is vital that all of your communications are as integrated as possible. The advantage of the Branding Idea is that it provides the springboard for every creative execution, across every media channel, thus ensuring overall creative coherence. It's no accident that some of the most distinctive and compelling brands – across whatever category – have a strong Branding Idea at their heart.

The job of actually creating the Branding Idea is undertaken by the creative team within the lead communications agency. It is essential, therefore, that this team is fully aware of the project background, including the overall plans and objectives for the brand. The best way to achieve this is for this team to play an active role in the Day One, helping to develop the Brand Funnel and Brand Vision.

Postcard analogy

At JWT, the Branding Idea is expressed in the form of a postcard. The analogy runs as follows:

Postcard	=	Strategic/creative proposition
Addressee	=	Target audience
Writer	=	Brand/company
Written message	=	Desired consumer response
Key visual		
(and line, where appropriate)	=	Branding idea

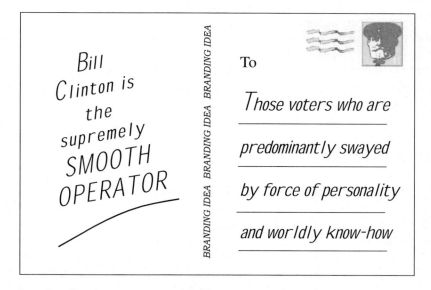

Figure 4.6   The JWT Brand postcard applied to Bill Clinton

Figure 4.7   The JWT Brand postcard applied to Bill Clinton

For the purposes of continuity, let's see how the Brand Postcard works for our earlier Bill Clinton example (see Figures 4.6 and 4.7).

As you see, the postcard encapsulates those pillars of the strategy which have now been agreed – the target audience, the brand identity and the desired consumer response – and shows how the Branding Idea relates directly to this framework.

Once the Branding Idea has been approved, the postcard is sent to every member of the core team, in order to provide an instant, at-a-glance reminder of the agreed direction.

Brand properties

We are moving towards an 'attention economy', where the consumer's increasingly short-lived attention is the primary limit on supply. This means that brand memorability will remain at a premium; strong brand properties could well make the difference between success and failure. Don't assume that screaming louder and brighter will get you attention. It may work while you are shouting, but you will have to keep spending at a high level to maintain awareness. And if your shouting has annoyed people (which may well be the case), that awareness may not convert to anything more valuable.

In developing your Branding Idea, you therefore need to audit what Brand Properties, if any, you already have, and resolve how these could/ should be used. These Brand Properties can stem from many different sources, including:

▦ *Name*: All brand names tend to fall into one of three broad groups:

1. Abstract, for example Yahoo.com. Usually, a distinctive and attractive collection of letters which, at a stretch, convey a general mood/attitude. However, in order to convey what the site actually is and does, these types of name need to receive strong investment in terms of their visual identities, advertising campaigns and so on.

2. Associative, for example Handbag.com, Ask Jeeves. These types of name go a little further towards indicating their brand's overall role and benefit. They are inherently symbolic, carrying a ready-made set of associations (Handbag is a female-targeted portal, which seeks to become as indispensable to women as their handbags; Ask Jeeves is an information provider which aims to be as knowledgeable and helpful as PG Wodehouse's famously consummate butler).

3. Descriptive, for example Dictionary.com; Letsbuyit.com. These types of name provide the clearest possible description of the brand's overall function (a dictionary site and a retail site, respectively). However, they lack any inherent personality; these qualities therefore have to be acquired via other elements of the marketing mix (for example design and advertising).

▦ *Line:* for example 'A woman would be lost without her handbag.com'
▦ *Logo:* Again, Ask Jeeves is a consummate example (the characterful illustration speaks volumes about the brand's tone and personality)
▦ *Colour:* for example the bright pink of the new women's portal, Ready2.com
▦ *Character:* for example Asda's Captain ValueMad
▦ *Music:* for example the strong sonic branding of the Intel Pentium Processor
▦ *Geographical provenance*: for example Vatican.va: the Pope's own Web site, direct from Vatican City
▦ *Graphic style:* for example the clean-cut computer graphics of First e, a recently launched Internet-only bank.

Ask yourself:

For each Brand Property, whether brought by a long-existing brand, or newly created:

- What is it saying to consumers about your brand?
- What response is it eliciting?
- Does it reinforce the brand's individuality?
- How is it working?
- How could it work?
- Is it still relevant? Why/why not?

How, when and where to reach your audience – the communications plan

You now need to resolve the media by which your Branding Idea will be communicated to your target audience.

The key questions:

- What media do our target audience consume, and why?
- What types of media should be we using?
- What is their role?
- What budgets are needed?
- What will it achieve? How will success be measured?

The communications plan is developed via the following four steps.

1. Define your communications objectives

What do you want your target audience to think and do?

- Act: Go and visit it/buy it now

- Seek information: Find out more about you and your offer

- Relate your product to their own needs and wants: See it as something that will help them in their lives (see 'solution' and 'lifestyle' in the 'Consumer Discoveries' section)

- Have your brand top-of-mind: Be reminded that you are still there

■ Modify their attitudes/change their view of the world. This is the aim of much public education advertising (for example the 'Drink-Drive' campaign). Given the amount of time that it takes to change attitudes, it may be quicker to try and change the behaviour, and then see attitudes change to fit with the new behaviour.

■ Re-confirm their attitudes: That they have made the right choice by coming to you, for example. This objective underlies much of the advertising of established brands.

2. Identify specific communications tasks that allow you to achieve your objectives

For example, your primary goals might be to raise awareness and encourage trial. Within this, you may have a range of different audiences:

■ The people who are buying the product/brand
■ The people who are using the product/brand
■ Opinion or style leaders: the people who you want to wear/use/talk about your brand (for example journalists and editors).

For each of these audiences, think about their lives and what they are looking for, where is the best place to communicate with them, and what is the appropriate tone of voice/mood.

3. Explore the optimum blend of communications vehicles

The choice of media is ever-expanding. Gone are the days when the media solution always seemed to resolve in a 30-second TV execution, backed up by a national press campaign.

Potential media channels could, for instance, include:

■ Television   ■ Print   ■ Papers
■ Magazines   ■ Radio   ■ Cinema
■ Internet/email   ■ Posters   ■ Postcards
■ Direct mail   ■ Sponsorship.

In particular, several powerful marketing opportunities are available through the Internet medium itself:

- *Exploiting Web alliances*: Where there are synergies between the profile of a site and the dot.com brand, Web alliances can be used to reach the target audience in a subtle but effective manner. They allow the new brand to communicate with a ready-established audience, increasing the brand's association with its allied partner. For example, when DLJdirect (the online stockbroker) launched in the UK last year, they established sponsorship alliances with The Motley Fool (a site for share-dealing novices).

- *Co-branding*: Where the advertiser and the Web site come together with a joint voice on a subject/service, the brand gains an increased association with its allied partner, and can exploit all sorts of synergies between the two brands. For example, during last year's Wimbledon championships, IBM provided real-time results in association with Sky, through the medium of a desktop 'results ticker'. And the user benefited from the best of both worlds: the technology of IBM and the sports-reporting expertise of Sky.

- *Leveraging links to/from other sites*: This is a relatively cheap and simple way to increase traffic between two sites. In practical terms, Brand A 'rents' a space on the screen operated by Brand B, using this space to encourage Brand B's visitors to give Brand A a try. In particular, Brand A and Brand B often save on media expenditure by coming to reciprocal or revenue share arrangements.

- *Internet-specific marketing*: This spans a plethora of online tools, ranging from online advertising to affinity portals and portal deals. Although at present the most common form of online advertising is the placing of banners and buttons on sites, the approaches are bound to become more sophisticated.

To generate awareness, the best approach is to gain presence on high traffic sites such as ISPs and large portals. To generate a particular response, the most effective tool is to purchase keywords, create category-specific banners on search engines and use vertical portals. For example, take handbag.com, the UK's first women's portal, which launched last year:

- It generated awareness by placing banners on women's channels in major ISPs and portals.
- It generated response by purchasing relevant keywords on search engines (for example 'fashion', 'shopping' and 'horoscopes' on Excite).

The major benefit of online advertising is that it can be highly targeted and offers brands the opportunity to communicate with consumers on a one-to-one level, within relevant environments about specific subjects. Plus it creates the opportunity for detailed accountability and evaluation, as we shall see later in the chapter.

If you have a transactional offering, then you should also consider affinity programmes. Portals and ISPs are steadily building their portfolios of partners in order to increase the breadth of services on their sites. These programmes provide brand owners with access to an established customer base. And because these arrangements tend to operate via revenue-sharing or contra deals, they can often be incremental to the fixed media budget. For example, Yahoo!'s merchant partnership deals offer a virtual department store to advertisers, based on cost-per-click-through.

Establishing portal deals, where a brand becomes totally integrated into the site, can be particularly beneficial to new brands. In many cases, the advertiser will provide content for the portal, which increases the interactivity with the brand. And of course the advertiser also gains exposure, courtesy of the other site's traffic.

Budgets

Your media choice may well come back to budgets. Advertising space costs money.

As a rough guide, current prices are outlined in Table 4.1. Remember, however, that media inflation is calculated to carry on running at up to 5%, year on year, so these figures may become increasingly out of date. Also bear in mind that these media charges are additional to the cost of producing the communication in the first place. Whereas radio advertising represents particular value-for-money in this respect, the production of certain types of TV/cinema advertising can lighten your purse by a cool £1.5m.

4. Put the plan together

To construct the final plan, you should:

- Re-appraise your target audience (including any sub-groups) and the respective communication tasks
- Identify which vehicles you are recommending

Table 4.1   Outline media costs

	UK $	Germany $	Italy $
30 second TV ad aimed at ABC1 men (3–6 week campaign)	4.4M	2.1M	1.7M
Black and white full-page ad in major national newspaper	87K	28K	25K
Large poster, nationwide (10–15 day campaign)	908K	839K	600K
Bus stop poster, nationwide (10–15 day campaign)	1.3M	1.9M	375K
30 second radio ad aimed at ABC1 men (1–3 week campaign)	382K	1.4M	115K
30 second cinema ad (4–8 week campaign)	875K	2.1M	170K
Home page banner on a major portal (4 week campaign)	40K	50K	30K

Source: MindShare, 2000

- Describe the communication tasks they will help accomplish and how you intend to measure their effectiveness
- Calculate a timing plan and an estimated budget.

Ask yourself:

- Have you made a promising start/significant improvement in the way your brand communicates with its customers?
- Have you really capitalised on the Branding Idea?
- Have you made the most of non-traditional media, in such a way that you will really capture your target's attention?

Bringing the branding idea to life – creative execution

This is when the Branding Idea takes on a whole new momentum, as it is developed into specific creative executions, across the specific media channels now identified. The process starts with a creative brief.

The creative brief

Together with the Brand Vision, the Creative Brief is a key focal point. It is where the thinking on the brand, the consumer and the media is distilled into a key thought which will help inspire the creatives to convert the Branding Idea into compelling executions across the defined media mix.

As the name suggests, the brief should be brief:

- A single-sheet distillation of the process
- Single-minded.

Equally inherent in the name is that the brief should be instructive:

- Take decisions
- Give direction

Although the actual wording of the Creative Brief form tends to vary from agency to agency, most of these forms focus on the same six key issues:

- *Role for communications*: for example reinforce existing behaviour, provide information, gain trial.

- *Target market definition*: for example demographics, lifestage, lifestyle.

- *Consumer insight*: the aspect of your target audience's belief or behaviour which you are going to leverage (the stronger the insight, the stronger your key message).

- *Key thought*: the single-minded proposition which you wish to communicate (this is the most important entry on the entire form – and the one which the creative team always look at first!).

- *Rationale*: the key evidence which supports the 'key thought' (although this information won't necessarily need to be communicated to the target audience, it still creates the vital discipline of ensuring that your key thought is valid and substantiated, and therefore likely to be credible in the real world).

- *Executional issues*: for example tone-of-voice, or any mandatory inclusions, such as phone number, Web address, or a slogan.

The most distinctive creative idea isn't just the responsibility of the creative people; a poor brief invariably results in poor creative work, so think hard about what really matters. This is especially important if there is little time for the brief to be polished and refined. Here are some additional tips for giving the creative team the best possible direction:

- Find ways of bringing the brief to life, using whatever stimulus you need (props, locations, and so on). The emphasis is on the brief as a creative launch-pad. You will fail if you think of it as a dry and static marketing document.

- You will also fail if you demand that the advertising should perform impossible miracles. Be realistic.

- Don't sit on the fence, without a point of view. Be courageous.

- See everything from the consumer's point of view (yes, again!). Write in the way you feel they would express themselves. Think about how they will respond to your communication.

- Avoid the category's 'communication generics' – revisit your Brand Vision (which, by definition, should be wholly distinctive) and bring this to life. Does this Vision succeed in permeating the entire communications task?

The creative development process

Don't keep a dog and bark yourself. Everyone can be an 'advertising expert', but given that you have hired highly-qualified professionals to undertake the creative execution, give these people room to develop their ideas. ('Co-creation' does not mean that every member of the team should actively work within every stage of the process. There are times when certain members of the team should be given the room to concentrate on their core expertise, using the remainder of the team as an informed source of opinion and encouragement.)

Don't use the creative process as a way of trying to refine your thoughts about the overall brand strategy – this is a very expensive and irritating way of doing business, and risks shortening everyone's life expectancy.

Assuming, therefore, that your brand strategy is sound, you'll be able to judge the creative ideas entirely against this pre-defined framework. If *you* don't like the proposed creative idea, stop and ask yourself whether this matters. The key question is: will your *customers* like it/notice it? If your target audience has a different taste and outlook to you, it may even be right that the proposed creative idea makes you, personally, feel uncomfortable.

Ensure that clear lines of communication and decision-making responsibility are maintained:

- Because the time pressures are usually so great, ensure that everyone is kept informed.

- Decide up front who will take the final decision. Although teamworking can be vital, timing may mean that you have to nominate one person who takes primary responsibility for these decisions (and this is where you will later find that everyone else in the company becomes an instant expert, claiming that they themselves 'wouldn't have done that'). Get all of this sorted out up front and life will be easier for everyone.

- Working meetings are important – often the best way is for the client and agency to work more closely together than they would on campaigns within more traditional categories, when longer lead times mean that there can be a greater independence. But remember that the point of this proximity is for you to act as a useful sounding board for the agency's work-in-progress, rather than to get involved in the actual creative ideation.

- Understand how the process feels for creative people – the idea is their creation, born of much blood, sweat and tears, and they may be very protective of it. See the world from their point of view and think very carefully about how you criticize their 'child'.

Creative development research

Providing you have sufficient time and budget, you may find it useful to research the proposed creative ideas among a representative selection of your target audience. No matter how well you may think you understand your customer/advertising responses in general, this type of research can still prove invaluable in further strengthening the campaign under development.

This research can be undertaken either by the communications agency (usually led by the Account Planner, whose overall role is described later in this section), or alternatively by an independent Research Specialist.

During the earlier stages of creative development, the creative proposals are likely to be shown to consumers within small-scale discussion groups or one-to-one interviews. This format provides the most flexible way for the consumer to respond in their own words to the proposed campaign. If appropriate, this type of research can be held within a specialist facility, allowing the discussion to be observed by interested parties through a special screen (yes, this is legal, but only providing you adhere to the various terms and conditions stipulated in The Market Research Society's Professional Code of Conduct).

Towards the later stages of creative development, you may also wish to undertake a so-called 'pre-test': a larger-scale, quantitative survey, which attempts to provide a statistical prediction of how your campaign will actually perform, in-market. This exercise would be handled by a specialist Research Agency. Although this type of research can have its uses, beware treating it as an exact science: each Research Agency has its own particular methods and philosophies, and any creative idea ultimately eludes a strictly numerical analysis.

For campaigns which are going to run internationally, it is clearly important to ensure that this wider target market is reflected within the research process. Crucially, this doesn't mean that the campaign has to be researched within every single market in which you intend to operate, not least because such an undertaking would wreak havoc upon your timing plan and budget. Instead, identify those markets which are most important to you. From that list, you should then select the core group of countries which, in your judgement, embody the greatest cultural or behavioural differences (for example for a pan-European business, you might consider restricting your research to a representative country in each of Northern, Southern and Eastern Europe).

Who can help – communications experts you are likely to meet/call upon

The communications business splits into many different elements. Some companies seek to offer all services (so called 'one stop shopping'); others focus on one particular discipline.

Whatever the structure and philosophy of the companies you might be working with, it is essential that everyone works to the same Brand Vision and Branding Idea. If the different elements of the communication look as though they've come from different companies, then your brand risks looking indecisive, even schizophrenic, assuming that anyone notices it in the first place.

International businesses should, of course, check that each of their suppliers is able to operate across each of the countries within the marketing plan. Moreover, a supplier's claimed 'international credentials' should not be taken at face value: are their international operations a wholly-owned, organic part of their organisation, or are there certain countries in which the operations are delegated to a third party? If the latter is the case, then how, exactly, does the process work, and how successful has the relationship proven in the past?

A brief list of the disciplines is outlined below.

Design
- Packaging design
- Brand identity design and corporate guidelines
- Graphic design of materials
- Website design.

Advertising
- Account handlers – manage the relationship between the agency team and the client
- Account planners – understand the consumer and develop the brand strategy
- Copywriters – develop the creative ideas, focusing on the words/copy
- Art directors – develop the creative ideas, focusing on the look/design.

Media
- Media planners – understand the media landscape and how to reach the target audience
- Media buyers – buy the time and/or space from the media companies.

Public Relations
- Media relations (journalists)
- Opinion-former relations
- Lobbying.

Promotions
- Create and manage special promotions
- Produce the materials and handle the distribution.

Events
- Manage launches and specific events
- Work on the concept and design
- Organise the practicalities.

Collateral materials
- Design and produce all the supporting materials
- These can include brochures, product specifications and internal communications materials (for example sales support, communications guidelines).

Direct mail
- Send materials direct to the consumer – usually in the form of a personalised communication
- Also responsible for database development and management, ensuring that the company has the appropriate information about their customers to make more effective contact in the future.

Customer Satisfaction (CS)
- Gauge customer satisfaction, usually via research
- Develop CS programmes to improve performance
- Handle staff training to improve service levels.

Customer Relationship Management (CRM)
- A current fashion for trying to encourage customer loyalty and long-term relationships
- Involve all aspects of the customer's buying process, and sophisticated information management
- Develop management processes, including call centres/support.

Market Research
- Used throughout the various stages of development
- Qualitative research: small-scale in terms of numbers of people (focus groups, interviews); produces in-depth findings, psychological insight and information in the customer's own words
- Quantitative research: large-scale surveys or polls. Less depth, but the large numbers mean that the results tend to carry a greater statistical significance. A sample of 1,000 is generally seen as giving a representative sample for the UK. If you want to look at sub-groups (that is, not just 'all adults', but a segment such as 'women aged 19–34, who use the Internet at work'), then you may have to increase your sample size to make sure that each of the sub-groups is large enough to provide robust conclusions.

Did you get what you wanted? – evaluation and refinement

The final stage of the communications development process – are you getting where you wanted to go? The last stage, but vitally important if your communications are to continue to improve and drive you towards your ultimate business goals. Once you've spent an arm and a leg for example televising, direct-mailing and event-marketing a small blue frog that you are confidently told represents all that is good about your brand, you will presumably be anxious to know whether it worked or not.

At this stage, you need to re-visit some of your earlier thinking and hypotheses, and see if these have been validated. There may be new insights or knowledge which cause you to evolve your thinking. The Internet is so new, no-one is yet sure how it will work most effectively as a business medium. So keep looking and listening, and keep challenging all of the conventions.

The process of evaluation is continuous – you need to keep checking on what is happening and whether things are progressing as expected. And, whether things are going well or not, there is always valuable learning to be gained. This is because feedback from what has happened is vital to developing each successive stage of the campaign.

Communications are a live and active process – they're about people, their responses and their feelings. It is not an exact science, and because of this it is important to be clear about your own assumptions, as these will drive your individual interpretation of the results.

Remember, also, to monitor all of the routes and methods by which you're communicating with your consumer. There's no point obtaining detailed feedback on your poster campaign, if you have no idea how your direct mail initiative and your sponsorship programme have performed. Ideally, you should be able to build a picture of which media have worked most effectively for you, and why.

The 'classic' questions

The communications plan will already have identified key tasks and measurements. Using this framework, the evaluation of the campaign tends to focus on:

- *Communication*: How well does your target audience notice, remember and understand your message?

- *Involvement*: How have your communications affected the way your target audience feels about your brand? What drove that perception?

- *Action*: How has your target audience responded to your communications? For instance, bol (Buy On Line) consider their most recent advertising a success, since its sales increased while the campaign was 'live'.

Questions specific to dot.coms

Measuring the success of a dot.com's campaign is largely similar to the process you would undertake for more traditional businesses, not least because you are still fighting with these businesses – as well as other dot.com brands – for an awareness of your brand and its offering in the minds of consumers (who usually have something better to think about). You will still need to be differentiated and memorable, and to respond to the needs of your consumers as they develop.

However, there are of course a number of objectives specific to dot.com brands, which will influence how their campaigns are evaluated:

- Web address – you will need to know whether your marketing is establishing the address firmly in your target audience's mind. This doesn't just apply to the newcomers; the better known access points (for example amazon/yahoo) also need to maintain and increase their awareness.

- All dot.com marketing falls into the 'direct response' category, because you will be directing your consumer to your site, first and foremost. This is equivalent to inviting consumers to pick up a brochure, in the offline world. Some learning from relationship marketing should therefore help to guide measurement: you will need to establish how the progress of the brand is pulling people through a 'trial – purchase – repurchase – recommend' cycle, and what you can do at each stage to improve pull-through. When your customers visit the site, how likely are they actually to use the service offered? And do they then use it again? Why/why not? As they continue their relationship with your brand, how do their perceptions of you change? Do they tell their friends about you? Can you encourage them to do so?

- As a dot.com brand, you will inherit a massive amount of data regarding the users of your site and brand. This will range from which paths people are taking through the site, to whether the user was from the UK or abroad, and whether they are likely to type 'playboy' into a search engine or not. Some of this data can be provided by your hosting company. In addition, there are agencies (for example Webtrends and netpoll) who specialise in very detailed analysis of who visits your site. However, although this will tell you an awful lot about how your site is being used and by whom, it cannot reveal what your targeting opportunities are in the future; this can only be accessed by talking to people who are not yet using your brand.

What do you want to know about your customers?

During the 'Key Discoveries' process, you will have found out a great deal about your customers. At this stage, think about the sorts of questions you need to ask those customers. What do you want to know about them, both in order to establish whether your communications are working, and to improve your service/build stronger relationships in the future?

Many companies set up a questionnaire. However, most of these are not only very dull to complete, they actually reveal little about the customer and their relationship with your brand. Even fewer questionnaires manage to reflect the brand's values – most are asked in the pseudo-scientific language of research.

Once your appropriately worded and impeccably structured questionnaire has yielded its results, keep that information and make it accessible to people who are handling customer service. Information is a memory and should be treated as such; do not fall into the trap of 'corporate amnesia', asking your customer to re-tell their relationship every time they contact you. If your customers have a problem, having to retell this six times before they can talk to someone who might be able to help is likely to remind them of how annoyed they are with you – unlikely to promote loyalty and positive word of mouth.

What measurements will you use to assess your achievements?

The temptation is to focus on what is easy to measure. However, this may not give you any insight into what is really valuable to your customers.

Allow people to tell you what they want – this will be worth its weight in gold, even if you don't like what they are saying. But don't just take their comments at face value – look at the 'why' as well as the 'what'. It's unlikely that your customers will either wish or be able to place their experience of your brand into any wider context; this vital extra level of interpretation needs to be contributed by you and your team.

So keep asking the questions, but always check them back against your vision, the objectives you've set and the business results. No-one is liked by everyone all of the time; it is better to stand for something than it is to be forgotten because no-one is quite sure what you do, or why they should choose your brand.

Sources of information

There is almost no limit to the breadth and depth of feedback on offer. At the very least, you should make use of the information which, as an Internet brand, can automatically come your way:

- Sales data
- Internet throughput/click-through
- Customer information gained at registration
- Feedback from customer services
- Chat rooms and discussion groups.

Depending on your time-scales and budgets, you may also find the following types of research invaluable:

- *Ad hoc surveys and polls*: Omnibus surveys are a particularly cost-efficient and quick way of putting a few questions to a large audience, but the questions themselves have to remain relatively top-line.

- *In-depth qualitative research*: This could be carried out online, perhaps using a specially-recruited consumer panel. But remember that the whole point of this type of research is to allow consumers to respond in their own words. Try, therefore, to avoid asking questions which require a simple 'yes/no' answer and concentrate, instead, on creating questions which are more probing and open ended.

- *Tracking studies – large scale, continuous quantitative research*: The research company will conduct surveys of the general public (or specialist segments thereof) either on doorsteps, in-home or in the street. Usually interviews are carried out throughout the year, asking about awareness of the brand and advertising, what is being communicated, and the nature of any brand images/perceptions.

- *Tracking studies vs omnibus surveys*: While it is possible to track brand awareness among various audiences by using an Omnibus survey, it is worthwhile in the long term investing in a full brand tracking survey. While an omnibus can give you a quick snapshot of how many people have heard of you, a full tracking survey, with either continuous data or a series of 'dips', will allow you to track awareness over time and detect any changes more accurately. It will also allow you to isolate each individual driver of those uplifts (for example TV/press/radio ad, point of sale (POS) material, sponsorship and so on).

▪ *Econometric analysis*: This is the most sophisticated – and most expensive – option. The unique benefit of this approach is that it aims to strip away all 'outside' factors which might possibly have affected your campaign's performance (such as a competitor suddenly lowering their prices, or launching their own high-profile communications initiative). The result – in theory – is that you can measure those effects which were specifically caused by your own campaign.

▪ *'DIY' econometrics*: Taking the same time period, place the following three different measurements together: the opportunities your audience had to see/hear your campaign; what actually happened to customer awareness; and what actually happened to site traffic. If your campaign has been effective, these three factors should reveal some sort of positive correlation. However, although this is a useful exercise, remember that it ignores the crucial 'outside' factors which a proper econometric study would take into account.

Separating the different elements of the marketing mix

Many dot.coms include as part of their registration forms, or in an online survey, questions as to how the person found out about them. Triggers such as buttons on search engines, online banners, or a friend's advice, are all useful prompts to action. In the offline world, similar triggers would be found in media such as direct response mailings and competitions. However what consumers will not tell you at this point is how your triggers were helped on their way by an overall approval of your brand; this you will have to investigate in other ways.

Most consumers will also misattribute their media. Television will often receive a substantial score in tracking data for a brand that has only ever used posters. It seems that if people remember advertising for a brand, they tend to assume they 'saw it on the telly'.

It is relatively simple to detect whether your online media are prompting click-through. However, it is not so easy to see how they are contributing to brand imagery, particularly since the Internet world cannot accommodate regional tests. Some companies have tried to use separate Web addresses in different media (just as addresses for companies may appear differently in various direct response press ads), but current evidence shows that this does not really help to provide an accurate estimate of which media are driving traffic.

Stanley Pollitt, one of the founding fathers of Account Planning, described effective advertising as being 'concerned with consolidating or modifying brand personalities to exert greater influence on the struggle that consumers were facing in reconciling personal beliefs and habits with both their buying behaviour and their attitudes to brands.' (*Pollitt on Planning, 2000*). Perhaps the deliberately complex nature of this definition is responsible for the fact that thirty years on it is still largely ignored in the evaluation process. Communications are still usually measured in terms of what can be quantified, despite the fact that much of the consumer's response remains unquantifiable. The temptation with dot.coms, where so much hard data is available, is to concentrate on the figures and to forget how people feel.

This is particularly regrettable, since Internet companies currently occupy some of the most emotionally charged territories (such as trust, self-confidence, freedom, independence, and changing societies). A woman in a group recently conducted for an Internet bank commented: 'It all sounds great – I'll have some when I'm clever enough'. It is important to measure qualitatively how your brand interacts on these emotional levels if you are to understand fully how your marketing is working, and is likely to work in the future.

The 10-minute strategy

What is your dream? What do you really want and how will you know when you have got it?

Find out:
- Who is buying and using?
- Why are they buying and using?
- How are they buying and using?
- What else are they spending their time, money and energy on?
- Why should they spend their time, money and energy with you?

Funnel the information into the key insights:
- How does it fit with your dream?

Focus and define your brand vision:
- 2 words, or write it in your own blood – no pain, no gain.

Fan the message:
- What do you want to say?
- How do you think people will respond?
- Which media should you use to fan fastest and furthest?

Feedback:
- Keep checking what is working and what is not
- Apply the learnings to make your plan even more successful.

Fidelity:
- Consistency matters
- Stay true to your dream, to your customers and to your strategy.

CHAPTER 5

'Fulfilling the Promise'

David C Lane, ANDERSEN CONSULTING, MEDIA AND
ENTERTAINMENT, UK AND IRELAND

You walk confidently into the venture capitalist's office, sure your business plan has
survived scrutiny. It has to. After all, you have nurtured the business idea for almost
a year now. Not to mention the hours of work you've put in, bouncing ideas off
your professors, friends and family, soliciting feedback. Not to mention, too, the
hours of 'espionage' you've invested in visiting your competitors' sites, pretending to
be the innocent customer. And the friends you've convinced to join you in the
adventure of your life. Your idea has to be an eWorld winner! Of course, it helps
that the venture capitalist is your rugby mate from college.

Then, the fateful words crash over you: 'A really good idea, Adam. Good market
potential, strong forecasts, great team. Except for one missing link... where are
your fulfilment plans? Just how are you going to make sure your customers get
what they want, when they want it, how they want it?' This chapter should help
answer these questions.

Introduction

How many of us hear the cash registers ringing without thinking hard
enough about what it takes to make online consumers part with their
money, not just once, but again and again? What makes our online
consumers who they are? What makes them buy our product, repeatedly?
To what extent is this dependent on how we get to our consumers what
they want, when they want it, where they want it, how they want it? And at
what cost? These questions touch the heart of the online fulfilment challenges facing Internet start-ups today.

These fulfilment issues are especially acute for European online start-ups
and US online retailers looking to enter the European market. Unlike the
US, Europe's online markets are more diverse in terms of online penetration,[1] growth rates,[2] Internet access costs and payment habits. In the UK,
more than 90% of online transactions are paid by credit card. This compares

to less than 20% for Germany and the Nordic countries. Compared to the relative homogeneity of the US online market, European structures are typically more fragmented, characterised by distinct national norms. While every doorstep in North America is reached by one parcel carrier, UPS and one post office, USPO, European postal and carrier networks are fragmented with substantial variations in coverage and quality.

Thus the European Internet entrepreneur has to consider the issue of eFulfilment near the top of his/her business priorities. This chapter hopes to provide some thinking points behind:

- what changes are revolutionising the European eTailing market
- which forces make or break consumer online demand
- what Internet businesses have to do to stay ahead of the eFulfilment game... and keep consumers coming back.

The eTailing market: eTailing does not equal online retailing

The cosy world of retail – as our parents knew it – is quickly becoming a relic of the past. Time, space and location are no longer constraints to when we buy, what we buy and where we buy. This is because the Internet has revolutionised the shopper's lens, creating a new breed of shoppers called online consumers. As online consumers usher in different buying patterns, retail businesses have to change in response. While the Internet has enabled consumers to change they way they buy, it has also enabled a new breed of eTailers to influence what and how much consumers buy.

The consumer, not the retailer, decides on the relevant product range

How often have you heard a retailer say to you, 'Sorry, M'am, we don't stock that particular range', or 'We don't stock that title in this store, Sir, but if you would like to wait three weeks, we'll have it ordered from the central warehouse for you'? Typically, consumers would have resigned to their fate and either reconsidered their purchase or given up altogether. Traditionally, the retailer has retained the right to edit the product range available to you. If what you want doesn't fit the retailer's profitability margin, or doesn't sell in sufficient volumes to the masses, chances are you'll have to prepare for lots of legwork to get what you want.

In the online world, however, your bargaining power has turned the retailer's priorities upside down. Because the Internet is not constrained by time, space or location, consumers can buy what they like, not just what is available. Consumers can buy from whoever gives them more choice, not just from the nearest available high street store. In short, consumers can now buy on personal preference, not mass availability; consumers can satisfy lifestyle needs, not market-defined needs.

What does this mean for eTailers? The imperative is to offer a lifestyle proposition to consumers. The power to edit product range is now with the consumer. The eTailer now has to provide solutions, not just products. While a 'bricks-and-mortar' competitor will strain to stock 60,000 music titles, the eTailer can now provide a catalogue of some 500,000 titles. The eTailer can cater for personal favourites, from the oldest jazz classics to the latest Oasis album; consumers will be relieved at the freedom to ignore the latest 20 chart toppers typically stacked along high street store fronts. Most importantly, eTailers can explore a whole range of lifestyle products to proposition consumers. An entertainment company no longer stops at selling CDs. A preferred entertainment eTailer could provide a solution comprising music albums, theme restaurants, clubs and even holidays. Think how the Ministry of Sound has influenced the way we think about having a good time!

Pick-Pack-Deliver becomes the responsibility of the eTailer

Home delivery is a natural corollary to home shopping. As long as the bargaining power is with the consumer, he'll expect lots more. This includes the role of the eTailer to pick, pack and deliver single or multiple unit online purchases direct to the consumer's front door. The eTailer has just been promoted as the modern milkman. Like the days of old, the consumer expects delivery to cost no more than the milk.

The implications for eTailers are twofold. First, eFulfilment costs are real and can reach 30% of sales (excluding VAT).[3] While consumer buying has gone virtual, delivery remains physical; the related labour and transportation costs will be nothing but real. Traditional retailing has taught best practices in managing economies of scale, teaching middlemen (like retailers) in the supply chain of goods to optimise cross-industry infrastructure and aggregate supply. The bulk-breaking of goods necessary for single unit pick-pack-deliver creates additional costs of sales in the online world. In the cybershop of competitive margins, the eTailer's challenge is to deliver single units over the 'last mile' with speed, at a low cost.

Table 5.1 Capturing demand vs fulfilling demand

Characteristics	Capturing consumer demand	Fulfilling consumer demand
Economic drivers	■ Finding and building on consumer relationships	■ Economies of scale (infrastructure) ■ Product picking densities ■ Package delivery densities
Operating capabilities	■ Creativity ■ Branding	■ Consistency ■ Low cost execution
Focus/Culture	■ Consumer focus ■ Entrepreneurial	■ Process focus ■ Continuous improvement

Second, eTailers need to understand eFulfilment skills. Consider the familiar HMV store at the corner of the street. When you walk in, you are bombarded by 'Buy Me' messages coming out of every square foot of shop space. You pick your own CD or video, queue up to pay, are given a cursory packing service, and there's no delivery to speak of. Therefore, as a retailer, you work on skills which make the consumer decide to buy.

In the online world, however, the retailer needs new operating skills. As the Web develops, we are witnessing a growing split between players who capture customer demand, and those who fulfill them. Capturing consumer demand (hearts and wallets inclusive) is primarily in the hands of media windows, like Web sites and TV stations. These players are focused on finding and sustaining consumer relationships, focusing on lifestyle centric offerings. The core capabilities behind capturing consumer hearts rest with creativity, branding and content. On the other hand, eTailers have increasingly moved into fulfilment roles. This requires operating skills focused on process efficiency – comprising the twin challenges of speedy, customised delivery and economies of scale – and continuous improvement to meet with rising consumer expectations. Making that 'last mile' to consumer homes, at a high quality of service and low cost, defines the eTailer's drivers of success.

eTailing is different from online retailing:

■ The consumer, not the retailer, decides on the relevant range of products
■ The eTailer is responsible for the costs of pick-pack-deliver to the consumer
■ Industry players will polarise around demand capture and fulfilment roles; these are distinguished by very different operating skills and economics

■ eTailers will need to focus on the 'last mile' delivery of single units to manage high levels of service quality and low cost.

The eFulfilment challenge: managing information flows that, in turn, manage money and physical flows

Fulfilment focuses on everything that happens from the time the order is taken, to the time the product is received and the consumer is satisfied

As eTailers move closer towards fulfilment roles, it is important to understand what fulfilment entails. Taken simply, fulfilment focuses on everything that happens once the decision to purchase has been made to the time the product is received – and the consumer is satisfied. eFulfilment encompasses the flows of physical goods, information and money. Despite the majority of eFulfilment value being occupied by physical flows (which include shipping and manufacturing), money flows and information flows will occupy approximately 16% and 17% respectively of total eFulfilment value in Europe. The European online fulfilment market is estimated to total $6.5bn in 2002.[4]

From the point of view of managing information flows, the eFulfilment process can be divided into five distinct categories: consumer management, catalogue management, order management, delivery management and inventory management (see Figure 5.1).

The *consumer management* operation captures and organises information required for building and sustaining a relationship between eTailer and consumer. This includes information to support fulfilment. Take, for example, the online clothing shop, iFitU, and its long-time consumer, Mr Smith. The eTailer would have basic data about Mr Smith in its system, including his first name (and that he prefers to be addressed by his first name, Brian), delivery address and past payment details. The data will also show that Brian has a solid credit history and prefers payment by credit card. Consumer fulfilment history would reveal that he recently complained about a pair of trousers delivered in the wrong colour, subsequently sent back to iFitU as a return. Account maintenance information would show that iFitU still has an outstanding order to fill – that of the replacement pair of trousers in the right colour, khaki – within three days. Otherwise, a refund would be due back into Brian's credit card account.

The *catalogue management* operation provides content that helps Brian make his purchasing decisions with iFitU. Brian wants to buy a new jacket

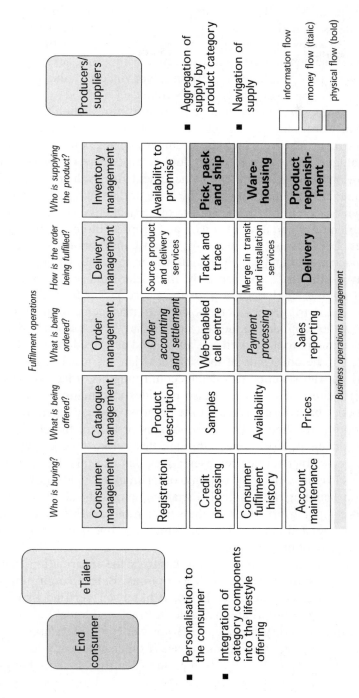

Figure 5.1 The information driven fulfilment value chain

for his girlfriend, Kim. He looks up product descriptions in the online catalogue, and sees a fleece jacket in a screaming red which he knows she'll love! He skips the language options in German and French, and reads with amusement a customer's review on how the jacket is 'thick enough to keep two people warm'. Brian is convinced by the video clip that the fleece will be a good fit for Kim's frame.

The *order management* operation next captures information that is relevant to Brian's order and consumer support. This vital function links to other management functions such as consumer management for consumer details, catalogue management for product details, delivery management for shipping options and inventory management for product availability. Back to Brian: after finding out about the price of the red fleece – which is broken down onscreen into the basic cost of the jacket, VAT and shipping charges – Brian clicks on the jacket icon and drops it into his virtual shopping basket. Looking out the window, Brian congratulates himself on having avoided a cold and wet 30-minute trip to the mall. On top of that, he's just saved himself £5! Immediately after Brian's placed his order, the system collects his 'click-and-drop' of the fleece jacket from the virtual shopping basket. A trigger is sent to the delivery management function that manages how the supplier and the courier company pick, pack and deliver the order. Settlement to third parties is automated as agreed in commercial agreements. On the other side of the screen, Brian has just had his credit card authorised. He is alerted that details confirming his order will be sent to his email address. The message also provides information on how he can send queries both during and after the order process via email. Brian is given the option to choose the email address or cancel the correspondence – he cancels it. Brian's been through this before – he knows there are also live consumer service representatives that can take his questions about credit clearance, delivery options, order tracking, and most importantly, returns handling. Very quickly, Brian completes the short consumer survey before logging off. Back in the server room at iFitU, the system sends the sales-related data to the marketing department for future sales targeting and promotion planning.

The *delivery management* operation controls the information that is required to manage the physical delivery options. Before confirming the order for the red fleece jacket to Brian, it has been verified that both product and delivery options are available. A 'track and trace' link is built into the physical delivery service, so Brian can track the status of his order online. The system also checks to see if other orders are due to the same destination within the time frame, and identifies Brian's bungled order of the last time. At the warehouse, the jacket and trousers are physically picked and packed. This process includes the printing of delivery labels and value added services – a little 'Happy Birthday' gift tag for Kim, which Brian will be glad about! Brian's khaki pair of trousers and the red fleece jacket for Kim are consolidated into a single delivery booking. Two days later, Brian receives his trousers and Kim's jacket, with a complimentary smiley-face 'Happy Birthday' gift tag next to the jacket. Brian beams in satisfaction.

Behind the scenes, the *inventory management* process captures information and activities that are required to accurately state the availability of the product for on-time shipment. Real time data confirms there is just one red fleece jacket in stock in the size Brian's ordered; the next shipment of red fleeces in assorted sizes is due in two days' time. It is also confirmed and communicated to Brian at the time of ordering that delivery will take three days; this information is vital in Brian's buying decision, since Kim's birthday is a week away. In the case of Brian's previous returned pair of trousers, this warehouse operation also saw to the receiving, unpacking and reconditioning of the returned good. Inventory management, physical storage and product replenishment functions follow after, geared to optimise product availability while avoiding excessive inventory costs.

The eFulfilment challenge is multi-functional:

- It involves managing information, money and physical flows to satisfy customers
- It includes all processes from the time the order is taken, to the time the product is received and the consumer is satisfied.

The online consumer: broken promises mean broken relationships

Consumer lifetime value is IN; transaction-based retail model is OUT

As much as the Internet has changed the retail market, thinking around consumer value and consumer relationships has also evolved. Consumer lifetime value is predicated on a company's ability to build and sustain a long-term relationship with a consumer. The vital ingredient to this relationship is trust. Among other reasons, intense retail competition and shorter product life cycles have pushed successful retailers and eTailers alike to justify investment expenditure against consumer lifetime value. The economics are simple: repeat purchases increase revenues, while customer loyalty reduces acquisition costs.

Repeat purchasing is the prize of every retail campaign. To keep consumers coming back, you must give consumers reason to perceive greater value in your products and services compared to the competition's. This value perception is influenced by the:

- *product* – description, choice, personalisation
- *convenience* – accessibility, range, delivery
- *service* – ordering, after-sales support, returns procedure
- *price* – retail price, taxes, shipping charges.

Keep your consumer promise all the way, all the time

The currency of a lifelong eTailer–consumer relationship is trust. Once lost, trust is expensive and difficult to reinstate in a consumer. It is expensive to win back a consumer because consumer acquisition costs are high. Multi-channel retailers in Europe reported that on average, customer acquisition cost was $22, while the amount for pure-play eTailers was $42. Customer acquisition costs can range from $108 for newcomers to $29 for established players.[5] Pure-play online retailers spend as much as 58% of advertising expenditure on customer acquisition, compared to 3% on customer retention. In contrast, multi-channel players spend about, on average, 51% on customer acquisition and 16% on customer retention.[6] While the embryonic eTailing market has embraced valuation methodologies based on consumer base, long-term targets of profitability will call for careful management of consumer acquisition costs. And managing a satisfying relationship in the eyes of the consumer is the key to reducing such skyrocketing acquisition costs.

While losing a consumer is easy, winning back a consumer is difficult. This is because a consumer's switching costs are close to zero in the eWorld. Competitive offerings are only a click away. These competitors will be focused on creating and sustaining relationships. They will be making the investments to get their fulfilment right. If they succeed in building trust, why would the consumer consider returning to you as a customer? To tempt consumers back, the approach is typically to reduce prices and buy volume – an approach which may lead to other difficult relationships, such as with shareholders.

Remember the little things that keep the relationship strong

Just why do online consumers leave? Recent market research show that failings in online fulfilment – or weak eFulfilment – contribute significantly to consumer attrition. Over the US Christmas season in 1999, it was found that 25% of sites that were explored could not take the consumers' orders.[7] Some crashed, others were 'blocked', under construction or were otherwise inaccessible. Recent research also indicated that $325m was spent online by UK Christmas shoppers in 1999, but that only 65% of those orders were estimated to have been fulfilled as promised.[8] Worryingly for eTailers, 35% of shoppers who experienced problems on a Web site subsequently left that Web site for another.[9]

The 'little things' that we take for granted at bricks-and-mortar stores aren't so little in the eyes of online consumers. As consumers, we never expect shops to be closed during advertised opening hours. Since the Internet is a 24/7 medium, why should eTailers ever find an excuse to be closed? When we make a purchase at a high street store, we get 'instant fulfilment' upon payment by walking out of the store with the goods in our hands. Since eTailers take payment online anytime of day, why shouldn't delivery time countdown from the moment of payment as well? If the net is better than the store, should delivery be 'free' on the net, too? Unfortu-

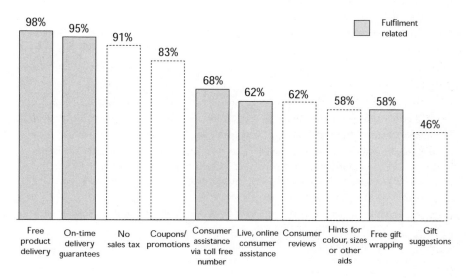

Figure 5.2 Factors most likely to encourage a repeat purchase by US online consumers[10]

nately for the eTailers, most high street shoppers don't consciously cost their own time and money spent in making their way down to the mall, sifting through product alternatives at multiple stores, then transporting purchases back home themselves.

The most powerful statement to emerge from the 1999 online Holiday shopping is this: when consumers were asked which type of products or services would increase the likelihood of their making repeat purchases, five of the top ten recommendations depended upon improved fulfilment (see Figure 5.2).

Across the Atlantic: breaking promises and running foul of the law
'Toysrus.com Slapped With Class Action Lawsuit'
(*eCommerce Times*, 12 January 2000)

The $2.5bn toys retailer is reported to be taken to court on behalf of a consumer who ordered Christmas gifts from the retail giant Toysrus.com's website, but never received the goods. Toysrus.com is just one of many US online retailers that might be operating in violation of the FTC's Mail Order Rule, a 1975 measure that governs the performance of mail order sales and that is now deemed to apply to online retailers as well.

The US Federal Trade Commission's Mail Order Rule
The FTC's mail-order rule seeks to protect consumers who shop by mail. Under the rule:

- A mail-order company must send ordered goods within the time period specified in its ads, or within 30 days if no shipping date is given. The time requirements go into effect when the company has received the completed order. This means that the company has received the consumer's cash, check, or money order, or charged a credit account, and that it has all the information necessary to process and ship the order. Failure to specify essential information, such as the size or color of an ordered item, would make the order incomplete.

- If the company cannot meet the shipping deadline, it must notify the consumer and provide the consumer with the option of either receiving a prompt refund or agreeing to a delay. The notice must include the new shipping date, instructions on how to cancel the order, and a postage-paid means of reply.

- If the consumer agrees to a new shipping date and the company is again unable to meet it, the company must send a second notice as soon as possible. Unless the consumer signs and returns this postage-paid notice, the company must automatically cancel the order and issue a refund.

- If a company cannot ship on time and does not notify consumers as required, it must deem the order cancelled and issue a refund.

- If a consumer chooses to cancel an order, the company must refund the consumer's money within seven business days after receiving the consumer's request (for orders paid by cash, check or money order) or credit the account within one billing cycle (for credit card orders).

The online consumer relationship is built on kept promises:

- Think consumer lifetime value
- Keep your consumer promise all the way, all the time
- Remember the little things that keep the eTailer–consumer relationship strong.

Consumer expectations: competition and your own performance will continue to 'raise the bar' on you

Your fulfilment solution must meet your consumers' expectations; competition and your own performance will act to continuously raise their expectations

Consumers only get tougher. Consumer demand for 'cheaper, quicker and better' never lets up. Retailers through the ages have known that consumers are tough masters. Yet, the differences between pressures faced by eTailers today and traditional retailers are that first, an online consumer expects eTailers to respond faster and more directly to their changed individual demands – patience is no virtue online; and second, online consumers make stepwise changes *en masse*, leaving an eTailer in the lurch completely if it fails to match the competition immediately.

An eTailer like Amazon.com could introduce its services years ago with a two-week delivery promise. Tomorrow, anything less than next day delivery (or the perceived commitment to achieve this target) will trigger a visit to competitor sites. Before the Internet, poor service took its time to travel by word-of-mouth. Today, chat rooms and online community sites spread 'corporate dirty laundry' like wildfire. Today, eTailers face the pressure to match every competitor innovation in real time. Because consumer switching costs are low or non-existent, failure to match competitor offers easily leads to overnight diminishment of consumer bases. Every start-up's nightmare is a halving of its share price with a news announcement of service breakdown. Common sins against online consumers include cumbersome registration procedures before checkout, submission of credit card numbers before being provided with shipping charges or the total tab, and ambiguous messages about actual delivery.

Consumer expectations arise from sources where they perceive value in product and services. These include areas of product, convenience, service and price. Key expectations are summarised in the table below, alongside implications for eTailers.

Table 5.2   Online consumers' expectations

Sources of consumer value perception	eConsumer expectations	Implications for eTailer

Product	■ Accessibility to full range of products, across depth and breadth – fulfilment of lifestyle propositions
	■ Availability of easily navigable product catalogues
	■ Personalised products
		■ Cost of catalogue development (especially where industry standards are lacking, for example building materials)
		■ Development of 'market-of-one' proposition
		■ Just-in-time production and delivery capabilities:
		  – Customised products
		  – Tailored delivery

Convenience	■ Promise of speed, cost and time of delivery specified at point of order confirmation ■ 100% availability ■ Home delivery for all product types	■ Integration of information sources in supply chain to fulfill promise to customer ■ Integration of systems with suppliers ■ Reliance on third party execution standards ■ Investments in alternative delivery solutions, for example drop boxes
Service	■ Option of direct contact with consumer service representatives – multilingual services with 24/7 access ■ Proactive remedial action when fulfilment failures threaten ■ Goods return with ease, at no additional expense	■ Multiple contact channel strategy, for example phone, fax, email ■ Contingency plans built into fulfilment chain to identify and act on problems early ■ Returns management: 2-way logistics channel
Price	■ Perceived price online may include shipping ■ Perceived price should not exceed high street's	■ Management of additional costs of sales, especially for single-unit deliveries

The physical flow of products: influence of product and supply chain characteristics

Consumer expectations continually 'raise the bar' on you:

■ Short reaction times and increased costs come with every stepwise shift in consumer expectations, triggered by competition or oneself

- Expectations of products: eTailers must evolve towards lifestyle propositions which typically integrate product, service and content from many sources of supply
- Expectations of convenience: eTailers must provide a promise on the speed, cost and time of delivery at the point of order
- Expectations of service: eTailers must provide levels of consumer service which match or surpass high street retailers
- Expectations of price: eTailers should expect consumers to perceive price to be inclusive of shipping and tax
- The eTailer needs to opt for eFulfilment solutions that scale and improve to meet challenges of ever-increasing consumer expectations.

Net multiplier effects... what works for good news works for the bad, too!

Imagine you're the CEO of an eTailer start-up. You wake up one morning and the world starts screaming 'Murder!' at you. All you did was disappoint a couple of online consumers. What could you have done? You didn't expect demand to shoot through the roof! Before you can get onto the phone to work out your corporate PR crisis plan, your brand name has already been 'vandalised' many times over on virtual walls. Virtual demonstrators are urging boycott... not just at home, but all over the world.

Scary, but a very real nightmare for every eTailer. For ToysRUs, the rude awakening about online consumer satisfaction crashed down days before Christmas 1999. While Reuters meekly reported that ToysRUs would be 'dishing out $100 coupons to some disappointed Internet shoppers who will not be getting their gifts in time for Christmas', irate parents were smearing the ToysRUs name all over the walls of free chat rooms:

> There is NO substitute for a disappointed child on Christmas morning... This was the WORST online shopping experience of my life. Not only will I never buy from ToysRUs online again – but I'll shop other brick and mortar stores before stepping foot in another ToysRUs... And customer service is terrible. ToysRUs didn't even notify shoppers of the problem until last week. My wife is angry because we had everything else all wrapped and we were faced with uncertainty. We ordered early to ensure that we got the 'difficult to find' gifts and so that we would not be doing things last minute. Instead, we found ourselves planning 'contingencies' 5 days from Xmas. 100 "Geoffry" dollars?! Are you kidding?' (Anonymous. New Jersey, USA. Works in Internet Medical Marketing)

> I've received an email from ToysRUs and the stupid thing is they should have been able to tell me they couldn't ship the order when I was e-checking out (like LL Bean). But no, I get an email the day after I place the order (and I don't get the $100 in coupons). NO wonder they can't compete with Etoys. (Anonymous. Cincinnati, USA. Works as Industrial Designer)

Not only are dissatisfied consumers showing their anger in full force, they're instantly forming lobby groups against you. And recommending your competitors to all who may care to listen. No doubt not all your consumers will feel the need for bitter revenge. How you wish bouquets (like the following posting) would work their magic… fast!

> A satisfied customer. I ordered toys from ToysRUs four times in November and I had no problems whatsoever. I even got free shipping and great prices. Everything came within one week. I am not sure what all these dissatisfied customers are ordering, but I had a great experience with TRU. (Anonymous. Illinois, USA)

Online consumers have extremely high expectations and extremely low tolerance levels for poor eFulfilment. And they're not content to keep negative feelings to themselves. The once-fallen eTailer may choose to salvage consumer faith by spending on increased capacity. Indeed, ToysRUs CEO John Bardour announced a tripling of web servers to cope with anticipated Christmas traffic way back in November 1999. Failing to anticipate consumer demand or expectations came at a high price, though. On 15 November 1999, ToysRUs reported that profits for the third quarter fell 25% in part due to expanded Web site costs. Repeated outages also eroded what existed of consumer loyalty. Cormac Foster, analyst at Jupiter Communications in New York commented, 'If I'm going to wait until the middle of December to buy a toy for my nephew, to make sure he doesn't already have it, I'm not going to go to a site that couldn't handle the traffic in the middle of November.' (Quoted in 'ToysRUs: Our Site "B" Slow', *ZDNet News*, 17 November 1999).

Effects of breaking fulfilment promises can go beyond bad press. For some eTailers, eFulfilment problems can lead to larger financial and organisational issues. Value America, the online reseller of thousands of brand name products, went through a watershed period in the fourth quarter of 1999 due to fulfilment delays and transition issues. While consumer demand increased, the company failed to keep its promise of next-day delivery to consumers. This was attributed to the installation of new technology infrastructure (including the addition of inventory management software) intended to scale capabilities with growth. By 3 Jan 2000, its stock price was $5.25. (When Value America went public in April 1999, its stock price was $23.00.) What ensued was a complete restructuring of its business. Value America eliminated what it called 'all nonproductive product categories', including housewares. The company would concentrate on categories in which the mix of product selection, product fulfilment, customer service and gross margins was strongest; this includes computers, office supplies and consumer electronics. Two of its founders resigned, and half the workforce was laid off. However, the nightmare didn't go away. As at 5 April 2000, Value America's stock price was $2.88, and the company faced doubts about its ability to stay in business.

Your physical fulfilment chain will be influenced by product characteristics and cyclicality of demand

Your physical fulfilment chain – encompassing product sourcing, ware-housing, distribution and delivery – will be determined by the characteristics of the product you sell. Figure 5.3 segments some online product categories according to ease of fulfilment and manufacturing strategy. Ease of fulfilment refers to the ease with which products can be made available, distributed and delivered. Manufacturing strategy refers to the level of customisation in the product which determines if it is best built-to-order or built-to-stock.

Fulfilment options take into account service, convenience and delivery costs. These depend on product characteristics, both quantitative (size, shape, weight) and qualitative (value, fragility, perishability). Just-in-time (JIT) manufacturing of a new music chart release makes no sense; however, this is potentially ideal for an obscure back catalogue jazz album. Single wrapped CDs with a delivery lead time of two days can be sent via the postal service, while a $2000 Armani suit for next day delivery would best be sent via special courier, tracking facility optional. Items that are built-to-order are best shipped directly to the consumer, for example Dell computers. For more standardised built-to-stock items, simple fulfilment contracted to a third party would suffice.

Demand cyclicality adds complexity to fulfilment options. Products like music albums are prone to cyclical demand: consumer purchases peak upon new album releases or just prior to a gifting season like Christmas. Knowing that consumers demand nothing less than 100% availability and next day delivery, eTailers could manage demand by conditioning consumers to pre-order new releases. This could be complemented by prior agreements with suppliers and delivery contractors to cater to expected peak seasons. Conditioning consumers' buying pattern is most suitable for cyclical demand created by artificial events, such as new product launches or promotional events. The sudden surge of demand at the launch of Playstation 2 in Japan caused Sony's site to crash: about 500,000 users per minute accessed the site during the midnight hours of the launch date, 17 February 2000.

Align existing offline supply chain structures to the online world

The challenge for eTailers is to align the existing offline supply chain to the new demands of the online world. eTailers aggregate shopping needs

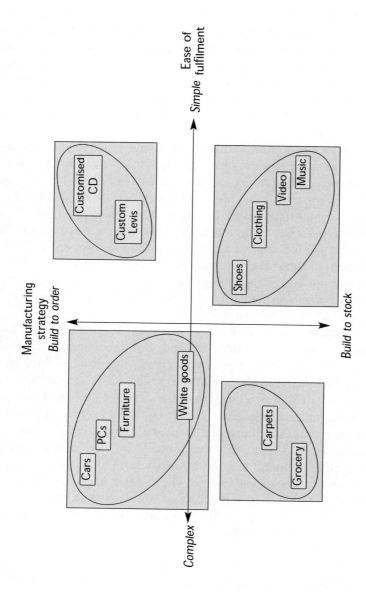

Figure 5.3   Product range segmentation according to key fulfilment characteristics

to create lifestyle solutions for online consumers in much the same way as supermarkets aggregate the 'weekly shop' for offline consumers. Distribution centres can either be dedicated online fulfilment centres, or integrated sites such as Valley Media (US-based music and video supplier to store retailers and eTailers) that fulfil both online and offline product warehousing and shipping. Having sourced a product from the manufacturer or wholesaler, that product will be stored in the distribution centre, from where it will be despatched to the consumer after picking, gift wrapping, multi-unit order consolidation and packing.

eTailers have pursued several options to fulfill distribution needs:

1. Distribution centres can be owned and managed in-house, for example Webvan.

2. The distribution function can be outsourced to a third party, for example QXL's contract with iForce.co.uk.

3. A third option is to use both in-house and outsourced distribution centres. Amazon uses such a hybrid solution. It manages its book fulfilment in-house, but outsources fulfilment of CDs to Valley Media.

4. An alternative is to create a 'virtual' solution, shipping directly from the manufacturer to the end consumer. For Dell Computers, which builds-to-order, this solution is fundamental to their business model. However, this option is viable only if the supplier maintains a distribution centre with online fulfilment capabilities. There should also be strong relationships and compatible technical infrastructure among partners, incorporating JIT manufacturing and a fully integrated supply chain.

Physical delivery of the product to the consumer is most commonly outsourced

The Internet frees the consumer from the constraints of space in terms of what they buy and where they buy. The irony is that delivery brings space and distance back to life for eFulfilment. In fact, the eTailer is faced with more delivery complexities compared to his bricks-and-mortar counterpart: while the high street store can dictate a delivery zone, eTailers are expected to fulfill orders across national, regional and sometimes international distances.

Due to the economies of scale created by threshold drop densities, a relatively small number of large logistics organisations[11] have developed the capability to execute door-to-door delivery across varied distances and scale. Most eTailers outsource delivery to these third party organisations. eTailers find it feasible to take on delivery in-house if the catchment area is restricted. Kosmo of the US, for example, restricts within-the-hour delivery to specific metropolitan areas. In densely populated areas like New York, Kozmo brings goods to its consumers by foot or bicycle. While consumers may be delighted at swift deliveries, the firm has to bear the cost of hiring delivery personnel.

Create a reverse distribution system to manage returns

In the offline world, returns are usually accepted by the store that sells them. Pure Internet eTailers, however, usually employ one-way supply chain solutions that are not equipped to receive, assess and dispose or repackage single unit returns from customers. Market research from The Yankee Group indicates that nearly 45% of online shoppers today have concerns about their ability to return purchased goods.[12] Many eTailers have written off returned products by selling returns off at cost, donating them to good causes or simply disposing them as waste. Ironically, the growth of consumer online purchases will see an increasing number of returns, and most of these will be in perfect condition. Treating returned goods carelessly will mean money wasted for many eTailers. Also, fast and reliable delivery is one of the most effective ways of reducing returns.

To cope, eTailers should develop a strategy towards treating returns, either good or faulty. Good products can be returned to the manufacturer directly or to the fulfilment centre. In many cases, a Central Return Centre (CRC) can consolidate returned goods. An outsourced CRC can prevent returns from clogging up an eTailer's main distribution system. The eTailer may find that they are responsible for dealing with faulty products. This may include the act of recycling, possibly mandated by regulation in countries such as Germany where there are strict environmental laws.

The physical flow of products is influenced by product and supply chain characteristics:

- Product features and cyclicality of demand determine physical fulfilment options
- Align existing offline supply chain structures to the online world
- Physical delivery of the product to the consumer is commonly outsourced
- Create a reverse distribution system to manage returns.

Your eFulfilment options: build, buy, rent, pay-as-you-go

As an Internet start-up, you want first mover advantage. You need speed to market. Your fulfilment capabilities may or may not be readily available in the market, packaged as a solution for you. Three major issues will guide your thinking around feasible fulfilment options for your business.

'What are my requirements?':Your fulfilment capabilities will be defined by your consumers' expectations

What do your consumers expect of you? Is it premium service? Or is it a low cost, 'no frills' provision? The more you understand your consumers' expectations, the more you can target capabilities which can enable you to keep your promise to consumers and seal a long-term relationship. Your fulfilment capabilities will be defined by the:

- depth and breadth of the product range you offer the consumer
- characteristics of the supply chain which support your product
- level of delivery service you promised your consumer
- cost of service provision.

'What solutions are available in the marketplace?': Keep your eye on what is achievable

Having defined your fulfilment capabilities, it is time to cast your eyes to solutions which are available in the market. There is, of course, the option to custom-make solutions from scratch. However, for reasons of speed to market and cost efficiency, this may not be the best option for an Internet start-up. This debate will be further developed later.

Be mindful that the European online fulfilment market is still in its infancy. There are only a handful of players who are beginning to address the precise issues that today's eTailers face. It is important to differentiate your eTailer business-to-consumer focus from business-to-business solutions available in the marketplace. A number of businesses have attempted to adapt existing business-to-business/mail order fulfilment solutions to the intricacies of direct-to-consumer online fulfilment – the result may be a service that fails to meet your consumers' expectations.

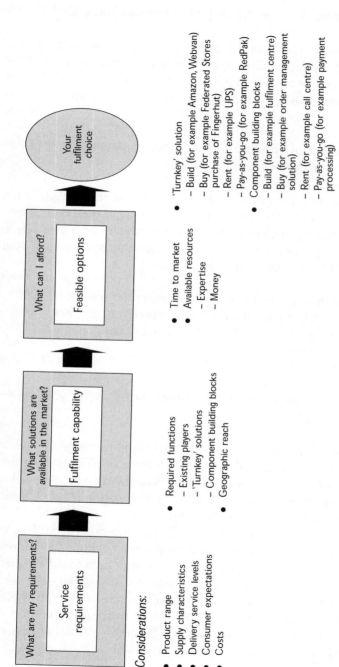

Figure 5.4 Framework for identifying your fulfilment solution

'What can I afford?':Your business constraints of time, money and know-how will limit your options

Every start-up must face up to three fundamental constraints in its early days: time, money and know-how. Speed to market will keep your eyes on the clock. Your financial backers and benefactors will no doubt be watching their returns on investment closely, thus precluding any extravagant capital infrastructure dream on your part. Most significantly, you may lack expert skills to select, implement and manage your fulfilment solutions. Constraints of time, budget and expertise may lead you to decide to outsource the critical fulfilment services you need.

'But beware growing too big for your boots...':The softer sides of eFulfilment take time and planning to perfect

In eSpace, everyone moves at eSpeed. With sufficient money, ready-made physical assets of fulfilment – like equipment, facilities and warehouses – can be bought and adapted readily. However, the softer elements of software infrastructure development take time. The '100% availability' mantra means that consumers expect perfect fulfilment regardless of demand peaks or rapid growth in eTailing volumes. The successful eTailer almost has to acquire flexibility, scalability and reliability from the start.

The heart of the issue is *scalability*. One of the most common problems facing successful eTailers is that of growth outstripping their initial capacities. Fulfilment capabilities must be conceived to match rapid growth from the start. Entering the market without fully testing systems infrastructure can mean fulfilment glitches; one glitch can scar the eTailer's brand in the eyes of consumers forever. High profile music eTailer, Boxman, had spent a significant proportion of their UK marketing budget to create a public relations splash before its UK launch. While consumer expectations were fuelled, adequate fulfilment capabilities were not in place. The result was a communications campaign that persuaded customers to order a product that was slow to arrive and frequently damaged. In response to eTailer needs, online fulfilment operations such as iForce.co.uk now offer start-ups flexible agreements that allow them to scale their businesses quickly as consumer demand grows.

As your business evolves, so will your eFulfilment requirements. The faster you grow, the more often you should re-evaluate your requirements

Selecting your eFulfilment option will not be a one-off decision. As business objectives and constraints evolve, so will your eFulfilment requirements. There's no running away from constant re-evaluation of your business requirements to keep your eye on what's most important – keeping your insatiably demanding consumers continually satisfied.

By default, many start-ups find themselves plugging into existing third-party systems and infrastructures to get quick access to new fulfilment capability. Companies have identified eTailers' plight by packaging products to meet eTailers' growing needs. Muze has spent many years building its music catalogue, offering a valuable resource to start-up music eTailers. Experion's and Equifax's consumer credit and risk databases have also been compiled over a considerable length of time. The capabilities that these service firms offer are often, cleverly, not for sale; they are only for rent. The eTailer is often faced with plugging together a range of 'pay-as-you-go' services to meet their fulfilment needs.

Other eTailing players have found outsourcing agreements inadequate with rapid business expansion. Amazon.com made the decision to invest in its own eFulfilment centres around Europe and the US. Any eTailer faced with decisions on evolving eFulfilment requirements must trade off objectives against constraints. A look at Amazon's life cycle of eFulfilment (Figure 5.5) shows how service quality has been and is likely to be maintained as the supreme business objective.

'Eenie-Meenie-Minie-Mo': Your eFulfilment options to build, buy, rent or pay-as-you-go

Now you have decided on the eFulfilment capabilities you need, and you have a clear view of where you want slack capacity in your solution. The next step is to source as high service a solution as possible. Your options are fourfold: build, buy, rent or pay-as-you-go. Whatever the final decision, the heavy investment involved will be sure to cause many a sleepless night as you think through your options thoroughly.

The weighing of pros and cons can begin with thinking about 'build vs buy'. Table 5.3 summarises some arguments around building your eFulfilment capabilities from scratch.

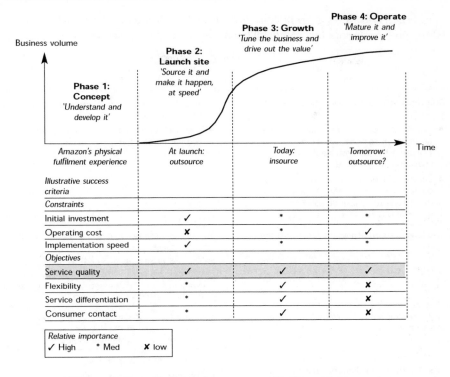

Figure 5.5   Amazon's physical eFulfilment life-cycle

For the majority of start-ups, the constraints of time and expertise bias the eFulfilment decision towards renting or 'pay-as-you-go'. Some of your soul-searching may include the arguments in Table 5.4.

Your eFulfilment option will be influenced by your consumers, the solutions marketplace and your resources

■ 'What are my requirements?':Your fulfilment capabilities will be defined by your consumers' expectations
■ 'What solutions are available in the marketplace?': Keep your eye on what is achievable
■ 'What can I afford?': Your business constraints of time, money and know-how will limit your options

Table 5.3   'To build or not to build?' – arguments for and against building eFulfilment capabilities from scratch

BUILD	
Pros	**Cons**
You retain full control over the fulfilment processes: ■ No reliance on external fulfilment sources during peak seasons (for example Christmas) when restricted product allocations might occur ■ Direct control and visibility levels allow tighter management and more accurate forecasting to ensure demand and expectations are met	Your skill as an eTailer is in capturing demand, not fulfilling demand: ■ Your lack of expert fulfilment skills will leave you with a beast you can't tame
You limit system incompatibilities with third parties	You might be slow to launch, and compromise time to market: ■ You will need to invest time to build and test physical or IT infrastructure, train human resources to manage, and integrate or build systems from scratch
You can achieve lower overall costs at higher transaction volumes	You have to invest significant money and management time in the development of facilities, systems and human capital
You can customise your solution to your specific needs and requirements	Your customised solution will not be flexible: ■ Volumes could increase rapidly ■ Your business model and supporting operations could shift in response to market realities ■ Lifestyle solutions dictate a need to move into alternative product categories, often with radically different product characteristics.

- Think Big: build scalability into your fulfilment solution from the start
- As your business evolves, constantly re-evaluate your eFulfilment requirements
- Keep your eyes on your business objectives as you decide one of four options: build, buy, rent or pay-as-you-go

The European fulfilment services marketplace

The European fulfilment services market has both specialist and generalist providers. Their services range from full 'turnkey' fulfilment to 'compo-

Table 5.4   Arguments for and against rent/'pay-as-you-go' options

Pros	Cons
You can launch quickly by 'plugging in' your system to the third party's existing infrastructure	You lose aspects of the direct relationship with the consumer if delivery is outsourced to a third party
You can channel scarce resources to best/most urgent use: ■ You can minimise investment into fulfilment infrastructure ■ Cash and management time can be channelled towards other business priorities ■ Consumer services and logistics activities typically depend on scale for cost effectiveness, something start-ups are unlikely to have	You may find integration and volume transaction costs stacking up, eroding initial savings: ■ Transaction costs for high volume products may be significant ■ Technical integration of IT infrastructure among the partners can be highly complex and expensive
You can harness the expertise of niche industry players in areas such as tax or physical fulfilment: ■ Facilities and infrastructure by third party providers are more likely to be leading edge since the fulfilment process will be their core competence ■ Good systems take years and experience to build	You may compromise your service standards: ■ Reliability on services can become unpredictable ■ Dynamic forecasting for inventory can be difficult because of delays in processing orders among partners
You can benefit from flexible agreements which cope with peak and volatile demand: ■ Scalability can be achieved without system interruptions ■ In particular, 'pay-as-you-go' does not penalise you for dips in demand as you pay only for what you use	You may be locked into a weak bargaining position: ■ True online fulfilment capability is currently a scarce resource, giving the third party a strong negotiating position ■ Buying/negotiation power can be critical in getting sufficient supply in times of product shortages or high seasonal demand ■ Today's deal structures lock the dot.com into the relationship for considerable periods of time to justify capacity investment by the third party

nent' plays that aim to solve a very specific fulfilment issue. Fulfilment players can be segmented into four groups of service providers:

1. *Incumbent logistics providers*: players like national postal services and UPS have developed more comprehensive order, delivery and inventory management roles.

2. *Incumbent mail order companies*: players like Otto Versand and Quelle in Germany have expanded their existing direct-to-consumer operations into the online world.

3. *Specialist service providers*: players like Verisign, Experion, Muze and OrderTrust are component specialists who offer specific components and an overall fulfilment service.

4. *'Turnkey' solution providers*: players like Redpak, iForce.co.uk and PFSWeb offer complete fulfilment solutions to dot.coms. Offerings address specific online retailing fulfilment needs.

Figure 5.6 shows some of the players in the European eFulfilment services marketplace. Companies like national postal service company Deutsche Post and couriers UPS Worldwide offer mainly physical fulfilment, while Equifax supports money flow services. New players like Redpak offer information driven eFulfilment service, which in turn drive physical and money flow fulfilment activities. Profiles below illustrate the difference in eFulfilment services offered by players in the distinct areas of managing information, physical and money flows.

Company profile #1: RedPak – managing information, thus facilitating producer and supplier relationships as well as physical and money flows in a complete eFulfilment solution offering

RedPak is a new company setting up to enable producers to provide an order management and delivery service to emerging eTailers and other online outlets. RedPak enables eTailers or online 'sales windows' to source products directly from producer inventories across Europe and to deliver these directly through the letterbox or front door of consumers' homes. This allows the producer and eTailer/'sales windows' to capture more value in the supply chain. With RedPak, eTailers are relieved of administrative tasks behind fulfilment, and can thus concentrate on core activities of creating and maintaining relationships with consumers.

A distinct advantage of RedPak is its ability to give eTailers turnkey access to key European markets. RedPak's offering is flexible enough to support different commercial relationships between producers and eTailers. RedPak leverages producers' existing infrastructures and existing quality third party services to provide a low cost, low risk, easily implemented and highly effective online fulfilment solution to online retailers

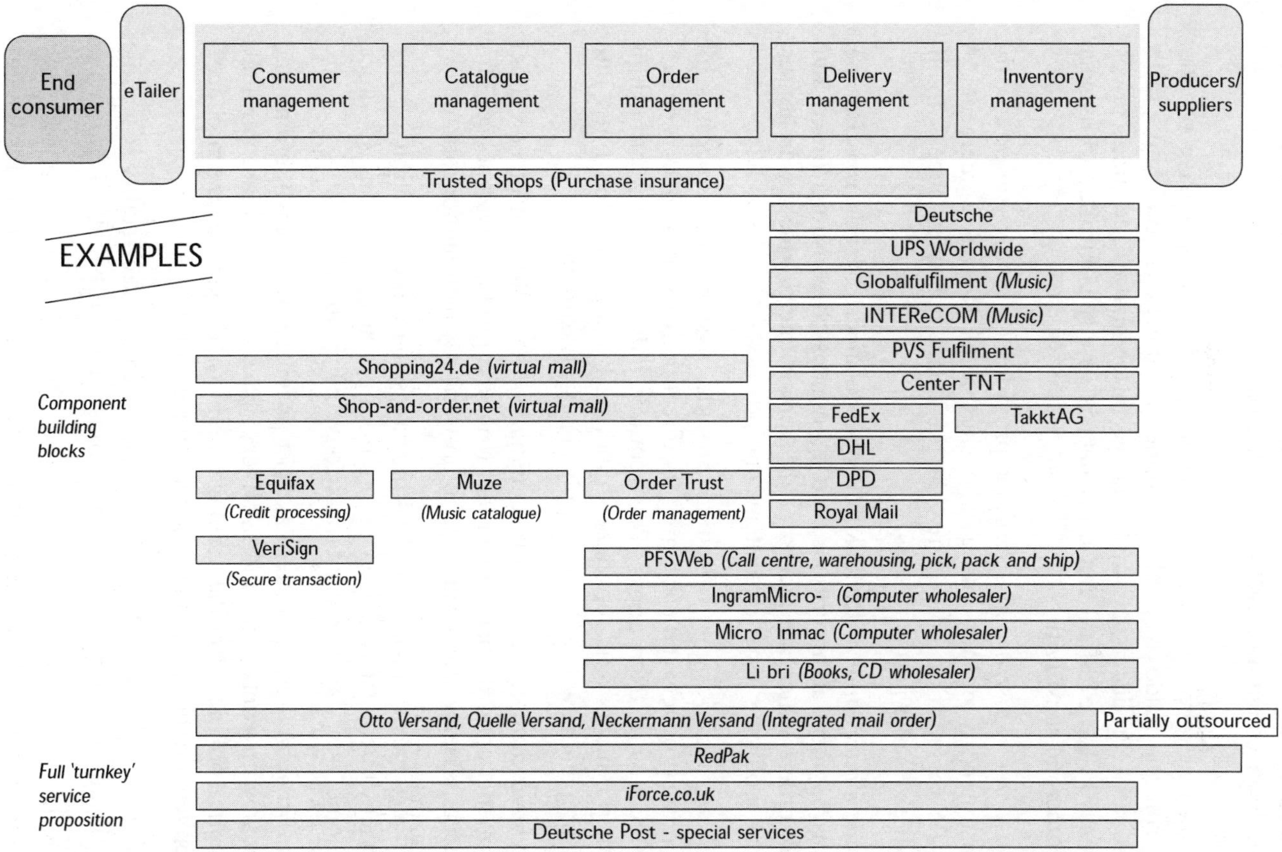

Figure 5.6   Examples of players in the European online fulfilment services marketplace

and 'sales windows'. RedPak service modules can be implemented in part or full. Services within RedPak's offering include:

- *Catalogue services* – RedPak enables producers to manage product information made available to online consumers via different eTailer Web sites. Producers can also manage differential eTailer trade prices. Access to the eTailers' consumer data is strictly controlled to manage commercial sensitivities.

- *Consumer registration* – RedPak provides a standard interface for consumers to register with eTailer sites under RedPak agreements. A single registration could provide the consumer with access to all RedPak eTailer partners' sites.

- *Order management* – RedPak collects consumer orders across Europe, gains payment authorisations, and aggregates all consumer orders into bulk orders which are picked at the appropriate producer warehouses, using producers' existing systems and processes.

- *Sourcing management* – RedPak provides systems and processes for sourcing products and packaging for direct delivery through consumers' letterboxes or front doors. This requires industry-wide relationships with producers and suppliers supported by sophisticated links into existing and new warehouse/supply chain infrastructures.

- *Payment processing* – RedPak manages the collection of consumer payments upon despatch of orders from the producer warehouse. This process is quick and secure due to up-front payment authorisation.

- *Delivery management* – RedPak manages the relevant national postal services to collect consumer orders from producer warehouses. Direct-to-home, next day delivery brings convenience to the consumer.

- *Returns management* – RedPak will provide returns instructions and labels with each consumer delivery, based on individual product/ supplier policies. RedPak manages returns (through to the producer/ supplier warehouse), replacements and refunds.

- *Consumer services* – RedPak provides a call centre facility to handle email and telephone queries from consumers on behalf of individual eTailers.

- *Financial services* – RedPak manages financial settlements for the key parties in the process. RedPak collects consumer payments and manages periodic settlements with producers, eTailers and third parties.

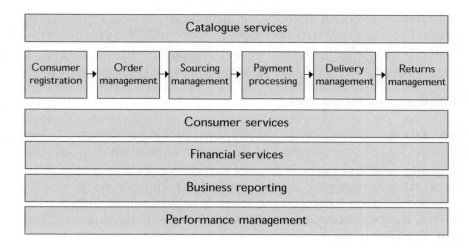

Figure 5.7   The scope of the RedPak service

■ *Business reporting* – RedPak gives the eTailer and producer/supplier access to consumer segmentation data, not accessible through other channels. Detailed reports on sales, financial, returns and other operational matters are provided. This is executed in accordance with Data Protection regulations.

■ *Performance management* – RedPak monitors and reports key performance indicators. Redpak also manages adherence to service level agreements with producers/suppliers, eTailers and third parties.

Figure 5.7 shows the full scope of the RedPak service.

Company profile #2: United Parcel Service (UPS) – managing physical flow

UPS is one of the few truly global players in logistics. UPS' strength is in its home delivery experience in the US – UPS has a big presence in the US home shopping market, and has reaped benefits from the growing online shopping business. Today, UPS operates an international small package and document network in more than 185 countries and territories, spanning both the Atlantic and Pacific oceans. In the UK, however, it has focused on business-to-business, international and intercontinental express deliveries. UPS views Europe as a lucrative market for expansion. To support this strategy, UPS has acquired some small European logistics firms. It remains likely to acquire larger players in the region.

UPS's logistics management services

Besides operational efficiency and reliability, UPS has continued to expand its basic services, from pricing and service options, to whole new categories of business. UPS can store customer's merchandise, then ship them 'just in time'. UPS also offers a comprehensive consulting service in which it assembles services based on the customer's individual needs, which might include freight payment, customs clearance, warehousing, carrier selection, rate negotiation, tracking, information systems, Electronic Data Interchange, fleet management, order processing, and inventory control.

UPS' ground forces handle physical fulfilment processes

The first step in UPS' fulfilment process is pickup. UPS delivery drivers are assigned a specific route, making regularly scheduled stops along the route. Typically, the driver delivers packages in the morning, and picks up packages in the afternoon. Large-volume customers, who might ship thousands of packages a day, may have a UPS tractor-trailer stationed on site. Lower-volume customers, who might ship as few as 2–5 packages a week, are served by the UPS package car.

To transport packages most efficiently, UPS has developed an elaborate network of 'hubs' or central sorting facilities located throughout the world. Each hub is 'fed' by a number of local operating centres, which serve as home base for UPS pickup and delivery vehicles. Packages bound for a specific geographical region are all consolidated. Every day, feeders, or tractor trailers, transport thousands of packages from the hub where the package originated, to the hub nearest the package's destination.

At the hub, when packages are loaded onto package cars for local delivery, they are loaded in the same order in which they will be delivered. This process is called the 'preload.' By delivering packages in sequence, from one address to the next closest address, drivers complete their routes as quickly and productively as possible. Each driver is assigned a specific route, or 'loop.' To optimise the driver's effectiveness, UPS industrial engineers continually research and analyse delivery trends and traffic patterns for each route. When the package is delivered, technology helps ensure that the package has arrived at the correct address, and provides customers with useful information. Using a hand-held computer device called a DIAD (Delivery Information Acquisition Device), the driver electronically captures information about each package, including the time of delivery, and even the signature of the person receiving the package. This information is transmitted via cellular telephone directly from the package car to UPS computers, where it is available for customers to trace their packages or to verify proof of delivery.

UPS' ecommerce offering to etailers

UPS has separate eCommerce offerings that aim to improve customer service, reduce costs, add Web site functionality, increase consumer surf time on your site and empower consumers.

This is enabled through a suite of services which include:

- *Tracking*: Letting consumers track their shipments right from the eTailer site, using their unique reference or order number

- *Rates and service selection*: Displaying for your consumers all the UPS shipping options and rates, giving them the flexibility to choose the service that best fits their needs and budget

- *Address validation*: Reducing shipping and billing address errors by validating the city, state and postal code at the time of consumer order entry

- *Time in transit*: Enabling your consumers to know exactly how long it will take for goods to reach them via UPS Ground service

- *Shipping and handling*: Offering customised shipping rates, tailored handling charges, discounts or standard UPS rates to fit your eTailing business and unique consumers

- *Service mapping*: Letting shoppers choose the best shipping service by viewing a colour-coded map showing ground shipment transit time

- *Electronic manifesting*: Giving your eTailing business flexible billing options, referencing number tracking capabilities and other feature benefits by uploading shipment detail to UPS

- *Branding through 'UPS Graphics'*: Reassuring your online consumers that your eCommerce site has the expertise and reliability of UPS behind it.

Company profile #3: WorldPay – managing money flow

WorldPay is a UK-based payments processor and bureau with global reach. It is targeted at small eCommerce start-ups which lack track record or credit ratings. eTailers who find themselves unable to obtain an Internet merchant account with a normal bank would likely employ WorldPay's services to launch your eTailing business within 48 hours.

Payments bureau

WorldPay provides the eTailer with a complete payments facility. Typically, services include authorisation, interface with the bank acquirer, settlement (usually within 30 days) and a degree of protection against fraud risk. WorldPay also offers consulting, fast implementation, Web hosting and wallet services.

Payments processor

As a payments processor, WorldPay is similar to an old-style card processing bureau. Its shared services offering includes merchant acquisition processing, card issuer processing, credit references/assessment/scoring services and address verification. To the small Internet start-up, WorldPay delivers quality outsourcing of the processing element by experienced third parties, thus negating the need to develop and run an in-house payment system. This also speeds up time-to-market.

Merchant software switching

WorldPay.com also offers software components that provide the interface between the eTailer's systems and the acquirer. Processes include floor limit checking, authorisation, draft storage and submission. These processes provide building blocks for whole payments systems to develop.

Conclusion

As eTailing takes off, eFulfilment will become a more complex and challenging issue. Not only do consumers expect products of all shapes and sizes to reach them at their doorsteps, they also expect to dictate when and how their purchases get delivered to them. Morning or afternoon slots are no longer good enough; consumers want the convenience of a two-hour delivery time slot, often outside normal nine-to-five delivery hours. In addition, the value of the 'doorstep experience' – otherwise described as the last metre of the delivery chain – has pushed eFulfilment companies to think about 'sugar coating' their eFulfilment offering by including customised services, like gift packing and specialist packing.

The online consumer seals his or her perception of the eTailer brand through the quality of his or her experience during eFulfilment. This consumer experience is fully influenced by the quality and efficiency with which information, money and physical goods exchange hands. As an eTailer, you must bring a holistic, first-class fulfilment experience to your online consumer. Otherwise you risk being relegated to worst-class eTailer in the limited memory space of the fickle online consumer.

Notes

1. Internet penetration ranges from a high of 54% in the Nordic countries to a low of 16% in France and 18% in Spain. IDC, 'An IDC consumer survey: European Internet and eCommerce – Ready for 2000?', December 1999
2. In 1999, the slowest growing online markets were in Switzerland (110%) and Italy (145%); the fastest growing were Belgium (420%) and the UK (280%). Boston Consulting Group, 'The State of Online Retailing 2.0', 1999
3. Andersen Consulting Analysis
4. Figures apply to online fulfilment for the following products: entertainment, apparel and footwear, software, health/beauty, consumer electronics, toys, sporting goods, speciality gifts, furniture, housewares, small appliances, home improvement and office supplies. Analysis culled from IDC (Internet Usage and Commerce in Western Europe, December 1998), Jupiter (Shopping Online Projections, November 1999) and Andersen Consulting Analysis
5. 'The Internet in Europe', Warburg Dillon Read (France) SA, January 2000
6. ibid.
7. Andersen Consulting, eSanta study, 20 December 1999
8. Cited by Reuters, 3 January 2000
9. Andersen Consulting, Christmas online shopper survey, 10 January 2000
10. Andersen Consulting, Christmas online shopper survey, 10 January 2000. Values reflect the percentage of respondents out of the 1,492 US online shoppers surveyed. Respondents were asked which proposed product or service feature would increase the likelihood of them making future online purchases
11. These logistic companies include national postal service organisations (for example Royal Mail of the UK), major mail order firms (for example Otto Versand), international couriers (for example DHL, UPS and FedEx) and other national parcel carriers (for example Deutsche Post in Germany, and TNT in the Netherlands)
12. Cited by PlanetIT, 12 January 2000

CHAPTER 6

Start-up Technology

Ceri Carill, Eduardo A. Krumholz
and Daniel Deganuti, ANDERSEN CONSULTING

The Internet has opened up dramatic possibilities for new types of business, and exciting new ways for existing businesses to expand their reach and scope as never before.

This revolutionary business impact is achieved through a complex interaction of technologies and standards that together provide near universal connectivity for businesses and their customers, and a common technology framework within which, at last, hardware and software from almost all major vendors can interact seamlessly.

This chapter aims to provide you with an introduction to the most important technologies and standards used today to develop eCommerce sites on the Internet, so that you will be in a position to understand much of the terminology used by the Internet technologists with whom you will work. It also provides an overview of approaches to getting your business connected to and managing security on the Internet – something that cannot be overlooked. It does not seek to be a complete Internet technology reference.

Evolution of Internet architectures

Before you select the architecture for your site, it is important to develop a basic understanding of the options available. This will help you balance the necessity of speed to market with the advantages (and cost) of robust, mission critical components when considering different architecture designs for your site.

As an entrepreneur, you are responsible for the ultimate success or failure of your business, and you must take ownership of the site architecture decision, whether it is your own team that is building these critical components, or you are contracting with an outside company. Do not forget that, when working at Internet speed, this is a decision you will only make once – so take care!

Since the inception of the Internet, three major generations of architecture have evolved for building Web sites. Each generation has built on the previous technologies to achieve new capabilities. This section provides an overview of each of these architecture generations, and how they have contributed to increased robustness and scalability in Internet applications.

In parallel with the development of the Internet, many businesses have deployed Enterprise Resource Planning (ERP) systems (such as SAP). When the power of these ERP systems is combined with that of the Internet, even greater value can be generated for businesses. In the later sections, Enterprise application integration, B2B opportunities and The importance of XML, the power of some of these integration technologies are described.

First generation Internet architecture

It is important to remember, when considering the simplicity of the first generation of Internet architecture, that the original intention for the Internet was to allow remotely located researchers to share information. In its earliest days the Internet was used mostly as a network to support email and discussion groups. In the early 1990s, however, a combination of two efforts led to the creation of the first generation Internet Architecture. In 1991 Tim Berners-Lee posted the language of the World Wide Web (WWW) in an Internet discussion group called *alt.hypertext*.[1] And between 1991 and 1993, Marc Andreesen and a group of student programmers at NCSA (the National Center for Supercomputing Applications located on the campus of University of Illinois at Urbana Champaign) worked to develop a graphical browser for the WWW called Mosaic.[2]

The first generation Internet Architecture provides the ability to serve formatted words and pictures to remote locations over the Web. The two

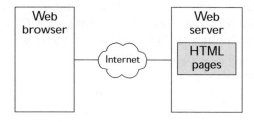

Figure 6.1   First generation Internet architecture

major components are the browser and the Web server (see Figure 6.1). The conversation between the browser and the Web server is initiated when the user types in or clicks on a new Web address, or Uniform Resource Locator (URL). Browsers send URLs to the Web server in the form of a request in HyperText Transfer Protocol (HTTP) that tells the Web server where to find a specific page in its directory structure. The page is written in a special language called HyperText Markup Language (HTML), which allows the author to specify certain formatting attributes, as well as links to other Web pages on the Internet. The Web server then replies to the browser's request by returning the desired HTML page and any graphic files that are included with that page.

The first generation Internet architecture published static electronic documents with a simplistic approach, one that encouraged millions of developers to start publishing on the Web. While there are many complex business functions that are not realistic to implement with this simple architecture, it is the perfect design for your new company's first steps on the Internet. It is never too early to launch a Web site and your company's first site should be fast to build, fast to deploy, low cost, and disposable. All you need is a few HTML pages and a Web server to start advertising your mission on the Web, announcing to the world who you are, what you are doing, and why they need to know!

Second generation Internet architecture

Late in 1995, the introduction of Common Gateway Interface (CGI) programs[3] to the Internet changed it from a medium that could only publish static electronic documents to a medium that could support dynamic client/server applications. The CGI standard allows the browser to send URL requests that, instead of returning static pages, launch an application located on the Web server. It is this application that generates, on demand, the HTML that is returned to the browser, instead of simply reading a file. Upon receiving a CGI request, the Web server launches the application and returns its results to the browser. CGI opens up a broad range of new possibilities, as Web sites using it are able to:

- return dynamic data
- query files or databases for information
- send email
- launch other applications.

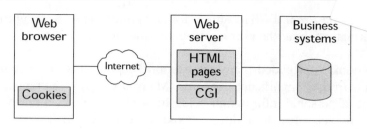

Figure 6.2   Second generation Internet architecture

Put simply, CGI enabled business on the Web, and fundamentally changed the nature of what could be done on the Internet (see Figure 6.2).

CGI applications can also be developed in any programming language although scripting languages like PERL are the most popular. As CGI applications are easy to write, seemingly overnight developers and entrepreneurs around the world began to incorporate these programs into thousands of Web sites, bringing the Internet to life.

Powerful as it is, CGI also has significant limitations for more complex applications. For example, because a CGI application is run from scratch every time the Web server needs it to generate a page, it has no memory of any previous runs. In other words, it is 'stateless'. This is not a problem if a user can enter all required information in a single HTML page, but useful applications typically require a seamless flow from screen to screen, page to page – they require the ability to remember, at a minimum, who the user is.

This limitation was quickly circumvented through the use of 'cookies'. A cookie is a small file created by the user's browser on the user's machine at the request of a CGI program. Introduced by Netscape, it 'permits a server to tell a browser to store a block of information on the user's hard disk, and to give it back on subsequent visits to the same server.[4] No information in a cookie is sent to a server that wasn't first put there by the same server.' With cookies, Internet applications can remember information across browser sessions (that is, different page accesses). Typical uses of cookies include:

■ *Sessions* – The ability to provide a Web based service that maintains information across multiple forms or pages. Thus, users can 'log on' once to an application and then use it straightforwardly.

■ *Automatic User Recognition* – Even many third generation architecture applications still use cookies for automatic user recognition. This is how some sites know your name as soon as you enter the URL without your having to log in explicitly.

■ *Client-side Profiles* – The ability for an application to store a profile of information about the user on the user's machine.

While cookies provided many application benefits, this browser mechanism also raised significant concerns. Many users were outraged by the amount of personal information being tracked on their own machines by unknown Web sites. In addition, cookies created could be searched by companies to discover how employees were using their computers. To deal with such privacy and security concerns, browser makers were forced to provide the option of disabling the cookie mechanism. We will see below in the discussion of third generation architecture how this issue is resolved by enabling application servers to store profile and session information on the server side.

As the number of users of CGI applications continued to rise, a further limitation of CGI began to be realised – poor performance caused by the overhead of having to run a separate program to serve each and every browser request.

Finally, serious programmers, used to the benefits of modern object oriented tools, found that CGI's simplistic protocol was slow and cumbersome to code.

Third generation Internet architecture

The third generation Internet architecture seeks to overcome the limitations of CGI to enable development and deployment of industrial strength applications. Its key features are Application Program Interfaces (API) and application servers (see Figure 6.3). Third generation Internet architecture introduces application servers that:

■ avoid CGI performance issues through the use of server APIs
■ avoid many security and privacy concerns by minimising use of cookie technology
■ provide off-the-shelf business objects for complex general-purpose functionality
■ enable object oriented frameworks for the development of robust custom business objects for company specific logic
■ support the dynamic generation of HTML pages
■ improve high availability and the ability to handle large numbers of users.

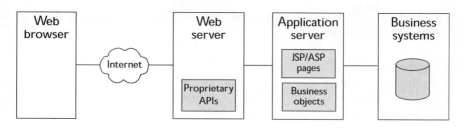

Figure 6.3   Third generation Internet architecture

Performance

A major performance improvement of the third generation Internet architectures is the use of server APIs to avoid the limitations of CGI programs.
Because server APIs are often specific to the particular Web server in use
(for example Netscape or Microsoft), they are commonly referred to as
proprietary APIs (NSAPI for Netscape, ISAPI for Microsoft and Open
Market's FastCGI for Apache). Although the detailed implementation of
these APIs differs, each yields much higher performance than the original
CGI programs by enabling separate browser requests to be handled
without the need to start up a new program each time.

Privacy and security

While third generation Internet architectures still rely on cookie technology for automatic user recognition, all other session and user profile
information can now be stored within the application server and the back
end database. This approach addresses the security concern of cookies
while reducing the dependency on the user's machine. For example, if a
user connects to the application from one machine today and from a
different machine tomorrow, the system can still retrieve that user's
profile. With this approach most of this session and profile information is
now stored within the server side architecture components.

Business objects

Application servers will provide many general purpose business objects as
standard, as well as provide tools for developers to build their own busi-

ness objects. Common general purpose objects supported by today's application servers include:

- Content management
- Session information
- Personalisation
- Online catalogue
- Shopping cart
- Order management
- Clustering and load balancing.

Both custom and off-the-shelf business objects can access back end business systems that may include databases, file systems, or other off-the-shelf applications. While the out-of-the-box functionality provided with many application servers enables developers to build significant applications with little coding. The real power of these application servers is realised when the out-of-the-box functionality is combined with the object oriented, standards based frameworks for custom development.

On Microsoft platforms, business objects are known as server-side ActiveX controls. These are special software components, written either in the C++ or Visual Basic programming languages, that can be used within Active Server Pages (see below) to assist in the dynamic generation of Web pages. ActiveX controls use a mechanism known as DCOM (Distributed Component Object Model) to 'plug into' the Web server. A benefit provided by DCOM is the fact that the business objects need not run physically on the same computer as the Web server – they may be accessed across a network, typically within an enterprise.

Other application servers use different mechanisms to integrate business objects. One common mechanism is known as CORBA (Common Object Request Broker Architecture). CORBA components, like DCOM components, need not run physically on the same computer as the Web server – they may be accessed across a network.

Dynamic generation of HTML pages

Application servers allow Web pages to be custom created using either Microsoft's Active Server Pages (ASP) or Sun's Java Server Pages (JSP) technologies.

While these are the basic emerging development standards for third generation Internet architecture application servers, each application server should be carefully examined since their implementation approaches will differ slightly. A brief description of each third generation Internet development technology is given below.

Active Server Pages

ASP pages, typically used on Microsoft Web servers, are a mixture of static HTML (for parts of the page that do not change), ActiveX controls (special program components written to the Microsoft ActiveX standard), VBScript, and JavaScript. ASP pages require a special language processor, defined by Microsoft, to be embedded in the Web server. When an ASP page is requested by a browser, the special language processor in the Web server executes the ActiveX components in the page and runs any server-side VBScript scripts and server-side JavaScript scripts. Each of these actions work together to create HTML pages that are returned for display in the user's browser.

Java Server Pages

JSP pages are similar in principle to ASP, but use different specific technologies to achieve their results. A JSP page is a mixture of static HTML, Java, and JavaScript. These pages require a special language processor (defined by Sun) to be embedded in the Web server. When a JSP page is requested by a browser, the special language processor executes the Java components in the page and runs any server-side JavaScript scripts. Each of these actions work together to create HTML pages that are returned for display in the user's browser.

Application servers often support 'clustering' to provide the highest levels of scalability, expandability, and high availability. Clustering is the ability for many application servers run at the same time to share the work of a given application. One of the applications servers acts as the 'master' to direct new requests to the application server with the lowest load. If one of the application servers should crash, the master application server redirects requests to servers that are still available. When new application servers are started up, the master application server is notified and starts sending it new requests. Performance and scalability are the major benefits to clustering as the master applications server works to balance the traffic load equally across all applications servers. This mechanism allows a business to increase the capacity of their Web application by adding more computers to the back-end architecture.

Complexity

With third generation architectures, development teams are presented with many options for secure, robust, high performance, personalised, object oriented application development. While this is a powerful framework, the sheer number of options available quickly introduces complexity. An important point to note when designing your architecture is to pay attention to the details of application version compliance. It is common for one version of an application to work well with only a certain version of another application. Tracking all the different applications, their versions, their compatibility requirements, and their system dependencies quickly becomes a Web of its own. It is a wise move to document all your existing applications and their versions before purchasing software. Once this list is documented, submit the list to each of your software vendors for their review. Only once they have provided written confirmation that your environment is sound, should you start building your architecture. This extra step in the design phase will save you many headaches down the road.

While third generation architectures have brought many benefits to businesses setting up on the Internet, their robust, flexible (and often complex) architectures mean that the days of building an Internet site in a day are no more. What was a simple task for one person has become a potentially high-risk, complex and large scale project. For those who are able to deliver these complex projects with good speed, flexibility and reusable assets, the rewards can be huge.

Enterprise application integration

It is critical for an executive to consider the Internet an extension of core business. Integration between hyperspace and the 'real world' is critical. At some point in the life of every eCommerce transaction, a product needs to be shipped, an aeroplane needs to be boarded, actual money needs to be exchanged.

The Amazon.coms of the eWorld must not only build innovative Web sites that can manage thousands of transactions per second, they must also integrate these eCommerce applications with traditional back-end databases to keep track of their customers and their orders, and with fulfilment systems to deliver the products and services the eGeneration is buying in ever-increasing numbers.[5]

Even more challenging than building your new Internet architecture is understanding how to integrate it with your existing systems. Start-ups are typically considered the luckiest members of the Internet revolution since their existing systems are limited or non existent. Many existing systems are a generation or two behind the Internet applications, making integration even more difficult. This has caused many established companies to upgrade their back office systems to newer applications with more open interfaces.

Bricks-and-mortar companies looking to extend their brands into cyber-space often have made enormous investments in mainframe-based systems, ERP applications, and data centres. They need to integrate and automate their existing billing, accounting, and order processing systems with each other, with their new Web-enabled eCommerce applications, and often with other companies across the Internet. And they need to manage the business-to-business transaction chains that many new eCommerce business models require – whether it's Web-based supply chains or industry-to-industry trading exchanges. The fact is, every eGeneration business is unique, with a different set of requirements.[6]

Enterprise Application Integration (EAI) tools attempt to simplify the daunting task of bring the Web and existing systems together (see Figure 6.4).

B2B opportunities

The visionary executive knows that all these Internet tools keep building on top of each other raising both the risks and rewards exponentially at each level. For those who make it this far, the benefits are about to start paying off with tremendous competitive advantages.

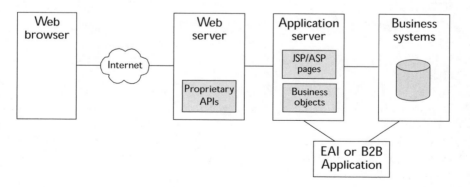

Figure 6.4   Third generation Internet architecture with EAI

Using the Internet to simplify or automate business-to-business (B2B) transactions provides the greatest potential for value creation in eCommerce today.

'Nearly 95% of all goods and services purchased by corporations are purchased with paper based processes.'[7] For companies who have made the investment in B2B to enable their business systems, the opportunity to gain competitive advantage by lowering purchasing costs is tremendous. At the same time, sellers cannot afford not to build channels to the exploding digital market.

B2B infrastructures like Ariba and CommerceOne provide buyer/ supplier networks that companies can plug into (see Figure 6.5). The idea behind these solutions is to lower costs and streamline the supply chain, delivering benefits to all trading partners.[8]

The importance of XML

Potentially one of the most important technologies to emerge in the area of B2B eCommerce (and eCommerce in general) is XML.

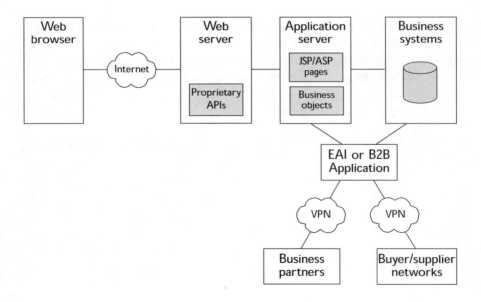

Figure 6.5   Third generation Internet architecture with EAI and B2B

XML stands for eXtensible Markup Language. It is a standard, generalised language for the structured storage and transfer of information. Its importance comes from its potential to become the *lingua franca* for business information on the Internet.

Background

XML is a simplification of SGML (Standard Generalised Markup Language). SGML is a so-called meta-language which has been used to describe thousands of different document types in many fields, from the technical documentation for stealth bombers to musical notation. HTML is just one of these document types – a markup language written in SGML, and used to describe the presentation of documents on the Web.

Unfortunately, one of the casualties of SGML's flexibility is that it is a huge and complex language. XML is an abbreviated version of SGML, omitting the more abstruse and less commonly used parts of the language in return for being easier to use in applications, and easier to understand. XML should be thought of as a subset of SGML rather than an extended version of HTML.

eXtensible Stylesheet Language (XSL)

XSL is a language to facilitate the transformation of XML documents into another form. This can be a different XML document format, an HTML document, or just about any other document format. The use of XSL for translation between XML languages is often referred to as XSLT, or 'XSL for Transformation'.

One of the main uses for XSL is to take the information from an XML document, merge it with specific presentation information, and create a document specific to a given medium. For example, an XSL stylesheet can be used to transform an XML document into HTML for display in a conventional Web browser.

In addition to formatting for presentation, XSLT can be used to transform XML into other formats, allowing delivery of information across multiple channels from a single source, and de-coupling applications from volatile interfaces.

eXtensible Linking Language (XLL)

XLL is a standard language to describe links to resources, and to reference locations within those resources. XLL expands on the linking functionality of HTML by allowing more complex and flexible links to be constructed, in addition to the simple hyperlinks of HTML.

Relationship between XML, HTML and EDI

Markup languages such as HTML rely on a pre-defined set of tags, which can be used to describe parts of a document. In HTML for example, these tags are focused on presentation, that is, text can be tagged as 'bold' or 'Times Roman font'. XML does not define a set of tags. Instead, as a meta-language, it defines rules by which users can define their own tags, in effect defining their own languages. This makes XML far more powerful than HTML, as XML languages can be extended and modified without requiring revisions to XML-enabled browsers and parsers.

EDI, or Electronic Data Interchange, has been used for many years to transfer information between parties involved in a business transaction. EDI itself is a broad concept rather than a standard, in much the same way as 'eCommerce' does not refer to a specific standard. This has led to a number of proprietary implementations, each using different data formats and requiring special software. Data interchange is just one of many possible applications for XML, where it offers the possibility to create a common, standard language and structure for the exchange of EDI data. The XML EDI Group (http://www.xmledi.net/) is dedicated to implementing EDI dictionaries in a standard XML framework.

What is the significance of XML?

XML is having a significant impact on both business and computing. It is changing the way in which systems perform business functions, and it is changing the technical solutions adopted to build these systems.

XML technology will affect the following four main business areas:

- Business-to-'channel' (business-to-business and business-to-customer)
- Integration
- Knowledge management
- Infrastructure components.

The following sections describe the use of XML in these business areas and the advantages that XML confers over more conventional technologies.

Benefits of XML for multi-channel commerce

eCommerce includes both business-to-business (B2B) and business-to-customer (B2C) commerce. XML will affect both of these areas, but perhaps more importantly, the inherent flexibility of XML will begin to blur the distinction between them. In place of separate B2B and B2C eCommerce, we will have the concept of 'business-to-channel' eCommerce because the same systems can be used to interact across the entire eCommerce spectrum. These channels include both communication with a user via a browser, and direct transfer of information between 'backend' applications with no user interaction.

Standardisation

One of the primary aims of XML is to increase standardisation. XML allows the creation of specialised languages, that is, tag sets and structures relating to specific industries or applications. These languages are descriptive of the data *content*, rather than the data *presentation*. XML documents express records such that both the field data and meaning are captured, and as such can be used for multiple purposes. For example, a document describing customer order records could be used within a company's own ERP systems, for communication with external suppliers, and for display on an order-tracking Web site. When these languages become standard, the effort required to build, interface and maintain systems will be reduced, while retaining XML's inherent flexibility.

The key to this standardisation is the concept of schemas. Schemas, also known as Document Type Definitions (DTDs), define a set of tags for a given document format, essentially creating a new XML-based language.

At the time of writing, industry groups are collaborating to define schemas specific to their business. For example, FIXML is an XML-based language which describes transactions and activity in the Financial Markets industry. Organisations such as XML.org and BizTalk.org will act as repositories for these standard schemas and DTDs, encouraging system builders to use them to build standard, de-coupled interfaces between their applications. This will facilitate the more widespread adoption of eCommerce at a lower cost.

These standard schemas will be particularly applicable to EDI. Using XML as the data format for EDI will mean that companies sharing the same schema will produce compatible interfaces by default.

However, standardisation of languages (that is, schemas) is not the be-all and end-all of XML. One of the big advantages is that the data can be parsed by any XML-enabled application, as long as it has access to the relevant DTD. Further, XSL has been designed to facilitate transformation from one XML document type to another, so if your data happens to be in the 'wrong' standard, it is still possible to convert it to something more useful.

Extensibility

Another key aspect of XML is its extensibility. If you require content description which is not available in a standard schema such as FIXML, it is possible to define your own and extend the capabilities of the language without costly software changes. This is in contrast to HTML, where any changes to the tag-set require a new version of the browser software, and lends great power to XML as a data description format.

Device independent presentation

For B2C eCommerce, one of the most common requirements is to publish data to the customer via a variety of channels. These channels may include a Web site, printed documentation, telephone information systems or mobile devices (personal digital assistants, or PDAs). Because XML separates data content from presentation, the same XML data content can be used to present across all of these channels. The use of XSL allows an XML document to be transformed into a different format. This could be HTML for display on a Web page, Postscript for publishing, or another XML language to interface with a different system at a business partner. Any changes to the content can be made in the single XML source, and reflected through the multiple presentation channels.

Simplified client-side processing model

XML data can be transmitted to the client with no loss of content or structure. Consider a Web site giving access to flight timetables – in the HTML world, every query from the user requires a new data-set to be returned from the server to the browser. Users rarely receive the data they want with their first query, requiring multiple calls to an HTML server. In an XML solution, the entire timetable could be sent in one shot as structured XML data, which can be queried multiple times offline by a Java applet, thereby reducing load on the server and network.

International character handling

Unlike HTML, XML is capable of expressing the full international character set. The XML 1.0 specification is based around the ISO-10646 character set, which includes virtually every character used in every written language in use today. In addition, most XML parsers support multiple character set encodings, for example, European, Japanese, or Chinese, meaning that your business transactions can contain street names in Arabic and customers' names in Japanese.

More effective search agents

With XML content tags, more complex tasks can be performed on the data than simple full-text searches. Imagine searching online for documents by Albert Einstein. A simple search of HTML data will return all documents which contain the text 'Albert Einstein', whereas the same search of XML data could allow us to search for documents where our <author> tag contains 'Albert Einstein'. Microsoft have already begun to exploit this capability by embedding XML meta-data (author, date, content information, word specific functions) into HTML files created in Office 2000.

In current internal Knowledge Management systems, a document management tool such as Documentum is often used to manage and search repositories of documents using meta-data in this way. However, XML meta-data will allow more efficient access to document repositories and, more importantly, the content or knowledge within the repository. Document management systems manage business objects (documents), while knowledge management systems manage the content or knowledge in those objects. XML can allow for simpler, standardised use of meta data about business objects, and the flowing of this knowledge over the Web.

For external searching across the Web, XML meta-data should ensure that search engines return more relevant hits, requiring fewer bandwidth and processor intensive searches. Again however, success depends on the adoption of a standard set of meta-tags, and efforts to re-tag the huge volume of HTML data which already exists.

Compatibility

Another benefit of XML lies in compatibility between applications, and between different versions of the same application. This can be illustrated by Microsoft's use of XML in its Office 2000 products.

When an Office 2000 HTML document is viewed in a browser, only the HTML-compatible formatting is displayed. However, when the same file is loaded back into an Office 2000 application, all headers, footers, cross-references and fields are correctly regenerated from embedded XML data. This means that Word 2000 documents, for example, no longer need to be stored in a proprietary format viewable only by Word users. In HTML/XML format, anyone can view the document with simple formatting, but Word 2000 users need not lose access to more complex document features. This is because in XML, tags which are unknown to a particular device are ignored. When the document is displayed in a browser, the tags describing Word-specific information are ignored.

This capability has important ramifications for forward and backward compatibility. Future Office 200x documents stored as HTML with XML meta-data will be readable by Office 2000, as the nature of XML means that tags which are not understood can be ignored. Likewise, Office documents can be viewed on a variety of platforms by only reading the compatible tags.

More flexible linking

In order to make XML as general and extensible as possible, functionality such as linking has been abstracted from the core specification. Instead, XLL has been developed to provide linking capability equal to and beyond that offered by HTML. This is a set of tags which can be used to describe hyperlinks, and reference absolute and relative locations within XML documents. In addition to the simple, unidirectional links offered by HTML, XLL allows bi-directional links, and links to non-specific locations within a document – for example, a link to the second paragraph of a document. Another XLL concept is that of 'link groups'. These enable link destinations to be separated from the main document content, thus simplifying maintenance when resource locations change.

XML industry standards and frameworks

One of the areas which will be vital to the success of XML is standardisation. The primary aim is to produce a standard framework for the development and distribution of XML schemas, both horizontally (cross-industry) and vertically (industry-specific), to accelerate the widespread adoption of XML for eCommerce and application integration.

Two main organisations have emerged which aim to facilitate this standardisation:

- http://BizTalk.org/
- http://XML.org/

It should be noted that these organisations have very similar aims and ideals, and industry players are beginning to side with either BizTalk.org or XML.org. Both have the support of traditional industry 'heavy-weights', and it is not yet clear which will emerge the victor in the latest round of posturing.

Conclusions

From its simple yet powerful beginnings as a globally distributed hypertext system, the World Wide Web has emerged as possibly the most powerful force for change in the business world since the industrial revolution.

The combined forces of technological progress, real-world business needs and the recognition of the power of standardisation have led to the development of a number of architectures and technologies that enable applications of enormous power to be deployed on the Internet today. We have presented here a snapshot of the current state of thinking around Internet architectures, and some likely directions for those technologies.

If we cannot predict the future of the technologies themselves, there is one thing we can predict with certainty: the pace of technological change fostered by the Internet revolution is not slowing, and we may expect many exciting developments over the coming years.

Hosting your site

Joining the revolution

Today, no one can deny the Internet's dramatic power of expand business. The opportunity to reach new markets on a truly global basis and to establish new relationships in existing markets has opened a vast avenues of commerce. And this opportunity is spurring growth not just within Internet companies, but within large scale enterprises in virtually every kind of industry, from healthcare to software to financial services. Recently more and more companies are starting to realise that with the growing complexity of Web sites, managing the explosive growth of the Internet operations is neither the most efficient nor the most cost-effective use of their available internal resources. This understanding has tipped the scales toward a solution with greater business benefits: supporting mission-critical Internet operations by outsourcing their management. Today the hosting market is expected to grow 76% per year.[9]

Hosting options

The implications of your hosting strategy are significant not only for the performance of your system but also for the planning and development of your system. In order to connect your business to the Web, you must decide both what type of relationship to forge with your Internet service provider (ISP) and indeed which ISP is best suited for your business needs. As the Internet continues to expand, four primary types of relationships have emerged for connecting businesses to the Internet. These primary hosting options are presented in order of cost below:

■ *Internal hosting*
  Many large organisations choose to host their Web sites internally. For companies that already have a capable IT staff well tooled with system administrators, network administrators and database administrators (DBAs), internal hosting is a leading option. These organisations purchase hardware and software directly from the vendors and arrange for network connectivity from the ISP. Generally, ISP arrangements for network connectivity guarantee a certain level of Internet bandwidth with optional bursting capabilities to ensure that both planned and unexpected demands are met. It is also very common for many busi-

nesses to host development and testing environments internally as no Internet bandwidth is required for these environments.

■ *Co-location hosting*
Co-located servers consist of customer provided, pre-configured hardware and software. Businesses choose to pay the premium for co-location service over internally hosting production systems in order to benefit from the fast, reliable network connections and high quality facilities that are common among ISPs. The two primary considerations with co-located hosting are the fact that customers must purchase and configure the software and the ISP generally cannot guarantee the same level of service that is supported for ISP purchased and configured machines.

■ *ISP hosted solutions*
ISP hosted solutions consist of a customer leasing ISP provided hardware and software. Customers benefit from fast, reliable network connections and high quality facilities that are common among ISPs. In addition, since the ISP provides and configures the hardware and software, a standard service level is guaranteed by the ISP. While hosted service is more expensive than co-located service since in this case the ISP provides significant value added by purchasing your equipment and installing a standard software configuration, ISPs generally try to make the financial arrangement more attractive by spreading the cost over monthly payments after a one time set up charge.

■ *ASP service*
Application Service Provider solutions attempt to manage and deliver application capabilities to multiple entities from a data centre across a wide area network. ASP service consists of packaged software applications, professional services, computing hardware and network connectivity, for a monthly fee. The major difference between the ASP offering and the hosted service is that the ASP provides much if not all of the development effort. While this added value increases the cost of service, ASPs also generally spread much of the cost over the monthly payments. While the ASP offerings are extremely promising, this new line of outsourcing has been slow to take off, especially in Europe. The value of the European ASP market was only $14m in 1999.[10] 'The likes of Corio and USi have never done anything else and have specifically constituted to prosecute the ASP opportunity. From an investment perspective, there must be a play for an indigenous European ASP funded and formed to do nothing else.'[11] The ASP market faces significant challenges trying to provide ASP service with traditional packaged

applications. Traditional packaged applications are not easily customised by businesses located in remote locations and the market has not yet delivered new applications structured for the ASP model. Additionally, for many large scale applications many of the difficult challenges are different from business to business depending on the internal operation of that business. These challenges often result in unplanned costs. While the prospect of ASP hosted solutions that significantly lower your up front investment cost and remove your organisation from many of the technical headaches is very appealing, it is important to ensure detailed requirements are agreed upon by all parties before committing your business to a long term agreement, especially since the typical ASP arrangement ranges from one to three years.

Hosting implications

The following are several principles one should keep in mind when designing your Internet interconnection, or hosting solution. Over time these will become less relevant, however today, with varying Service Level Agreements (SLAs) available between ISPs, there are several things a start-up need consider with regards to interconnecting to the Internet.

Network performance

The first is how close can you get your Web servers to the Internet backbone. Since the Internet is a collection of networks that interconnect with each other, some ISPs are closer to the backbone than others. The tier-1 ISPs can generally provide the fastest Internet connections since their backbones combine to form the actual backbone of the Internet. These tier-1 ISP backbones connect both at the Public Internet Peering Points and via private peering relationships. Even if you select a tier-1 ISP, it will be important for you to understand how your target customers are connecting to the Internet, since the effective bandwidth between your site and your customers depends not only on your ISP, but also on your customers' ISPs and all ISPs in between. Minimising the hops (number of routing points your data streams must transit) between your Web applications and your customers' browser will increase the performance for your end users. This means you will need to do some market research as to who your customers are and where they connect to the Internet. This picture will vary greatly if your customer market segment is more B2B or

B2C focused, and will be different based on which countries within Europe you will be targeting. ISPs leverage the following practices to increase the performance of their networks:

- Direct presence at public internet peering points

- Private Peering Relationships – As the Internet continues to explode, traffic is often delayed at the designated public peering points due to the massive number of requests that must be supported. An astute ISP operator will arrange private peering relationships to avoid the Public Internet Presence Peering Points when traffic is intended for their private peering partners.

- High quality routers

- Satellite links – High speed satellite Internet links avoid existing international bottlenecks, and can be customised to meet specific Internet-related needs.

Many of the larger ISPs are equipped with global load balancing and global caching techniques to improve the user's perception of your systems' performance. Global load balancing works if you have decided to replicate your environment in multiple data centres around the world. Even though your users in Europe and in Asia may enter the same URL to access your site, the European users can be directed to the data centre in London while the Asian users can be directed to the data centre in Tokyo. With global caching, static content can be cached in servers between your users and your Web server. This practice also increases performance on the network and within your application architecture by intercepting users' requests for content that does not frequently change and returning the desired Web pages.

After you know the major ISPs which your customers use, you should research and understand the telecommunications company's or ISP's routing practice – some go through the US in order to go between European countries, and a Trans-Atlantic bi-directional hop can cause considerable delays. Based on this information, you will need to design the physical location of your Web and application hosting site or sites, and you should take into account that these design considerations of location of your Internet access points can directly affect your operational costs in major ways. This is the 'network interconnect effect' that comes from the fact that some European countries still have dominant monopoly providers who charge largely different fees for big Internet interconnections.

In terms of sizing the Internet interconnection, along with sizing the telephone lines you will need to buy from a telecommunication carrier, and potentially the number of modems or access points you will need to support customer connections – you must do volume estimations to ensure you are not overspending on the network operational costs which you will need to include in your business plan. You will need to calculate volume estimates by building a realistic start and growth plan for the number of concurrent customers by country/local area. This estimation is needed to build realistic operational cost estimates, and also so that your customers can have a good performance/perception of your company's presence.

Security

There are many security features that must be defined for a hosting solution, from physical security of the building to network security to system level security. Many ISPs provide state of the art smoke detection and fire suppression systems as well as fully redundant power supplies with multiple backup generators to protect against natural disasters. Aside from natural disasters, there is also a real concern that at the ISP site a hacker or competitor might try to harm or copy parts of your Internet solution. For these reasons video surveillance, man traps at entrances, fixed and roving security guards, electronic key access, pin codes, biometric identification systems, motion and heat sensors, and 24/7 secure access are all used to protect against intentional or unintentional on-site human activity that could be harmful to your solution.

ISPs also provide network security and system level security measures ranging from usernames/passwords, support of secure protocols, and firewalls.

Failover, high availability, and fault tolerance

Hosting solutions offer several levels of support in the case your Internet solution becomes unusable or inaccessible. Failover solutions maintain an up-to-date copy of a database on an alternative computer system for backup. In the event that a failure occurs, all traffic is redirected to the alternative system. There are many ways to provide failover solutions that vary significantly in cost and effort. Determining the mechanism that is right for your solution will depend on both your operating budget and the value of the data within your solution.

The term 'high availability' or RAS (reliability, availability, service-ability) refers to a fault-resistant solution used to describe environments that can quickly recover from failure. High availability is also an important concept when maintenance is required. Often high availability strategies will be used to shut down one or more components in order to perform maintenance while ensuring that the overall solution is still available for users. However, high availability solutions are not as secure as fault tolerant solutions.

When the value of data in a solution is extremely high, fault tolerant solutions must be employed. These are most often used with financial institutions. A fault tolerant solution ensures that in the event of failure at any level in the system, no data is lost, and the state of the user is maintained. The cost of a fault tolerant solutions typically range in the millions of dollars since end-to-end redundancy must be built into every aspect of the system.

While very few start-up companies require fault tolerant Internet solutions, it is good to understand the different levels of failover and how these levels are often supported. Some of the common ways to support failover leverage cold standby sites, hot standby sites, and load balancing on top of redundant application components.

The placement of a 'cold' server is a remote location provides a mechanism for recovery in the event of failure by your primary server. In the event of failure, applications and content would need to be loaded onto the server. When defining the procedures for recovery with a cold server, the backup solution plays a critical role since the applications, content, and data need to be restored from the last available backup of the system. While the frequency of backing up the system must be determined by how often the system components change, common backup procedures include daily differential backups (only modified content/data), weekly full backups, and off site storage (for example in underground, environmentally controlled vaults) of the backup tapes. The frequency of backups is important since the cold server can only be restored to a level as good as the latest backup. Once the cold server is restored, a phase of regression testing is required on the new environment. And finally traffic can be redirected to the new environment. This is less expensive that a hot standby site solution, however, as you can see from the many process steps involved that the recovery time is much longer.

The placement of a 'hot' server at a remote location provides an immediate solution in the event of failure to your primary solution machines. The 'hot' servers are located at a remote location and turned on. These servers are preloaded with all content and applications. The entire machine is configured and pre-tested to be ready in the case of failure. The major issue with 'hot' standby sites is how current the transactional data is at the time of failure. Several levels of manual or automated replication procedures exist to minimise the loss of data when failures occur.

In order to load balance a site, the ISP will need to configure duplicate network, systems, and application architectures for the production environment. It is important to work with the ISP to understand if the redundancy is build in at the network level, Web server level, application server level, database server level. Common solutions to save costs load balance sites up to the database level. If database redundancy is also required then a primary database and a hot standby database must be configured where database replication services keep both databases in sync.

When failure occurs, many manual and automated tasks will need to be performed in a short amount of time to minimise the loss of usability for your solution. It is always a good idea to set up failover planning sessions between your developers, operations group, and network providers. These session should ensure that the proper procedures are in place and tested before failover occurs.

Monitoring and reporting

Many ISPs provide monthly reports describing usage monitoring, URL monitoring, network monitoring, and application performance monitoring. These provide useful information about site usage and site performance. These reports should be analysed in order to improve site usability.

Most application specific monitoring requirements will need to be defined by the application development team. The monitoring tool can be configured with the target error numbers, and so on.

Certain defined events that are detected by monitoring systems will require your IT department to be notified. Some common response times are 15 minutes for security threat situations, 1.5 hours response time to replace faulty or downed systems with a warm swap box, and 2 business days response time for configuration and policy changes. Many ISPs allow customers to add more escalation procedures for additional cost. Since site errors and security threats happen at all hours of the day it is critical that your hosting solution is equipped with 24/7 help desk facilities. These help desk facilities must be equipped with trouble ticketing systems capable of capturing your call details and tracking issues to resolution.

Location of production servers

Will the purpose of your Internet site be to sell merchandise? If so, you need to be aware of that the physical location of your production servers where eCommerce transactions are made may be the location of your tax base for these customer transactions. This is a strategic choice which should be made early in the start-up phase, since you could conceivably put your servers in other European locations, and still market and sell to other countries. For these reasons, it is important to involve your chief financial officer (CFO) and external legal and auditing agencies to advise you on your direct situation for the best location for your Web presence.

DNS and search engines

When development of your site is complete, and it is tested and ready to launch, it will be important for your users to connect to your site from around the globe using the desired URL for your company. The Domain Name Service (DNS) is used to translate hostnames such as www.your-business.com to an IP address such as 10.280.71.5. Most ISPs will take care of registering a domain name and registering your site URL and site description with the major search engines.

Security

Information security is a vast subject, more worthy of a small library than a small chapter. Therefore, the goals of this chapter will be modest. The intent is to convince the reader (assumed to be interested in creating an Internet business) that information security is:

- Important
- Difficult
- Achievable.

Once thus convinced, the reader is referred to the bibliography for more precise advice and detail on implementing effective information security in one's own enterprise.

The security imperative

Today's business environment is in the throes of being revolutionised by electronic commerce. While these changes generate tremendous new opportunities for business gain, the law of risk and reward warns of a correlated increase in risk. Information security constitutes one area of significant eCommerce risk, driven by increasing:

- Technology pervasiveness within new business solutions
- Enterprise reliance on information accuracy and availability
- Volumes of sensitive enterprise data
- Value of commerce conducted through electronic channels
- Visibility of electronic vulnerabilities
- Demand for distributed networked access to data and systems
- Technical knowledge and skills of adversaries
- Threats of legal liability.

Security is an imperative in this risky environment.

Security is frequently perceived as a mechanism to prevent someone from doing something. While this view has a noble aspect (crime prevention, accident prevention, and so on), the general perception is that security controls create additional cost and effort that interfere with the legitimate pursuits of the majority.

Nonetheless, for as long as there are bad or stupid or careless people in the world, there will continue to be a need for security. Perhaps it is more compelling, then, to transpose the established view – to consider effective security as an enabler that allows someone to do something that might otherwise be impossible (or at least, ill-advised).

In this sense, information security enables successful eCommerce. It:

- Facilitates development of a trust relationship between buyer and seller
- Recognises information as a business asset
- Protects the confidentiality of involved parties
- Reduces the threat of fraud
- Ensures that important information and systems are available when needed.

Insufficient attention to security can result in:

- Direct financial loss due to fraud or theft
- Opportunity cost related to system downtime

- Embarrassment
- Loss of credibility with customers and suppliers
- Civil and/or criminal charges resulting from failure to protect sensitive information
- Depending on the information involved, perhaps even physical harm or loss of life.

Thus, it is (at least) ill-advised to pursue opportunities in eCommerce without being sufficiently enabled with information security safeguards.

In an electronic economy, information is not merely by-product: it is an asset. Indeed, for many eCommerce enterprises it is the primary asset. Organisations must protect their information with the same care that they have traditionally applied to their tangible assets of plant, property and equipment.

Information security is indeed important. Unfortunately, achieving excellent security is not easy.

The security challenge

Security is difficult, and not just in the virtual world. Consider that banks have existed for hundreds of years, yet they continue to be robbed even today. The automobile has evolved considerably over the last century, but accidents are still commonplace. It would be naïve to believe that information security challenges will disappear in the foreseeable future.

This should not imply that Internet eCommerce is reckless. The bottom-line is that some level of risk is associated with anything worth doing. The extension of credit, for example, has changed the face of modern business practice despite the fact that credit carries inherent risks of fraud and default. The goal of information security is not to create an environment of zero risk, but rather to manage risk to an acceptable level.

To appropriately manage risk, however, one must first have a solid understanding of the risks at hand. 'Hackers' tend to get the lion's share of current information security headlines, whether they have defaced a Web site, stolen credit card numbers from an online merchant, or subjected popular Web sites to prolonged Denial Of Service (DOS) attacks. Yet even today, hackers remain a relatively minor security threat. According to the Gartner Group, 'Most instances of computer crime involve insiders who abuse existing processes and circumvent control measures to take money or cause damage.'[12]

Too often, security is equated with the application of technology-based controls. Firewalls, encryption, biometrics, smart cards, and so on are hot security devices today. And, for the most part, these techniques and technologies adequately fulfil their stated functions. Unfortunately, specific technologies are only individual links in the security chain. The most advanced technologies available can not protect against a password taped to a monitor; against an employee who unwittingly discloses sensitive information to an outsider; or against a flawed back-up and recovery process. People and processes tend to be weaker security links because humans are more vulnerable to misjudgement, mistakes, and manipulation.

Effective information security risk management requires a holistic view of security. Holistic security recognises that the security of a solution must be measured by the strength of the most vulnerable component, as this is the component most susceptible to failure or attack. A fortified front door will not protect a home if a window is left open. Likewise, a heavy-duty lock does not protect a bicycle that is secured to a sapling.

Further, criminal activity constitutes only one category of threat to information assets. Natural and man-made disasters, negligence, carelessness, honest mistakes, and innumerable other circumstances can place information and information systems at risk.

A holistic view of security promotes the optimal deployment of people, processes, and technologies toward a common security goal. Personnel must be trained. Policies must be communicated and enforced. Processes must be reviewed and refined. Technologies must be integrated and tested. Holistic security focuses on the strength of the chain, rather than the strength of any particular link. Such a comprehensive approach is difficult, but it is achievable.

The security solution

Development of a complex solution demands a structured approach. Otherwise, it is easy to become enmeshed in the specifics of the solution and lose sight of the original intent. As the old adage goes, 'When you're up to your ass in alligators, it's easy to forget that your original goal was to drain the swamp.'

As with most truly difficult challenges, there are no easy solutions for information security. There are, however, approaches that one can follow towards a quality solution.

This section will describe a method and an architecture that will support the definition, implementation, and iteration of a holistic security solution.

The method describes the actions to be taken. The architecture provides a framework that describes an overall structure for the solution. These two components can be used together much in the same way one might use both a set of written instructions and a schematic diagram to assemble a complex piece of machinery.

Security method

For any task, the best place to start is at the beginning. With respect to information security, the beginning is the security policy, the statement of 'original intent'. The security policy describes, at a high level, the goals that are to be achieved through the protection of information and why these goals are important. The policy, at a more detailed level, encompasses the guidelines, standards, and procedures to be employed to achieve the security goals.

Lack of clear and precise policy leads to inconsistent behaviour and, ultimately, security gaps. Therefore, there is near universal agreement among security professionals that a well-crafted security policy constitutes ground zero for the protection of information assets. Nonetheless, organisational security policies, if they exist at all, are too often incomplete, inconsistent, unusable, or out-of-date. Good policy is challenging for many reasons:

1. Security policy is boring. Written words on a page do not engender the same level of excitement as does the latest hardware device or a flash, new software package. Even within the realm of the written word, one is unlikely to find a security policy on a best-seller list.

2. Security policy depends on people. And people are a notoriously difficult bunch. They are most difficult at the extremes: consider the exceedingly clever and the exceedingly stupid. Somehow, effective security policy must be appropriate across the continuum.

3. Security policy is not available off-the-shelf. Commercial product feasibility is based on the concept that a reasonably specific set of features can satisfy the needs of a broad range of potential customers. Unfortunately, since each organisation is unique, a one-size-fits-all approach to security policy serves only to generate exceptions, which in turn require specific policy.

4. Enforcement is unpleasant. The existence of (even a good) policy is insufficient. Policy must be enforced or, eventually, it will be ignored. For example, airlines are notorious for failing to enforce carry-on baggage limits and boarding priorities. The result is that most passengers ignore the policies, resulting in chaotic loading and, often, delayed departures.

5. We live in a dynamic world. Organisations change. Technologies change. People change. It is a catch-up world, and documents never seem to keep pace. Yesterday's policy may already be out of date. Last year's policy almost certainly is.

A quality security methodology must begin with security policy that respects the policy challenges described above.

Exactly such an approach has been developed by the Center for Education and Research in Information Assurance and Security (CERIAS) and Andersen Consulting in a joint research effort titled PFIRES[13] (Policy Framework for Interpreting Risk in E-commerce Security.) The PFIRES lifecycle model is shown in Figure 6.6.

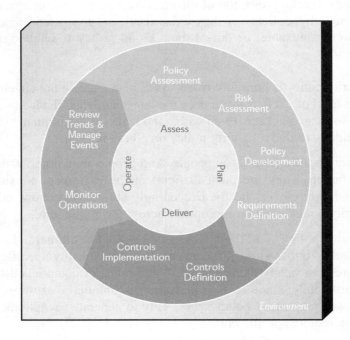

Figure 6.6   PFIRES Lifecycle Model

The complete PFIRES research paper is available on the CERIAS Web site, http://www.cerias.purdue.edu. The following paragraphs describe, at a high level, the PFIRES model as a method toward a holistic security solution.

The PFIRES life cycle is defined by four phases closely tied to the software development life cycle: Assess, Plan, Deliver, and Operate. Each phase is then divided into two steps that define high level actions necessary to develop and maintain security policy, and the controls necessary to monitor and enforce it. Feedback loops are introduced to validate the output of each step against the requirements for that step.

The *Assess* phase represents the starting point within the life cycle, either for a proposed business change or for an initial security assessment. The purpose of this phase is to assess the proposed change against the existing policy environment (Policy Assessment) and existing infrastructure (Risk Assessment). In addition, human performance considerations are addressed in an Organisational 'As-Is' assessment.

The *Plan* phase prepares the organisation for the implementation of the change, the policy updates brought about by the change, and the risk mitigation measures chosen to support the change. Policy Definition is the step in which the security strategy and security policy are created and updated. The Requirements Definition step outlines the requirements for the new or updated policy and the controls needed to secure those changes.

During the *Deliver* phase the security policy, controls and training are designed, built and rolled out to the organisation. The phase consists of two steps: Controls Definition and Controls Implementation. The Controls Definition step designs the security infrastructure to meet the changes in security policy. In the Controls Implementation step, the security infrastructure designed in the previous step is built, tested and rolled out along with the training to support the solution.

The *Operate* phase is the phase in which policy compliance is monitored and events and trends are handled. The phase consists of two steps: Monitor Operations and Review Trends and Manage Events. The Monitor Operations step monitors the controls that are in place to ensure policy adherence for violations. The Review Trends and Manage Events step handles the violations or events and also reviews trend data and external forces such as regulatory changes, industry trends, changes in business direction, technological advancements and new security threats, for opportunities to update security policy and controls.

In summary, the PFIRES approach emphasises that:

- Effective security policy must be managed through an iterative life-cycle-driven approach
- Effective security requires that security controls are driven by security policy, not vice versa.

No security policy is ever perfect or ever complete: hence the need for ongoing iteration.

Security framework

Whereas the Security Approach describes the actions required to develop holistic security, the Security Framework describes the security solution itself. The use of a framework is important, as it avoids a 'list' approach. While lists are certainly handy, one can never be certain there is not at least one item missing from the list. A list may also contain items that are not necessarily required. A framework, on the other hand, is a rationalised structure designed for both conciseness and completeness.

An excellent example of a Security Framework is shown in Figure 6.7.

The Security Framework comprises technology and non-technology components, including:

- Business assets
- Risk management
- Security strategy
- Security management
- Security policy and standards
- Security awareness
- Security compliance
- Security administration
- Security development
- Security operations
- Security services
- Security infrastructure.

This view of a comprehensive information security solution is intended as a thought trigger and completeness check for the design of a security architecture. It describes the set of security components that must be incorporated into the plan, design, build and operation of a business capability and how those components fit together. The open framework allows for products and technologies from numerous vendors to be implemented and

Figure 6.7   Example of a security framework

integrated into a complete security architecture. Each of the security areas are described briefly in the following paragraphs.

Business Assets at the core of the Security Framework are items of value to be secured and protected. Assets can be tangible (such as systems, networks, facilities, people and customer data) or intangible (for example, the reputation of the business).

Risk Management ensures that an organisation employs reasonable risk/reward and cost/benefit analysis to the design of the overall security solution. A security risk assessment is performed as part of the Risk Management function. It involves evaluating threats to Business Assets, identifying security vulnerabilities or weaknesses that can take advantage of those threats, and prioritising business risk.

Security Strategy sets the future directions for information. The primary goal is to give an overview of the future business directions and the security controls which should be in place to support these business functions. The Security Strategy must be aligned with other business strategies to ensure that security is considered when new business capabilities and acquisitions are planned, new alliances are made and when new markets are entered. All strategies must work together.

- Security Management initiates and manages security programs to support an organisation's business goals. Security Management develops, builds and maintains the security organisation and shapes its structure.

- Security Policy and Standards form the foundation for all security related activities. Their aim is to achieve consistency in architecture and to reduce the risk, effect and cost of security incidents. The Security Policy and Standards must follow the general security directions in the Security Strategy. Once developed, the security policy will be used to drive all other infrastructure decisions in the security framework.

- Security Awareness is a key component of a secure solution because people often constitute the weakest link in the chain of securing information. The Security Awareness plan describes the organisational expectations regarding information security, and communicates each individual's responsibility for ensuring the confidentiality, integrity and availability of Business Assets.

- Security Compliance includes all necessary elements required to ensure that the Security Policy and Standards are created, followed, measured, enforced and updated as required.

- Security Administration performs administrative processes, primarily oriented towards managing users throughout their life-cycle within the organisation.

- Security Development encompasses the design and implementation of security solutions. It supports and enables the building of new security technologies, architectures, applications, systems, and business capabilities, as well as new Security Services and Security Infrastructure.

- Security Operations provides for the ongoing monitoring of security components and security events. Security monitoring refers to the tracking of relevant events and the subsequent actions to be taken when such events occur.

- Security Services are re-useable common security architecture components which have been documented and packaged to facilitate easy re-deployment. The objective of the Security Services is to achieve consistency and standardisation across an organisation for common security functions such as authentication, encryption, and so on.

- Security Infrastructure describes the actual security components which provide protection for the Business Assets. Security Services such as an authentication service or encryption service are implemented using the security components in the Security Infrastructure. Examples of Security Infrastructure components include: firewalls; smart cards; public key certificates; encryption devices; biometric authentication devices; virtual private networks; and so on.

Not every area of the Security Framework is equally relevant to every organisation. And likewise, each organisation will have unique priorities across the set of relevant areas. Nevertheless, each area must at least be considered by every organisation to ensure the completeness of the overall security solution.

Conclusion

Information security is, indeed, important and difficult.

Information security is also achievable, given a risk-management-driven approach.

The security method and architecture described in this chapter are examples of tools that can be used to structure a comprehensive and holistic approach to information security. Myriad other tools, approaches, philosophies and perspectives can be provided by vendors, security consultants, researchers, and authors. Regardless of approach, the following four principles are key to effective security:

- Start immediately to reduce risk
- Invest time and resources commensurate with the level of risk reduction they provide
- Avoid 'snake-oil' solutions that claim to make security easy or effortless
- Emphasise continuous improvement.

The actual implementation of a secure Internet eCommerce solution is left as an exercise for the reader.

Top 10 ways to begin with quality security

1. *Know what you need to protect*
   Unless you identify the assets that require protection, you are at risk of leaving assets exposed to information security risk. These assets may be tangible (for example hardware; software; inventory; funds) or intangible (for example credibility; privacy; reputation; morale.)

2. *Take a holistic view*
   Effective security is pervasive, so consider security not only in terms of technology, but also as it relates to your strategy, business processes, and employees.

3. *Recognise people are your weakest link*
   People includes employees, customers, suppliers, and anyone else with access to your information and systems. Consider how to protect against the bad, the stupid, and the careless.

4. *Create a security policy*
   The security policy describes management expectations for information security and the specific responsibilities of each individual to protect information assets.

5. *Ensure that controls are policy-driven*
   If an envisioned security control is inconsistent with the security policy, then either the control is not appropriate, or the policy needs to be changed. Keeping security policy up-to-date avoids the risk of fragmented security and policy irrelevance.

6. *Build security into each new business capability*
   It is easier to build security in than it is to add security on, so consider the security implications of each business change as early as possible.

7. *Monitor constantly*
   Security logs and events are useless unless they are reviewed and acted upon in a timely manner.

8. *Prepare for incident response*
   Prepare your organisation on the steps required in the event of a security failure. Quick action may permit you to minimise the damage from the attack.

9. *Upgrade*

Security vulnerabilities are posted by vendors, CERT (Computer Emergency Response Team), and hackers. Ensure that the latest security patches have been applied to all of your systems.

10. *Iterate*

Security is a never-ending responsibility.

Bibliography

Amoroso, E. G. (1994) *Fundamentals of Computer Security Technology*. Prentice Hall. ISBN: 0131089293

Chapman, B. D., Zwicky, E. D. and Russell, D. (eds) (1995) *Building Internet Firewalls*. O'Reilly and Associates. ISBN: 1565921240

Cheswick, W. and Bellovin, S. (1994) *Firewalls and Internet Security – Repelling the Wily Hacker*. Addison-Wesley. ISBN: 0201633574

Feghhi, J. and Williams, P. (1998) *Digital Certificates: Applied Internet Security*. Addison-Wesley. ISBN: 0201309807

Garfinkel, S. and Spafford, G. (1997) *Web Security and Commerce*. O'Reilly and Associates. ISBN: 1565922697

Krause, M. and Tipton, H. F. (eds) (1999) *Handbook of Information Security Management*. CRC Pr. ISBN: 0849399742

Pfleeger, C. P. (1996) *Security in Computing*. Prentice Hall International. ISBN: 0131857840

Stallings, W. (1998) *Cryptography and Network Security*. Prentice Hall. ISBN: 0138690170

Security web sites

Andersen Consulting Security Homepage	http://www.ac.com/services/security
Deploying Firewalls – CERT	http://www.cert.org/security-improvement/modules/m08.html
Information Systems Security Association Inc. (ISSA)	http://www.issa-chicago.org/security_links.htm
Microsoft Security Advisor	http://www.microsoft.com/security/default.asp
Information Security Magazine	http://www.infosecuritymag.com

Faulkner & Gray	http://www.faulknergray.com
Rainbow Series Library	http://www.radium.ncsc.mil/tpep/library/rainbow
(ISC)2	http://www.isc2.org
SANS	http://www.sans.org
ISSA Tools	http://www.uh.edu/~bmw/issa/Tools.html
BugTraq archives	http://www.securityfocus.com/
CERIAS	http://www.cerias.purdue.edu/
CERT	http://www.cert.org
COAST	http://www.cerias.purdue.edu/coast/
Computer Security Institute	http://www.gocsi.com
W3C Computer Security Resources	http://www.w3.org/Security/
Dynamic VPNs	www.tradewave.com/products/securevpn.html
InfoWar	http://www.infowar.com
ISS X-Force Vulnerability Database	http://www.iss.net/xforce/
NIST Computer Security Resource Clearinghouse (CSRC)	http://csrc.ncsl.nist.gov
Symantec Virus Hoax List	http://www.symantec.com/avcenter/hoax.html
NT Security	http://www.ntsecurity.net
Systems Internals	http://www.sysinternals.com
SC Magazine	http://www.westcoast.com
Symantec Norton AntiVirus Site	http://www.symantec.com/nav/index.html
How to design your Web site for availability	http://www.sunworld.com/swol-07-1999/swol-07-itarchitect.html
Verisign Guide to Securing Servers	www.verisign.com/whitepaper/onsite/server/index.html
FIRST	http://www.first.org/
IETF Security Area	http://web.mit.edu/network/ietf/sa/
ISF	http://www.securityforum.org/menu.htm
SIA	http://www.siaonline.org/
AntiOnline	http://www.antionline.com/

RISKS Forum	catless.ncl.ac.uk/Risks
HNN Hacker News	www.hackernews.com/
Network World Fusion Focus	www.nwfusion.com/focus
security focus	www.securityfocus.com/
ZDNet devhead Security	www.zdnet.com/devhead/filters/0,,2133245,00.html

Notes

1. http://www.pbs.org/internet/timelime/
2. ibid.
3. Robert Orfali, *Client Server Programming with Java and CORBA, Second Edition*, Wiley Computer Publishing, New York, 1998, page 36
4. G. Winfield Treese, *Designing Systems for Internet Commerce*, Addison Wesley Longman, Inc., Reading, Massachusetts, 1998, page 77
5. http://www.bea.com/products/weblogic/server/datasheet.html
6. ibid.
7. Walid Mougayar, *Opening Digital Markets: Battle Plans and Business Strategies for Internet Commerce*, McGraw-Hill, New York, 1998, page 25
8. http://www.ariba.com
9. Forrester Research, February 1999
10. Richard Wendland, *Application Service Providers: Researching the Future… Investing Today*, Durlacher Research, July 1999
11. ibid.
12. Gartner Group, Inc., 'The Information Security Strategy Five-Year Scenario', copyright 1999
13. Policy Framework for Interpreting Risk in eCommerce Security, copyright 1999 Andersen Consulting and CERIAS (Center for Education and Research in Information Assurance and Security)

Glossary of terms

Definitions for the following key computer and information security terms are referenced from the SANS Institute NSA Glossary of Terms Used in Security and Intrusion Detection http://www.sans.org/newlook/resources/glossary.htm

Authenticate	To establish the validity of a claimed user or object.
Availability	Assuring information and communications services will be ready for use when expected.
Back Door	A hole in the security of a computer system deliberately left in place by designers or maintainers. Synonymous with trap door; a hidden software or hardware mechanism used to circumvent security controls.

Confidentiality	Assuring information will be kept secret, with access limited to appropriate persons.
Crack	A popular hacking tool used to decode encrypted passwords. System administrators also use Crack to assess weak passwords by novice users in order to enhance the security of the Automated Information System.
Cracker	One who breaks security on an Automated Information System.
Cryptography	The art or science concerning the principles, means, and methods for rendering plain text unintelligible and for converting encrypted messages into intelligible form.
Denial of service	Action(s) which prevent any part of an Automated Information System from functioning in accordance with its intended purpose.
Firewall	A system or combination of systems that enforces a boundary between two or more networks. Gateway that limits access between networks in accordance with local security policy. The typical firewall is an inexpensive micro-based Unix box kept clean of critical data, with many modems and public network ports on it, but just one carefully watched connection back to the rest of the cluster.
Hacker	A person who enjoys exploring the details of computers and how to stretch their capabilities. A malicious or inquisitive meddler who tries to discover information by poking around. A person who enjoys learning the details of programming systems and how to stretch their capabilities, as opposed to most users who prefer to learn the minimum necessary.
Integrity	Assuring information will not be accidentally or maliciously altered or destroyed.
Intrusion detection	Pertaining to techniques which attempt to detect intrusion into a computer or network by observation of actions, security logs, or audit data. Detection of break-ins or attempts either manually or via software expert systems that operate on logs or other information available on the network.
IP Spoofing	An attack whereby a system attempts to illicitly impersonate another system by using IP network address.
Key	A symbol or sequence of symbols (or electrical or mechanical correlates of symbols) applied to text in order to encrypt or decrypt.
Non-repudiation	Method by which the sender of data is provided with proof of delivery and the recipient is assured of the sender's identity, so that neither can later deny having processed the data.
Penetration testing	The portion of security testing in which the evaluators attempt to circumvent the security features of a system. The evaluators may be assumed to use all system design and

implementation documentation, that may include listings of system source code, manuals, and circuit diagrams. The evaluators work under the same constraints applied to ordinary users.

PGP (pretty good privacy)

A freeware program primarily for secure electronic mail.

Private key cryptography

An encryption methodology in which the encryptor and decryptor use the same key, which must be kept secret. This methodology is usually only used by a small group.

Proxy

A firewall mechanism that replaces the IP address of a host on the internal (protected) network with its own IP address for all traffic passing through it. A software agent that acts on behalf of a user. Typical proxies accept a connection from a user, make a decision as to whether or not the user or client IP address is permitted to use the proxy, perhaps does additional authentication, and then completes a connection on behalf of the user to a remote destination.

Public key cryptography

Type of cryptography in which the encryption process is publicly available and unprotected, but in which a part of the decryption key is protected so that only a party with knowledge of both parts of the decryption process can decrypt the cipher text.

Rootkit

A hacker security tool that captures passwords and message traffic to and from a computer. A collection of tools that allows a hacker to provide a back door into a system, collect information on other systems on the network, mask the fact that the system is compromised, and much more. Rootkit is a classic example of Trojan horse software. Rootkit is available for a wide range of operating systems.

Sniffer

A program to capture data across a computer network. Used by hackers to capture user ID names and passwords. Software tool that audits and identifies network traffic packets. Is also used legitimately by network operations and maintenance personnel to troubleshoot network problems.

Spoofing

Pretending to be someone else. The deliberate inducement of a user or a resource to take an incorrect action. Attempt to gain access to an AIS by pretending to be an authorised user. Impersonating, masquerading, and mimicking are forms of spoofing.

SSL (secure sockets layer)

A session layer protocol that provides authentication and confidentiality to applications.

TCP/IP

Transmission Control Protocol/Internet Protocol. The suite of protocols the Internet is based on.

Tripwire

A software tool for security. Basically, it works with a database that maintains information about the byte count of files.

	If the byte count has changed, it will identify it to the system security manager.
Trojan horse	An apparently useful and innocent program containing additional hidden code which allows the unauthorised collection, exploitation, falsification, or destruction of data.
Virus	A program that can 'infect' other programs by modifying them to include a, possibly evolved, copy of itself.
Worm	Independent program that replicates from machine to machine across network connections often clogging networks and information systems as it spreads.

CHAPTER 7

The Rise of Mobile Commerce and WAP

Paul Eijkemans, ANDERSEN CONSULTING

If you are setting up an Internet business you will have heard about mobile Commerce (mCommerce). This chapter discusses mCommerce and the Wireless Application Protocol. It details what they are, the services that they will enable and the roles that your business could play in mCommerce. There is a brief snapshot of the status of mCommerce and a discussion of the future developments that will shape this market.

The rise of mobile datacommunication

Watch the trends

One of the largest trends in the past few years has been the growth of the Internet. Stories about the success of the Yahoo!s and Amazons of this world are widespread. And it is true, the Internet grew from an estimated 16m worldwide users in 1995 to an astonishing 240m in 1999. But only some realise that another trend has been even more successful than the growth of the Internet. In 1995 there were about 8m users of mobile phones worldwide, while in 1999 this number has grown to a thrilling 450m users. And that means that telecommunications companies such as Nokia and Ericsson backed the right horse.

Converging technologies

Over the last few years the Internet and telecommunications trends have started to converge. Network operators consider wireless datacommunication to be a huge opportunity, realised by offering mobile services to their customers and thus compensating for the declining margins on voice based networks. In addition, progressive customers demanded easy access to information anywhere at any time. Convergence started when users connected their mobile phones to their laptop computers. The connection itself was done through a cable or a fragile infrared connection, and after installing all kinds of proprietary software that needed several prayers and curses to get working, they were able to watch the bulky content from the Internet downloading at a slow 9,600bps speed. Then there were the attempts to integrate the browser itself in the phone. Early attempts, such as Nokia's Smart Messaging, were not successful because it was not an open standard. The expensive multi-purpose device that came with this technology never attracted large masses. Although software and hardware developments all focused on producing solutions for downsizing purposes, such as Java, the Network Computer and Personal Digital Assistants (PDAs), it looked impossible to come up with a simple solution for a usable data communication-able wireless device.

The Wireless Application Protocol (WAP)

Why WAP?

And then there was the Wireless Application Protocol, an open standard for browsing through WAP enabled Internet-sites with a wireless device. In general WAP is a set of specifications that define how the client, a mobile device, and a server communicate with one another and how a user communicates with the mobile device. In essence there are three reasons why this set of specifications was conceived:

1. To set a global standard that will enable global services.
2. To set an open standard that is not controlled by one party.
3. To set a standard that is optimized for the limitations of a wireless device.

The first reason is clearly to create a global network of WAP sites working with standardised technologies that can be reached by devices that know these standards. The economies of scale are huge for those companies that will only have to support one major global standard instead of dozens of small local non-standards that all deviate in characteristics. For the customer this is also great news since it means that he or she will also be able to access any WAP compliant site with the wireless device.

Unfortunately, since WAP is still evolving there will be multiple standards within the standard itself. But we will get to that later.

With many large phone manufacturing companies such as Motorola, Philips, Ericsson and Nokia, it is almost impossible for one company to dictate to the market what the de facto standard is. Setting an open standard that can be implemented by everyone reduces the risk of one single company backing the wrong horse and throwing away millions of dollars on investments. And luckily for us, the side effect is that the evolution of wireless technology as a whole is put in a higher gear. The driver of the WAP standard is an industry association called the WAP Forum. This association was originally founded in 1997 by Nokia, Ericsson, Motorola and Phone.Com, formerly known as Unwired Planet, to conceive a communication standard for wireless data access. At this moment it consists of over two hundred organisations in various fields of computing and wireless, including for example AT&T Wireless, Oracle and IBM. The WAP Forum is open to everyone who is interested in implementing WAP in its products.

New standards had to be invented for wireless devices, instead of using existing Internet technologies. This reflects the wireless device limitations.

- The size of the screen
- The input facilities of the keyboard and other navagational tools
- The limited computational capabilities such as CPU power and memory size
- The restricted bandwidth.

Of course, screen sizes of mobile devices will grow larger and larger. But these small screens are unlikely to have the same display capacity as a normal 15-inch monitor. Applications on the wireless device have to take into account this limited screen size when trying to show tables and graphics to the user.

When your are behind your computer you can use your mouse and keyboard to control your system. Unfortunately, most mobile phones only have some buttons that you can press. Since current Internet standards assume that you have a mouse and a keyboard at your disposal, a new standard that takes these usability issues into consideration had to be invented to make up for the loss. Still, the input facilities of most wireless devices can sometimes be a pain. Anyone who ever tried to type in a list of contacts including their phone numbers, knows what we are talking about. The keypad of a mobile phone is just not made for easy data entering, although the browsing buttons on a WAP enabled phone work surprisingly well. Voice recognition on the device itself, touch-screens and smart data entry mechanisms already exist or will be introduced in no time but can never capture all the required inputs. Simple data entry will still be one of the major input types in the coming years. Hopefully new usability concepts on top of the current WAP standard will be invented to meet these shortcomings.

Although Gordon Moore's law, or prediction, that the capacity of microchips doubles every eighteen months still holds true after 35 years, the computers integrated in the mass market wireless devices do not have the same computational capacity as their larger counterparts on the desktop. Much more power than that presently in wireless devices is needed to increase application functionality.

Another restriction is the limited bandwith of the network. The speed of most common networks that are in use for wireless communication, such as GSM, cannot really be compared with fairly standard 56kbps dial-up lines or 10Mbps cable modems that suck information from the Internet at an astonishing speed. Network characteristics range from country to country and from operator to operator, but the speed of most networks is limited to a mere 9,600bps, although new standards with higher speeds are on their way. First, in most countries there will be General Packaged Radio Service (GPRS), that is capable of using multiple slots to transfer data at a maximum theoretical speed of 115kbps, about eight times the speed of GSM, depending very much on the actual version of GPRS that is implemented. GPRS will require only minor additions to the current mobile network. Second, there will be third generation standards, under the umbrella label UMTS (Universal Mobile Telecommunications Services), that will push speeds up to 2Mbps. GPRS will be launched in most European and some Asian countries at the end of 2000 and UMTS is expected to be introduced somewhere in 2003, with frequencies for it to be auctioned at this moment. UMTS will require major changes in the mobile network infrastructure and will probably only run in populated areas for the first few years. Until the introduction of new technologies there has to be a standard that deals with the low data transfer capacity by demanding a much lower bandwith for transfer than current Internet content standards do.

WAP as a standard

WAP specifications range from transport specific standards to specifications that define mobile device application languages. Although these specifications are based on well-known Internet standards. Companies have to do additional coding to make their sites WAP enabled. Browsing through the same information as you do with your Internet browser is not possible with a WAP-enabled device. The WAP specifications are not hard to understand if you have some knowledge about how the Internet works.

The way information is exchanged between Internet sites and a WAP device is similar to the way you communicate through your Internet browser, via your Internet Service Provider (ISP), with Internet sites. The main difference between browsing through your existing browser and through your WAP-enabled wireless device is the WAP gateway. While your ISP is facilitating retrieval of information from the Internet with your browser, the WAP gateway will not only get the information that you have requested but will also shrink it into a more compact format to save bandwidth, before sending the pages to the wireless device. In theory a WAP gateway would also be able to retrieve HTML pages from the Internet and compile them into a format that is readable by the microbrowser in the device but unfortunately practice shows that there is more to Internet surfing than just simple HTML.

The common way to gain access to a WAP gateway is by dialing up the access server of the organisation that provides this service (see Figure 7.1). The server will assign a unique IP address to your phone, just as your ISP does when you dial in through your modem. After that the phone is able to retrieve information from WAP sites over the network that the WAP gateway is connected to, which will be the Internet most of the time. You will probably be billed for the seconds that you are connected to the dial-up server, but this completely depends on the billing strategy of the mobile network operator.

WAP technical

To tickle the technical expertise of those interested we will explain some of the standards that are involved with WAP and compare them to the Internet standards that we know. On top of the architecture standards shown in Figure 7.2 there is the Wireless Application Environment (WAE) that contains both Wireless Markup Language (WML) and WMLScript. These languages can be used to create applications that will work in the micro-browser that is built into the wireless device. WML is actually a subset of XML (eXtensible Markup Language) a sophisticated successor of HTML. Under the WAE there is the Wireless Session Layer (WSL) and Wireless Transaction Protocol (WTP). These protocols are necessary for the actual communication between the client and the server and is comparable to the HTTP-protocol that we know from the Internet. Next is the Wireless Transport Layer Security (WTLS), which is a security layer that

210

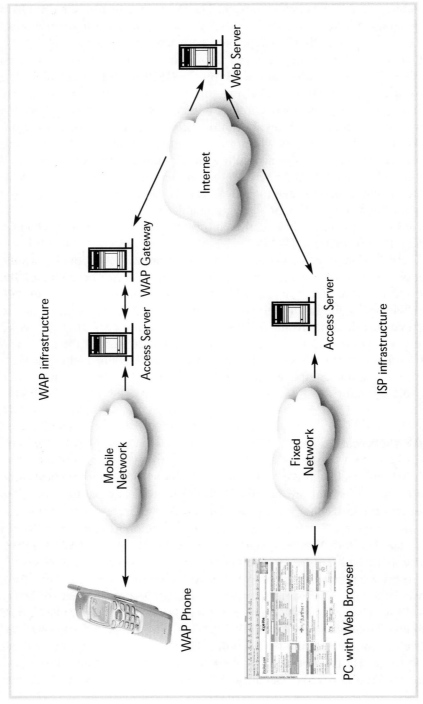

Figure 7.1 Communication model

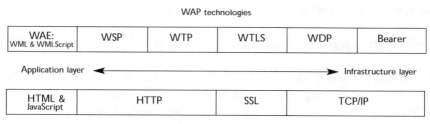

Figure 7.2 The WAP Stack

enables WAP to secure the communications between the client and the server. The transport is taken care of by the Wireless Datagram Protocol (WDP), which is network independent, and the bearer, which is the actual network. With WAP the bearer could be GSM, CDPD (Cellular Digital Packet Data), CDMA (Code Division Multiple Access) or a dozen other network types.

What to convert?

If a company already has a solid Internet presence and controls content that is interesting to offer as a mobile service, it is not so difficult to start offering WAP services to customers. The largest challenge would be to determine what kind of service could be offered. A second challenge is to convert the content that is used on the Internet site into content that is suitable for a WAP phone since the desired characteristics of information shown on a WAP phone can differ from information shown on a desktop PC. For instance, reading an in depth article on tulips in a Web browser is completely acceptable for anyone interested, but one can doubt whether any WAP user is interested in doing the same thing on the small screen of a WAP device. Challenges such as usability, user recognition and security issues also need to be addressed. Fortunately, converting HTML Web pages into WML Web pages can be done by any programmer with some HTML experience. And the infrastructure for offering WML pages to a customer is already there since the existing infrastructure for offering Internet services can be used.

Mobile services: which services are possible?

The additional value of mobility

If you want to know which services can be offered through a mobile infra-structure you will first have to define the customer benefit.

With mobile services the customer benefit usually derives from:

- any time; because I carry my mobile phone with me 24 hours a day
- anywhere; because wherever I am, my mobile phone goes with me
- in an easy way; because my mobile phone is a small device that is easy to use.

Let's start with the any time component that is of course interweaved with the 'anywhere' component. Just as you almost always carry around your wallet, your mobile phone goes with you almost everywhere. A WAP-enabled mobile phone makes it possible for you to access information at any moment you feel a need to – not only when you are behind your desktop PC browsing the Internet.

And then there is the 'anywhere' component. When you have your laptop right in front of you, you can access the Internet through a dial-up connection. During lunch, you can visit the nearest Internet café and check those pages that you are interested in. When you are driving and get stuck in a traffic jam WAP will enable you to find a way round the blockage, or avoid it in the first place.

The 'in an easy way' component has everything to do with usability concepts. Connecting to the Internet with your notebook and using your phone as a modem is not easy, partly since the combination is much more cumbersome than a simple all-in-one device such as a mobile phone. In addition, accessing information through Short Message Service (SMS) is not very user-friendly since cryptic keywords have to be typed in to get a message that will contain the information that you need.

Dichotomy of services

In general two types of WAP services can be offered. The first is an Internet-like service that we will call Personal Services that is open to everyone. The second is an Intranet-like service, that we will call Business Services and that is often only open to a specific group of people, such as the employees of a certain company.

Table 7.1   Some personal services

Sector	Service
Financial services	■ Banking services, such as money transfer ■ Brokerage
Retail	■ Tracking and tracing of orders ■ Accessing product information
Entertainment	■ Games
Reservations	■ Movie tickets ■ Hotel room reservations
User-to-user	■ email access ■ Text based chatting
News and infotainment	■ News, traffic, weather reports ■ City guide
Portals	■ Horizontal (wide) portal services ■ Vertical (specialised) portal services
Search engines	■ Price comparing mechanisms ■ Route information

Personal Services are services that all customers can use. Table 7.1 lists only some of the possible services that can be offered to consumers. For most services, like brokerage, the process has similarities with how consumers use Internet services. With brokerage, a customer would use a mobile phone to access the WAP-enabled page of the financial institution and after authentication he or she will be ready to do simple transactions by just selecting a fund, a transaction type and the amount in money or in pieces. Confirmation of the execution of the transaction could be sent to the customer through SMS.

Which Personal Services eventually will prove to be succesful is hard to say. Although, it seems that the financial institutes will be among the first to deploy serious wireless services that will be used by large numbers of customers, reflecting the importance of accessing their product anytime and anywhere.

Although the opportunities for consumer services are huge, one should not overlook the possibilities for companies to create Intranet-like services that can be used by employees, or other authorised users, to retrieve all kinds of information that they are able to use in their day-to-day jobs. It is not very difficult to come up with some interesting services that a company could offer to its employees, throughout the value chain. Table 7.2 lists some of the possibilities.

Table 7.2   Some business services

Business process	Service
Logistics	■ Stock information ■ Tracking and tracing of orders
Sales	■ Sales information ■ Entering orders at a client's site
Service	■ Routing service mechanics
Human resource management	■ Retrieving information on colleagues such as e-mail and phone number
Firm infrastructure	■ email access ■ Reading company news ■ Help desk requests

Although the technology used is very much the same, there are some differences between Internet-like services and Intranet-like services. A company is able to completely control the standards and the type of phone that the employees use because it can supply all employees with the same device. This differs very much from the world outside the company where consumers have various preferences resulting in the purchase of different phones which can all be WAP compliant but deviate on small variances in the implementation of the WAP protocol in the microbrowser. A second issue is security because, although strong security is also needed within a company, there are far more security components involved in offering services to consumers than in offering services to your employees. One of these security components is the fact that the users of Business Services will generally not access the service through an open-to-everyone infrastructure, such as the Internet, but will use these services through the company's own access server and WAP gateway which will make identification of a single user less difficult.

Business roles

Structuring the various roles

Before deciding where the money can be made, it is important to map the various roles you can adopt as a company, and especially as a start-up, in the mobile commerce arena. Looking at Figure 7.1 and some additional brainstorming results in the following categories: network operator, access provider, portal provider, WAP site provider, billing party, phone manufacturer, consultant, system integrator and software developer. All these roles will probably make money somehow, the question is: Which role do you see as the most interesting and most logical to adopt?

Network operator

The network operator is the company that operates the mobile network and can be regarded as the spider in the Web. The network operator sells mobile subscriptions to its customers, mainly for voice communication. In the highly competitive mobile market there is downward pressure on the margins for voice communication and most network operators regard data communication as a welcome addition that will not only polish their name as an innovative company but also as a new revenue source. Even if the access server and WAP gateway server are operated by a completely different company that has nothing to do with the mobile operator, the latter will earn money because its mobile infrastructure will be used for transporting data. Today most network operators earn their money by billing the seconds that a customer is online. In the future, when customers have a permanent open line between their wireless device and the network, billing will probably be done by the size of the data transferred. Over the years the network operators made their networks suitable for low speed data communication, but to offer high speed or broadband data communication much greater investment has to be made. Progressive network operators are experimenting with high speed additions to their current network, such as GPRS, and some network operators are already involved in the national auctions for broadband frequencies. If you wish to start-up as a network operator you should hold your breath since finding a way to make money as a start-up in a saturated market will be very hard. Maybe an acquired UMTS licence could be converted into a start-up since for UMTS everyone would have to build an almost completely new mobile network.

Access provider

The access provider enables you to dial up a WAP gateway and access WAP services. At this moment the access provider is in many cases the same organisation as the network operator because offering WAP gateway access is an extension to offering voice services. For a network operator it is easy to connect an access server and WAP gateway server to an existing mobile infrastructure. Network operators already have easy access to their current customer base and may therefore be the first to be considered by the customer when he or she chooses an access provider. If a network operator has an access server and WAP gateway server in place, a simple SMS (as is the case with the Nokia 7110 mobile phone) or a less simple change of settings on the phone is enough to set up the phone to dial up the access server. However, because some network operators still do not offer WAP gateway access on their networks or because network operators want their customers to access only WAP sites approved by them, other companies may jump in and provide access services themselves. Most of these companies will be existing Internet Service Providers (ISPs) because they will already have the infrastructure that is needed to offer an access service.

Portal provider

Portals play an important role on the Internet. In general they are nothing more than collections of links to other sites, often decorated with additional information such as news services or related topics. A portal is a starting point for most, often first-time, users that wish to surf the Internet. The large ISPs especially, such as America On Line (AOL), that provide their subscribers with software that is adapted to provide the homepage of the ISP when loading up, are able to attract large crowds.

When a user is directed to an ISP's portal there are no limitations to surfing to another portal. When he or she wants to navigate from the AOL homepage to Yahoo!, nothing is blocking that. But this flexibility of choice, that is so evidently available when surfing the Internet , may not be abundant when a customer is using his or her phone to access WAP services. The first thing the user will see is the startup screen of the access provider. The address of this home page is set up in the phone's memory by the same configuration SMS that was sent to set up other items such as the dial-up number of the access server. The home page address can be changed to another, of course, but it depends completely on the access provider whether a customer is able to access other WAP sites. If we look at the WAP services offered in various countries at the moment it is clear that most portals are 'closed' and do not offer any possibility of choosing WAP sites beyond the menu that is offered as standard.

The chain of dependencies looks very interesting. If you buy a phone in a shop you will almost always buy it with a subscription from a network operator. This network operator will probably offer WAP gateway service as a standard service. Sometimes your phone will be pre-configured to make use of this service, or else a configuration SMS can be sent to your phone by the access provider. This configuration SMS also includes the address of the portal's home page. And if you change this, the operator is unwilling to provide you with data from WAP sites that are not included in the selection possibilities. It is almost impossible to break this chain! Indeed many customers will not even be interested in breaking it because they are happy with current services. Besides that, setting up the phone for accessing other sites is far too complex for the masses. But as soon as customers start noticing that there is a lot more information outside the portal that there is inside, things will probably change and an open portal will be a distinguishing factor for the service offered. Regulatory boards will probably also focus on the non-voice monopolies of the network operators and their power over customers.

You could start your own portal service and offer it to mobile phone users. But you will have to be aware of the solid iron chain described above. Even if all technical problems are solved, it will still be very hard to lure customers to your portal if it is not integrated with the comfort of just buying a phone and wapping right away. Partnering with a network operator seems to be a key solution here.

WAP site provider

We have already described the possibilities of offering various WAP services to customers: the number is almost unlimited. Most sites that will be conceived in the following years will be additional WAP sections of existing sites. But there will also be sites that will be completely focused on WAP and that will only use an Internet presence for marketing and configuration purposes. Configuration of a customer's WAP site settings through the Internet will be a hot issue since the user interface of a wireless device is too clumsy to do time-consuming configuration. A challenge is how to attract customers with your service in order to create a solid customer base. Key for the WAP site provider is to join a mobile portal. And since these portals will be run by network operators or ISPs most of the time, it is essential to team up with these companies.

How you will earn money by offering WAP services is still not very clear. The trend of giving away everything free blocks the possibility of earning big time money by billing customers for basic services. In a competitive environment it will be especially hard to make customers pay for basic services such as news or real-time quotes. But specialty services are a completely different story and you are sitting on a pot of gold when you are able to invent a unique WAP service that customers value. It seems hard to make money with traditional advertising. A phone is a very personal device and customers will probably be very reluctant to get bombarded by advertisement SMSs, as is the case with spam, or have most of their device's screen eaten up by still very small banner advertisements. If you want to make money here you should put more effort into gathering information on the client to create profiles that will enable you to offer the exact services required. Advertising is usually only a significant revenue for main market portals that reach a large target audience frequently. Another source of wealth could be the whole setup of kickback fees that can be offered by the mobile operators. Why can't the mobile operator pay you a percentage of their earnings when customers are online with your service for several minutes? The only thing you have to do is to prove that you were the one that made the customer go online.

Consultant

In the next few years there will be increasing revenues from consulting on mobile commerce. But what is there to consult about WAP? For a company that doesn't already have a clear eCommerce or multi-channel strategy and does not already have a full scale presence on the Web, WAP will not be the next step. But there are also many companies that have a strong eCommerce presence and who think that WAP could add an extra channel between them and their customers. And who will those companies choose to do their WAP business with? Right – those consultants who helped them on the Web in the first place. Probably in the first few years the WAP pot will be too small to provide for a whole evening dinner and WAP will be a component of larger offerings most of the time, including eCommerce or call-centre technology.

But either way, only those consultants that already have a strong client base in those sectors where WAP will first take off, such as the financial sector, are able to attract enough revenue to compensate for the costs of gaining knowledge on wireless technologies to stay ahead of competition. For the smaller consultants, finding a niche is of the utmost importance. These niches could be the safety aspects of WAP, knowledge on payment systems or other areas that require deep knowledge that differentiate from bigger competitors.

Billing party

The fact that the network operator bills its non pre-paid customers every month is a good starting-point for billing customers for other services than voice seconds. As a billing party you could act as a clearing house for the companies that offer WAP services to their customers, eliminating the need for all different WAP site owners to set up their own billing systems for small payments. Through the billing system the customer could be billed for small payments such as for accessing pay-by-view information. This, however, requires an integration of the WAP site with the billing mechanisms of all WAP access providers. In terms of payment safety this solution is quite interesting since the access provider is able to safely identify the customer. It is a different story when it comes to pre-paid cards. Before there is a mechanism that is able to subtract money from a pre-paid card for payment purposes it will be very difficult to safely identify a customer who dials in with a pre-paid card.

Phone manufacturer

To some, WAP stands for 'Where Are the Phones?' Since WAP was officially introduced in the summer of 1999, until April 2000, hardly any mobile phone manufacturer, except Nokia with its 7110, has deployed WAP enabled phones on a large scale. Ericsson has a WAP-enabled handheld-like phone and Motorola and Siemens are very busy getting their act together but, as far as I know, no large scale deployment has yet taken place, although this is changing quickly. Because of the small differences in usability aspects of the phones the WAP sites will probably have to slightly adapt their code to support every type of WAP phone that will be used to access the site. The phone manufacturer with the first large scale deployment of WAP phones will set the standard.

Many manufacturers, such as Philips, claim to be waiting until GPRS is widely available. However, building a microbrowser into a phone is a complex process, some manufacturers are still not capable of building a phone with a bug-free microbrowser, not even if they buy a ready-to-go microbrowser from Phone.Com. On top of that software costs are a large part of the construction costs of a mobile phone and making bad software choices could lead to enormous losses resulting from an erroneous development process. An interesting case is the Siemens S25 phone. When Siemens launched the S25 it supported the WAP 1.0 standard. Unfortunately for Siemens, the WAP Forum decided to declare WAP 1.1 as the de facto standard, rendering the S25 effectively useless.

System integrator

The role of the system integrators will be to connect the current eCommerce infrastructure or the company's legacy systems to the WAP infrastructure. The strategic asset that makes this business successful is the client relationship. If you do not already have a stronghold with those clients wishing to move to WAP, you will not have a strong case. In addition, WAP starts with consulting on strategic and process related topics, not with system integration. Only if you, as a company, have advanced technological skills or are prepared to team up with a consultant or move towards consulting, will you have a stronger case.

Software developer

The Siebels and Oracles of this world will make money by marketing products that will enable their customers to establish WAP presence in their specific area. Additional modules attached to existing software products will make them open to access through mobile devices. An example of this is the additional WAP module to Siebel 2000. Also completely new products will be developed, such as easy-to-use WAP development kits or software that is focused on offering a very specialised service.

Even for smaller companies, as is the case with most Internet startups, there are huge opportunities to grow by developing software that fulfils the needs of other companies that wish to offer WAP services to their customers. Again, niche is a keyword here. Large companies are good at developing products that they can sell many times. Small companies are good at developing very specialised products. A small company could, for instance, focus on developing specialised software to access legacy systems or to develop very specialised WAP services.

What's happening in the world?

Analyst predictions

Unless you have a crystal ball, it is very hard to predict the future of WAP. In most countries, except for Japan, there is hardly any experience with mobile commerce.

I would like to share some of the analysts' predictions with you:

- In July 1999, Ovum reported that smart phones and data-centric terminals will account for as much as two thirds of the estimated $67bn handset market in 2004

- Forrester Research expects that 10% to 15% of the mobile phones sold in 2000 will be WAP-enabled phones

- Datamonitor expects that around 2005, 69% of the GSM subscriptions will be WAP enabled

- According to Gartner Group, mobile phones are expected to be the most common client device worldwide by 2005

- Datamonitor calculated that in 2004 more than 13.9m Europeans will be able to access financial services through WAP

- Nokia expects that in 2004 more mobile telephones will be connected to the Internet than PCs

- Forrester Research expects that, in Europe, Italy will be the largest mCommerce market with a size of €4.8bn, followed by Germany with €4.1bn and the United Kingdom with €3.4bn

- IDC analysed the market and claims that, in Western Europe, 30m WAP-enabled phones will circulate in 2004.

These numbers indicate an exciting future for WAP.

Real-world picture today

A recent press release from Vodafone shows that it is planning to give away Nokia 7110 WAP phones to lure consumers into registering for the Vodafone Interactive service. After launching WAP gateway access in November 1999, Dutch KPN still only hosts about 6,000 WAP users from a mobile customer base of about 3m. Does the consumer need more time to get accustomed to using a mobile phone as an information device? Is the low availability of WAP phones restricting the growth?.

Customer acceptance is restricted by the cost of the handsets. The going rate for a WAP-enabled phone in April 2000 was approximately $450. Compare this to iMode, the Japanese counterpart of WAP. iMode enabled handsets are priced at a lower level than a normal Japanese handset resulting in mass acceptance of the service. Such a price-sponsoring strategy is most likely to work in markets where a mobile operator had a near monopoly on mobile services or where phones could be configured only to be used with the mobile network of one operator. Since in most other countries there are not such strong monopolies and in some countries hacking SIM-locks is a national sport, this strategy may be difficult to pursue.

Customer surfing online may not meet the expectations of most network operators. Experience in Scandinavia shows that most consumers do not use their mobile phones for surfing from WAP site to WAP site but rather for accessing situation-relevant information that can be retrieved in the blink of an eye. WAP services used this way show more similarity with Teletext than with the Internet. The same applies for iMode where it looks like people only access services for quick reference. Business models will have to change accordingly.

Geographic snapshot

Netherlands

In November 1999 the former state owned telecommunications company KPN, with a market share of about 50% of the Dutch GSM market, introduced M-Info. M-info is a WAP portal through which subscribers with a WAP-enabled phone can access a limited number of primarily Dutch services. The portal of M-Info is 'closed', meaning that no services beside those approved by the network operator, can be accessed. In March 2000 KPN decided to start selling, by auction, the slots in the portal for a period of half a year. In my opinion this is a non-consumer-driven decision that will prove incorrect, but it is still an interesting proposal. As one of the first European network operators to offer a WAP portal, KPN received a nomination for most innovative operator at the GSM World Congress 1999 in Cannes. The other four operators do not offer a WAP gateway to their customers yet, although Libertel, the second largest, is cooperating with ING Bank to introduce financial services through WAP in mid 2000, which in practice means that Libertel will also have to introduce its own WAP gateway by then. Because of the resistance of the non WAP-enabled network operators to introduce WAP gateways, and the closed nature of M-Info, several operator independent initiatives for offering WAP gateway services have been introduced by ISP-like companies.

Germany

In Germany the three largest network operators with a combined customer base of 21.2m, D1 of Deutsche Telekom and D2 of Vodafone and E-Plus, are all offering WAP gateway access. One of the most interesting WAP services is the brokerage service of Consors. The company offers real time quotes, portfolio viewing, order placement and order information through WAP. For security purposes Consors makes use of WTLS, the security layer that is similar to the SSL found on the Internet. ComDirect, another German brokerage service, offers quotes, market news and a market overview but no trading yet. Sixt, a large car rental company, offers the possiblity of reserving a car through WAP, something which is rewarded with 10,000 Lufthansa (Germany's largest airline) miles.

Finland

In Finland, the land of Nokia, the network operator Sonera is taking a lead in mobile commerce. With its wholly owned subsidiary Sonera Smart-Trust, the company is trying to set a standard for safe wireless authentication through the Internet. The company is co-operating with several other companies to set standards in the wireless arena. An example is the co-operation on UMTS with the Japanese network operator NTT DoCoMo.

Singapore

SingTel Mobile launched its WAP services on 11 January 2000. SingTel Mobile's subscribers have access to services like news updates, a bus guide, a phone directory, share prices, IPO enquiries, a home loan calculator, local weather information, horseracing results from the Singapore Turf Club, a lucky pick random number generator for lotto and toto, and the sending of free Internet SMS and pages. The required text information is retrieved from the various content providers such as Channel News Asia and Singapore Bus Services. SingTel Mobile is also currently working very closely with SingTel (what a surprise) to enable its customers with WAP phones to access services like email, eBanking and eFood to be launched on the 'My SingTel' portal. The next milestone is the introduction of GPRS in the third quarter of 2000 as one of the first in the world or, as SingTel Mobile's CEO Lucas Chow put it at the introductionary speech of the WAP gateway access, 'This is going to be an exciting year for us and our customers'.

Japan

In Japan there is iMode, a WAP-like text-based information service that is provided by NTT DoCoMo, Japan's largest network operator. iMode is not based on WAP but is a different standard that relates more to compact versions of current Internet technologies and puts more emphasis on usability than WAP does. iMode was launched in February 1999 and managed to attract more than 3m subscribers within a year. Through this service about 250 applications authorised by NTT DoCoMo and about 2,500 unauthorised applications can be accessed. The portal offers a great number of services such as banking, travelling and entertainment, but the most successful application on iMode is a screensaver created by toy manufacturer Bandai. About US$400,000 is paid every month by users that want to have the daily picture of toy figures Tare-Panda and Kitty on their display. Colour has just been introduced to the iMode terminals that are produced by various Japanese electronics companies. Support for the Global Positioning System (GPS) and Java will be implemented in the iMode terminals this year, effectively introducing localisation and an advanced form of interactivity.

USA

The patchwork quilt of various wireless infrastructures is not helping the North Americans to cover the gap between them and the European and Asian countries, who take the lead in mobile data communication. Only some GSM 1900 network operators offer WAP gateway services and as far as is known no frequency spectrum for third generation networks, such as UMTS, has been assigned yet. An interesting mobile network, however, is the Mobitex radio shared network that is operated by BellSouth and is running on Ericsson technology. Users of the Palm VII with a built-in Mobitex-modem are able to view news and their emails, do banking and access dozens of other services.

Scepticism

There is a lot of scepticism around, as always when new technologies are introduced, and that's good since an unprejudiced mind is necessary to separate nonsense from well-considered reasoning. Unfortunately, some of the scepticism is based on incomplete understanding of the WAP. To provide you with ammunition to ward off at least some of the ill-founded scepticism I have collected some of the most interesting statements that I have encountered. Of course, this ammunition is largely based on personal opinions and I challenge you, the reader, to formulate a rejoinder if you think differently.

'WAP will soon vanish when bandwidth-increased technologies such as GPRS and UMTS take off'
The respectable Dutch computer magazine that was quoted, forgets that WAP was designed to be network independent. In general this means that GPRS and UMTS will enable your WAP device to retrieve information at a far higher speed than currently possible, rather than replace the current WAP standard. The increased bandwidth of these technologies enable you to do more advanced things, such as having full-motion video on your screen, and will mean that future versions of the WAP protocol will have to include technologies to address new uses. Just as HTML and SSL are still basic components of the Internet today, with other more advanced technologies such as XML and advanced encrypting broadly available, the technologies included in WAP will not become obsolete over night.

'Competing technologies such as Windows CE, Palm VII and iMode have a far better chance to become leaders in mobile eCommerce'
First, we need to address the way in which these technologies are competitors of WAP. Windows CE is basically an operating system and only competes with WAP when it comes to user interface capabilities. Adding WAP compatibility in its micro-Internet Explorer will make a wireless Windows CE device WAP compliant. In addition, Microsoft has joined the WAP forum and publicly announced full support for WAP in its future products.

Palm, on the other hand, doesn't only provide an operating system but also offers its own services through Palm.net, which any user with a Palm VII device can access. Palm.net is accessed through the built-in Mobitex modem and uses the operator dependent BellSouth Mobitex network. The extent to which users will like the closed nature of this system depends on the quality of the content offering.

iMode is a Japanese standard, only supported by the operator NTT DoCoMo. Although it is clearly the most advanced solution when it comes to functionality and the number of users, this closed nature limits its potential for worldwide deployment. NTT DoCoMo also realises this and is planning to adopt and integrate WAP into its future services.

'The Stone Age user interface WAP provides now will not be sufficient to attract large masses of customers'
It is true that WAP looks like it was invented in the Middle Ages. But do not forget why it looks the way it does now: the size of the screen, the limited computational capabilities and the restricted bandwidth will not allow a fancier user interface. The question is whether this plainness restricts customer's usability to simple transactions such as seeing stock prices change, retrieving their email and other services that do not rely on a flashy user interface. If the characteristics of the user interface can change because of enhancements in the current restrictions, they will. Perhaps voice recognition will enable this.

'As technological evolution progresses, wireless devices will be more powerful. And at some moment a wireless device will be able to run the same software as the desktop PC'
This is right – at some moment the wireless device will be capable of running the same applications as the desktop PC… as we know it now. The rapid cycle of technological change belches up smarter and faster gadgets. But this is also true of the desktop PC in the study and thus there will always be a gap between these classes of computing power. This gap specifically creates the need for a stripped version of its larger sister. Maybe a wireless device will have enough power within a few years to run Internet Explorer 5.0 without sweat, but at that time we will have version 8.0 with new features, running on our desktop PC.

The future of WAP

Evolution of WAP

All owners of WAP phones should know that the standard itself is still evolving and that the WAP phone they bought for big bucks about a month ago, will not be able to support future versions of the WAP protocol, unless the phone can be easily flashed with new software. Most of the new features in the WAP 1.2 standard have already been approved by the WAP

Forum and the specifications of the new WAP 1.3 standard are on their way. New features included in the WAP 1.2 standard are push-technology and the possibility of handling incoming and outgoing voice-calls using WML and WMLScript, something which can be of use in a situation where companies offer multi-channel services.

Has WAP been invented too early, before all technology and standards have been given time to crystallise? Probably, but you have to start somewhere if you wish to set a worldwide standard. The WAP 1.1 standard supports today's technology perfectly and as soon as new standards are needed to enable advanced technology, they will be there. A problem could be the large number of legacy phones supporting the WAP 1.1 standard when the various players in the mCommerce arena are already trying to support WAP 1.3. Fortunately, a customer buys a new mobile phone at an average rate of about one every fourteen months.

Push functionality

With push functionality a service will be able to send you information even if you have not requested this information. You can compare push functionality with SMS. However, an SMS message is limited to about 160 characters while push functionality enables complete documents to be sent to your phone. Push functionality will prove to be extremely useful for receiving fax-like messages or to accept messages from systems that are triggered by previously set events. Push functionality would basically require a permanent connection between the device and the mobile network.

Localisation

Another huge area of opportunities concerns localisation capabilities. The capabilities can be used to localise the mobile phone and predict within an acceptable range where the user is at that moment. If applications are able to use this information, the service offered can be adapted to the user's location. If, for instance, a department store is able to detect that a known customer is entering the building, it can easily send a message to the customer's phone with information about new products the customer would be interested in. Another example could be a WAP site that provides information on hotel reservations. With localisation information this site can push information on vacancies within a one mile vicinity of the user. Or think about a well-known fast-food chain that has restaurants all over town. If this chain keeps a list of customers that are befriended and it is able to detect whether two of these customers are near one of its restaurants, it could send both customers a notification that one of their friends is near, including an invitation to grab a discount burger in the restaurant right around the corner. Of course these applications will require a complex integration of the systems of the mobile operators and those of companies that wish to use the localisation data. These applications also raise questions about the privacy of the individual since one can doubt whether customers wish to be constantly spammed with advertising messages from the shops they pass while leisurely loitering in the shopping mall on a Sunday afternoon.

WAP as a user interface

An interesting side effect of having a flexible and programmable user interface especially designed for mobile phones is that this interface can also be used for other purposes than browsing through WAP sites. For instance, when a phone is able to control other devices, the WAP user interface could be used to send commands to these other devices. With Bluetooth, a technology invented by Ericsson, it is possible to connect to other devices over a low cost radio link. When the WAP specifications are defined such that there is an easy way for programmers to access the Bluetooth technology that is built into a phone, for example through a Bluetooth WAP API, this phone can be the master control of many other devices. This is not only about having a remote control for your Bluetooth compliant TV but it is also about paying your parking fee through the WAP user interface by just holding your phone near the parking meter and following the instructions on your display.

Payment systems

Another interesting development is how the SIM-card in mobile phones can be used to make small payments. Suppose you would like to view information on a WAP site that is not capable of billing you through the billing system of the network operator. In a worst case scenario you have to leave your credit card details on this site. With a WAP Payment API that is simple to access by software, the microbrowser in your phone would be able to subtract small amounts of money from the SIM-card in your mobile phone after you have acknowledged the payment. Through a similar system you would also be able to reload the SIM-card with money when there is no longer enough credit on the card. The field of payment systems is so diverse and complex that a book the size of this is barely enough to cover all the related topics.

Broadband technologies

The evolution of faster ways of transporting data to a mobile phone will in most countries be spread out over two phases. The first phase is GPRS. With GPRS you will be able to combine multiple slots to transport data over the mobile network. GPRS also enables you to have a permanent connection between your phone and the network. In general everyone refers to GPRS as a 2.5 generation technology, where the first generation is an analogue mobile network infrastructure and the second generation is a digital mobile network infrastructure. It very much depends on the actual version of GPRS which transfer speeds you can maximally get, but in general the speed will be 115kbps. The second phase is UMTS, the umbrella name of the third generation of mobile infrastructure. Although UMTS will enable data transfer at a speed of about 2Mbps, it is questionable whether UMTS will be successful within a period of ten years. First, UMTS needs considerably more technical changes to the physical infrastructure than GPRS and these changes require vast investments. Second, the data transfer speed offered by GPRS will be enough for most applications, unless mobile video conferencing establishes itself. UMTS will probably only be deployed in urban areas where the customer base is large enough to support the huge investment. However, most network operators are already investigating the possibilities of UMTS.

Conclusion

There is much more to mobile commerce and the WAP than was covered by this chapter. And as always with technologies that still have to prove themselves, it is very hard to comment on the results of all these developments. All the hype that is created around wireless technology, and WAP in particular, clouds the fact that WAP is only the first station on a very long track. WAP is the enabler, the kick-starter, the driving factor for mobile eCommerce, but is certainly not the terminus. This chapter provides you with a framework for understanding WAP and, to a larger extent mobile commerce, and I hope that it will be helpful when you want to make a decision on whether the mCommerce market is an attractive one in which to start your own Internet company. I do not claim to have a monopoly on WAP knowledge and hope that if you have any remarks, even critical, you will contact the author at paul.c.eijkemans@ac.com or at mail@eijkemans.com.

Acknowledgements

I wish to thank my colleagues in the m-Commerce Focus Group Netherlands at Andersen Consulting, Wouter Evers, Jeroen Langendam and Bart van Ginderen, for their enthusiasm in working with me on new mobile technologies. I would also like to thank Joris van Dongen, Torsten Klein, Joel Osman, Mika Saastamoinen and Richard Siber for their contributions to this chapter or for providing me with expert information.

The views expressed in this article are personal and do not necessarily conform to the views of Andersen Consulting.

References

Internet references

www.wapforum.com	On the official site of the organisation that controls the WAP standard there is a lot about the various specifications that are contained in WAP
www.gsmag.com	The GSMag regularly publishes an interesting newsletter on what is happening in the GSM market
www.ericsson.com	Home of the well-known Swedish phone manufacturer and source of a lot of information and a toolkit
www.yahoo.com	Yahoo! is one of the largest portals around
www.amazon.com	Earth's largest bookstore has just launched a WAP service as an addition to its Web site
www.symbian.com	Symbian is a company that develops core software for mobile devices and tries to set standards in the wireless community. The company is jointly run by Ericsson, Motorola, Nokia, Panasonic and Psion
www.palm.com	Surf to this Web site if you wish to see the latest models in the very popular Palm series
www.gelon.net	For those who can't afford to buy a WAP enabled phone, Gelon.net offers a virtual phone through which you can

access various WAP enabled sites. You can also find a huge collection of links to WAP sites

www.nokia.com   This well-known Finnish phone manufacturer also offers a lot of information and toolkits through its Web site.

webopedia.Internet.com   A great resource for getting descriptions of new technologies

Literature

Mann, S. (2000) *Programming Applications with the Wireless Application Protocol: The Complete Developer's Guide*. New York: Wiley Computer Publishing

Nordan, M. M. (1999) *Europe's mobile Internet opens up*. Forrester Research

Phifer, G. (1999) *Enterprise management alert: a winning e-business strategy*. Gartner Group

Porter, M. J. (1980) *Competitive Strategy: Techniques for Analyzing Industries and Competitors*. New York: The Free Press

Torris, T. (2000) *Offering the right content to WAP users*. Forrester Research

Zohar, M. (1999) *The Dawn of Mobile eCommerce*. Forrester Research

Glossary of terms

API – application program interface

An interface by which an application program is able to access an operating system or other applications. An API enables an application to retrieve information from another application without knowledge of the business rules encapsulated in this other application

Bps – bits per second

A common measure of expressing the data speed of computer modems. The speed in bps is equal to the number of bits transmitted or received per second. Kbps: kilobits per second; Mbps: megabits per second. Another common measure for determining data speed is baud, which refers to the number of times a digital signal can change in one second

CPU – central processing unit

The brain of your computer. A CPU can be told to execute the instructions included in a software program.

GPRS – general packet radio service

A high-speed packet data technology

HTML – hypertext markup language

A document format language used on the Internet

Java

A computer language that enables applications that are coded in Java to run on various platforms. It was invented by Sun

PDA – personal digital assistant	A handheld device that combines several functions such as computing, telephony or networking. Until 1999 the success of PDAs was limited, however it is widely thought that PDA sales will become very popular in the future
SMS – short messaging service	A method of sending small text messages to or from a phone.
UMTS – universal mobile telecommunications system	A collection of broadband communication technologies
XML – eXtensible markup language	This markup language is a specification developed for Web documents. Programmers are able to use it for definition, transmission, validation, and interpretation of data

CHAPTER 8

Legal Aspects of Setting Up an Internet Business

David Griffiths, Kirsty Foy and Toby Hornett
CLIFFORD CHANCE

This chapter will outline some legal issues commonly facing an entrepreneur starting up an eCommerce business. There are a number of practical steps outlined below which could usefully be followed in the preliminary stages of setting up an eCommerce business but it is important to note that for most issues, specific legal advice will be needed at the appropriate time.

Protection of ideas: confidential information, copyright and patents

Many Internet entrepreneurs start their business with one asset: an idea. The Internet has spawned many ideas for new services, better ways of providing existing services, innovative ways of selling goods and many others. The ability of a business to succeed with a new idea will often depend on getting the idea to market before its competitors and to some extent on preventing competitors from copying what it has done. One of the first legal issues an entrepreneur will face is to determine whether he can obtain any legal protection of his ideas and business plans and to take any steps necessary to obtain this protection.

There are three basic forms of legal protection an entrepreneur can use for this purpose. Each protects different types of intellectual assets and different steps must be taken to obtain protection. These are:

- *Law of Confidence*: which protects confidential ideas and information from unauthorised use or disclosure and is particularly important in the initial stages of developing a business idea

- *Copyright*: which protects the expression of ideas (rather than the ideas themselves) and is key where software or the content of site (for example text or design) are the basis of an eCommerce idea

- *Patents*: which protect ideas which are new processes and which, despite the considerable formalities required to obtain and preserve a patent, are increasing in the context of eCommerce because a patent holder has a monopoly in respect of a patented process.

Confidential information

The ability to get an idea to market first is particularly important for eCommerce businesses as many are able to obtain funding far beyond the level available to bricks and mortar start-ups on the strength of a business plan which may be little more than an idea. Even where a business is more developed, the relative ease of entry to many eCommerce businesses makes protection of ideas a crucial issue for entrepreneurs. Keeping the idea entirely secret is clearly not practical as the business will need financing before it has been launched and people will normally need to be hired to establish the business. It is possible to disclose the information and retain legal protection from unauthorised use or further disclosure if:

- the information itself is not trivial and
- it was disclosed in circumstances where an obligation of confidence exists.

The first requirement will generally be met if the information is not something that could reasonably be thought of without access to the confidential information for which protection is sought. The second requirement will be satisfied most easily if a non-disclosure agreement is signed by every potential recipient of the information before it is disclosed. If these requirements are met, it will normally be possible to get an injunction to prevent unauthorised disclosure of the confidential information or to get damages for any loss caused by unauthorised disclosure. One significant drawback however is that third parties who are not aware of the confidential nature of the information can use and disclose it without any restrictions. While it is usually possible to sue the person or company which made the initial unauthorised disclosure, the damage will often be irreversible at that point. A further drawback is that the idea will usually be disclosed to the public when the business is launched and after that, the restrictions on use and disclosure will normally cease to apply.

Practical steps

Everyone to whom confidential information is given should be asked to sign a confidentiality agreement *before* the information is disclosed (see appendix A for an example) and information should be disclosed only to those who need to know it. This will establish a clear duty of confidence. In addition, all relevant documents should be marked 'Confidential' and as few copies as possible should be made. Care should be taken when storing and disposing of confidential documents to ensure no-one will have unauthorised access to them.

Copyright

Copyright is a collection of rights in relation to a piece of work which allow the owner of those rights to do certain things with that work and to prevent others from doing certain things.

The main types of material for which copyright protection can be obtained are literary, dramatic, musical and artistic works, typographical arrangements of published editions of works and sound recordings. Computer software is considered a literary work for these purposes and therefore is protected by copyright. Copyright will only be available if the work is original.

A copyright owner has the exclusive right to copy the work, issue it to the public, perform it, make adaptations of it and, for certain types of work, distribute it. These rights enable the copyright owner to exploit the commercial value of a piece of work and to prevent others from exploiting that value. Where the owner of the copyright is not able to carry out activities himself, he can permit others to do certain things and will usually charge a fee. This is called 'licensing'. Where a piece of work has commercial value, the copyright owner will almost always grant licences as he would not be able to exploit the full value of the work by himself. For example, an author of a book often licenses the rights to publish the book to a publishing company which can make more money from the publication than the author could himself. Payment for licences can be one-off fees but are often royalties, that is, fees calculated on the commercial success of the work such as a percentage of gross receipts on copies sold.

The creator of a work will usually be the first owner of copyright in relation to that work. However, where the creator has been commissioned by someone else to create the work, the parties might agree that the person commissioning the work will be the owner of the copyright. It is also possible for a copyright owner to sell (or 'assign') the copyright entirely. The new owner (or 'assignee') will then have the same rights as the original owner in relation to copyright. However a creator of certain types of work has additional rights which cannot be assigned. These further rights are known as 'moral rights' and they are the right to be identified as the author of the work and the right to prevent the integrity of the work from being degraded. The former right entitles the creator to a work protected by copyright to be credited for that work. The latter right is not commonly relied upon, particularly in the context of a piece of work produced in a commercial context. These rights have, however, been used by a renowned Canadian sculptor when he was commissioned to make a sculpture of Canada geese for a department store. The sculpture was put on display at the store and, at Christmas, the store's staff put red bows around the necks of the geese. Although the store owned the sculpture, the sculptor was able to obtain a court order forcing the store to remove the bows because they degraded his work. Moral rights, although they cannot be assigned, can in some circumstances be waived, that is, the author can agree not to exercise or assert his moral rights.

After a period of time has elapsed, the copyright will expire and the work will fall into the public domain. In the UK, this period is in most cases 70 years after the death of the author. A work which is in the public domain can be exploited by anyone. The work will, however, be less attractive commercially at this point because competitors would also be able to exploit the work. It is possible for new copyright to be created in relation to a work which is in the public domain. This might happen where, for example, a photographer takes a photograph of the *Elgin Marbles*. Although the *Elgin Marbles* themselves are not protected by copyright, the photographer would own the copyright in the photograph. A licence would therefore be required to copy or publish the photograph.

There are some exceptions to the restrictions on using protected works which allow certain types of use such as for educational purposes, for criticising or reviewing a piece of work or for reporting current events. It is also possible to use a part of a protected work as long as it is not a substantial part. This is known as 'fair use'. Whether any particular part of a protected work would be considered substantial for this purpose depends on the comparative quality of the part taken rather than the quantity. As an example, the *Mona Lisa*'s smile is a small part of the work in terms of quantity but would likely be considered a substantial part of the work for fair use purposes (although of course, the *Mona Lisa* is not a protected work).

Where a breach of copyright has led to a loss of profits, the copyright holder may make a claim for damages for that loss. Other available remedies include delivery or destruction of infringing copies.

Copyright laws vary in different countries although most developed countries are bound by international conventions on copyright which give a basic level of protection for works created in other countries. The European Commission intends to adopt a Copyright Directive by the end of 2000 to further standardise copyright protection across the European Union.

Practical steps

Authors commonly send a printed copy of new works they have created by registered post to themselves. The unopened envelope should be kept in a safe place and can then be used to establish when the work was created.

If the company wishes to use a substantial part of material created by someone else, it can purchase an assignment of the copyright in the material or obtain a licence from the copyright holder. This is commonly referred to as 'clearing' the material. Each licence must be negotiated with the copyright holder who will charge a fee based on the perceived value of the work and the extent of the licences. If the work will be carried out by someone else on commission, a written agreement should be signed making clear who will own the copyright and what rights each party will have in relation to the material.

Patents

A patent is intended to protect the inventive kernel of a product or process. Patents require formal registration and will only be granted to an applicant whose invention involves an inventive step and is capable of industrial application.

A patent gives the owner the right to sue another person who uses the same process even if that person did not copy the patented process or even know that it was patented. A patent can be sold or licensed to other companies which may provide a valuable royalty stream. If the value of an Internet start-up companies' business is derived from a unique technological application, such as a unique combination of software applications and systems that provides a site with a unique order processing mechanism, it might be able to register a patent to protect the process and to prevent other Internet companies using the same mechanism.

There are, however, a number of drawbacks to relying on patent protection. The details of the invention must be disclosed to the public as part of the registration procedure therefore when the patent expires, others will be able to exploit the invention freely. In addition, the application process can be complicated, lengthy and expensive and once the patent is registered, a patent holder must be vigilant in taking action against infringers. In the Internet domain, Amazon.com is currently engaged in a dispute with Barnesandnoble.com over Amazon's one-click shopping process for which it obtained a patent in the US. Amazon has obtained a preliminary court order forcing Barnes and Noble to use a two-click process until the dispute is resolved. In addition, Priceline.com is in dispute with Microsoft over Priceline's 'name your own price' auction process. These disputes can be costly and time-consuming but since patents for 399 Internet-related business methods were granted in the US in 1999, it is certain that the number of disputes will escalate.

Practical steps

A company which intends to register a patent in connection with an invention must ensure that the details are kept confidential until registration. Advice should be sought as early as possible on registrability from a patent agent. If another party such as a web site developer is involved in the development process, the development agreement should specifically assign any new product to the client company.

Protection of names: domain name registration and trademarks

A company's name and the names it gives its products enable customers to recognise that company and its products. When someone sees a soft drink with the name Coca-Cola on the side of the can, he knows what it will taste like and therefore whether he wants to buy it. Establishing brand recognition is an essential part of building a business and the value of a brand can be enormous. In fact, Coca-Cola is believed to be the most valuable brand name in the world and the name itself had an estimated value of $83.8bn in 1999 (source: Interbrand). The value of names is just as important for Internet companies, possibly more so given that the Internet is a passive medium, so a memorable domain name is needed to allow users to find the site. The name Amazon.com is believed to have one of the fastest growing values ever and the value of the name itself in

1999 was estimated at $1.3bn (source: Interbrand). A priority for any Internet business will be to establish the right name for its web site and products and to protect those names. This is done by registering domain names and obtaining trademark protection.

Domain name registration

Registering domain names is one of the first things an Internet business needs to do. A short memorable name which readily identifies a company and/or its services is ideal.

A domain name represents a web page's Internet Protocol (IP) address. The IP address is used by computers to locate a particular file or page and the IP address for each page is unique. However an IP address is usually a 32-bit number (for example 123.123.123.12) so names are allocated to each number to make them more memorable. Domain names are organised around a hierarchy of names. The top level domain identifies the general type of domain usually by type of organisation (for example .com for commerical, .edu for educational and .org for non-commercial organisations) or by country (for example .uk for the United Kingdom, .fr for France and .de for Germany). The second-level domain identifies a specific administrative owner for certain pages and includes the top-level domain (for example cliffordchance.com).

IANA (the Internet Assigned Numbers Authority) was originally responsible, under contract from the US government, for administering allocation of IP addresses and managing the domain name system. These functions have been transferred to ICANN (Internet Corporation for Assigned Names and Numbers), a non-profit, private sector corporation formed by a broad coalition of the Internet's business, technical and academic communities. Responsibility for allocating second level domain names has been given to various private entities known as registries (such as InterNIC and Nominet UK) and there is some overlap in the ability of the registries to allocate names within the top-level domain (for example both InterNIC and Nominet UK can allocate second-level domain names within the .co.uk top-level domain).

Each registry has an application process for registration of a second-level domain name. This is a fairly simple process and can be done online through a registry's web site. An applicant will be asked to provide basic contact information and credit card details for payment of the registration fee which is generally in a range of £75 to £125 per name registered. If the application process is followed and the chosen name is not identical to one which is already registered, an applicant will be given that name.

Some registries for top-level domain names have further requirements, particularly those which relate to countries. Some examples are:

- *Italy*: an applicant must have a branch or office in Italy (www.nic.it)

- *Australia*: to obtain a top-level Australian commercial domain (.com.au), there must be a 'distinct 1:1 correlation between a domain name and an applicant's registered commercial name' and the applicant must prove it has the rights to the commercial name or that it is registered with a recognised (Australian) government or industry authority (www.domainregistration.com.au)

- *Ireland*: domain names are not permitted if they consist of generic names, words or descriptions which in the view of Irish Domains, the Irish registry, would be misleading if given to the applicant or would imply that the applicant had trademark or other rights in the name (www.irishdomains.com)

- *The Netherlands*: only organisations based in or which have a subsidiary in the Netherlands and which are legally registered there may register .nl domain names (www.domain-registry.nl).

Cybersquatting/competing legitimate claims

There has been much publicity around the practice of registering names of well-known companies or trademarks as domain names with a view to selling the domain names to that company or the owner of the trademark. This has become known as 'cybersquatting' and is possible because most registries allocate names on a first-come-first-served basis.

Most registries have been and are developing systems of dispute resolution to deal with the problem of cybersquatting. For example, registrars in the .com, .net and .org top-level domains (including Network Solutions Inc. and InterNIC) have adopted ICANN's Uniform Dispute Resolution Policy. In general, if a trademark owner can show that it owned the trade mark before the allocation of the domain name and the owner of the domain name has no legitimate interest in the name, the registry will transfer the name to the legitimate trademark holder.

Most registries will also cancel or transfer a registration pursuant to a court order. Playboy Enterprises Inc. was able to obtain a court order in the US requesting Network Solutions Inc. to cancel the registrations of a web site publisher which had registered domain names matching trademarks owned by Playboy and to transfer them to Playboy Enterprises Inc. Network Solutions Inc. complied with the order.

Conflicts can also arise between 'legitimate' applicants for the same name. Before the rise of the Internet as a forum for business companies with the same name but involved in different businesses or locations could usually use their names without conflict because they were operating in different markets. However, some companies are now finding their name or brand name has been registered by another company of the same name or using the same brand names and the registries' dispute resolution processes generally do not apply in these circumstances. For example, Nissan Motor Co. has been involved in a dispute with Nissan Computer Corporation, a small American supplier of computer equipment which has been doing business under that name since 1991 and has had its site registered as www.nissan.com since 1994. Nissan Motor Co. is currently suing the computer company in the US courts in an attempt to get the domain name. There is a great deal of uncertainty in this area of law and most disputes are settled without reaching court, often when the bigger company buys the domain name from the smaller company. Recently Compaq settled a dispute which had been running for several years over the domain name www.altavista.com which Compaq wanted for its search engine of the same name. Alta Vista Technology Inc., a small software company, had registered the name before the search engine was launched and resisted Compaq's attempts to force it to hand over the name. Compaq eventually paid an amount reported to be more than $3.3m to buy the name.

The various dispute processes are generally available only to applicants seeking to register a domain name which they have already established as a trade mark. These processes will not assist an applicant simply because the current holder of the domain name is not using it in business unless the applicant can establish prior use of the name as a trade mark. A company establishing a new business may find its chosen name has already been registered by someone else whose sole intention is to sell the domain name. Usually the holder of the domain name wants simply to sell the name to the highest bidder but sometimes the domain name holder has other motives. An unusual bidding war took place between Dell, IBM, Novell, VA Research and others for the domain name www.linux.com. The companies wanted to use the domain name in connection with the linux operating system. The system had been developed by a community of programmers and access to its programming code had been made available freely so no-one was using 'linux' as a trademark. The holder of the domain name asked bidders to present a business plan setting out how they intended to develop the system. In the end, he gave the name to VA Research reportedly for considerably less than the highest cash bid of $5m.

As well as time and cost, disputes over names can generate bad publicity, especially where the owner of the domain name is not a commercial enterprise or is not willing to sell the name. E-Toys, the online toy seller, which does most of its business through its site www.etoys.com, became involved in a bitter dispute with a group of Swiss artists who had registered the domain name www.etoy.com before the toy seller was founded. The trademark rights to the name had been registered by another business before the artists' site was registered and that business was subsequently purchased by E-Toys which gave E-Toys a prior right to the name as a trademark. On that basis E-Toys was able to get a court order in the US blocking the artists' site. The artists fought back with a counter-suit and a publicity war which included a press conference held in the Museum of Modern Art in New York. They also published a game on the Internet making fun of E-Toys. The artists rejected an offer of up to $400,000 for the name and eventually E-Toys dropped its action but agreed to pay the artists' legal expenses.

Various proposals have been put forward to alleviate these problems, including introducing new top-level domains such as .eu, but we can expect that the global reach of the Internet and its increasing demand will continue to generate domain name disputes between companies from all over the world.

Domain names: practical steps

A company should register domain names as early as possible (and consider .org, .net, .com and any country name with which there may be any possible connection in the future). Registrations can be done on the Internet by entering the search term 'domain name registration' into a search engine and then selecting the registry for the chosen top-level domain. A company should also check that the chosen name and similar names are not being used either as domain names at other levels or as trademarks if this could lead to confusion.

Trade marks

A trademark is 'a sign capable of being represented graphically which is capable of distinguishing goods or services of one undertaking from those of other undertakings'. It may be a word, design, shape, colour or even a sound or smell and its purpose is to distinguish goods or services from one provider from those of another. The owner of a registered trade mark can prevent others from using it or from using a confusingly similar mark.

To qualify for registration a mark must be distinctive and not identical to an existing mark for similar goods or services. To distinguish a name as a trademark, it must not be merely descriptive of the goods or services it represents. For example, 'The Coffee Shop' would not be permitted as a trademark for a coffee shop but would be acceptable for an online chat site.

As mentioned above in relation to domain names, it has been common in the past for different companies to own and use the same name or trade mark in different areas. This does not cause a problem if each company is providing goods or services within distinct markets. However, if the markets overlap, confusion can arise over the source of the goods or services and this confusion needs to be resolved, usually by one party using a different name. For the most part, a web site through which a company offers goods or services may be accessed from all over the world therefore disputes over the use of particular trademarks in different territories will be much more common.

As well as establishing its own trademarks, a company needs to make sure it does not infringe trademarks belonging to others. Using a trademark belonging to someone else in connection with the sale of goods or provision of services will infringe that person's trademark rights. It is important to note that use of the trade mark in a metatag could constitute a trade mark infringement. Metatags are sections of programming code within a web site that highlight particularly important words in relation to the content of the web site. These highlighted words are used by search engines to connect search requests to particular web sites but they are not visible on the site. Site builders have tried to benefit from the popularity of particular brands by inserting those brand names as metatags. Search engines will list that web site high in the results of a search for the famous trademark and this can provide valuable selling and advertising opportunities. If the name is being used in the metatag simply to attract users who are looking for that brand name, this would probably be a trademark infringement and the trademark owner could get a court order to prevent this use. The trademark owner may also be able to get an award of damages for the trademark infringement. However not all uses of a trademark belonging to someone else will be an infringement of that trademark. Playboy Enterprises Inc. brought an action against Terri Welles, a former 'Playmate of the Year', who had set up a promotional web site that included the terms 'Playmate of the Year' and 'Playmate of the Month' as metatags. The court's view was that the use of the metatags did not affect the trademarks of Playboy Enterprises Inc. and that Ms Welles had a legitimate reason to use the names as a description of herself and to catalogue her site properly with search engines. The court did accept, however, that the use of trademarks in metatags could result in a trademark violation.

Recent cases involving trade mark infringement in the electronic environment include electronic use of a registered mark on a web site, use of a registered mark in a domain name and use of a registered mark as a link to a site operated/authorised by the trade mark owner without consent. Ticketmaster brought an action against Microsoft which had inserted in its Seattle Sidewalk site a hypertext link to the Ticketmaster site which avoided Ticketmaster's front page and main advertising area. Ticketmaster claimed that this linking diluted its trademark. Microsoft argued that linking 'is an intended consequence of and fundamental to the nature of the World Wide Web'. Ticketmaster has altered its web site to prevent the univited linking from Sidewalk while it awaits the outcome of the case.

Trade marks can be transferred or licensed for use by others. A transfer gives the purchaser exclusive use of the mark (subject to any licences which have already been granted) whereas a licence would usually be non-exclusive and restricted in scope.

Trade marks: practical steps

A company's trade mark registration strategy should be very closely linked to its strategy on domain name registration and a company should check the availability and register any relevant marks as soon as possible. A basic search of all European registers for identical marks would cost approximately €500. However it may be worth carrying out a more detailed search which would pick up any similar marks as well. This search would cost approximately €3,250. It is now possible to carry out some searches of European trademark registry databases online.

Registrations may be made at a national level for a particular class, which in Europe cost (taking account of agent's fees) approximately €1,000–1,200 per jurisdiction plus a further €400 per additional class. Alternatively an application could be made under the European Community Trade Mark System (which would give trademark protection across the European Union). Such an application might be expected to cost approximately

€2,000 to prepare and file an application in up to three classes, with a further €250 per additional class thereafter.

Corporate structure/investors

Choosing a structure

The most basic and commonly used types of business structure in the United Kingdom are partnerships and limited liability companies. A partnership is an agreement between two or more persons to conduct business together whereas a company is a separate legal entity created by following a statutory procedure. The principal differences between the two are:

- The owners of a company (that is, the shareholders) are not liable for the debts of the business whereas the owners of a partnership (that is, the partners) are liable

- The income or losses of a partnership are treated as the income or losses of the partners for tax purposes whereas the income or losses of the company are treated separately

- A partnership will (unless otherwise agreed) be dissolved if a partner leaves the partnership or sells his interest in the partnership whereas a company will continue to exist even if the shares are sold

- The assets of a company are owned by the company itself whereas the assets of a partnership are owned by the partners.

The choice of structure for a business is often tax driven and specialist advice should be sought when planning a structure. There can be some advantages in using a partnership structure in the early stage of a business if the business is making a loss and the partners have other income as they will be able to deduct the loss from that income for tax purposes. In general, however, a corporate structure (that is, a company) will be more suitable for a business where investments will be made by persons who are not actively involved in running the business due to the concern about liability for the business debts and the desire for the ability to sell their interests more easily. In some cases more unusual structures such as unlimited companies or limited liability partnerships may be appropriate.

A company can be formed by the owners by filing certain documents with the relevant authority. The required documents in the UK are the articles (which set out the shareholders' basic rights and how the decisions will be made for the company), the memorandum (which sets out the number and classes of shares and the business objects of the company) and two forms, one of which contains details about the first officers of the company and the other containing a declaration by a solicitor or one of the officers stating that the requirements of the Companies Act have been met. A fee of £20 must be sent with the documents for filing. For a very basic corporate structure, the standard articles contained in the Companies Act can be used although it is normal to make some modifications to simplify administration of the company. The Companies House web site (www.companieshouse.gov.uk) has more detail on the registration process. Alternatively, companies can be bought 'off-the-shelf' from law firms or other corporate service companies. An off-the-shelf company is one which has been formed but it has never traded and it can be transferred easily by selling the issued shares.

Initial investments

In general, and particularly with traditional start-ups, the first round of funding for a company will mainly be from investors known to the company's founders such as friends and family and these investors are usually granted shares in proportion to their investment. At this stage, the corporate structure is usually fairly simple with only one class of shares and all shareholders having the same rights. Investments may continue to be made by these investors until the company has established a successful business (which may take years) to the point where it can attract 'professional investors' such as venture capitalists. Many Internet start-ups, however, have been able to attract investment from venture capitalists before the business has been established and this results in a more complicated corporate structure at an earlier stage. Venture capitalists will often want to have different (more favourable) rights than the other shareholders, particularly in relation to voting on corporate decisions, appointing directors and receiving dividends (that is, a share of the profit) and a share of the assets of the company when it is wound up. To achieve this, it is normal to create different classes of shares with different rights attached to each class.

Where outside investors are involved, particularly venture capitalists, the standard provisions of the articles may not be sufficiently detailed to deal with the relationship between the shareholders. In this situation a shareholders' agreement will be used. This sets out more detailed provisions such as restricting the rights of the founder-shareholders to sell their shares or to issue new shares without the consent of the venture capitalists and giving the venture capitalists a specified level of representation on the board of directors. Another reason for using a shareholders' agreement is that the articles are a public document which can be read by anyone whereas the shareholders' agreement will usually be private. These documents vary greatly from company to company depending on the bargaining strength of those involved and legal advice is essential at this stage for all concerned.

A common investment mechanism used by venture capitalists is convertible debt. This is a loan from the venture capitalists to the company where the venture capitalist has an option to receive shares at a set price in place of being repaid on the loan. This benefits the venture capitalist because if the company fails there would usually not be enough assets to pay back all the company's creditors and return the shareholders' investments. The company's creditors would be entitled to be repaid before the shareholders receive any share of the company's assets. However when the company is successful, a shareholder will share in the profit of the company whereas creditors are only entitled to receive the amounts they are owed, regardless of the company's success. The venture capitalist will want to be a creditor while the company is going through its early stages and then convert the loan to shares when the company becomes successful.

Another source of financing available to Internet companies is from 'incubators'. Incubators are companies set up (often by venture capitalists) to invest in early stage Internet companies and they provide a variety of services including office space, equipment and sometimes mentoring assistance and capital to new businesses. Venture capitalists are finding that incubation provides an organised way to finance and monitor their 'fledgling' companies. An investment by an incubator would be similar to those of a venture capitalist but the incubator will want shares or payment for its services as well as for its financial investment.

Share options

Share option schemes are a common way for Internet start-up companies to recruit experienced managers from traditional companies without having to match their previous salaries and benefits. A share option is a right to buy shares in the future at a price which is set when the option is granted. This means that if the price goes up, the option holder will have a right to buy shares at below their market value. This can produce a substantial benefit with no risk.

In traditional companies share options are usually given only to the most senior directors and executives. In Internet companies however share options are often granted to a much wider group of employees. It is hoped that share options will encourage employees to stay with the company during the initial risky period and motivate them to work harder by offering a benefit from an increase in the share price.

Typically, when an employee joins the company, it will grant him the right to purchase a specified number of shares in the future at a price per share equivalent to the market price on the date of grant. The employee therefore gets the benefit of an increase in the value of the shares without having to make a financial investment. If the shares increase in value, the employee can exercise his or her right under the option to buy shares and then sell those shares on the same day creating an instant profit. Usually, a company will impose a waiting period before the options 'vest' (that is, become exercisable). Commonly this would be one year for an initial block with other blocks vesting in periodic instalments (commonly monthly or quarterly). If the options are granted before the company is listed, the option agreement might provide that the options may only be exercised on a specified event such as a sale of the company or listing on a stock exchange. However, in virtually all schemes, options must be exercised within ten years of the date of grant (if they are to be exercised at all).

The scheme rules can be drafted so that the employee cannot exercise the options after his employment has been terminated and the provisions might differ depending on the reason for the employee leaving. A company may deal with these issues as it sees fit in the rules of its scheme.

A degree of tax relief can be obtained in relation to the benefit received from share options of the scheme has been approved by the Inland Revenue.

There are a number of requirements for approved schemes and at the time of writing the government was reviewing tax treatment of employee option plans. In practice, however, many Internet start-ups adopt unapproved plans. In either event it is important to get appropriate advice before setting up the scheme.

Share option schemes are not without their disadvantages. Staff (particularly less senior staff) may be tempted to leave if they get a sudden windfall from their options. If the share price falls (especially if it falls below the exercise price), staff may become disgruntled and demotivated. However, share options are becoming a standard or even essential element of compensation for Internet companies and in most cases an

Internet entrepreneur will want to consider implementing a scheme at a relatively early stage in the business.

Contracts

Binding contracts and letters of intent

Contracts will be at the cornerstone of any business. A person who breaches a binding contract can be sued in court therefore a binding contract enables parties to the contract to perform their side of the agreement with the comfort that the other party will perform its obligations. Effective contracts will be essential for businesses where the payment and delivery of the goods or services do not happen simultaneously.

Under English law, there are four ingredients necessary to create a valid contract:

- *Offer*: a statement of willingness to enter into a contract on stated terms (for example 'I will sell you this car for £1000').

- *Acceptance*: an unconditional acceptance of the offer on exactly the same terms as the offer.

- *Consideration*: each party must agree to do something it is not legally required to do or refrain from doing something it is entitled to do.

- *Intention to create legal relations*: this element is not usually an issue in commercial situations but prevents agreements which are clearly not intended to be binding from forming a binding contract.

In many European jurisdictions, consideration is not required and a contract may be formed where the other three ingredients are necessary (some countries may however have additional requirements). An Internet business must be careful that an offer is not made unintentionally to users in other countries where a binding contact might be formed even though the user is not giving anything in exchange.

In some situations, an understanding or agreement which is not legally binding can be useful. A non-binding agreement is called a 'letter of intent', 'memorandum of understanding' or 'heads of agreement'. It is used to set out the intention to enter into an agreement in the future. Although an appropriately worded letter of intent cannot be enforced in the English court, it can be convenient to set out the commercial intent of the parties and provide a framework for future negotiations. Letters of intent can be particularly useful for a new business caught in a catch-22 situation in that it is unable to get investors to commit to making their investment before the business has signed up some customers or partners but customers and partners do not want to commit their business until the company has financing in place. If the investors have signed a letter of intent to provide funding, the customers might feel more comfortable entering a binding contract and vice versa.

The parties may, however, want certain parts of the letter of intent to be binding, particularly any confidentiality provisions. It is important to make clear which parts of the document are legally binding and which are not. Using the words 'Subject to Contract' or 'nothing in this agreement creates or should be deemed to create legal relations between the parties' will normally show that the document is not intended to be binding.

In some cases, the parties might not originally intend the letter of intent to be legally binding but then start to trade on the basis of the letter without signing a formal agreement. In this case, the document might assume a binding nature if it becomes clear the parties intend the document to be binding and the other elements for forming a binding contract (as outlined above) are met.

Key commercial contracts

A new Internet-based business will often commission someone else to develop the web site on its behalf. In almost all cases, it will also need an Internet service provider which will host the site and provide other services. These services will provide the business with its 'premises' and are therefore it will be very important to make sure the agreements produce the desired result.

Web site development agreement

This agreement will be very important for an Internet company as the work produced will be the key interface between the business and its customers. At a basic level, the site must work properly and must be designed to suit the particular business. It is important to consider how much control the company wants to have over the web site when it is produced. The resulting web page will almost certainly be protected by copyright (see above) and it is likely the copyright will initially be owned by the developer, not the Internet company itself. The Internet company will need to agree an assignment or a licence of the copyright. An assignment would be preferable because the Internet company would be able to modify the design and prevent others from copying the site. If an assignment of the copyright is not obtained, the Internet company would need a licence which should specify whether the company can modify the site and whether the developer can use the same design for its other clients.

If the web site contains original works (literary, including software, music or artistic) created by someone other than the developer or the company, the developer or the material company will need a licence from the owner of the copyright in that material. The development agreement should specify who will be responsible for obtaining the licence and what will happen if it cannot be obtained or is too expensive.

Internet service provider

Successful operation of eCommerce services is dependent on the reliable service provided by the network of the Internet Service Provider or Providers (ISP) selected to provide connectivity, hosting and email services. A company will need to find an ISP which matches the company's requirements. This match may be based on a variety of factors including the ISP's 'acceptable use policy' for connectivity, service level commitments, whether it has an upgrade guarantee for bandwidth to remain competitive with other ISPs. The networks used by the ISP and its telecommunications service providers must be reliable and sufficient for the type and volume of business the company expects to do. In any agreement with an ISP it is important to consider future use of the ISP selected and build flexibility into the agreement to cater for the company as it develops.

Transacting online

Most successful Internet businesses rely on business conducted (that is, contracts formed) online. An Internet company might enter contracts with customers or act as an intermediary to bring two parties together. It is essential, therefore, to ensure that the requirements for forming a binding contract are met for transactions conducted using the Internet.

It is perfectly possible to form a valid contract for many types of transactions using the Internet. However it may be more difficult to prove later that a contract was made, and what its terms are, than would be the case with contracts formed offline. Server logs and other records can be helpful to proving the existence and terms of a contract made electronically.

Where the business involves contracting online (for example online retailing), the business must be careful to ensure that all the relevant terms have been incorporated into the contract. One method of dealing with this is to design the site to make sure customers scroll through a set of terms and then click on 'I agree' at the bottom of the page. For some sites where a high volume of transactions is being processed, this process can make the site unattractive to customers. For fairly straightforward contracts (such as for the sale of a book) the site might be designed in such a way that a customer must click on a link with 'Proceed' on it which has text such as 'By clicking on Proceed, I acknowledge that I have read the applicable terms and conditions'. A link to a page setting out the terms and conditions should be near the 'Proceed' link to allow customers to read them at that stage if they choose.

The draft eCommerce Directive (discussed more fully below) will require the contract formation process to be 'clearly and unequivocally' explained to customers. If the Directive is adopted in its present form, an online contract will become binding when the customer has received an electronic acknowledgement of the customer's acceptance of the offer. This is not required for contracts currently and will not be required for offline contracts when the Directive is introduced. Many Internet companies already follow the Directive as a matter of customer relations policy particularly as many people are still hesitant about transacting online. If customers understand the contract formation process and receive a confirmation of the transaction, they will feel more comfortable transacting online and there is less likely to be a dispute later.

European regulatory framework

The European Commission has targeted eCommerce as its most important priority for the future of business in the European Community. Various eCommerce related Directives are likely to be in place before the end of 2000. These include the eCommerce Directive, Directive on distance marketing of consumer financial services, copyright Directive and Directive relating to eMoney. The overall intention of these Directives is to harmonise member states' regulatory environments so that consumers and businesses can transact safely and securely online.

Where a customer is located in a different country than the business there could be a dispute over which country's laws apply to the contract: those of the customer or those of the company. The eCommerce Directive (due to be adopted during 2000) in its current form will make businesses subject to 'home country control' which means that a service would be regulated by the laws of its country of establishment rather than the customer's country. Exceptions are likely to be made for linguistic or cultural reasons, public policy, security, health and, notably, protection of consumers.

Companies trading over the Internet should include a specific choice of law clause in any online contract, usually the legal system with which the country is most familiar. This is possible where the other party is a business, however if the other party is a consumer, consumer protection legislation in the consumer's country is likely to apply. An Internet company offering goods or services outside its own country must be very careful to seek advice in those countries.

Digital signatures

It is difficult to identify other people who are using the Internet and this creates problems for eCommerce businesses who need to know the identity of the people with whom they are doing business. It is possible to verify the identity of Internet users by using a certification authority. These authorities verify the identity of users on a network by issuing a unique digital certificate to each user which can be used as a method of authentication of the user's electronic signature when used with an Internet communication (such as email). The European Commission has introduced a Directive on Electronic Signatures which aims to make electronic signatures legally recognised throughout Member States and to establish a legal framework for certification authorities and many member states have already introduced legislation on electronic signatures. It is hoped that these measures will facilitate eCommerce by giving an electronic signature the same effect as a written one and helping to establish trust in certification authorities and their procedures.

Distance selling

The Distance Selling Directive contains important restrictions on Internet companies involved in selling goods or services on the Internet and it will be implemented in 2000.

The Distance Selling Directive applies to contacts concluded under an organised scheme for distance sales or service provision where the supplier uses exclusively means of distance communications for the purpose of concluding the contract. For these purposes 'means of distance communications' means any method of communication where the supplier and the consumer are not physically present at the same time (and includes email and the Internet).

Suppliers will be required to provide the following information before the contract is finalised:

- the name of the service provider
- the address (if payment is to be made in advance)
- the main particulars of the goods or services
- the price (including taxes and delivery charges)
- arrangements for payment and delivery and performance of the contract
- that the consumer has a right to withdraw from the contract (see below for more details)
- the cost of using the distance communication (unless it is charged at the basic rate)
- the period for which the offer is valid
- the minimum duration of a supply contract (if any).

The information must be provided in a clear and comprehensible manner. Suppliers of contracts for the supply of food and drink or other regularly supplied goods (for example newspapers) or for accommodation, transport, catering or leisure services on a specific date or for a specific period are not required to give this information (nor to give the withdrawal period described below).

The supplier should also send the consumer a confirmation of key information relating to the contract in writing or in another durable manner. This information should be sent in good time or, at the latest, at the time of delivery. This information should include:

- confirmation of the conditions and procedures for exercising the right of withdrawal
- the geographical address for complaints
- information on after-sales services and guarantees
- the mechanism for cancelling contracts which have a term of one year or more or which are indefinite.

However, this requirement does not apply to one-off contracts fulfilled and invoiced through distance communications (such as information provided over the Internet).

Other important provisions include the following:

- *Right of withdrawal*: Consumers will have an absolute right of withdrawal for seven working days after receipt of the goods. If the contract is to provide services, the period will run from the day of conclusion of the contract or the day on which the written information referred to above is given, if it is given after the services have been supplied. If the supplier has not given the consumer the written information, the period for withdrawal will be three months (although if it is given within the three month period, the seven day period will apply from that date). The consumer will not be required to give a reason for withdrawing and the supplier will only be permitted to charge the direct cost of returning the goods. A consumer will not be permitted to withdraw if:
  - the contract is for the provision of services and performance has begun (with the consumer's agreement) before the end of the seven-day period
  - the price depends on fluctuations of financial markets
  - the goods are: custom-made or have a limited life; audio or video recordings or computer software which were unsealed by the consumer; newspapers, periodicals or magazines; or
  - the services are gaming or lottery services.

  If the contract is cancelled, associated credit agreements must also be cancelled without penalty.

- *Performance*: Unless otherwise agreed, an order must be performed within 30 days of the order being made. If the goods are unavailable, the consumer must be informed and must be able to obtain a refund within 30 days. Local laws will be able to permit a supplier to provide substitute goods or services if the consumer has been informed of this possibility prior to the conclusion of the contract or in the contract. If a consumer rejects the substituted goods or exercises the right of withdrawal in respect of the substitute goods, the cost of return must be met by the supplier and the consumer must be informed of this.

- *Card payment*: Consumers will not be responsible for fraudulent use of a payment card.

- *Prohibition on inertia selling*: Suppliers will be prohibited from sending goods which have not been ordered and making a demand for payment. In such a case, the consumer will not be required to pay for the goods.

- *Restriction on certain means of communication*: Automatic calling machines without human intervention and faxes can only be used by suppliers with the prior consent of the consumer and other means of communication may not be used if the consumer clearly objects.

- *Waiver*: A consumer cannot waive rights or lose protection due to choice of a non-EU governing law if the contract has a 'close connection' with the EU.

Some types of contract are excluded from the Distance Selling Directive including financial services contracts, contracts relating to immovable property (for example land) contracts concluded by automatic vending machines, by telecommunications operators via public payphones or at an auction.

The draft Financial Services Distance Marketing Directive (which will be implemented in June 2002) applies to financial services contracts and contains similar provisions to the Distance Selling Directive however there is no duty of good faith relating to the provision of information and member states may not implement any further levels of protection other than those included in this Directive.

Network service regulation

In some countries it may be necessary to obtain a licence to provide an Internet service. For example, an electronic communication network may require a telecommunications licence in some jurisdictions and some services may be classified as broadcasting requiring a licence.

Liability for content

Liability for own content

A company will be responsible for the content it publishes on its site and must take care that it does not infringe third party trademarks or copyright. Where a licence has been obtained to use third party trademarks or content on a site, the licence agreement will probably contain restrictions on how the material is to be used and these restrictions must be followed or the company will face legal action. In addition, if defamatory material were published on the site by the web operator, it would face legal action.

Some sites contain 'chat rooms' or bulletin boards where visitors record comments onto the site. If the operator of the web site has no control over material posted by users this should be clearly indicated and a disclaimer of liability should be displayed on the site. In addition, the web site operator should review material regularly and delete material where necessary, particularly if a complaint has been received that the material is defamatory.

Some sites feature links through to external sites over which the operator of the referring page has no control. The operator of the referring page must take care that the material on the external page is not confused with material on the original site or that a link may be viewed as 'facilitating' any potential illicit activity taking place on the other site. A company should only include links to external sites which it has reviewed. It should also make it clear that the visitor is moving to an external site and that it is not responsible for the content of external sites to which it provides links. Another point to note on links is that they should be to another web site's home page, unless the operator of the external site has agreed otherwise. As mentioned above, the operator of the external site might claim its trademarks have been infringed if the link refers the user to a page other than the home page.

Liability of an ISP

There has been a great deal of uncertainty over whether ISPs are liable for content published by third parties on a site using the ISP's services. The general position in England is thought to be that ISPs depending on the precise services offered will not be liable for defamation if they took reasonable care to ensure the defamatory material was not published and they took steps to remove the material when they became aware of it. Demon Internet recently settled a defamation action brought against it for statements made about an individual on a newsgroup which was on Demon's servers. The individual asked Demon to remove the statements but the ISP refused.

The draft eCommerce Directive in its current form restricts the liability of ISPs for defamation or infringement of copyright or trademarks in respect of content on sites using their services in the following circumstances:

- *Conduit*: a company is a mere conduit for information (for example a telecoms service provider or an Internet access provider) and it:

  1. did not initiate the transaction
  2. does not select the receiver of the transmission
  3. does not select or modify the content.

▦ *Caching*: information is cached (that is, a copy of information is temporarily stored on a local server to allow faster access) if the ISP:

1. does not modify the information
2. complies with applicable access conditions
3. complies with rules and industry standards on updating the information
4. does not interfere with access technology
5. acts expeditiously to remove or bar access if it knows the original information was removed or access barred or a competent authority has order it to be removed or access to be barred.

▦ *Hosting*: where an ISP stores information provided by a user of its service and:

1. the ISP has no knowledge that the activity is illegal and is not aware of facts or circumstances that indicate illegal activity
2. upon obtaining such knowledge acts expeditiously to remove or disable access to the information. This exclusion does not apply however if the recipient of the service is acting under the authority or control of the ISP.

Practical steps

The draft eCommerce Directive is not yet in force and will require national implementation, therefore these protections cannot yet be relied upon. ISPs should therefore include in their standard terms and conditions a warranty from users of the service that no defamatory material or material that infringes trademarks or copyright will be published on the site and obtain an indemnity from users for any liability incurred as a result of any claim relating to any content. An ISP should also remove all material as soon as it is aware of any potential dispute rather than waiting for the dispute to be resolved.

Data protection

Where an Internet company takes personal details from customers or visitors to a site the person from whom the details are taken is described as a 'data subject'. The data subject should be aware that the recording and use of those details is very likely to be an activity controlled by privacy protection laws. The Data Protection Directive (which has been implemented in most EU member states) controls the use of personal data and will have much relevance to businesses carrying out business on the Internet. The main provisions are summarised below, however as with all directives regard must be had to its practical implementation in each member state. There is also a specific directive in relation to telecoms which is outside the scope of this chapter.

Principles

Personal data (including information that would identify a particular person) should be processed fairly and lawfully. Certain information should be provided to a data subject at the time the data is given including the name of the company collecting the data and the purpose for which the data is being processed. This can be done by an email notice or on an appropriate notice on a web page.

Personal data should be collected for specified, explicit and legitimate purposes and not further processed in a way that is incompatible with those purposes. In some countries it is necessary to make a registration with a regulatory authority to process data for specific purposes.

The personal data collected should be adequate, relevant and not excessive in relation to the purposes for which it is collected and/or further processed. Many web site operators require visitors to register before gaining access. A web site operator should explain why non-essential questions are being asked and whether a response is optional. For example information regarding gender, marital status, income or age is likely to be irrelevant or excessive for a site selling books.

Personal data should be kept in a form which permits identification of data subjects for no longer than is necessary for the purposes for which the data was collected or for which it is further processed. This is difficult in relation to large databases which may contain a vast repository of information the accuracy and timeliness of which may vary. Also, many businesses find it cheaper to retain all digital material indefinitely than to ascertain what should be destroyed because it has served its purpose and is no longer relevant. Strict compliance with this requirement could require systematic email archive destruction.

Use of personal data

The Directive defines 'processing' data very widely including collection, recording, alteration and use. Personal data may only be processed in specific circumstances such as with the 'unambiguous' consent of the data subject. Processing sensitive data (including details on religious or political beliefs or on an individual's health or sex life) would require 'explicit' consent.

Rights of data subjects

Under the Directive a data subject is granted certain specific rights which may impose indirect obligations on companies taking or using data.

Right to notification

A company processing data must provide the data subject with details about the company and the purposes of the processing. The information provided must be sufficient to guarantee fair processing of the data. This could include details of recipients of the data, the existence of the right of access to the data and the right to rectify the data concerning them and whether replies to questions are obligatory or voluntary.

Right of access

An individual must have a right of access to data held by a company including the right to have such data rectified, erased or blocked where it is incomplete, inaccurate or fails to comply with any other provision of the Directive.

Right to object to processing

Individuals have a right to object to the processing of data 'on compelling legitimate grounds', at least where processing is carried out 'in the public interest' or 'in the controller's legitimate interests'. Where such an objection is justified, the company must stop processing the particular data. In addition, individuals have either an absolute right to object to processing for direct marketing purposes or a right to be informed before data is disclosed for direct marketing purposes and to object to its disclosure free of charge.

CHAPTER 9

Valuations and Building the Financial Model

David Russell, PRICEWATERHOUSECOOPERS

Si possis recte, si non, quocumque modo rem (Horace)
(By right means, if you can, but by any means, make money)

Horace seems pretty much to have caught the current mood among eBusiness entrepreneurs as they seek funding for ever more unusual ideas and ambitious schemes. Every day I get an email newsletter from Venture Finance News (www.vfinance.com) which describes the next $100m or so of investment in eBusiness ventures. So how does a value get attached to an eBusiness or to a business plan? What are the valuation methods? And what sort of financial model is required as part of the business plan?

You have an idea or the outline of a business case and perhaps you have a team ready to make it happen. How do you your express your plan and growth prospects in terms of pounds and dollars? And how will investors value your idea and plan? Perhaps some background information and some step by step guidance will help you. This chapter discusses the questions above, and others, under three broad headings:

■ Valuations in the dot.com world: techniques, difficulties with traditional approaches and discussion of some of the alternatives

■ Spreadsheet modelling: it will all be presented in a set of spreadsheets (the financial model itself) and so its important to do this well – some tips are described here

■ Building the financial model: description of the key financial statements and detailed guidance on how to put them together.

Valuations in the dot.com world

There are obviously a range of valuation methodologies that are in vogue
to different degrees and a range of challenges in valuing an eBusiness. In
particular, how do you value a company with no proven track record,
limited revenues and no profits or immediate prospect of profits? How do
you take account of the enormous initial expenditure required, particularly
in marketing and in the acquisition of customers? Why is first mover
advantage so important and will this continue? What influences value?

In this section we discuss some of the principles and techniques applied
in the valuation of eBusiness ventures together with their respective drawbacks. As will quickly become apparent, there are no right answers in this
area. However, the background on the different techniques will, at least,
provide you with:

- some context when constructing the financial model for your business
- some understanding of the perspectives that investors might take.

The section begins with the consideration of traditional valuation methods.

Traditional valuation methods – do they work?

The press today frequently covers the question of valuing Internet businesses and laments the break down of traditional valuation tools and
techniques. However, the investment maxim 'Cash is King' may be
overused but is as valid in the Internet world as in plain old bricks and
mortar. At bottom, a business is worth the present value of its future cash
flows and there are a number of techniques which are variants on this
basic theme. Therefore the cash flow analysis and projection is critical to
any business plan.

The reason that we appear to have departed from this tradition is that for
most Internet businesses significant positive cash flows are in the distant
future and, as a result of this and many other factors, subject to massive
uncertainties. Clearly in the short term, other investment considerations –
profit taking, the herd instinct, sentiment, favourable press coverage (such
as a mention in the Gilder Technology Report) and so on – are to the fore
particularly in the day trading community. Thus Internet and more generally telecoms and technology valuations have been driven ever higher as
investors seek, in effect, to guess the future and, in particular, to forecast
the 'winners' who will dominate a particular market or sector.

But in terms of fundamentals, investors ultimately and in the long run expect to recover cash flows that justify their up front investment. In theory, investors are looking ahead to a more mature eBusiness marketplace in which each sector, whether business to consumer (B2C) or business to business (B2B), has consolidated around a smaller number of major players. Today's plethora of start-ups will have gone through a shake-out period in which some will have been taken over, some prospered and dominated and others gone bankrupt. Clearly, this shake out phase and the more mature marketplace beyond it are still some way off, perhaps a decade or more in some sectors. And so the investment community must make a judgement of likely future success based on a selection of data available now. Since we are considering cash flows in the future, investors are forced to look at a series of leading indicators which, they hope, provide reassurance that the cash flows will be there in the future. Estimating the cash flow for next year for a nascent eBusiness is hard enough: accurately forecasting free cash flow five years hence is near to a hopeless exercise. Instead, subscriber numbers, revenues and visits are thus all indicators of progress towards the scale and domination required to deliver cash flows in future. Consequently, first mover advantage takes on great significance in the minds of an investor.

Let's consider a hypothetical example to illustrate the point. Let's look at a business to consumer market segment worth £10bn in the UK and an eBusiness start-up targeting this segment. Now if the business has started recently but successfully then perhaps it is capturing 10% of the online business in this area and that 1% of the market has already gone online – in other words turnover of £10m per annum and, no doubt, significant losses because of extensive marketing spend and set up costs. But let's now look ten years into the future: the business in question has capitalised on its first mover advantage and built a market segment dominating brand. It now has 10% market share of the segment in question – £1bn turnover in the UK before considering other European prospects. It should also be more than competitive with its physical world competitors because of various Internet related cost advantages. With such a turnover and high margins, this would be a very attractive business and the sales and margin fundamentals in ten years time would justify significant valuations. This is the future that the investment community is attempting to predict.

So, in summary, the traditional approach to valuation (principally discounted cash flow techniques such as the calculation of net present values) still applies, even in the world of eBusiness. However, the uncertainties involved and the probabilities that must be considered, often five to ten years into the future, make it insufficient, on its own, as a valuation tool. A range of proxy methods and predictive tools has arisen in addition to the traditional methods. Not surprisingly, therefore, the best approach to valuation is to take a combination of the traditional discounted cash flow (DCF) together with some of the newer approaches depending on the circumstances of your business.

To understand the DCF method in much more detail, I recommend ploughing through a copy of *Valuation: Measuring and Managing the Value of Companies* by Copeland *et al*.

Some practical approaches

Practical approaches to and techniques for the valuation of an eBusiness include:

- Turnover multiples – valuation based on a standard or agreed multiple of current or forecast revenues
- Metrics-driven valuations such as on a per subscriber, per visitor or similar basis using benchmarks or standard valuations
- Relative valuations: basing your valuation on parameters derived from comparison with similar businesses which have already been established.

We consider below each of these techniques in turn along with some of their shortcomings.

Turnover multiples

Different valuation techniques are more appropriate for some business models than for others. For example, the valuation as a multiple of turnover that eBay will trade on will be significantly greater than that of CDNow or Amazon for very good reason – turnover for eBay represents commission earned from which only operating costs need be deducted. For CDNow, cost of sales must first be taken into account with operating costs then deducted as well. To put this more generally, for most B2C business models, turnover represents the value of goods or product sold. For consumer to consumer (C2C) business models (eBay) and consumer to business (C2B) models such as Priceline, however, turnover represents only the commission or transaction fees taken on the transactions arranged through the site – a tiny percentage of the total value of goods and services.

A step up from analysis on the basis of revenue multiples would therefore be analysis on the basis of gross margin multiples. This is done by estimating an overall gross margin percentage for the business and applying this to the sales achieved or forecast. Even this model is overly simplistic as the operating costs of different business models will vary – digital versus physical distribution, site visitor volumes and other such factors will influence the level of operating costs and thus the free cash flow and valuation.

Let's illustrate with two of the famous names – Amazon and eBay. If we look at revenue multiples in comparison with gross margin multiples (figures based on recent valuations and published results):

Company	Revenue multiple	Gross margin multiple
Amazon	15 to 20	75 to 90
eBay	70 to 90	90 to 110

Clearly, gross margin multiples offer a more reasonable basis for comparing valuations of different business models than revenue multiples do.

However, it is important to note that the metric of importance is the long term gross margin, sustainable in a more mature business. Clearly, during the start-up phase and during early high growth, margins may be compromised because processes are being established, sales returns being managed or economies of scale have not yet been achieved. It is important therefore to forecast this 'steadier state' margin rather than base a valuation on the gross margin achieved in the first few months.

Similar issues arise in determining the appropriate turnover figure to use – current year actual turnover or forecast turnover for future years. Since the valuation multiple (of turnover) reflects predicted future growth, as a general rule the valuation multiple will reduce the longer the business has been in existence.

Table 9.1

Year	Turnover($m)	Valuation multiple	Valuation ($m)
1	2	500	1000
2	20	100	2000
3	100	50	5000
4	300	20	6000

The trend described above (for the valuation multiple to reduce with time) will be partly (but only partly) offset by the fact that as actual turnover growth is delivered, investors can have more confidence about future performance and therefore ascribe a higher overall value to the business.

In short, valuation on the basis of a turnover multiple (or, more sensibly, a gross margin multiple) is an easy to use but simplistic method which can be applied to many different business models (with appropriate adjustment of the multiple used) and will quickly give a ballpark figure valuation.

Metrics driven valuations: user or visitor multiples

In favour of this method is the fact that most sites will have this information. But against it is a whole range of problems: difference in definitions; lack of certified numbers and most importantly no assurance that an increase in visitors is clearly and causally linked to an increase in revenue. For a subscription-based ISP (for example AOL in the US), there is a pretty obvious link – more subscribers or users means more subscription revenues. However, for an eTailer, repeat visitors and first time visitors will convert to buyers at different rates.

Unique user numbers (as provided by MMXI Europe) tackle the problem of definition and, to some extent, reliability but not the more fundamental causal problems with this method. So this method gives you an indication of value only.

Relative valuations

At first sight it may appear that all Internet stocks trade at similarly preposterous valuations. On closer examination, however, the same forces that cause specific stocks to trade at a premium or discount to their sector average can also be seen in the Internet sector, and even in the sub sectors for the different business models. Of course, fashion and rumour among the day trading community can distort these patterns but, in general, there are a number of factors that have a consistent influence on value such as:

- Market leadership or market domination – seizing the space to be number one or two in the marketplace – it worked as a strategy in the physical world for Jack Welch at GE and it applies 100-fold in the eWorld

- Pan European or international reach – outside of the US, individual national markets are smaller scale – cross-border capability opens doors to significantly greater growth

■ Growth – most eBusinesses are growing rapidly but some more than others – the higher the growth potential, the greater the valuation premium.

Thus identifying a similar model in the marketplace and performing a comparative valuation can be a worthwhile exercise. The revenue, gross margin or subscriber valuation multiples of the benchmark business already valued by the market can be adjusted to reflect the particular circumstances of the business under review. Let's consider an example.

We have already seen that Amazon trades on a valuation multiple of up to 20 times revenues. Let us say that your business model is also that of an eTailer. By year 3, you are forecasting revenues of £40m. Your starting point is a multiple of 20 times revenue per Amazon. On the plus side, you are at an earlier stage of development than Amazon and therefore with more growth to factor into the valuation – this implies a higher multiple. On the minus side, you are operating in the UK, a much smaller market and you are second to market and therefore less assured of market domination. Moreover, your market sector is one which lends itself less readily to home delivery (garden equipment, for example, which is more difficult to ship than books due to bulk and chemical content). So a more appropriate multiple of revenues to value your business might be five to ten.

So this is a very useful valuation method but there is a high degree of subjectivity in determining the adjustments relevant to the comparison with the established business.

Summary

What this last example illustrates is that there is as much art to the valuation process as there is science. Fundamentally, a business is, of course, worth whatever a buyer is prepared to pay for it. It is important to understand the different techniques and to be able to apply them to your own business. More important, however, than the valuation method itself and any arguments about it are the activities of preparing a business or business plan for sale and marketing it to potential buyers or investors. And remember that the person valuing the business, venture capitalist, angel investor or otherwise, will consider your valuation and study your financial projections in detail, but they will also spend much of their time pondering the quality and determination of the management team and, related to that, the probability that the forecast cash flows will actually be achieved. The valuation they place on the business will reflect their assessment of these factors.

Spreadsheet modelling: best practice

The spreadsheet-based financial model is going to be a critical input to negotiations about value, projections of financing requirements and estimations of options and shareholdings. All the more important, then, that it is accurate and does not have a vicious bug or error hidden in one of the supporting schedules. Here are a few guidelines to help you avoid those mistakes in vital calculations. This is not a guide to spreadsheet mechanics themselves – these are assumed knowledge and the focus here is more on matters such as how to ensure that the calculations are logically consistent and how to prevent the model from becoming unwieldy and difficult to maintain.

Even for the simplest of financial models it is important to think in terms of the separate stages of model build, namely:

- Specify and design
- Build
- Test.

Key questions to consider during the design phase include:

- What is the most effective layout or structure of the model?

- How will sensitivity analysis be carried out – in other words testing the different valuation and cash flow outputs in different scenarios by varying the key input assumptions?

- What will the key outputs be – all the schedules or just headline financial schedules discussed above such as the cash flow and forecast profit and loss account?

- What assumptions are required to complete the required calculations?

Example output schedules are included at the end of this chapter.

Why specify and design?

It can be very tempting simply to begin with a couple of sheets of calculations. Put together a few calculations and column headings and off we go. After all, spreadsheets are easy to use – what's so difficult?

Well, if you have not thought through the required outputs, the level of detail, the difference between assumptions, inputs and calculations and many other such details, then you expose yourself and the model to a number of risks of which the risk of errors is just one. And let's not forget that this model is one of the first building blocks of a significant business that you plan to grow. One obvious outcome of the casual approach is that unnecessary iterations are introduced into the building process. You are bound to be under time pressure at this stage. Perhaps you are making a range of updates prior to the next meeting with you potential venture capitalist – frequent changes against the clock lead to errors. And this does not help your credibility as a reliable custodian of millions of pounds of venture capital funding.

In addition, the design is likely to become increasingly disorganised making the model difficult to maintain and making sensitivity analysis more and more cumbersome. Equally important, the model is one of the crystallised outputs of your idea and business plan – it will be the subject of review and, no doubt, revision during financing discussions and start-up. Why risk the blow to credibility of needless errors being unearthed at this stage?

The model can be seen as having three key component parts:

- Inputs
- Calculations
- Outputs.

Defining the outputs

The broad outputs will be obvious from the rest of the business plan. It is now important to define the items to be included in output schedules from the financial model and getting the level of detail in these correct.

Contents of output schedules will typically appear in the rows of worksheets. It is important to work out here the level of detail required. For example, will cost of sales be shown as analysed by sub-category or in aggregate; will staff costs appear as a single line or will salary be separated from bonus, and other on-costs, and so on.

The columns of the output sheets will typically represent time – either months or years or perhaps both. Again decisions are required – is a monthly cash flow required? Or is annual sufficient? Or perhaps the model must begin with a monthly cash flow for the first 6 months and then switch to quarterly? And is each column showing the movement for the period or the balance at the end of the period?

Specifying the workings of the model

The core of the financial model will be a set of formulae and calculations which link the inputs provided to the specified outputs. A systematic approach is required. Either within the model or separately, construct calculation reference tables which show how key calculations within the model are derived. The calculation table should include the cell reference, a description of the cell and its purpose, and a description of the calculation.

Constants such as the interest rate or the tax rate should not be hard coded into formulae and calculations. Instead a separate input should be created and calculations should reference this input. This allows maximum flexibility in the model.

When building the calculations in the model, try to keep formulae short and concise – and break long calculations into intermediate formulae.

In specifying calculations be careful when the column specification changes in terms of the time period for example from monthly to quarterly and this may require elements of the formula to change. For example if you have input a monthly accommodation rental, accommodation costs will change from being one times this input to three times this input.

Input requirements

Once the calculations required in the model have been defined, it is possible to determine the input data required. Typically the data used in the model will fall in to one of the following categories:

- Firm or factual figure: a given or agreed quantity typically sourced from some separate and incontrovertible document

- Agreed best estimate: uncertain quantity for which an estimate has been made based on comparable statistics or data

■ Assumption/variable: quantity subject to considerable uncertainty and for which few or no comparable statistics are available – often these will be key to a business plan.

Design structure

Correct layout and design of the spreadsheet model will make it easier to navigate and to update and will reduce the risk of errors. It will also make it easier for users to understand the purpose and operation of the spreadsheet model. The usual layout of a worksheet is as follows:

■ *Documentation area:* this does not include data or calculation information – instead this area will include descriptive information on the name of the worksheet, its purpose, version and date information and an index of the major sections.

■ *Input area:* this section is used to capture data input and assumptions which will be used in formulae and calculations. This can be done by means of data input screens but simple entry into the spreadsheet area is probably sufficient.

■ *Calculation area:* it will often be possible to capture most calculations in the output area. However, for complex calculations, a separate calculation area can be of benefit in showing how particular outputs are arrived at. Calculations should in general proceed from top to bottom.

■ *Output area:* cells in this area should typically contain text or formulae (including simple references to cells in the calculation area). As a general rule, they should not contain direct entry data as this compromises the flexibility and maintainability of the model. This area will be organised in the form of the relevant outputs of the model such as cash flow and profit forecasts.

It is likely that these areas will be spread over multiple linked worksheets. The same principles nevertheless apply. Macros, to the extent required, would typically be held in a separate area of the model. The most common use of a macro is to run a valuation calculation to support, for example, sensitivity analysis and to construct a range of valuation outcomes.

Building the financial model

The financial schedules or the financial model will be the subject of close scrutiny by the potential investor. Fine words and creative ideas count for much in the rest of the plan but at this stage they must be boiled down into a set of numbers. At bottom the reader is keen to establish if and when you are going to make money.

Financial statements come in a standard format and it is best to keep to this for the most part. Lenders and investors will expect to see financial information presented in a particular way and so there is little value in innovation in this area. By all means be innovative in the derivation of the numbers themselves, but for the formats and structures, keep to the traditional.

If you do not have an accountant or finance professional on your prospective management team then it is worth considering some expert advice in this area, at the very least to verify the calculations and assumptions. Most incubators will be able to provide this service along with other support in refining your business plan.

In most circumstances, the key schedules required will be:

- A pro forma profit and loss account
- A pro forma balance sheet
- A statement of forecast cash flows.

Typically these will cover a five-year period and in the early stages of the business (the first year for example) should be monthly or quarterly. Less detail is required for future years.

Each of these statements is described in more detail below and a set of examples is included at the end of this chapter. The examples are based on B2C eTailer but the formats would be similar for different business models.

Profit and loss account

This is a statement of the income and expenditure (or revenue and costs) of the business for a specific period (month, quarter or year). Figures are determined on an accounting basis and are therefore not necessarily the same as cash inflows and outflows. A few examples will illustrate this point.

- *Revenue:* revenue is typically recognised in the profit and loss account at the point of sale – not at the point of receipt of payment.

- *Stock:* if the business buys goods for resale, then these are recognised as a cost in the profit and loss account only at the point of sale. Up to that point, the business will show this stock as an asset with no profit and loss account impact (even though there has been a cash outflow).

- *Fixed assets:* the accounting method for dealing with an asset used over several years (perhaps IT hardware) is to spread the cost over the life of the asset (a technique known as depreciation). A proportion of the cost of the fixed asset is shown as a cost in the profit and loss account over the estimated life of the asset. This is clearly not a cash cost as there is only a single initial cash outflow for the whole cost of the fixed asset.

Balance sheet

This is a statement of the assets and liabilities of the business including accumulated profits and losses at a set point in time, typically at the end of the accounting period (such as the year end). It is not a valuation of the business but rather a summary of the accumulated accounting assets and liabilities.

Cash flow statement

This is a summary of the cash inflows and outflows of the business for a specific period (month, quarter or year). It will include the net cash position in terms of borrowings or cash balances. This is a more important schedule in terms of valuations than the balance sheet as we have already discussed how cash flows form the basis of traditional valuation methods.

For your own purposes, you will almost certainly want to construct a valuation model or models – whether these are included in the financial model shared with others will obviously depend on circumstances. This would include modelling the potential exit strategies and valuations and thus the returns available to management, equity investors and venture capitalists. The valuation model is typically based on the cash flow forecast, at least in part. However, as discussed already, different valuation methods can be used depending on circumstances – thus a valuation based on multiples of turnover would draw its base data from the revenue line in the profit and loss account.

In addition, an important use of the model, definitely for yourself and perhaps to share with investors, is 'what if' or sensitivity analysis. The model should be such that it allows you to vary key assumptions and study the results in terms of cash flow and valuation effects. This will allow you to identify the most important ratios and assumptions (the key sensitivities) and also establish a range of likely outcomes and consider how this would, for example, influence your financing requirements. This sensitivity modelling should include varying key inputs and assumptions such as gross margin achieved, rate of sales growth, average revenue per visitor and such like.

A number of supporting schedules will be required to allow you to arrive at these front-line schedules and these may or may not be in report format. Likely schedules include:

- *Revenue or market model:* assess your present and future market and the share that your business will take.

- *Cost of sales model* (where appropriate): consider the cost of the goods you will sell, the margin that you will achieve and how that will change over time.

- *Operating costs model:* in addition to the direct cost of sales, your business will have sundry other operating costs such as management salaries, accommodation, web hosting and design and so on.

- *Asset model:* as the business starts and grows, you are likely to accumulate assets – the most obvious are fixed assets such as computer equipment and stock of goods sold.

- *Financing requirements:* this may be part of the cash flow statement but clearly the business needs to raise funds either through debt finance or equity investment. This may be over two or more rounds of financing. Equity investment involves the sale of a stake in the ownership of the business (typically a shareholding) to an investor. Debt finance involves the business borrowing money – the lender does not directly take a stake in the ownership of the company.

Revenue or market model

Bottom up

What sort of turnover will your business have? How many visitors will come to the site? And how many will buy while they are there? What will the average buyer spend? These and many other similar questions are what you must address in building your bottom-up revenue model. Factors such as the number of buyers (and thus orders), average order size and so on will also be important in determining the cost profile of the business.

The bottom-up model will clearly differ considerably based on the underlying business model. Thus, for example, a model based around advertising and sponsorship will not need to consider looker–buyer ratios but will need to forecast visitor numbers and average page views per visitor as advertising rates are typically based on per thousand page views.

Also of importance will be the rate at which these key assumptions change with time – the growth rate for customer numbers, increases in the average spend per customer, and so on.

Let's work step by step through an example for a B2C eTailer:

1. Determine the number of visitors to the site by reference either to Web outreach statistics or established sites – for example, iVillage. These are typically expressed as a proportion of the total Web population. Projecting into future years, therefore, you will need both estimates for growth in the Web population and estimates in growth of the Web outreach of your business. The first is reasonably easy to come by (many of the investment banks such as Deutsche Bank and Morgan Stanley Dean Witter publish such statistics). The second will require judgement on your part and, perhaps, reference to experience in the US which Europe still tends to lag by one or two years.

2. Determine the ratio of lookers to buyers. Again some comparable statistics are available for this measure (such as from the US) which will allow you to make a sensible estimate. It may be necessary to distinguish between first time visitors and repeat visitors as they tend to have a different propensity to buy. This might require you to take a more sophisticated approach to Step 1. This estimate is the number of buyers that you have in any set period (and in theory also the number of orders you need to process, and the number of shipments you need to make – assuming one shipment per order and so on).

3. Determine the average purchase per customer – this can be a transaction figure or a per annum figure and represents the amount the customer spends with your business. This will be influenced by the sector in which your business operates – a holiday will typically cost more than a few CDs.

The process for a B2B market site would be similar. Key statistics would be overall transaction volumes in the relevant market sector, average transaction size, and proportion of the overall population of buyers and sellers joining the market. For a business model based around advertising, turnover will depend on the popularity of the site and the number of page views. Therefore the calculations of Web outreach and visitor numbers will still be important. For a commissions-based business model, the potential online trading market size needs to be estimated – again by reference to number of visitors, the number conducting transactions and the average transaction size. Of course turnover in this respect is simply the commission percentage applied to the value of transactions occurring. For example, if Goinggoinggone.com, an auction site, handles transactions between subscribers of $150m in a year and charges an average commission of 1.5% on transactions conducted through the site then Goinggoinggone.com will record turnover of $2.25m for the year (1.5% of $150m).

Again there are a number of sources that allow you to research these sort of details. Mediametrix.com, for example, provides statistics such as unique visitors per month while Red Herring, Yahoo Finance, NOP Research and the usual suspects such as Goldman Sachs and Morgan Stanley Dean Witter provide a wealth of background of market size, online population, comparisons with the US and such like.

Top down

The top-down revenue or market model is an essential check on your bottom-up estimates and calculations and a reality test for your longer term growth aspirations for your business. The technique involves taking a macroeconomic view of the overall market value of the category in question, considering the total value online and reviewing the longer-term projections of your turnover against this total potential market.

Again let's take an example. Consider the market for garden equipment and flowers – total projected market size in the UK of £3bn in five years time. Looking at US experience and making a forward projection, we estimate that 3% of this market will go online by 2005. That gives us a total potential online market size in the UK of £90m in the year 2005. Now if your bottom-up model and growth forecasts have given you turnover of £60m by that year, then you need to question whether a 67% market share is realistic and attainable. Alternatively, you need to take a look at some of your assumptions and forecasts.

The top-down forecast therefore also allows you to make an assessment of your competitive position as the market matures – what sort of share of the market are you targeting, and what sort of share is required to justify the projected valuation of the business?

Accounting presentation

As a final note on revenues, remember that accounting has always offered presentational opportunities and building the revenue or financial model is no exception. Accounting techniques will almost never affect forecast future cash flow, the truest measure of value, but they can distort revenues and, as we know, valuation on the basis of revenue multiple is common. One example of this would be in advertising barter deals in which two businesses exchange advertising space on their respective sites. Each then books additional advertising revenue (and advertising expenditure) despite the fact that no money changes hands. Do not miss an opportunity to show your business in the best light possible – more sophisticated investors will look more closely at fundamentals but, notwithstanding such scrutiny, continued positive press or 'turnover' growth are powerful stimuli, short term, to value growth. Of course, you should stay within the bounds of the regulations and therefore professional accounting advice can be important in this area, particularly with more complex issues.

Cost of sales model

Having determined the revenue from the sale of goods through your web site, you must now consider the cost of those goods. This is distinct from the operating costs of the business such as management salaries, marketing, web site design and so on. To illustrate with the Amazon example again, cost of sales would cover the amount paid by Amazon to publishers or distributors for the books sold to its customers. Operating costs (described in the next section) would cover the salary, infrastructure and marketing costs that make the Amazon empire tick.

The simplest way to arrive at the cost of sales is to determine it as a percentage of the sales which you have already calculated – thus if you achieve a margin of 30% on sales of £1m then your cost of sales is £700,000. You can determine the margin percentage in a number of ways. Perhaps the most obvious is to consider margins achieved in the appropriate sector of the market in the physical world and make appropriate adjustments. In the context of cost of sales, there are few fundamental reasons for big differences in gross margin between the physical and virtual worlds. All the physical world costs of bricks and mortar stores and retail staff fall under operating costs. In fact, the physical world business with its established buying power volumes may, in fact, be able to achieve better margins than the nascent eBusiness. So if you have the relevant information on existing gross margins, then you can apply this to estimate the margin your business can achieve. Consider reviewing financial information on the likes of Yahoo Finance or ordering annual reports for existing businesses. Brokers reports can also be a useful source of financial data. In addition to the factors such as supplier discounts dependent on volumes, you must also consider whether you are going to offer prices that are competitive with the physical world or undercut it (thus reducing margins).

An alternative method would be to build a margin estimate based on discussions with suppliers about the terms that you can achieve with them. This is more akin to the methods of the bottom-up revenue model. For a selection of the goods and services you intend to provide, you would have to work out the likely selling price and the terms on which you can source the goods and services. Cost of sales is determined by the terms of supply.

Of course, under a number of business models – advertising based, commission based – cost of sales is not relevant and this supporting schedule will not be necessary.

Operating costs

It is under this heading that items such as salaries, infrastructure costs and marketing expenses of the business are estimated and recorded. Cost items to consider when building up the estimates in your business plan are as follows:

- *Management salaries:* do not forget to include secretarial support in addition to the salaries that you intend to pay yourselves as the management team. Make sure to include the effects of inflation over the life of your plan, often five years. This applies equally to the other categories of cost which follow.

- *Salary-related costs:* this category covers the various benefits and related costs that accompany salaries. The most common on-costs are employer's national insurance contributions (allow 10% of salaries) and pension and sick pay costs. Also worth considering are bonuses, costs associated with share options and overtime. One further item that can be reflected here or separately are recruitment costs (typically about a fifth of first year salary).

■ *Call centre or call operator staff:* your business may provide a telephone interface for customers – either to make orders and enquiries or to seek help and guidance. This requires a call centre type operation with appropriate staff and equipment. In the early days, a few people and a few phones may be appropriate but in the longer term, something more like a traditional call centre may be required. The costs here can be built up by reference to the number of staff you think will be needed for a particular level of operations. From the number of orders, you can estimate the number of calls (proportion of orders placed by phone as opposed to Internet, number of follow of calls and so on) and then apply an average call handling time. In this way you can estimate the peak number of call centre operatives. As an alternative, you can approach an outsource partner as there are a number of companies that provide call centre services typically on a cost per seat or cost per call basis.

■ *Distribution costs:* again, depending on the business model, you are likely to incur costs in getting your product or service to your customers. This may just be the cost of postage or shipping or may cover more extensive home delivery services. It is not unusual for an eTailer to spend 10% of revenues on distribution.

■ *Warehousing costs:* if you hold stock then you also need somewhere to hold it – warehousing facilities. Your business might rent and staff warehouses or choose to outsource such operations to a partner such as Excel Logistics. Even if you do not hold stock, you may need some sort of warehouse to deal with collation of orders and processing of sales returns.

■ *Marketing costs:* marketing is discussed in detail in another chapter but the cost of your efforts to attract attention and win customers will be captured here. This will include bounty fees (typically a percentage of revenue earned from customers referred), online advertising and real world public relations and advertising. This cost estimate is likely to be more in the nature of an expenditure budget (an amount that you plan to commit to advertising) rather than an item by item costing based on volume of operations and supplier pricing.

■ *Sales returns and stock shrinkage:* if you hold stock, then inevitably some of that stock goes unsold or disappears. If you have purchased stock and cannot shift it to customers, then ultimately that stock becomes a cost to the business. Similarly, if a customer returns goods which you cannot pass back to the supplier or re-use, then again, the cost of those goods becomes a loss for the business. The plan should allow a small percentage for these costs and the amount allowed for will be influenced by the returns policy of your business.

■ *Content costs:* the business may employ a team responsible for generating content (journalist types for example) or may purchase content from a media source. Rates of £1,500 per syndicated article from a well known publication are not unknown.

■ *Web site design and operations:* these costs may have been captured as capital expenditure on fixed assets. In addition, however, you may employ staff or contractors in this area to support ongoing design upgrades and operations more generally. Alternatively, you may have outsourced this to a third party (someone like Hewlett Packard or IBM for example) – in this case you need to estimate the annual cost of this outsourcing arrangement.

■ *Support function costs* (finance, human resources, legal): how will your business keep its financial records and deal with debtors, cash and payroll? As with many of the cost items described, there is a choice to be made between staffing up to handle this internally and finding an appropriate outsource partner who will establish and operate financial systems. In the case of legal costs, provision should be made for the cost of establishing the business, ongoing legal advice on options, contracts and such like and significant legal costs in respect to acquisitions, alliances or flotation. Similar consideration should be given to tax advice and similar provision for cost included in the business plan.

■ *Accommodation and facilities:* will the business be based in office accommodation? If so, include the cost and do not forget to allow for growth. As well as the cost of space, there are a number of related costs such as security, rates, utility costs, insurance, cleaning and maintenance, telecoms and so on. Sometimes it is simpler to use a per employee average (working on the not totally invalid assumption that employees have an equal call on such costs).

■ *Equipment costs:* clearly staff need phones, desks, PCs and so on. Much of this might be captured under the heading of fixed assets (described above) but the cost of lower value items will still accumulate.

■ *Travel and expenses:* the management team will certainly have some travel and accommodation costs to consider whether it is visiting suppliers, customers or partners. But you may have a sales force or business development team to consider as well. If flight and hotel costs are involved, this can mount up to a significant sum.

These are just some of the cost types that may apply to your business. Some may be irrelevant and, more than likely, there will be some more specific ones not captured in this generic list. The same broad approach based on investigation of supplier prices and rational construction of likely volumes and activity levels should serve you well in constructing appropriate cost estimates.

Other profit and loss account costs are not necessarily included under the heading operating costs. Most common among such costs are depreciation (discussed under fixed assets), interest expense and corporation tax.

Asset model

The asset model is used to calculate how the likely assets and liabilities of the model will build up over time. As such it forms the basis of the balance sheet of the business and influences the cash flow statement. The assets and liabilities likely to be accumulated by the business are discussed below.

Fixed assets

The eBusiness will gradually accumulate fixed assets, typically physical equipment or land and buildings held for the long term. Of course, it is typically seen as one of the advantages of the eWorld that investment in fixed assets is so much less than in the physical world. That does not mean that such investments can be avoided. Webvan is spending millions of dollars on a network of distribution centres and Amazon, too, is investing in fixed asset delivery capabilities. Even the fledging eBusiness may invest in desktop equipment and office equipment. And although the hardware underlying the web site itself may initially be leased or rented, in the longer term, the new business may decide it wants to take ownership in this crucial area.

In accounting terms, fixed assets are depreciated over their estimated useful life: depreciation refers to the recognition as a cost in the profit and loss account of a proportion of the total cost of the fixed asset each year over its useful life. The value shown in the balance sheet should be the original cost net of the accumulated charges in the profit and loss account for depreciation.

Of course not all fixed assets are physical assets: other fixed assets include brands, long-term investments in other businesses and intellectual property. These are unlikely to feature in the initial business plan and model.

Debtors (or accounts receivable)

These are sales revenues not yet collected at any point in time. For a business making sales principally by credit card (typically an eTailer, but most B2C businesses will charge the consumer by means of credit cards), debtors will typically amount to one or two days sales as funds will be received from the credit card company in this time. Note, however, that operating costs should include the fee charged by the likes of Access or Visa (1–2% of sales value). However, for an advertising based business, advertising revenues need to be collected from other businesses, either online or real world. Depending on the terms agreed, these customers may have up to 60 days to pay your bills and in the meantime you will be showing a debtor for the outstanding amounts. Similarly with B2B plays, it is likely that there will be a time gap between the recognition of a sale and the collection of the relevant payment. The debtors figure can be estimated by reference to the turnover and the average delay till payment. Thus, if a business has turnover of $12m and typically waits 30 days for payment, average debtors will amount to $1m.

Stocks

As with fixed assets, received wisdom suggests that extensive stockholdings are for real world mugs and not for new eBusiness groundbreakers. Stock is accumulated when the business purchases goods for re-sale from suppliers and holds these goods prior to making sales to customers. Clearly this ties up capital and gives rise to risks that stock will not be sold – the end of season sale in every fashion chain is an illustration of this risk. Dell makes much of its business model under which it holds little or no stock: when an order is made by a customer, Dell places corresponding orders on its suppliers and the PC is rapidly assembled. As a result, Dell holds minimal stock of pre-assembled PCs. This is a valuable aspiration but the speed or reliability of service you wish to offer your customers may dictate that you hold some stock and not rely on the delivery timescales of your supply partners.

In such circumstances, the best way to estimate your stock holding is to consider it as a proportion of your sales turnover. Ask yourself what proportion of your sales (the products offered) you will hold as stock (rather than arrange delivery direct from suppliers) and then how quickly you expect this stock to turnover. Say you have sales of $60m in a year and half of your sales are from stock. You estimate that you hold stock for an average of two months (the gap between purchase from the supplier and sale to an end customer). Your average investment in stock will therefore be $5m ($30m of sales from stock, that is $2.5m per month, and an average of two month's sales held in stock).

Once again, B2B, commission and advertising-based business models are unlikely to hold stock and do not therefore have to worry about this area.

Creditors (or accounts payable)

Creditors are very much the equal and opposite of debtors described above. There will typically be a delay between your business making a purchase, whether for goods for resale or for various operational costs, and making payment for that purchase. The terms will depend on negotiation with your suppliers but 30 days remains common. The longer a period of credit that you can negotiate, the better for your cash flow. Thus, if your purchases from suppliers in a year amount to $36m (goods for resale of $30m and non salary operational costs of $6m), creditors (based on 30 day terms) would amount to $3m.

Other liabilities

Other liabilities that may apply include debt in the form of bonds, loans or a bank overdraft or amounts outstanding under lease agreements. The overdraft (or cash balance) will frequently be the balancing figure in the balance sheet and cash flow statement at the end of a period, that is calculation of all the other assets and liabilities will determine any remaining financing need (provided by an overdraft) or financing surplus, in other words cash in the bank.

Financing schedules

The financing required by the business should be summarised either on the cash flow statement or on a separate financing schedule. Financing requirements will typically be a calculation based on the likely operating losses during the start-up period, together with expenditure on fixed assets and working capital.

For example, if your business is budgeting an operating loss of £6m in the first nine months as well as expenditure on fixed assets of £2m then financing of £8m will be required. However, it may be that £1m of this can be covered through working capital creditors (subject of course to the business having a sound enough footing and prospects that creditors can see their money being paid in due course) leaving a requirement for £7m to be sourced as either debt or equity investment.

This sort of calculation will give the total financing requirement (which will clearly be changing from one month to the next) but it is also important to state the source of financing – management, angel investors, bank lending, venture capital and so on. Alongside this you should also include a draw down or implementation schedule indicating the timing of major financing requirements together with the related expenditures.

It may also be important to detail the ownership of the equity of the business and how that is likely to change over the period of the projections, for example as a result of subsequent rounds of financing.

You may choose to include here an indication of how the various investors are likely to get their money back together, of course, with their handsome profits. You should therefore make sure that the following points stand out in the financial schedules:

- The possible exit routes and their timing
- The projected timetable for the business to become cash flow positive
- The indicative timing for realisation of investments together with illustrative returns.

The most talked about exit route is the Initial Public Offering (IPO) or stock exchange flotation. The other likely route is acquisition which could be by a portal (Freeserve and Babyworld) or a real world business. It is a good idea to illustrate the potential returns available.

Table 9.2 illustrates the thinking of a potential investor. Across the top of the table is a range of values for the new business after two years. In the left-hand column is a range of potential investments. The percentages shown represent the share of the business that the investor would require to realise a return of 50% per annum. Thus, if you sought an investment of £4m and felt confident that your business would be worth £50m in two years time, then you might consider offering 18% of the business to a venture capitalist.

Table 9.2

Invested (£m)	Company Value (£m)					
	10	20	30	50	80	100
2	45	23	15	9	6	5
3	68	34	23	14	8	7
4	90	45	30	18	11	9
5	113	56	38	23	14	11
8	180	90	60	36	23	18
10	225	113	75	45	28	23

Note: All figures are expressed as a percentage.

Conclusions

So you are now equipped to build up some logical and supportable cost and revenue estimates for your business, to grow these over the life of your business plan and to capture this accurately and flexibly in a spreadsheet financial model. In turn, you can use this to model the likely valuations of your business and the different scenarios for future growth and prosperity. You are, in short, well prepared to make your case for funding in the investment community. You may be thinking that, if you can float after nine months, then why does this plan matter? But of course the flotation value will be influenced by the long term prospects of the business and this drives you back to the requirement to work these out and articulate them in a financial model.

Of course, as we discussed above, there is as much art to the valuation process as there is science and a range of softer factors will have a critical influence. The financial model is a critical 'get right' but the quality and determination of the management team, market positioning, operational plans and overall market sentiment are just as important. So you should be marketing yourselves, your business model or technology and your prospects at all times. The financial model is just a powerful tool that helps you do this and demonstrates that you know your market. The business is ultimately worth what a buyer or investor is prepared to pay for it, regardless of valuation methodology.

Example pro forma profit and loss account

	Launch 6 Months	Year 1	Year 2	Year 3	Year 4	Year 5
Revenues						
Product Revenue	–	1,500,000	10,000,000	30,000,000	75,000,000	100,000,000
Shopping links – referral fees	–	200,000	300,000	600,000	800,000	1,200,000
Online Advertising Revenue	0	–	250,000	500,000	1,000,000	1,500,000
	0	1,700,000	10,550,000	31,100,000	76,800,000	102,700,000
Cost of Revenues (Cost of Goods Sold)						
Product Offering	–	1,125,000	7,500,000	21,000,000	52,500,000	70,000,000
Warehousing and eFulfilment	–	225,000	1,300,000	3,300,000	6,750,000	8,000,000
	–	1,350,000	8,800,000	24,300,000	59,250,000	78,000,000
Gross Profit	–	350,000	1,750,000	6,800,000	17,550,000	24,700,000
Gross Profit %		20.6%	16.6%	21.9%	22.9%	24.1%
Product Margin %		25.0%	25.0%	30.0%	30.0%	30.0%
Operating Expenses						
Marketing Costs	–	1,000,000	2,000,000	3,000,000	5,000,000	8,000,000
Customer referrals (other portals)	–	50,000	250,000	350,000	500,000	700,000
Credit Card Fees (2% Revenues)	–	30,000	200,000	600,000	1,500,000	2,000,000
Marketing & Sales .	–	1,080,000	2,450,000	3,950,000	7,000,000	10,700,000
Content staff	50,000	100,000	150,000	200,000	200,000	200,000
Hardware and Systems Integration lease		500,000	750,000			
Technology staff	75,000	200,000	250,000	250,000	300,000	300,000
Hosting	–	50,000	50,000	75,000	100,000	100,000
Product Development	125,000	850,000	1,200,000	525,000	600,000	600,000
Corporate Infrastructure and people	625,000	1,120,000	1,375,000	1,625,000	1,925,000	2,250,000
Stockholding costs	–	50,000	125,000	200,000	275,000	350,000
Customer Service and order taking	–	200,000	600,000	1,600,000	3,000,000	3,500,000
General and Administration	625,000	1,370,000	2,100,000	3,425,000	5,200,000	6,100,000
Selling, General & Administrative Expenses	750,000	3,300,000	5,750,000	7,900,000	12,800,000	17,400,000
EBITDA (Earnings before Interest, Tax, Depreciation and Amortisation)	(750,000)	(2,950,000)	(4,000,000)	(1,100,000)	4,750,000	7,300,000
Cumulative EBITDA	(750,000)	(3,700,000)	(7,700,000)	(8,800,000)	(4,050,000)	3,250,000
Depreciation and Amortization (note)				333,333	1,000,000	1,666,667
Interest Expense	–	–	–	–	–	–
Income Tax (assumed 30%)						975,000
Net Gain (Loss)	(750,000)	(2,950,000)	(4,000,000)	(1,433,333)	3,750,000	4,658,333
Cumulative Gain (Loss)	(750,000)	(3,700,000)	(7,700,000)	(9,133,333)	(5,383,333)	(725,000)

Note: Initial site set up costs are shown as payments deferred to years 2 and 3 (that is, not capitalised). There is, therefore, minimal depreciation in the first two years. Depreciation in later years relates to major capital expenditure on a site upgrade at the end of year 2.

Example pro forma balance sheet

	Launch 6 months	Year 1	Year 2	Year 3	Year 4	Year 5
Assets						
Current Assets						
Cash and Cash Equivalents	250,000	250,000	250,000	250,000	5,605,000	10,975,000
Accounts Receivable (1)	–	35,000	150,000	375,000	825,000	1,150,000
Inventories		500,000	750,000	1,500,000	1,500,000	2,000,000
Other	–	–	–	–	–	–
Total Current Assets	250,000	785,000	1,150,000	2,125,000	7,930,000	14,125,000
Property and Equipment, net	–	–	–	1,666,667	2,666,667	3,000,000
Total Assets	250,000	785,000	1,150,000	3,791,667	10,596,667	17,125,000
Liabilities						
Current Liabilities						
Accounts Payable (2)	30,000	275,000	1,000,000	2,365,000	5,400,000	7,250,000
Accrued Expenses (Payroll taxes)	20,000	25,000	40,000	60,000	80,000	100,000
Bank overdraft	–	–	–	–	–	–
Total Current Liabilities	50,000	300,000	1,040,000	2,425,000	5,480,000	7,350,000
Long Term Loans	–	–	–	–	–	–
Total Long Term Liabilities	–	–	–	–	–	–
Equity						
Initial Equity Investment	350,000	350,000	350,000	350,000	350,000	350,000
Venture capital equity	600,000	3,835,000	7,460,000	10,150,000	10,150,000	10,150,000
Beginning Retained Earnings	–	(750,000)	(3,700,000)	(7,700,000)	(9,133,333)	(5,383,333)
– Net Income	(750,000)	(2,950,000)	(4,000,000)	(1,433,333)	3,750,000	4,658,333
Ending Retained Earnings	(750,000)	(3,700,000)	(7,700,000)	(9,133,333)	(5,383,333)	(725,000)
Total Equity (Deficiency)	200,000	485,000	110,000	1,366,667	5,116,667	9,775,000
Total Liabilities and Stakeholders' Equity	250,000	785,000	1,150,000	3,791,667	10,596,667	17,125,000

Notes:

1. Accounts Receivable applies principally to 'other revenue' as Product Revenue is collected via third party credit card administrators. Standard terms for 'other revenue' is net 30 days – the model uses 45 days to allow for the upward trend in revenue and has not been impacted by seasonality. Two working days of Product revenue have been included in debtors to allow for delays in receiving payment from credit card administrators.

2. Accounts Payable standard terms are assumed to be net 30 days and have not been impacted by seasonality for purposes of this model.

Example Statement of Forecast Cash Flows

	Launch 6 months	Year 1	Year 2	Year 3	Year 4	Year 5
Cash Flows from Operating Activities						
Net Gain (Loss)	(750,000)	(2,950,000)	(4,000,000)	(1,433,333)	3,750,000	4,658,333
Adjustments to reconcile net loss to net cash from operating activities:						
Depreciation and Amortization	–	–	–	333,333	1,000,000	1,666,667
Changes in Operating Assets and Liabilities						
Accounts Receivable	–	(35,000)	(115,000)	(225,000)	(450,000)	(325,000)
Inventories	–	(500,000)	(250,000)	(750,000)	–	(500,000)
Other Current Assets	–	–	–	–	–	–
Accounts Payable	30,000	245,000	725,000	1,365,000	3,035,000	1,850,000
Accrued Expenses	20,000	5,000	15,000	20,000	20,000	20,000
Net Cash Provided by (Used in) Operating Activities	(700,000)	(3,235,000)	(3,625,000)	(690,000)	7,355,000	7,370,000
Cash Flows from Investing Activities						
Purchase of Property and Equipment	–	–	–	(2,000,000)	(2,000,000)	(2,000,000)
Net Cash Provided by (Used in) Investing Activities	–	–	–	(2,000,000)	(2,000,000)	(2,000,000)
Cash Flows from Financing Activities						
Proceeds from (Repayment of)						
Long Term loans	–	–	–	–	–	–
Venture Capital Equity Investment (draw down)	600,000	3,235,000	3,625,000	2,690,000	–	–
Initial Equity Investment	350,000	–	–	–	–	–
Net Cash Provided by (Used in) Financing Activities	950,000	3,235,000	3,625,000	2,690,000	–	–
Increase (Decrease) in Cash and Cash Equivalents	250,000	–	–	–	5,355,000	5,370,000
Cash and Cash Equivalents, Beginning of Period	–	250,000	250,000	250,000	250,000	5,605,000
Cash and Cash Equivalents, End of Period	250,000	250,000	250,000	250,000	5,605,000	10,975,000

CHAPTER 10

Fundraising for Internet Ventures

Rahul Bhandari, ANDERSEN CONSULTING ALLIANCES &
VENTURES GROUP

This chapter discusses how to raise the funding for your Internet venture. First we
sketch out what venture capital is and where you may find it. We then look at what
motivates a venture capitalist (VC) and outline how they evaluate Internet investment opportunities. This leads to a pragmatic and innovative framework which will
increase your chances of getting the funding. Finally, we look at the tactical do's and
don'ts of identifying and meeting venture capitalists, pitching your idea and securing
the funding.

What is venture capital?

Venture capital generally refers to equity investments made for the launch,
early development, or expansion of a business, but it can also be used for
management buyouts and buy-ins (MBO/MBIs). The European venture
capital industry is the driving force behind the Internet revolution. In 1999
anecdotal evidence suggests that the growth and availability of funds has
been dramatic. Europe now has the money and the will to support entrepreneurs – use it!

Put simply venture capital provides money to help you succeed. The
money helps you dramatically enhance the value of your firm with the
investor sharing in the associated upside. Unlike banks who claim a legal
right to returns, Venture or equity investors' returns are dependent on the
successful realization of the business value. Any deal you do with a
venture capitalist (VC) should align your respective interests with theirs.

Of course, if a VC funds your business, you have to be prepared to give
away some of your equity. To do this you must believe that the value of
your remaining share ('cash in pocket') will be worth significantly more
because the venture money can be used to drive up the value of your business in a high growth market.

$$\text{Cash in pocket} = \text{Equity share} \times \text{Value of business}$$

VCs will also help you realise the business value by providing non-monetary assistance. They may help find the right team, introduce you to their portfolio partners and sit on your board providing financial and strategic advice but also acting as a sounding board for ideas. They will have no desire to run your business or hold majority stakes, rather they want to help you succeed. If you succeed, they succeed. If you fail, they fail.

Sources of venture capital

The four most common and practical sources of funding are from yourself, your team, a business angel and a VC.

Funding by yourself and your team

Frankly, if the team isn't investing then I wouldn't either. It is difficult to persuade a VC that you are a good bet if you are not certain enough to put your own money behind it. Financial commitment builds confidence in the venture and the team. If it all starts going horribly wrong, it is nice to know that the team can't walk away without some personal loss. The amount required depends on what you have. If you are a millionaire and you put in €50,000, it is far less commitment than if you re-mortgage your house and put in €25,000. The same goes for the teams and non-executives you have persuaded to join – will they stump up some cash? Do they really believe the plan enough to invest?

Business angels

These people tend to invest between £10,000 and £100,000 in start-up and other early stage financing. They can be your non-executives, family and friends, or high net worth individuals. This sized stake is unprofitable for VCs who would have to pay for due diligence and monitor the performance of your business for very little absolute cash return.

If you take family's and friends' money, just imagine the Christmas dinner when you have lost it all. Make sure everyone is happy with the risks involved and can afford to lose the money. Also, bear in mind that if your family want to be active hands on investors, they may not be the best people for the job. Money does not make successful businesses, people do. The best people to build your firm may not be the people with the money or your family.

There are many different types of angels; look for the angels that have been successful entrepreneurs and can add streetwise advice as well as money. Avoid taking money from many people that will seek to undertake in-depth due diligence, unless they are qualified to advise. You do not have time for this. Equally, a £10,000 investment does not secure a board seat paid at £20,000. This is not the way to select your non-executive directors and will not impress a venture capitalist.

If you don't know anyone who will invest a small amount of seed money, you can approach an investment club or matchmaking service such as Venturesite.co.uk, and matchco.com. Many of these high net worth individuals place their money with firms like Garage.com or e-Start.com who will match your idea with the appropriate investor.

Incubators

At the time of writing there are 170 incubators in London alone. A few European incubators such as Antfactory.com, Gorilla park.com and New Media spark are emerging as the likely front runners in this highly competitive arena. Most incubators will provide one or more of the following:

- Seed finance
- Office space and facilities
- Interim management
- Recruitment
- Legal and accounting services
- Marketing and PR expertise
- Access to a large network of contacts.

Perhaps the single greatest benefit of incubators is the opportunity to share in a learning environment with other people like you, doing things like you. Pick your incubator wisely, check out their financial backing and chat to their incubatees. With so many proliferating across Europe, it is not difficult to imagine an impending shake out.

Venture capitalists (VCs)

The majority of venture capital firms target companies looking for investments of over €500,000 with the average deal size over €3m, although half of companies funded every year receive less than €1m. Most Internet businesses are funded by VCs. VCs are acutely interested the high growth Internet industry and those market segments that promise the highest returns. VCs have a wide range of investment preferences and these will affect the sources you target. These preferences include the amount of capital you require, your industry sector and location, and your company's investment stage. Investment stages range from seed, start-up, early stage, and expansion to MBI, MBO and rescue/turnaround situations.

How venture capital works

VCs provide equity capital for high-risk business opportunities. They hope to acquire extraordinary returns on their investments, primarily through the appreciation of the underlying value of their equity (that is, their stake in an entrepreneur's business). If you want to use venture money, then you will have to prove high growth potential. The recent focus of venture money in the technology industries reflects the fact that high growth potential is obviously greater in a high growth market.

VCs raise money in many different ways. The most common is from a set of limited partners such as pension funds, insurance companies and major companies. They will put all of this money together, call it a fund and invest the money on their behalf, seeking returns of over 40%, with individual Internet investments doubling every year. Investors in the fund, the 'limited partners', will receive up to 80% of the economic benefit while the general partners, the VCs themselves, share the remaining 20%. In addition the VC will take a management fee of 1–3% of the fund.

To achieve these incomes the general partners have to limit the number of failures in their investment portfolio. We can explain this using the '5,000, 30, 10 and 1' rule. Of the 5,000 business plans reviewed, 30 are evaluated more closely and perhaps ten are invested in of which one becomes a successful Initial Public Offering (IPO). The others may be acquired, the management may buy out the VC or they may fail. While VCs recognise that some investments may become 'dogs', they never invest in a bad deal and always seek the 'pearls'. The key to success in this industry is generating a quality deal flow and identifying the most successful investment opportunities within it.

Most venture capital firms further manage their risk by sharing it around, co-investing with other firms. Usually there is a 'lead' investor and several 'followers' not only helping with risk management but also portfolio diversification, allowing them to invest in more deals. This syndication of the investments also helps the entrepreneur by speeding up future fundraising rounds providing additional credibility to the venture being funded, as well as enabling additional support, guidance and leverage where some of the investors are 'hands on investors'.

How VCs evaluate investment opportunities

VCs evaluate investment opportunities in many different ways. Some have formal evaluation processes in place while others are very informal. No matter how formal or informal, all VCs are short of time. If you get some use it wisely. Your challenge is to articulate the opportunity in an elevator pitch:

Illustrative OneSwoop.com elevator pitch

One Swoop.com is a much more convenient way for customers to buy cars up to 40% cheaper than their local dealer. This is achieved as the high value, high margin products can be bought through the Internet, finding the most competitive European dealer. Customers can now do what used to take a three-day round trip to Europe in 30 minutes from the comfort of their own homes.

This European business has a clear revenue model based on high value, high margin products. If the business takes 2% of all cars bought it would be the largest IPO in the history of the Internet. The founding team have unbeatable experience and in-depth knowledge of this market opportunity having worked in the industry most of their lives and spent many years lobbying the European Commission. The team have partnered with Andersen Consulting, the world's leading eCommerce consulting firm to deliver it to the market and have relationship with over 6000 European car dealers.

Sold – if I had the chance, OneSwoop.com would have my money.

Nearly all VCs focus on evaluating five core factors which determine the strength of the venture and the ability of the management team to exploit it. These are: the quality of the management team, the business model, technological, market and financial factors.

Quality of the management team

A VC will determine the strengths and weaknesses of the management team, whether additional management is needed, whether effective working relations can be established, and whether the commercial objectives and expectations of the entrepreneur and the VCs match. The strength of the team is the greatest factor a VC will consider. Remember that ideas are worthless, it is the ability to deliver them that is valuable. If you don't have a good enough team or can't persuade the best people to join you, then you are unlikely to be able to persuade VCs, and industry partners to join you. The team must present superbly and have a depth of knowledge that can reveal new thinking at every meeting. Equally, the team must demonstrate acceleration. If you are waiting for the VC money before you do anything else you are desperate. Remember that the person across the table needs to want to work with you – be insightful!

The business model

The business model needs to be ahead of the wave. Business-to-consumer (B2C) is rapidly moving out of vogue, business-to-business (B2B), wireless and technology infrastructure plays are in. The VC market operates ahead of the public markets. If the public markets are turning away from B2C markets, then VCs almost certainly will have done so.

Venture capitalists typically look for a venture that has the potential to quickly gain a significant share of a significant market. If you have a venture that is first in its category, providing a solution to a clearly identified need in the market which you can quickly dominate you stand a great chance of being funded. For Gorilla Park, a developing and well backed European incubator, ventures must have the potential to be a number one pan-European business within its category, and could achieve €100–200m IPO within 18 months.

VCs are more interested in the ideas that create new value rather than carve out value from old markets. Amazon created new value in the book market by enabling access to many more books than those available in the traditional market. Letsbuyit.com aggregates demand, something that never happened in the old world. Traditional retail 'catalogue' web sites that sell what the stores have always sold, but are now selling online carve out a little more market share, they do not create new value. If your business carves out value, try creating it.

Your revenue model must be very clear. Where will it come from and in what degrees? What are the margins in the industry, product mixes, returns...? I have seen so many business models relying on eight types of revenue, the greatest being advertising revenue. Advertising revenue as a major source of revenue is generally unrealistic for all but the sites with the largest and most frequent eyeballs. If you have eight revenue sources is it feasible that you can manage the complexity of this type of model in early scalable days? Can you clearly point to clear sources of significant revenue? Are there other businesses proving this revenue model? Do you have letters of intent from buyers who will pay those margins?

Your model must be structured to give VCs a reason to believe that you can achieve the revenue. There are a number of considerations:

- Do you have strategic assets to help your business to succeed? Do you have any strategic relationships? If you can, go to the VC with a systems integrator in place, your content deal, letters of intent from suppliers and buyers or one of the VC's portfolio firms. Without a doubt, major established bricks and mortar firms have enormous assets that can squash entrepreneurial start-ups. Internet retailing accounts for 1% of retail sales. The buying scale of a major retailer with 30% share of the 99% of retail sales is very, very powerful. Can you do deals with these firms to share their assets, while maintaining the freedom to move fast? UK-based ISP/Portal Freeserve took 30% of the UK ISP market within six months by distributing discs through bricks and mortar stores, not disintermediating them. The average cost of Freeserve acquiring its customers was approximately 100th of Amazon's initial customer acquisition costs.

- Can you stop your competitors replicating your model/assets? You won't be the only one on the market, you may not even be the first one. It is a fact of life that if you do well people will flatter you and flatten you by copying your plans. If you have an asset to help your business, is it exclusive? I see many plans that claim a point of difference dependent on easily available technology, content or other features.

- Is your model replicable across geography? Lastminute.com is one of a few concepts that got in early enough to set up a complex supply models with 1,200 suppliers, prove the concept in one country and then still be able to roll it out to other countries with minimal competition. These days are gone. If you have a complex model you may find it difficult to get money from VCs who want to invest in European businesses.

■ How can you minimise burn rate risk? Burn rate is the rate that you will spend the cash given to you. In many Internet investments it is fast. If you are ramping up a massive team you will have a significant burn rate, and consequently a significant risk. Try to minimise this by leasing rather than buying, avoid owning inventory where possible or secure a major client who will offset some of the cash requirement.

■ Is your business model attractive and realistic? Are you promising something interesting? Can you deliver this business case? What is the looker–buyer ratio versus your potential competitors? Is that level of growth realistic versus other Internet businesses? What are the most sensitive numbers? What is the best case, likely case and worse case scenario? You must deliver what you promise. There is a fine line between pitching high business cases to maximise value and minimise equity given and demonstrating an unrealistic and uncommercial brain.

Technological factors

These include systems development, proprietary aspects of the technology such as patents, and the ability to develop and implement the technical solution required to realise the business model. The VC may test for an understanding of the technical architecture, the ability to scale customer volumes and transitions, and the time taken to implement it. What components or software packages are going to be bought, or built from scratch. If your venture is a technical one, you need to explain the benefits in simple terms. The VC will ask an expert to check the feasibility and replicability later in the process. The first meeting will assume you can do it, and try to understand the attractiveness of the benefits. If you are investing significant money in research and development, VCs will only bear this risk if the upside is high. Often they will look for technology platforms, not products. Platforms have a greater upside as they spawn many products.

Market factors

These include the size and growth of the market, and the extent to which it is going online and is competitively intense. If there are clear competitors, the VC will want to know how you differ and how attractive these differences are to customers. If there are no competitors, they will try to asses why not – is it because it is a bad idea? Is the market large enough to yield a significant return on the investment? The VC will look for in-depth experience or knowledge within the market. Is it a cuddly cosy market where you will have problems realising supply contracts? Who are the key suppliers, what are the margins, what is the product mix? These factors are discussed further in the chapter on attractive markets.

Financial factors

These will determine the amount of capital need to achieve a sustainable market position, the initial amount of capital required by the venture and potential sources of capital required by the venture over its growth period. The VC will expect you to know exactly what you will spend the money on and when – hardly unreasonable! In addition, the VC will identify the potential exit routes where they could realise the returns on their investment. The most common are trade sales by a similar US business, a European business expanding across geographies, or an old world local laggard waking up. Some businesses will make it to IPO, which will put them in a position to do the mopping up of competitors across Europe.

Although all these factors must be addressed in detail within your business plan they must be addressed in the executive summary. The executive summary is the most important part of your business plan because it is the only thing most people will see. Think of it like a resumé (CV) which gets you invited for a job interview but doesn't get you a job. Sell your team's credentials and what can you do for the VC. The summary should tell the potential investor five things – the opportunity, the management team, your secret sauce, how you plan to make money and how much and what do you need the funding for. The summary should be as short as one or two pages like the CV. Any presentation in an hour's meeting should be no longer than ten slides. Mark Bernstein, CEO of Gameplay.com and serial entrepreneur presented his latest idea to investors on one slide – impressive and successful.

It is an inextricable fact that most VCs find most investment opportunities through people they know and respect. When you use lawyers, accountants who specialise in Internet ventures, systems integrators or visit networking events, ask for introductions to favoured venture capitalists. You are more likely to get the meeting. Attached is a sample one page executive summary form that effectively addresses many of these issues. There is another executive summary with a different style in the business plan chapter. Further examples can be found at bplans.com.

(Company Name)

(Contact Name)

(Address:)

Phone: Fax:

Email: Web Address: (if appropriate)

Management:
CEO
Sales/Mktg.
Product Development
CTO
CFO
etc…

Industry: i.e. Internet software

Number of employees: #

Bank:

Future auditor:

Law firm(s):

Amount of financing sought:
i.e. 2M euros

Current investors: (£amt invested)
Any venture capitalists, private investors, investment banks, or personal funds.

Use of funds: i.e. product development, marketing/sales, distribution, etc.…

Business Description: Briefly describe the general nature of your company. From this section the investor must be convinced of the uniqueness of the business and gain a clear idea of the market in which the company will operate.

Company Background: Provide a short summary of your company background.

Management: List senior management and prior experience.

Products/Services: Convey to the investor that the company and product truly fill an unmet need in the marketplace. The characteristics that set the product and company apart from the competition need to be identified (competitive advantage).

Technologies/Special Know-how: In this section, highlight whatever aspects of your product that may be protected by current IP or patent law. Provide evidence of how your offerings are different and will be able to develop a barrier to entry for potential competitors

Markets: Provide a clear description of your target market, and any market segments that may exist within that market. Include potential market size and growth rate. Also, mention your revenue model in this section.

Distribution Channels: Indicate which channels will be used to deliver your products/service to your target markets (i.e. website, direct salesforce, VARs, channel partners, and so on…).

Competition: List any current or potential direct and indirect competition. Briefly describe the competitive outlook and dynamics of the relevant market in which you will operate.

Financial Projections (Unaudited):

	1999	2000	2001	2002	2003
Revenue:					
EBIT:					

(currency in thousands)

Source: Mid-Atlantic Venture Association

Framework to improve chances of getting funded

The checklist below states the questions you have to answer 'yes' to before you can seriously expect Venture funding. They are listed in the likely order that you develop them.

Checklist	Yes	No
1. Can you define a business (revenue) model with the prospect of a venture capital-type outcome? (This means the market is big enough, available, and you have a sustainable advantage.)		
2. Do you have an executive summary you can send out that stands on its own as a compelling description of the business?		
3. Do you have a compelling stand-up presentation for investors?		
4. Can you defend your cost and revenue projections?		
5. Can you effectively demonstrate your business to show its customer appeal and revenue-producing capability? (demo, prototype)		
6. Can you validate the business model by believably pointing to actual partners and customers, letters of intent or research indicating potential?		
7. Can you build the management and technical team?		
8. Can you explain specifically what you are going to accomplish with the money raised? (milestones)		
9. Do you have an operating plan (covering development, launch, marketing, sales, and business operations) that makes one believe you can execute the business?		
10. Can you believably show you can launch the business with revenue-producing customers in a reasonably short period?		

After having assessed your readiness to secure funding using the checklist above I recommend you check your idea against the following five-step pragmatic framework of simple yet powerful formulae. Keep this framework in mind where preparing to pitch the idea to the VC. VCs will look for 'comfort factors' in your business plan. These comfort factors will be any particular element of these equations that give a good reason to believe that you can achieve the business plan.

Step 1:
Unique value proposition = (Idea with a unique Role in Value Chain) × (Targeted Customers) × (Financially Motivated Alliances)

A unique value proposition is created by focusing on three components. These are: an idea that has a unique role in the value chain, the number and quality of people in the target audience and the number and quality of the financially motivated alliances. Let's understand each of these components.

The primary component that makes up a unique value proposition is the role that your venture plays in the value chain of the industry or market you plan to serve. To accomplish this, you must understand the value chain; that is, how value is created in your industry and who the key players are. Mapping the value chain will help you better understand and communicate to potential investors how exactly your venture will add value to this chain by making things faster, cheaper and better. It will also help you evaluate the value of faster, cheaper and better to the customer and to your business. For example, does your new technology cut down paper-work by a factor of two or ten? What is the implication of this reduction in work to the customer? How does the target audience value that time? How much of that value can they share with you and how profitable does that make your business?

An attractive value proposition will only be profitable if the target audience buys it. This will increase with the size and growth of the audience and the extent to which they are online. This was covered further in Chapter 3 (Finding an Attractive Market).

The last component is to create financially motivated alliances. All strategic partners', investors' and employees' interests should be very clearly aligned with your own. If an alliance increases the probability of enhancing the value chain or bringing targeted customers to the venture, you should seek them out. Even if they fail, they may ease your progress to market, providing the 'comfort factor'. Partners may have a herd mentality; if you get one you are more likely to get another. Try to quantify the market value of the inputs into your venture and the benefits that the alliances are creating for you wherever possible. If you value your business at €10m and a partner invests €2m of services they could reasonably expect 20% of your firm. You must believe that you get more than a 20% increase in the value of your proposition to do this deal.

Step 2:
eSpeed = (small business velocity) × (well-rounded executive team)

Internet ventures are like books, everyone has one in them. Almost certainly 10–1,000 other people are progressing the same idea across Europe. eSpeed is your best and potentially only defence. The underlying thinking should be: think big, start small and scale very, very fast. eSpeed is driven by the management team and their ability to move those around them. That is why VCs invest so readily in serial entrepreneurs. If you can not demonstrate speed, go home. If you are an existing business, structure your business so you can move with freedom from your mature parent.

Step 3:
Dynamic Business Model = (Flexible business model + Revenue + Customer centricity) × Scalability

The four components of Dynamic business models are very attractive to VCs, as they drive the potential of the business and minimise the risk. The first component is flexibility. If the market dynamics rapidly change, how quickly can the business model be adopted to sustain leadership? Everyone is an Internet novice, so the learning curve is dramatic. If you can not respond to this curve you will lose your leadership. The second essential component is revenue. Clearly identify your five-year revenue streams in tangible segments, for example subscriptions, online purchases, advertisement revenue and so on, and ensure that you can deliver them. The third component is customer focus. You must understand and focus on identifiable needs of your customer segment and add value in a tangible and measurable manner. The more customers you have, the more valuable your venture becomes. And finally you must be able to scale-up rapidly while offering superb customer service.

Step 4:
Sustained Traffic = (Content + Community) × (Ad Spend) × (Channels)

In Internet-based business models generating and sustaining traffic is of critical importance. VCs want to know how you intend to cost effectively acquire and retain your customers. You can focus on three key areas to achieve sustained traffic. This includes providing relevant and current content focused on your customer segment, building a sense of community and interaction between your customers through providing email services, chat groups, bulletin boards, newsletters. Obviously the more you spend on advertising the more customers you will acquire, and the more channels you use, the more the customer will access your products and service.

Step 5:
High market valuations = Steps 1 to 4 + Smart Money + Barriers + Comparable Companies

Sell value, not high market valuations. Selling the latter implies that you
are interested in cashing out as fast as possible, rather than building a
sustainable business. High multiples and exit strategies will come from
healthy businesses. However, it is a fact of life that investors are more
willing to invest in high growth areas, and high growth generally leads to
high market valuations. In any discussion with a VC, it must be clear that
there are some likely exit strategies to realise this value.

VCs understand that all their investments will not have dramatic
growth, but none of them invest in a deal that they don't expect to be
successful. The best will help you become successful by adding more than
money. They will leverage their network, enable alliances, offer advice
and find the best people. This is smart money.

If you can develop barriers to entry then the value is protected. The
more specific you can be about the strategies to erect barriers to entry the
stronger your venture proposition looks for investment.

Finally discuss how comparable companies are performing in the market.
VCs will have their view; if you don't have one, don't expect any money.

Going for it

OK, now that you understand the motivations of VCs, investment evaluation criteria and how best to focus on and articulate the potential opportunity that your venture seeks to capture, the next step is to go for it. Here
are some tips:

- *Potential suitors:* It is very important for you to identify those VC that
  invest in your type of business, industry and stage of the venture. Create
  a short list of VCs that you would approach. To develop this shortlist,
  find out which businesses have launched where there could be some
  synergy with yours and find out who invested in them. Go to
  networking events to ask for advice from entrepreneurs, visit the major
  VC web sites and your country's equivalent of the British Venture
  Capital Association (BVCA). They will detail a list of VCs and their
  portfolio and investment criteria. Here is a useful check list that you
  could use to judge the match. Specifically, does the VC:

  - Invest in your sector (for example B2C, B2B, technology infrastruc-
    ture, wireless)?

  - Invest in your stage (for example, seed, first round...)?

▪ Invest in your industry (for example aerospace, retail)?

▪ Offer smart money?

▪ Bring major strategic assets to the table? Can they bring customers, branded content, match-make investments with great synergies... ?

▪ Provide value added services: do they help recruit, bring together a network, provide facilities, syndicate investments where necessary?

▪ Seem like the sort of people you want to work with?

Now figure out a way of meeting these VCs. Go to events where you are likely to meet them such as the entrepreneurial forums (for example First Tuesday, Upstart Europe, The Chemistry) or submit your business plan online (Matchco.co.uk, Garage.com, e-start.com). Make a list of the people you know within your network who may know VCs and will make introductions. Perhaps your lawyers, accountants and consultants who work in the area of high-technology and ventures are best suited to quickly get you an introduction.

If all else fails call them up. While this is possible, most people who call VCs will not be successful (the 5,000–1 rule), so you will be talking to a street-smart secretary who will expect to see an executive summary of your business plan prior to initiating the meeting.

▪ *The non-disclosure agreement (NDA):* Don't expect all VCs to sign NDAs. They will see the same idea, again and again, rejecting it because the team is no good. While many will sign agreements not to tell anyone about your idea, they will not sign those that restrict their ability to see and work with others who have a similar concept. This is an unreasonable expectation. Your defence is speed, not an NDA.

▪ *The pitch:* If the VC finds your team and idea appealing they will ask you to come in and pitch for an hour. All the hard work and preparation can now pay off. Take a presentation, but be prepared to speak without it. If you have an hour – you should take no more than 10 slides. Remember, it is you that is being evaluated – your vision, passion and ability to deliver your idea. Start with a high-level overview and be prepared to 'deep dive' on questions that the VC will invariably ask about competition, execution and so on. It helps you relate your venture idea to other ventures that the VC may have funded (from the research you did while compiling the list of VCs to approach). Although you want to project and convey a picture of confidence you also want to make sure you are not arrogant. If you don't know answers to questions the VC asks then admit it and promise that you'll look into it. If you bluff it, or are seen to be dishonest in any way possible then you will fail. Its also important that you identify the risks inherent in the venture and how you plan to address them. You want to show a mature and balanced approach to the venture, in a passionate and committed way. The first meeting is a getting to know each other meeting, although most will fall at this hurdle.

- *The interview:* Keep in mind that this is also your chance to interview the VC. So be prepared to ask them questions about what value they provide in their investments in addition to common money. Ask them if you could speak with the executives of a couple of ventures that they have funded. This will provide you with another perspective on how that VC firm works, and test their level of interest. Its critical that you have a sense of trust, confidence and chemistry with your VC. So treat it like getting into a long-term relationship which must be founded on mutual trust and confidence.

- *Subsequent meetings:* If the VC likes you, your team and your idea, they will carry out some preliminary investigations. They may call people who know you, and briefly check out the idea with industry gurus within their portfolio companies. After a few hours' discussion about the idea, they may invite you back for subsequent meetings involving other partners of the firm for a more in-depth analysis. If all goes well, there will be a discussion on outline terms. The term sheet includes the value of the company, how much the VCs are investing, and for what percentage ownership, as well as additional rights such as board seats, preferences, bankruptcy claims, and so on.

If this is agreed in principle the VC will progress due diligence. They will ask for references or call others within their network to conduct a legal, market and personal due diligence on you and your plans. This could be a six week process outsourced to a separate consultancy, or it could be 12 hours with a VC networked partner who checks out the idea. Bear in mind that many fail to get funding post due diligence and the terms can change to reflect the incremental risks that the VC has discovered. If you business case is found to be flawed or over optimistic, then at best the value of your business will be brought down, at worst the VC will not invest in you. Finally, the deal will be completed and the shareholder agreement drawn up. You get the opportunity to draw down the funds when required after this point.

■ The valuation process: A venture capitalist looking to seed your immature business will value your plan based on the many other deals he has done with similar potential. He will bear in mind the strength of your idea, team and financial rewards, but also your ability to go elsewhere. Go to more than one VC, or you will leave yourself in the position where you have to accept the terms sheet, because you have no fast alternative. See Chapter 9 for a more detailed discussion on valuation methodologies, but at the seed stage prepare to haggle based on comparables and walk away from unacceptable deals.

You should plan to raise as much money as possible, while giving away as little of your firm as possible. Equally VCs will try to invest what you need to make this business successful, but maximise their equity stake.

The percentage of your firm that a VC will take depends on the amount of money they are putting in as a percentage of the value of your firm. For example if your firm is valued at €10m, and an investor places €1m they will expect 10% of the firm. If they are an incubator offering value added services such as a physical location they will also attach a value to this and take it in further equity. Clearly, the uncertain elements are the value of your firm and the value of services invested in your firm.

Equity share (%) = (money and services invested/value of firm) × 100

Entrepreneurs will need to decide how much money to ask for. The cost of money is greater earlier in the development of the business (for example at the seed phase) because the risk is significantly higher. This reflects the lack of a trading record and uncertainty about your ability to set the business up, form supplier relationships and win buyers. There are also a set of risks that you can not control, such as the increase in competitive intensity or collapse in stock market prices. In the seed phase, most ask for enough money to get to launch but no more. The principle used is to define the money required over time and the key moments of risk. Always request enough money to get you to the point where the risk has significantly decreased (and hence the cost of equity), but no more.

Plan fundraising rounds to kick in at the key moments when risk decreases dramatically and the funding requirement increases dramatically. These are likely to be:

- *Seed funding:* You need some money to start, but the risks are very high. If you can develop 'comfort factors' (for example single large buyer, supplier letters of intent) before approaching VCs you can minimise the cost of equity and increase the chances of funding. You raise €1m.

- *1st round funding:* The business is set up in a single country. You have proven that you can form the relationships to set the business up and decrease the risk, but need much more money to market your business. As the competitive environment is still empty, you raise €10m to seize the market.

- *2nd round funding:* You have traded your business in a single country for 6 months and the response has been dramatic, proving that your concept has fantastic customer appeal. What is more exciting is that the European competitive environment is still immature. You raise €50m for an expansion into major European countries and to upgrade your scalable technology platform to enable personalisation.

- *Other rounds:* You are now planning an IPO, but need funding to get you there. The competition is increasing so you need money to continue your European expansion and customer recruitment and retention. An IPO will provide you with the tradable stock and cash

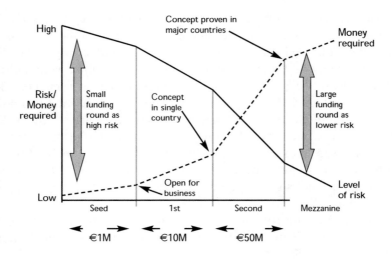

Figure 10.1　Illustrative fundraising strategy

to establish your business. The risk to investors is much lower as the concept is proven and an exit route is imminent.

As a final thought, VCs want you to succeed as it is the only way they can be successful. In my experience they are a very honest bunch of people who are interested in enabling you to maximise your firm. Of course, they negotiate very, very hard and are exceptionally experienced at cutting deals. I would strongly encourage you to employ professional advice to help you understand financing options and negotiate with VCs.

At the end of the day, VCs are placing a bet on you – don't let them or yourself down. Good luck.

CHAPTER 11

Leadership Capital Solutions for eSpace

Joyce Renney and Metin Mitchell
KORN/FERRY INTERNATIONAL

The search industry – considered formerly to be a specialist, niche business – is now one of the main players in the Internet-enabled world, both as professional service consultancies and – through one or two trailblazers – as players in their own right. Peter Drucker explains, 'The fastest growing eCommerce in the United States is where there was no 'commerce' until now – in jobs for professionals and managers... about 2.5m managerial and professional people have their resumes on the Internet and solicit job offers over it – a completely new labour market.'

The once mystical business of headhunting is now seen, and used, as a strategic corporate weapon. For far-sighted bricks and mortar companies it always has been, but why is the whole world now obsessed with hiring people? As *Information Week Online* puts it, 'People are the crown jewels. People can't be tallied on a ledger sheet, but it's the prime factor driving the new economy. More than ever in history, huge value is being leveraged from smart ideas – and the winning technology and business models they create. So the people who can deliver them are becoming invaluable, and methods of employing and managing them are being transformed.'

What this chapter seeks to do is give some orientation points in recruiting and retention in an environment where all the rules are different, still showing the links between professional experience, personality factors and corporate success. Bricks and mortar companies have focused on leadership, management, accountability and beating the competition. We have a new lexicon today – we talk of team leadership, empowerment, learning and even partnering the competition.

Our focus here is recruiting to help build a business, and we'll start from the bottom up; the founder, the dot.com Chief Executive Officer (CEO) – who may or may not be the same person – and the rest of the team. In terms of the leadership team, we are seeing a whole new ball game, from the Chief Information Officer (CIO) stepping up to become CEO, to the appointment – so far, mostly in the US – of Chief Commerce Officers (CCO) to work closely with the CEO. Chief Operating Officers (COO) are in high demand to make the lateral connections between functional specialists that have for so long been haphazard at best, and missing at worst. Lateral thinking is one of the most important success criteria among senior managers in this space – connecting the different parts of the organisation and harnessing its collective strength, ideas, commitment, knowledge and ability, form the foundation for success in the Net economy.

We will also look at the role the search firm has to play today. When funds are tight, what are the benefits of using a search firm? How can they help you find the people to make your dream a reality when everyone wants to hire the best? And the hardest question they may ask – are you the right person to run your business?

Search – what, where, how and why

First, a quick look at where the search industry came from. eCommerce is about making and claiming what is immediately a global market – which is how Korn/Ferry International began. The commercial world has always needed lawyers, bankers and accountants – and from this last stable came two of the brightest young accountants of their day. To Lester Korn and Richard Ferry, who created the search industry in the 1960s – calling their firm 'International' from day one – making and claiming a global market was fundamental. The same pioneering spirit was behind Korn/Ferry's launch of the first online search and assessment service for mid-level managers – Futurestep – which marries the speed and reach of the Internet with traditional search expertise. It is this human expertise – assessment and evaluation – that is missing from the job posting sites. Already, the market has fragmented.

Assessing people in this new environment is now the critical factor in hiring executives today. It is no longer a question of how to find them, it is evaluation that is the key – in terms of skills, experience and culture. But assessment and evaluation today are even more difficult – because everything is new. As a senior Internet executive with a leading Web retailer put it, 'There is little or no institutional memory here. While we have some Internet experience, almost no one has a lot of it. You can't look around you for the answers. You have to just get it done.'

So, who are the people who are getting it done?

The dot.com CEO

A study carried out by Korn/Ferry with Netscape Communications Corporation, *The Dot-Com CEO*, reveals new leadership and team structures in the dot.com world and profiles successful CEOs and their backgrounds.

Attributes of a dot.com CEO

The dot.com CEO is typically a young, aggressive executive who is well connected – electronically as well as personally – and is driving shareholder value. This group of 'young lions' is a unique breed and quite different to the stereotypical CEO of the last economic era. Today's dot.com CEO is flamboyant and often outspoken. Below are some of the more common attributes dot.com CEOs use to describe themselves.

Aggressive	Passionate	Charismatic
Communicative	Visionary	Driven
Outspoken	Tireless	Innovative
Outlaw	Rule Breaker	Paranoid

Background and education

Dot.com CEOs are generally young. If you are founding an Internet business as CEO, or are looking for a CEO to lead your company, there are many advantages to youth. However, experience is extremely important. As dot.com CEO, not only will you have to make decisions in a highly technological business environment, but you must also understand the customer and the Net economy marketing techniques.

In terms of experience, most good dot.com CEOs come from two areas: companies that have high customer service expectations and significant amounts of content; and management consulting – MBAs attracted away from the professional service firms towards Internet ventures.

Education plays only a part in the dot.com CEO's ability to manage and lead in the Net economy. The characteristics of the Net economy are such that they cannot be based on traditional business thinking. There is very little history to learn from and the digital economy continues to evolve in ways no-one is familiar with. A good knowledge of technology, coupled with an MBA, is an ideal background.

Style and motivation

The style of the dot.com CEO is one you no doubt know already – that of 'rogue warrior'. They do not like to be constrained by rules or follow traditional lines of thought. They look to the unusual and unconventional for solutions and approaches to business opportunities and problems. They possess a significant amount of charisma and other traits that give them the ability to motivate and immediately gain the trust of employees, business professionals and customers. They are decisive in nature and have the ability to handle situations that are both new and ambiguous.

The dot.com CEOs are motivated by the thrill of the battle. They are driven by the challenge of building a business and disrupting traditional competition. Their greatest challenge comes when they are told something cannot be done; they are not afraid to break some glass along the way to achieve their goal.

Specialised branding skills

Understanding the power of a brand and being able to develop that brand on the Web is a core capability for the dot.com CEO. Market leaders identify these five critical success elements for establishing a brand to attract and retain customers in eCommerce. These five capabilities are represented in over 85% of the top 100 US-based web sites.

With price, quality and product functionality now bywords of the past, competitive advantage in the Net economy is based on service and knowledge. The dot.com CEO must leverage the knowledge capital and digital assets they have led their organisation to create. These – coupled with the five critical success components – must be integrated into the branding and marketing message of the dot.com company.

The dot.com CEO as change agent

The dot.com CEO focuses on changing the fundamental underpinnings on which organisations are typically built – covering operating procedures, remuneration structure and interaction with colleagues and customers.

The dot.com CEO can play a critical part in attracting and retaining top executives. The organisation's strategy is, by and large, the basis on which decisions to join or to stay with the business are made. So whether attracting executives or leading existing ones, the dot.com CEO needs to possess a charisma that excites the team. After defining how progress will be measured, the CEO needs to loosen the reins and empower his or her teams, letting the company go forward.

Attracting senior start-up talent

Once the founder has the core team and funding in place, attracting senior start-up talent is fast, furious and fundamentally different. Following are the five key steps to winning the people you need to succeed.

Step One: Define what sets the company apart
The company must develop a clear vision of what it has to offer – what sets it apart from other organisations. If it has a unique idea or a hot new product in development, it has a much better chance of attracting great management. Highly qualified individuals need to be challenged and stimulated to build a dynamic team and, ultimately, a great company.

Step Two: Develop realistic expectations
It is important to recognise that in today's rapidly changing market, a CEO candidate may not have all the answers. A company must develop realistic specifications and be willing to accept trade-offs.

Step Three: Eliminate barriers to success
Having prioritised the skills that the leader must have and those that are secondary, the next step is to eliminate potential barriers to a candidate's success, for example, leaving the founder in place as Chairman, which will restrict the CEO's authority and autonomy. Instead, stay as a lead board director, or lead advisory board member and embrace the freedom to start another business. This generation's serial entrepreneurs now have a few ventures behind them.

Step Four: Be flexible
The shortage of top management talent has highlighted the need for flexibility in choosing a CEO. The law of supply and demand may require major concessions to bring the ideal CEO on board. For example, if the candidate is unwilling to relocate, would the company be willing to move?

Step Five: Recognise the importance of equity
Recent years have seen a growing number of individuals asking for equity in a company as opposed to cash remuneration. Some candidates may

already have a substantial amount in stock at their current place of employment, so money is not the primary motive for accepting a top position. However, a balance needs to be struck, and usually around age brackets. An established senior executive will have enough behind them to be able and willing to take a risk, often based solely on future shareholder value. However, with a large number of top candidates in their twenties or graduating from MBA courses, cash is still a very important part of the remuneration package. Equity builds loyalty, commitment and a sense of ownership, cash still makes the world go round.

Working with a search firm

Traditional companies and start-ups are going head to head to compete for talent, and the traditional role of search consultant as 'ambassador' is nowhere as important as in this space. Senior executives with proven eCommerce expertise are receiving calls all day, every day. Catching their attention is becoming more and more difficult – therefore, having a reputable firm known for its integrity and stature on your side can make the difference between being able to speak to these people and withering on the voicemail.

In this world of inter-connectivity, many people rely on the grapevine or their network of contacts to find and secure the people they need. But remember, your grapevine and your network is, today, everyone else's grapevine and network. How can you distinguish your opportunity from the plethora of others? What is more, what is your opportunity – do you know? Can you define it in the context of someone's already successful career?

In today's environment, a number of entrepreneurs will be using search for the first time. Due to the confidential nature of search, the industry is shrouded in a mystique that makes it hard to tease out exactly how search works.

Figure 11.1 sets out the main steps in a search assignment and gives you an idea – in very general terms – of the typical structure of an individual assignment.

So, what are the benefits of working with a search firm and how do you choose the best one for you?

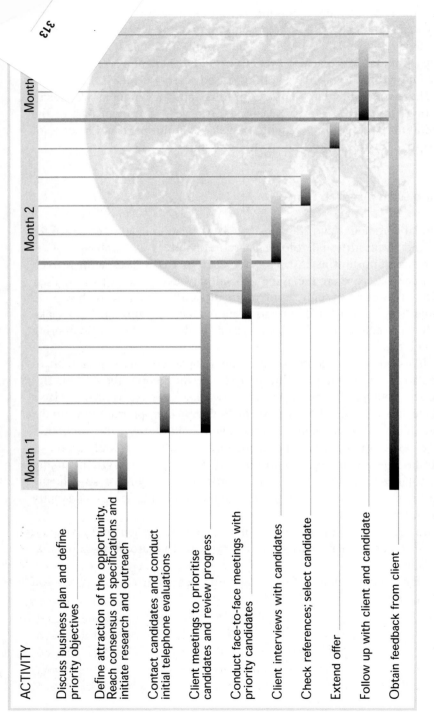

Figure 11.1 Typical stages of an eCommerce search

Source: Korn/Ferry International

Expertise

Executive search consultants are experts in recruiting. A search professional spends all of their time seeking out and evaluating senior executives against the strategic objectives of their clients.

Speed

A search handled by yourself, or by a colleague with many other responsibilities, is only one of a number of pressing problems. Executive recruiters, on the other hand, give their full and undivided personal attention.

Experience and network of resources

Recruiters, through years of experience, know where to find top talent, how to evaluate it in the context of the client's business and how to sell an opportunity to someone who doesn't need another one. It takes both skill and constant practice. Most entrepreneurs do not hire senior executives often enough to develop sufficient internal experience in recruiting at the highest levels.

Specialisation

One of the most important criteria in launching a competitor to a traditional business or industry, or a new model in itself, is industry knowledge and expertise. The head of E-Lòan didn't come from a technology company, he came from Direct Line – with the telephone banking experience providing an effective bridge to providing financial services on the Internet.

This industry expertise is reflected in the search industry. While most executive recruiters have general practices, many consultants specialise in serving clients in certain industries. At Korn/Ferry, each speciality practice is staffed by consultants with years of experience working in the same industries as their clients. All are backed by the research capabilities required to forecast industry trends, track economic developments and technological innovations, and identify future leaders within each specialty area. The beauty of this is that a range of expertise can be harnessed within the search team, so that technological knowledge can be coupled with, for example, financial, retail or healthcare expertise.

Choosing a Search Firm
From Executive Recruiter News:

- Will the consultant be a credible ambassador for your company?
- Does the consultant understand your business and the environment?
- Does the consultant have the right experience?
- Will the consultant give you top priority?
- Will the assignment be handled by the firm's best people?
- Are you comfortable with the consultant's approach?

Confidentiality

Executive recruiters work independently and confidentially. This is a significant advantage in the Net economy when you don't want to lose competitive advantage on the grapevine. The consultant's discretion will not expose the client's positions and intentions to competitors and – before time – to venture capitalists (VCs).

Objectivity

The search consultant sees the client, and his or her hiring needs, as an informed, experienced outsider. This perspective often results in recommendations for modifying the client's recruiting strategy or leadership structure.

Above all, remember that the search consultant is your ambassador. They help define what makes your opportunity attractive in competing for the best. They also help close the assignment – which means your new colleague starts without any emotional debris left over from the negotiation process – which can be protracted and unattractive, particularly with regard to equity stakes.

Competitive recruiting strategies

If you are planning to go public in the near future and you think you can't afford a search firm, think again. VCs recognise the importance of the leadership team, particularly with a view to going public, and a true VC partner should support your efforts to get the best people.

If you are at seed funding stage, you have a fine line to tread. VC firms are receiving dozens of business plans every day; there is no shortage of ideas. You may have what you think is the best idea in cyberspace, but if you don't have the people to bring it to life, it will be hard to get off the ground. It may be that you or your partner(s) need to be your own best search consultant. As Amazon.com CEO Jeff Bezos says, 'when I'm interviewing a senior job candidate, my biggest worry is how good they are at hiring. I spend at least half the interview on that.'

Founders of new businesses have always had to be good recruiters. In today's environment, the recruiting efforts have to be outstanding. Yes, the candidate is now king, but that doesn't mean anyone should lose sight of the basics – an easy trap to fall into in the Net economy, given the need for speed and decision-making based on incomplete information.

If you are at seed funding stage and driving your own recruiting efforts, primary areas to check are:

- *Learning capacity*: In the 'old economy' it was important to be a 'continuous learner'. In the new economy you need to be able to identify a palpable thirst for knowledge, new learning, future projections, three dimensional thought processes and relevant information.

- *Ad quotient*: Every company's every employee is an 'advertisement' for working with that organisation. Today we are really having to look at the soft, intangible factors in business life, and this is one of them. As founder, you are the ultimate 'advertisement', and your partners and your team are part of the subconscious reaction to working, or not working in your organisation. Therefore, it's everyone's job to help the hiring process – they are important ambassadors.

- *A sense of worth*: Ego and money, just as fire and water, are essential in the right quantities. It's a fine line in the Net economy – you need people with enough of these two key motivators to get results without making enemies along the way.

So, how do you assess the intangibles?

1. Make sure you see candidates in as many different settings as you can – particularly if for you they are a well-liked colleague or former colleague. You don't necessarily know your prospective partner, right hand person or international director as well as you need to.

2. 360 degree feedback in traditional companies is mainstream in the US, and gathering pace in Europe, for good reason. What subordinates,

counterparts, peers and project workers say can be highly illuminating to a boss who sees only a certain persona.

3. Everyone has a past. One of the things search consultants are so good at is due diligence – and also teasing out information and skills that may be buried in history. Someone's latest job is not necessarily the best indication of their future potential and harnessing skills they used a long time ago may be just what you need in a start-up that will depend on multiple skills.

However you go about your recruiting, it has to be said that for any company today, one of the top competitive tactics you can adopt is to work with a search firm – do your research, maximise the consultant's knowledge and expertise and retain that relationship as a long term partnership. More and more search firms are restructuring their pricing for the Net economy, building in the flexibility needed by today's entrepreneurs. Some firms offer a mix of part fee/part equity, or equity in lieu of fee, or some kind of delayed payment facility. It is worth finding out what the specifics are for your target firms; you may not wish to give away precious equity and could be better off negotiating a different arrangement.

More and more VCs are developing relationships with search firms both for hiring needs and evaluation purposes. As part of the business proposition assessment, the search firm is benchmarking the leadership against both strategic objectives and their peer group. In traditional companies, leadership team assessment is called 'management audit' and is usually part of a change process – typically in mergers, acquisitions, joint ventures and structural transition. In the Net economy, it is called 'meeting for breakfast' and IT IS the change process.

Recruiting and Retention in a Nutshell

Hiring in the Net economy is, as defined above, different. In summary, here are the top ten points to remember in getting your business off the map, and out into cyberspace.

1. The best talent is choosing from a number of opportunities – consider ethical, remunerative and lifestyle attraction and retention factors. Some dot.coms are differentiating themselves in ways that are meaningful to the hiring process – building fun into the culture, supporting family life, and recognising that even the most driven individuals need some balance.

2. Today, more and more of the world's most successful executives work not for the financial incentive, but for the stimulation. The opportunity to make an impact on how the business world is shaping up for the future is a key motivator.

3. eCommerce is immediately a global talent pool and a small talent pool – maximise your personal, professional and membership links across the world, or have a search firm do it for you.

4. You are not hiring with a defined job description – it's the person, their attitude, their commitment and their mix of skills as part of the leadership team that are important. You need a skilled professional to evaluate candidates in the context of your business objectives.

5. There are a lot of very young people in the eCommerce talent pool – it doesn't matter if they have less experience, as long as it is the right experience.

6. There is a large pool of people in the traditional business world – remember, most people are less entrepreneurial than they think, and can't always make the change from a traditional, team environment to leading an Internet business.

7. Venture capitalists make their decisions not on the idea or the product, but on the people behind it.

8. Most Internet roles are being filled by people with the same industry, not technological, experience.

9. When it's time for you to let go as founder CEO, it's time for you to let go as founder CEO. Your business will thrive and so will you.

10. A proven – successful – track record is what venture capitalists look for in Europe; a proven track record is what they look for in the US. Failure is learning, and the market will soon realise it. If at first you don't succeed, try again – but with the right team.

CHAPTER 12

Sample Business Plan

Steven Harpin
ANDERSEN CONSULTING STRATEGIC SERVICES

A great plan doesn't make a great business

This exciting plan was written in October 1999, well ahead of the business-to-consumer (B2C) wave for this category. It was used to recruit one of the most talented teams I have seen. In March 2000, the plan was dropped as the competition became too intense. The main US competitor arrived, not to buy the business as the entrepreneur had hoped, but to raise ten times as much money from the same venture capitalist (VC). The entrepreneurs saw three other similar plans in the market, the big five home retailers were all gearing up their eCommerce activities and a well funded pan-European portal was being developed in a UK incubator.

The real lesson from this plan was don't wait. The team started ahead of the wave; when the wave crashed over them they had been frantically moving around – on the same spot. I interviewed the entrepreneurs who learned 10 key lessons, which are worth sharing. This is what they said:

1. *You can do this*: 12 months ago I didn't think it would be possible to seriously consider recruiting the most talented people I have ever met, into a close knit and hard working team, meeting the CEOs of the world's leading firms and discussing the likelihood of them investing £3m in us, in addition to raising £4m from a VC. We came close, we had the confidence and we were convincing. We failed, but we can do this – we know that now.

2. *Sell to a team... if you can't do this you won't sell to a VC*: Go and recruit the best team you can find. If you don't have any money and can't afford a head hunter ring up the best people in the best positions in the best and most relevant firms and send them a letter/executive summary. You will never get serious partnerships or funding if your team isn't convincing. If you can't convince people to join you this will

tell you something about yourself, your idea or the person you're talking to. Non-executives can play a critical role in helping you succeed. Go to the best – they may say yes. We recruited the CEO of a major advertising company who knew this space very well, a serial technology entrepreneur and a board level retailer who knew the market in depth. All these guys have been very successful, and they were all wonderfully willing to help others follow in their footsteps. They opened doors and helped me decide what to say when I got through them.

3. *Get strategic partners even if the partnership may never work*: If you have the right partnerships, you will have some valuable assets and the money flows faster. You stand out from the thousands of other tiny start-ups. VC's, industry suppliers, buyers, and consultants will all take you very seriously because there is a reason to believe that you can dominate the industry, not die. We partnered with some of the best systems integrators, a well known VC, and tried hard to find a decent media company. Two of the media firms we spoke to couldn't make their mind up. The partnerships with these people could never have worked – they were far too slow. But they brought big money, and that brought success. You need to make sure you structure the deals so divorce can be cheap and fast.

4. *Go to all the potential partners at once*: Go to all potential partners at once, don't wait for them all to say no, until you progress to the next one. We went to the best blue chip media partner, who consistently said that they wanted to partner with us. The managing director then said no on the last day of a ten-week wait, while we presented our detailed plans for all aspects of the business to the whole of their organisation. There was no explanation at all, it was rude, unfair but tough. We felt as though we had been raped, our plans stolen and we were no longer ahead of the game. To make matters worse, the next partner was equally slow. Always get a next best alternative in parallel or you force yourself to do an expensive deal or worse, you have no deal. An alternative gives you the opportunity to walk away. The more you can walk away the stronger you are. Indeed if you walk away, they may call you back.

5. *The market talks to you*: If partners can't decide fast enough, VC's say no to first round funding ('but do consider us for second round funding'), suppliers say no and you can't raise a team you are unlikley to be successful. There is something wrong – work out why this is happening and fix it.

6. *Look bigger and faster than you are*: Get business cards printed and headed notepaper, register your firm, design the logo, recruit an advisory board, advertise around your potential partners, set up a web site or a prototype. If your business is called Inspiredhome, call your office Inspirational House and consider using serviced offices. If negotiations last more than a few days, you absolutely must demonstrate progress during discussions. Next time you meet people they will want an update – stun them with progress in their area of key concern. Rather than presenting all you have and pleading with people to come onboard, interview them, ask them about their business and the speed they can move at. Check out that they are absolutely the right people for you. This will make you look as though you have options – even if they are the only one.

7. *The issues are the same as bricks and mortar businesses*: No serious partner discussed the issues surrounding web site design, because everyone can imagine that you can do it. They discussed fulfilment and customer service issues, exactly the same as the real world. If you are setting up a direct business and can't estimate returns, then don't expect serious investors to take you seriously. If you plan to stock all your products in a warehouse and can't discuss stock turnover benchmarks, you are a risky bet. We were always quizzed in the areas we were weakest in. At one point we didn't have a fulfilment director, so we spent our life discussing fulfilment. We wished we had partnered in this issue area first, as it would then have dissapeared from the agenda. Anticipate these areas and compensate somehow.

8. *The VC will watch you dominate or fail*: If you can get the momentum snowballing you will win VC support. They will listen to what you say and sit back to see if you can deliver it. Say what you will deliver and do it.

9. *One thing leads to another*: Everyone from the team is doing something new that is connected to the plan. Some are consultants who are just better at their job and have moved into more interesting areas. Some have changed jobs to get closer to the technology, and some have gone to another start-up. We have started a journey of learning.

10. *This is with you for life*: Nobody lost anything, we all gained something. We have the bug. Meetings for our business were ten times better than normal when they went well. When they went badly they were ten times worse. It was a short roller coaster ride that we will all revisit. After all opportunity always knocks more than once.

All the names and CVs in this business plan have been changed.

Business Plan for a Unique UK eCommerce Pure Play Venture

'INSPIREDHOME'

'INSPIRATION AND THE ABILITY TO RECREATE IT IN YOUR HOME'

Address

Contact: Stephen Parker, Founder

Telephone number

January 2000

Copy _____ of _____ copies distributed

Table of Contents

EXECUTIVE SUMMARY

Company Name: Inspiredhome
Address:

Contact Person: Stephen Parker, Founder. Tel: 44 123 456 789
Date: 1 October 1999

Executive summary

(a) Vision: Inspiredhome.com will be the preferred UK destination for people whose intention is to create beautiful homes. It is an Internet vertical portal that will bring together content, commerce and community. *'It provides inspiration and the ability to recreate it.'*

(b) The business concept is unique: There is a strong and proven customer need to create beautiful homes and participate in female orientated communities:

- *Content*: There are 33 UK magazines based on 'home' themes with mass market circulation.[1] In addition, home television programmes such as *Changing Rooms* have over 7m viewings per episode.[2]

- *Commerce*: Our major UK commerce will be in decoration and furniture products. These are large (£8.5bn) and fragmented markets.[2]

- *Community*: US female community sites are very successful. Specifically women.com and iVillage female community sites are the 31st and 36th most visited Internet sites with over 4m unique visitors per month.[3] Hearst New Media (VC) back Women.com and have recently invested in a $50m US start-up called goodhome.com with a similar concept.[4]

Customers will find our service a unique one stop solution:

- *Integration of offering across sub-intentions*: Inspiredhome.com will beat traditional product-focused business models by integrating products and services to fulfil their intention to renovate their homes. This will include:

  1. to decorate
  2. to furnish
  3. to DIY

4. to have a beautiful garden

5. a set of home shopping channels (for example, home office, home entertainment).

At launch we will focus on the major markets of decoration (£2.7bn) and furnishing (£5.8bn), providing links to other intentions.[2]

■ *Inspiration, advice and the ability to recreate it in your home*: Inspiredhome.com will beat traditional retailers who focus on selling products and services and content aggregators (magazine publishers) by integrating content, commerce and community within the same site. Specifically we combine a magazines inspiration and advice with an ability to conveniently recreate it in the home.

■ *Depth and breadth of product range*: Inspiredhome will offer a greater depth and range of products and services than traditional bricks and mortar and direct mail retailers because we are not constrained by space. This objective will be phased in over time.

■ *Merchandising*: Inspiredhome will merchandise in a customer preferred way (for example wallpaper by period, colour, make, finish, style, mood, room, children/adult, special offers and top ten sellers). This is a competitive advantage versus current retailer merchandising (suppliers' wallpaper books).

■ *Strong sense of community*: We will build a very strong community among like minded individuals who will be able to communicate with each other, experts and suppliers of products and services. This will make them 'sticky' or loyal.

■ *New products and services*: Inspiredhome will develop 'own label' products and services as we develop scale and learning. This is likely to include exclusive high value ranges.

(c) *Attractive market*: The Internet market is large and delivering significant shareholder value. The furniture and decoration markets are large with low competitive intensity.

■ *The UK population is rapidly going online and buying more*: 1999 total online population of 13.1m people is growing dramatically (+47% on 1998). Total 1998 buying population of 1.0 m people is growing (+137% on 1997) fast. Each buyer is spending $248 per quarter (+58% on 1997).

■ *These positive fundamentals are driving high market valuations*: High market valuations are being driven to areas of Internet innovation. For perspective the top ten bricks and mortar retail firms are delivering 1.1 times market capital/revenue multiples, versus the top ten Internet companies delivering 57.9 times.[5]

■ *The core decoration and furniture markets are large*: The UK markets for the two core intentions are £8.5bn. We will launch in the large decoration (£2.7bn) and furniture (£5.8bn) markets as the key revenue drivers.

■ *Current competitive intensity is low*: There is no major Internet competition within this space in the UK. Speed is essential to take it rapidly. Those UK sites that are playing in this space either:

1. lack the ability to sell anything and/or
2. have no communication/community surrounding their offers.

(d) Achievable objectives: Inspiredhome.com will be the No. 1 UK vertical portal based on the home. Our focus will be on revene generating markets and achieving and retaining the No. 1 position. Specific objectives are:

Inspiredhome financial objectives

Financial objectives	Launch 6 months	Year 1	Year 2	Year 3	Year 4	Year 5
Gross revenue (£m)		1.6	9.5	29.1	66.7	92.0
Cost of goods (£m)		1.2	7.3	22.4	51.2	70.8
EBIT	(1.0)	(2.0)	(1.3)	1.6	8.3	13.3
Cumulative EBIT	(1.0)	(3.0)	(4.3)	(2.6)	5.6	18.9

(e) Stage of business: This business has secured a strategic relationship with a major UK content provider to rapidly move to start-up stage. It has seed capital from angel investors and the management team.

(f) Experienced management team with major strategic partnerships: Inspiredhome.com is a collection of major strategic partnerships. The combination of these partnerships and an experienced management team will minimise risk and increase speed to market.

Partnership strategy

Partnerships	Basis	They bring	We offer
Content provider	Equity	Rich and dynamic content Access to mass customers	Sell and continually promote magazines Equity Customer information
Systems integrator	36 month payment terms	Technology skills	Pure play reference payment
Strong management team	Wage plus options	Experience Commitment	Win/win options Motivating and dynamic environment
Access to suppliers ■ Retailers ■ Wholesalers ■ Manufacturers	% Revenue	Products Category knowledge	Margin Ability to leverage ■ Buying assets ■ Distribution/fulfilment system Internet learning and experience Customer information Speed to market

■ *The partnerships* bring the ability to make this happen and access to customers and suppliers

■ *The management team* is a set of outstanding proven achievers:

   ■ *Chief Executive:* Stephen Parker is the lead manager within a top five European eCommerce consultancy and has helped set up three B2C pure play businesses and one B2B business. Prior to this Stephen progressed a senior Brand Management career with Procter and Gamble and has started up two minor companies in his spare time.

   ■ *Finance Director:* Peter Wilkes is a principal consultant at McKinsey and Co within the Retail telecoms group where he manages major change programs and has worked with the executive boards of leading telecoms and media organisations. Prior to this he was Head of Finance at two British Telecom subsidiaries with a $180m turnover. He is a qualified chartered accountant.

   ■ *Technology expertise*: Adam Taylor is a main board and IT director of one of the world's largest trading firms. He was a co-founder of an IT consultancy and has won several awards for his specialist integrator and reseller results. His experience includes Systems and network integration, consultancy, configuration of servers, networks in multiple variants of Unix and NT. He has experience of many retail implementations.

▪ *Marketing and Trading Director*: Toby Gray is a partner in Andersen Consulting's consumer products practice. He is currently leading the development of a global eCommerce portal. He has extensive furniture retailing experience at board level having led strategic change programmes with three major 'home' retailers. Prior to Andersen Consulting, Toby had seven years Marketing experience in MFI where he was a European Marketing Director.

▪ *Chief Operating Officer*: Nikki John is Head of Logistics for GUS, one of the largest UK catalogue retailers. Nikki has overhauled direct delivery and payment systems resulting in a 30% increase in customer satisfaction and retention. Prior to GUS, Nikki set up her own logistics consultancy which grew to £12m fees.

▪ *Editorial Team*: This will be provided by the content provider.

▪ *Non-Executive*: Dickie Esher, a proven and serial entrepreneur, has invested in the seed phase of this project and will join the firm as a non-executive director. Dickie was co-founder of an IT services firm called Oxford Ltd which grew to 400+ professionals and $60m turnover through supplying niche database and systems technical expertise to enterprise clients. Dickie sold this business to the management.

We have targeted senior and respected industry experts to take non-executive positions. These discussions will be concluded on agreement of letters of intent.

(g) Financial arrangements: Venture capital funds of £4.5m in preferred stock for a 30% ownership which will take the firm from start-up to end of year 1 latest.

Financial arrangements

Partners	Investment	Equity
Founder	▪ £60K excluding loss of earnings of £440K during 3-year period	30%
Angel investors	▪ £250K	10%
Venture capital	▪ £4,500K	30%
Content provider	▪ Access to customers via major home magazines ▪ Content provided	15%
Employees	▪ Up to £200k and lower salaries	15%

- *Expected annual returns*: Venture capital CAGR are high, based on 10 times revenue multiple. They are exponential based on continuous revenue growth.

Expected annual returns

Venture capital	Input	Year 1	Year 2	Year 3
Annual returns (CAGR)	£4.5m	110%	234%	227%
Multiples of initial investment	£4.5m	×2	×11	×36

- *Exit strategy for venture capital investors*: There are two likely exit strategies in the Internet market:

  1. *Public offering*: We will actively seek a rapid Initial Public Offering within 12-18 months to drive our business forward and truly lock out the competition.

  2. *Acquisition*: We will be happy to look at a sale where it reflects the true value of the business and brings strategic assets to fuel its future growth and multiply future returns. Illustrative purchasers are:

     - *A major portal*: with access to many customers (for example Freeserve, AOL, Amazon). This will enable them to:

       - increase their customer loyalty by offering a leading vertical portal and
       - take a share of future revenues, for example the Freeserve/ Babyworld deal

     - *A US site*: (for example Good Home, Furniture.com) wishing to globalise its offer by entering the UK market as a foothold to Europe. Goodhome has expressed an interest in such a deal.

     - *A UK retailer*: Where they are slow to react to the market shift (for example B&Q have bought a direct mail DIY firm).

I. Unique business concept

A. Overview

Inspiredhome.com will be the UK's leading Internet vertical portal that will create a content rich community around people's intention to create beautiful homes. It will provide inspiration and the ability to recreate it within your own home. Customers will find our service a unique one stop solution;

■ *Integration of offering across sub-intentions*: Inspiredhome.com will beat traditional product-focused business models by integrating products and services to fulfil their intention to create a beautiful home. This will include:

1. to decorate
2. to furnish
3. to DIY
4. to have a beautiful garden
5. to enable home shopping.

■ *Inspiration, advice and the ability to recreate it in your home*: Inspiredhome.com will beat traditional retailers who focus on selling products and services and content aggregators (magazine publishers) by integrating content, commerce and community within the same site. The site will feel like a magazine with products linked to content.

■ *Merchandising*: Inspiredhome.com will merchandise in a customer preferred way for example by integrated solution (picture of a decorated room with furniture), wallpaper and furniture by period, colour, make, finish, style, mood, room, children/adult, special offers and top ten sellers. This is a competitive advantage versus current retailer merchandising (for example by suppliers' wallpaper books).

■ *Fulfilment*: Inspiredhome.com will offer a superior fulfilment service on key categories versus bricks and mortar stores. For example, we will deliver collated wallpaper sample orders within 48 hours.

■ *Strong sense of community*: We will build a very strong community among like minded individuals who will be able to communicate with each other, experts and suppliers of products and services.

■ *New products and services*: Inspiredhome.com will develop 'own label' products and services as we develop scale and learning by agreeing joint ventures with leading designers.

■ *Depth and breadth of product range*: Inspiredhome.com will build a greater depth and breadth of products in our key categories than traditional bricks and mortar and direct mail retailers. This will be phased in over time.

B. Vision

Inspiredhome.com will be the preferred UK destination for people who want to create beautiful homes.

- *Preferred*: We will be the destination of first choice. This will reflect our ability to offer inspirational solutions.

- *UK*: Our focus will be on the UK to rapidly build scale fast. This reflects the importance of speed to market. We will consider a European expansion after three months of UK trading.

- *People*: Our target audience will be mass market. Specifically, they will be women with Internet access who love their home and want to improve it.

- *Create beautiful homes*: This intention will be met by offering

  1. decoration
  2. furnishing
  3. DIY
  4. gardening
  5. home shopping information and products and services.

We will also become the preferred alliance partner for wholesalers and manufacturers of home-based products.

C. Business concept

Inspiredhome.com offers a unique proposition that will enable customers to find a one stop solution to all the advice, inspiration and products and services they need to transform their homes. We will be the primary point of customer contact. We will meet their needs by bringing together multiple cross-industry alliance partners. Specifically our key points of difference are:

(a) *Integration of offering across sub-intentions*: Traditional product-focused business models require customers to search for and buy products and services across many different retailers (for example DIY retailers, interior design stores, furniture shops, garden centres) to meet their intention to transform their houses into beautiful homes. We will offer a one stop solution by integrating products and services from their key sub-intentions:

1. to decorate
2. to furnish
3. to DIY
4. to have a beautiful garden
5. to shop for home-related products.

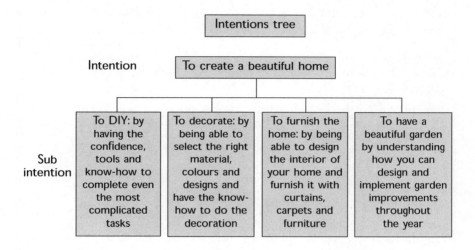

Figure 12.1   Unlike traditional retailers, Inspiredhome.com will integrate sub-intentions to provide a complete solution

(b) Inspiration, advice and the ability to recreate it in your home: Traditional retailers have focused on commerce, while content and community elements have been left to publishers. This is inconvenient for customers who find advice and inspiration in magazines, but need to approach retailers to buy the products and services. Inspiredhome.com will enable people to browse for inspiration and advice within the daily content feeds *and* purchase the relevant products.

(c) Merchandising: Traditional retailers merchandise their products by supplier (for example Dulux paint cards, Sanderson wallpaper books, power tools category). Inspiredhome.com will merchandise by customer buying insight. For example:

	To DIY	To decorate	To furnish the home	To have a beautiful garden
Content	• DIY 'How to' guides • Salvage finder • Expert directory (e.g. plumbers) • First aid and safety advice	• Interior decorating advice • Period looks arranged by rooms • DIY 'How to' guides • Product 'wizards'	• Colour coordination • Readers' houses arranged by style • Furniture renovation advice • Lighting options • Antique advice	• Contemporary and traditional garden pictures • 'How to' guide (build a pond...) • Seasonal guides to plants • Gardening encyclopedia
Commerce	• DIY Materials • Building materials • Plumbing and heating products • Electrical materials • Books • Insurance products	• 2000? wallpapers • 1000? paint colours • 1000? tile designs • DIY and professional decoration products • Other associated products	• Furniture • Soft and hard • Carpets • Curtain material/ready made • Lighting • Bedding	• Lawnmowers • Garden tools • Plants and shrubs • Fencing • Sheds
Interact/ community	• Ask 'Handy Andy' and other experts • Add customer top tips to 'how to' guides • Online bulleting board, chat rooms and lectures	• As DIY • Courses • Room colour match software (scan your room in) • IPIX examples • Period houses to visit	• As DIY • Design experts hold online discussion groups • Through the keyhole of a celebrity house (IPIX software)	• As DIY • Gardens to visit • Courses • Garden planning software • Garden season guides (this month...) • Great gardens for sale

Figure 12.2   The sub-intentions will integrate content, commerce and community

Customer insights and merchandising principles

Customer buying insight	Merchandising principle
'I want inspiration and the ability to recreate it'	Pictures of solutions by style, period, mood colour, finish, room, children/adult
'I want a bargain'	Top 10 offers
'I want some paint'	Sort by category
'I want to be reassured that I am buying a popular product'	Sort by best sellers within each category Sort by brand
'I want to buy a cheap product/mid-range product (for example rental market)'	Sort by price
'I want the latest fashion/style'	Latest product launches
'I want to buy the products and services that go with each other'	Colour matching suggestions, for example 'consider these fabrics with this wallpaper'
'I want a product with that feature'	Merchandising products by feature (for example wallpaper texture)
'Is there a slightly better one?'	'Consider this product' feature which identifies the next one up in the range (upsell opportunity)
'I want the accessories'	Display of relevant products and services (for example linen with the beds, tools to do the job)

▪ Products will emerge from 'magazine feed' content. This will be linked to a one-click ability to buy the products and services required to recreate the look within their own homes. For example, an article on Georgian homes will be linked to Georgian wallpapers and so on.

(d) *Fulfilment capability*: We will offer a 2 day (max.) wallpaper and tile sample service from our own (but outsourced) warehousing facility. This is a competitive advantage versus other stores where samples are ordered independently from suppliers and arrive at the customer's home at different times. We will stock a core range within our own warehousing facilities (30% of gross revenues) to ensure fast delivery. Other non-core items will either be:

1. delivered direct from supplier (large make to order items) or
2. be cross-docked within our warehouse (smaller items that will need collating).

(e) *Strong sense of community*: We will build a very strong community. Specifically, members can be discussion leaders in our chat rooms (6 months post-launch) and view bulletin boards. We will feature member reviews and houses. Members will be able to review products and services and offer each other advice on or creative tips. Members will be able to view each others homes for inspiration. This community experience will expand offline with exclusive courses and tours.

(f) *New products and services*: Inspiredhome.com will develop 'own label' products and services as we develop scale and learning. We will offer a set of unique value added services. For example there will be:

- 'Through the key hole' experiences to view decorated houses (for example typical Georgian house, country themes, celebrities' houses and members' houses) using IPIX 360 degree camera technology. Products and services viewed in these houses can be purchased.

- With scale we will partner with leading designers to develop our own exclusive ranges.

- We will give access to leading TV personalities, designers and interior decorators via community chat.

(g) *Depth and breadth of product range*: Traditional bricks and mortar retailers are constrained by space which restricts the range of products and services they sell. Specialist stores compete through a narrow but deep product range, superstores/hypermarkets (for example B&Q) compete with a broad but shallow product range, focussing on the high volume products. Inspiredhome.com is not constrained by space. We will have 'authority' in all ranges offered. This will develop over time by merchandising all products and services required to inspire our customers.

(h) *Our proposition for partners*: Inspiredhome.com will offer economic value to all our partners. Our knowledge of customers will be passed on to suppliers, who will be able to use it to develop new products and services.

(i) *Competitive parity on security and privacy*: We will match other Internet offerings in secure payments, and privacy. We will only pass on individual customer data if they wish us to do so.

D. Overview of sub-intentions

We will offer four intentions in detail and a general home shopping intention. Each intention will have a home page enabling easy access to online content, commerce and community offerings. We will focus on delivering a unique decoration, furniture and shopping intention for launch. DIY and garden intentions are a secondary priority. Inspiredhome.com will seek a partnership with a site that delivers against all of their DIY and Gardening needs. Until this is available we will provide affinity links to other suitable sites (for example 'Friends of Inspiredhome.com').

Inspiredhome.com sub-intentions delivered at launch and post launch

Intention	Furniture	Decoration	Shopping	DIY	Garden
At launch	'Authority' in major categories	'Authority' in major categories	Affinity partner links to major shopping intentions	Set of affinity partner links	Set of affinity partner links
	Concept rooms illustrating integrated solutions				
Post-launch	Rapidly build breadth and depth	Rapidly build breadth and depth	Rapidly build breadth and depth	One major affinity partner when a suitable site becomes available	One major affinity partner when a suitable site is available
	Build solution numbers and constantly refresh				

(a) *To decorate intention*: This will be our most important intention, reflecting the proliferation of products and services within it. Content will focus on generating inspiration, while products will enable customers to buy the products to replicate it in their own homes. This intention will look and feel more like a magazine, although there will be clear short cuts to purchase products and services.

■ *Content*: We will agree a content and editorial deal with a major magazine company with authority in home magazines. Content will drive people to the site to inspire the creation of a beautiful home. Key features will be developed with editorial expertise (from the content provider), but are likely to include:

■ Inspirational stream of content, structured in a similar way to a home magazine:

- Solutions (for example, pictures of home styles)
- Information on different styles (for example, concept rooms Victorian, country, 1960s)
- Information on the different types of products within these styles (for example, how to choose a wallpaper)

- Bright/creative ideas, 'how to' guides (for example, painting borders)
- News articles on product launches, fashion.

■ *Product and services*: Key categories include:

1. wallpapers
2. tiles
3. paints
4. tools for the job
5. fabrics
6. interior decorating features and woodcare.

Customers that require the tools to decorate (for example paint brush, ladders) will be able to 'one-click purchase'. Product wizards will guide customers through the choices to enable effective and fast selection (for example, choosing wallpaper).

■ *Community*: There will be a strong sense of community around interior decoration. This is reflected in the 33 UK home-based magazine publications and major TV shows on this subject. We will build on this to provide an effective community by offering:

   ■ Through the keyhole: into celebrities', members' and historic homes using IPIX 360 degree camera shots
   ■ Project-based chat, bulletin boards, expert/celebrity advice (for example Jane Churchill, Laurence Llewellyn-Bowen)
   ■ Offline courses based on design, curtain making and so on
   ■ Details of where to visit to see live examples of period houses
   ■ Customer reviews can be added to products and services
   ■ Customers tips can be added to the 'how to' guides.
   ■ Project based chat sessions, bulletin boards.

(b) To furnish intention: We will enable people to view and purchase furniture online.

   ■ *Content*: As with the decoration intention we will source inspirational content from a major home magazine company. Features will aim to achieve competitive parity with Furniture.com (US only) as the leading Internet site in this category. Illustrative content will include:

   1. style guides
   2. new product guides
   3. creative tips (for example, renovation tips).

▪ *Product and services*: These are likely to include:

1. finance
2. indoor furniture (by room, children's, specials, manufacturers, accessories, price and material and so on)
3. outdoor furniture
4. lighting
5. innovations.

Product wizards will guide customers through the furniture choices to enable effective and fast selection (for example choosing outdoor furniture).

▪ *Community*: This rich magazine-like community will be as decoration.

(c) To have a beautiful garden intention: We will enable people to view and purchase gardening products online through affiliate partnerships. Our competitive benchmark will be Garden.com as the leading Internet site (US only). At launch we will link UK garden retailers into our site. We will replace these links with a single well-developed site when it becomes available.

▪ *Content*: As with the decoration intention we will source content from a major magazine publishing company. Illustrative content will include:

▪ Monthly guides of what to do in the garden
▪ Designing a garden (for example city, water, topiary, herb)
▪ Gardens to visit
▪ Reviews of products and services.

▪ *Product and services*: These will include:

1. plants, trees and shrubs
2. bulbs
3. tools
4. seeds.

We will be driven by pragmatism, quickly agreeing affiliate partnerships with the best sites available.

▪ *Community*: We will offer a limited element of community (chat and bulletin boards) within this channel.

(d) DIY intention: A core intention of those who want to improve their home is to DIY. Inspiredhome.com will provide a wide range of content, products, services and community aspects to satisfy this intention. As this market is small we will provide links until Year 2. Should a major player develop this intention we will target a revenue sharing deal.

- *Content*: We will acquire DIY content from major aggregators. Illustrative content includes:

  - 'How to' guides: detailing step by step instructions for minor DIY tasks (for example, security, shelving and so on). These will include pictures initially, but as broadband Internet develops they will include video:

    - 'How to' guides will detail products required to do the job. Fast links will enable customers to buy these products

  - Directory services: Such as architectural reclamation yards and 'Scoot' for access to painters and decorators and other local traders, with the ability to rate them

  - First aid and safety advice: Such as what to do in emergencies (for example, broken pipe).

- *Product and services*: We will focus on the products and services that are:

  1. required for the most common DIY tasks outlined in our DIY guides
  2. can be cost effectively delivered (for example, excludes bulk orders of nails and screws). These will come from strategic relationships with Internet ready retailers (for example B&Q).

  Illustrative categories of products will include:

  1. hand tools
  2. adhesives, abrasives and finishes
  3. power tools
  4. security.

- *Community*: We will offer a limited element of community (chat and bulletin boards) within this channel.

(e) General shopping intention: We will meet a general Inspired 'home' shopping intention of products readily sold over the Internet to build revenue. Illustrative examples will include:

- Inspired office (for example Dell computing, Viking direct office products, office furniture)
- Inspired travel
- Inspired books and magazines (for example Amazon, all content providers magazines)
- Inspired entertainment (music/CDs)
- Inspired flowers
- Inspired gifts (with wrapping service)
- Inspired kitchen: kitchens, kitchenware, cooking
- Inspired bed linen
- Inspired money
- Inspired electricals
- Inspired utilities.

Where possible we will achieve a set of joint agreements (percentage of revenue) with an established Internet shopping intention (for example Shoppers Universe), or individual Internet ready suppliers (for example Interflora, Amazon).

II. Attractive markets

A. Overview

The UK Internet channel is attractive as online usage and buying is dramatically growing, supporting large market valuations which are significantly greater than those of traditional business models.

B. UK online usage, shopping projections and market valuations

The fundamentals of UK Internet business forecasts are very healthy. Specifically, online usage and buying is growing dramatically. These fundamentals are driving high market valuations.

(a) The UK population is rapidly going online: 1999 total online population of 13.1m[6] people is growing dramatically (+47% versus year ago). Forecasts do not include other new media channels (for example Inter-

UK online population 1997-2002

Online population	1997	1998	1999	2000	2001	2002
UK population (m)	58.6	58.8	59.0	59.2	59.4	59.6
% Population online	9%	15%	22%	28%	34%	38%
Total population online (m)	5.2	8.9	13.1	16.9	20.6	23.0
% Growth vs Y/A	N/A	73%	47%	29%	22%	12%

active TV) which will increase this further.

(b) Internet buying is increasing dramatically: Total 1998 buying population of 1.0m people is growing fast (+137% versus 1997). Each buyer is spending £155 per quarter (+58% versus year ago).[7]

UK Internet buying (per quarter) 1997-2002

UK Internet buying	1997	1998	1999	2000	2001	2002
UK online population (m)	5.2	8.9	13.1	16.9	20.6	23.0
% Buying over the Internet	8%	11%	14%[8]	18%	22%	26%
Total population buying (m)	0.4	1.0	1.9	3.1	4.5	5.9
% Growth vs year ago	N/A	137%	94%	63%	48%	29%
Amount spent per buyer/quarter (£)	£98	£155	N/A	N/A	N/A	N/A

US experience indicates that 47% of women spend over $100 per month versus 23% of men, suggesting that female portals may deliver significantly greater revenues than other portals as women come online.[9]

(c) These positive fundamentals are driving high market valuations: High market valuations are being driven to areas of Internet innovation. For perspective the top ten bricks and mortar retail firms are delivering 1.1 times market capital/revenue multiples, versus the top ten Internet companies delivering 57.9 times.[10] High Internet stock fluctuations do not change the fact that the market is rewarding Internet businesses to a much greater degree than traditional businesses. Clearly, the extent of these valuations may decrease, hence a conservative view of revenue multiples in our forecast Market Valuation.

The level of valuation multiple is dependent on the type of business. Inspiredhome.com is a vertical portal with an eCommerce revenue stream and could expect to achieve at least 5–100 times revenue.[11] To be conservative we have assumed only ten times revenue in the business plan. The table below shows an average valuation to revenue multiple of 37 for all Internet related IPOs as at May 1999 – the equiv-

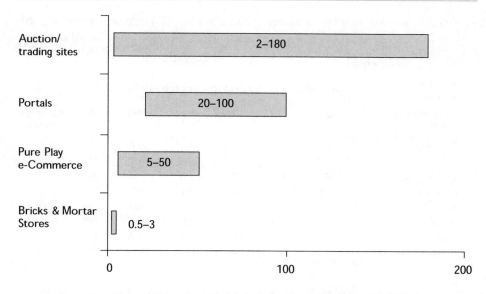

Sales multiple = current market value/annualised sales for 1999

Figure 12.3   Internet sales multiples depend on market type

alent figure (to the extent that updated information is available) as at October 1999 is still of the order of 30 times revenue.

C. Intention market sizes

(a) Overall: The UK market valuation for the major intentions chosen are £8.5bn. We will launch in the large decoration (£2.7bn) and furniture (£5.8bn) markets as the key revenue drivers and aim to dominate these categories. There will be considerable customer benefit in being able to decorate and furnish rooms from one site. In addition these are very fragmented markets where there is a significant benefit in being able to view large ranges online.

Total intention market sizes 1993–98

UK market size (£000)	1993	1994	1995	1996	1997	1998	% Change 1993–98
Decoration	N/A	2455	N/A	2591	N/A	2740	N/A
Furniture	5321	5488	5558	5721	5897	5817	+9.3%

(b) Decoration market: The decoration market is large and growing: all
key categories are growing. We will stock products within all of these
categories to ensure we offer a one stop shop.

Home decoration market by sector 1993–98[12]

UK market size (£000)	1993	1994	1995	1996	1997	1998	% Change 1993–98
Total market	N/A	2455	N/A	2591	N/A	2740	N/A
Paint	421	413	400	440	480	515	+22%
Wallcoverings	444	448	451	478	453	460	+4%
Chemicals	176	181	187	195	201	210	+19%
Tiling	175	178	181	183	189	195	+11%
Woodcare	123	130	138	150	168	180	+46%
Fabrics	N/A	930	N/A	950	N/A	979	N/A
Int. decorative features	N/A	175	N/A	195	N/A	201	N/A

■ Consolidated DIY outlets take major shares, but lack depth of
product range: the decoration market is dominated by the major DIY
multiples who stock high volume selling lines. We will beat these
stores by competing at the softer end of the decoration market
offering greater depth in the core categories of wallpaper, paint, tiles
and fabrics, especially at the higher margin, interior design end of
the market (for example Sanderson, Jane Churchill, Nina Campbell).

% Sales of decoration products by type of retail outlet, 1992–96

Retail outlet (% sales)	1992	1994	1996	% point change 1992–96
DIY multiple	53	58	60	+7
Paint specialist	19	18	16	−3
Non-specialist*	16	13	14	−2
Other independent DIY and hardware specialists	12	11	10	−2

* Includes variety stores, grocers and department stores

Currently DIY superstores have a smaller offering versus independents. We will be able to offer a bigger range than both the
DIY superstore and independent, with significantly better fulfilment service than the independent. 'Generally independent warehouses offer more choice' (Marketing Executive, wallcoverings
manufacturer).

(c) Furniture market: The furniture market is large: Total 1998 furniture sales were £5.8bn. We will achieve range authority in all six key categories.

Consumer expenditure on furniture, by sector at current prices 1993–98[13]

UK market size (£000)	1993	1994	1995	1996	1997	1998	% change 1993–98
Total furniture market	5321	5488	5558	5721	5897	5817	+9.3
Living and dining room	2090	2141	2142	2160	2180	2209	+5.7
Carpets and floorcovering[a]	1516	1585	1610	1669	1710	1572	+3.7
Kitchen furniture[b]	286	296	309	321	325	331	+15.7
Bedroom furniture	699	701	708	710	746	752	+7.6
Beds including mattresses	730	765	789	861	936	953	+30.2

Notes:
(a) Includes smooth coverings
(b) Excludes fitted kitchen furniture

- *The market is very fragmented*: The market is very fragmented making it difficult for the customer to shop. Inspiredhome will become a leading brand, stocking leading brands (content and product brands) that can compete versus these retail chains.

Estimated shares of furniture and carpets retailing by value by leading multiples[14]

Leading multiple	% value share
MFI	11.2
IKEA	6.4
DFS	4.2
Carpetright	4.1
Allied Carpets	4.0
Magnet	3.5
Courts	3.0
Harveys	2.3
UNO	1.4
Landmark	1.2
Furniture Village	0.9
Furniture land	0.8
Other	37.2
Department stores	11.0
Mail order/direct	5.0
DIY stores	3.8

■ *The furniture market is suitable for Internet selling*: 20% of people who have bought furniture in the past 12 months, purchased from catalogue showrooms (15%, for example from Argos or Index) and direct mail (5%) where customers do not have the opportunity to see the furniture first. This indicates a significant opportunity for Internet furniture sales. This is particularly so in the strategic online ages of 24–44 (47% of online population versus 37% of UK population) where there is an opportunity to get customers young and keep them for life.

Source of furniture purchases, November 1998[15]

Furniture purchase source	% of population buying furniture in past 12 months	% aged 24–34 buying furniture in past 12 months	Index 24–34 vs population
Specialist furniture and independent stores	16	20.5	128
Catalogue showrooms	15	31	206
DIY multiples/kitchen specialists	13	20	153
MFI	12	16.5	137
IKEA	10	17.5	175
Department stores, M&S, other variety stores	9	24	266
Mail order	5	6.5	130
Other	13	17.5	134

■ Direct sales and mail order are important parts of the furniture market, particularly in the bed sector. We will focus on building superior authority (versus bricks and mortar stores) in those sectors where there are high direct sales (beds, kitchens and lounge and dining room furniture).

Direct mail as % of total furniture value market sales[16]

	Total furniture	Carpets	Beds	Kitchen	Bedroom	Lounge/dining
Total market (£m)	5817	1572	953	331	752	2209
Direct mail sales	5%	N/A	16%	6%	N/A	3%

(d) Other factors: The market is also dependent on a number of factors outside the control of this business. The growth of these home markets will be a function of:

1. the economy
2. the housing market
3. demographic trends
4. fashion and design.

While all of these factors will effect this business plan, the finances are not sensitive to the speed of growth of the market.

■ *The economy will drive furniture expenditure*: Consumer expenditure tracks GDP growth, if the UK fell into recession this would slow the growth in the furniture market. Inspiredhome would suffer less as it will not have the bricks and mortar and inventory overheads of offline competition.

■ *The housing market is healthy*: The continued trend towards home ownership (1998, 67.6% of all homes owner occupied, +1.8% versus 1990[17]) will drive the decoration and furniture market. In addition the housing stock is increasing (+6.4% between 1990 and 1998 to 25m).[18]

■ *Demographic trends will support the market size*: There is a steady increase in the number of single person households (SPH) (1998 SPH account for 29% of UK housing, +23.5% versus 1990). This is reflected in the housing market figures above. This is likely to continue, driven by an ageing population, an increasing number of young people buying houses earlier, and lower marriage rates (1998 index 81.5 versus 1990).

■ *Fashion*: The 33 UK-based home magazines and programmes such as *Changing Rooms* drive fashion. Inspiredhome will stock both fashionable and enduring styles, beating retailers who focus only on fashion (for example Habitat).

D. Competitive assessment

(a) *Overall*: there is no major UK competitor occupying the UK Internet space in any of these intentions. Those who touch on the space are at a competitive disadvantage as without exception:

1. they only offer commerce or content
2. they offer no community aspects
3. they have a very narrow range.

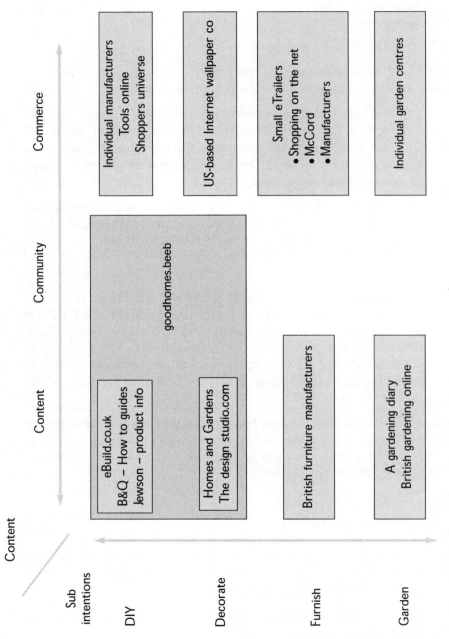

Figure 12.4 There is no major branded player on the Internet that plays the space we seek to occupy

(b) *UK Internet-based competition*: There is no major Internet competition within this space in the UK (see figure 12.4). Speed is essential to take it rapidly. Those sites that are playing in this space:

1. lack the ability to sell
2. have no communication/community surrounding their offers.

There are some moves in the market that may take some share from Inspiredhome should they be developed further. However, competitors are using their current brand that will appeal predominantly to current customers in a proliferated market.

▪ Kingfisher have purchased a direct mail DIY retailer and have a strategic relationship with AOL

▪ Sainsbury and Jewson have announced that they are starting a joint Internet venture, although this is a store-based venture being tested

▪ Argos/GUS have retail catalogues online selling furniture

▪ Debenhams plan to launch a home-based direct business in February 2000

▪ MFI and Ikea may develop their current limited offerings further

▪ There are 36 UK manufacturer and retail furniture sites that are not advertised. All of these are commerce only sites that are unlikely to be in a position to compete.

(c) *US sites that may be potential partners/competition*: We will ensure that our site achieves competitive parity versus the best US sites. These may be potential purchasers or competition:

▪ Garden.com integrates content, commerce and community

▪ Furniture.com integrates content, commerce and community

▪ Goodhome.com is described as 'everything for home decorating'. It has just achieved $50m venture capital funding and has a strategic partnership with Hearst New Media publications. We have discussed possible joint ventures with goodhome.com and they are a likely purchaser post US IPO.

(d) *Female portal sites*: There are a number of UK female portal sites under development by:

1. a major UK portal

2. a major UK content provider
3. a major US female portal
4. a UK retailer.

As these sites have not launched yet, we judge that they will lack substantial commerce capability in our categories. We also view them as potential partners that (1) will give access to customers and maybe purchasers within the next 12–18 months.

III. Marketing: targeting, objectives, strategy and plans

A. Target audience and positioning

(a) *Target audience*: Our target audience is female concentrated as 70% of interior decorating decisions are made by women.[19] Women currently represent 39% of UK Internet.[20] We will target the 4.5m that have access to the Internet today.

UK online females

Target Audience	1998	1999	2000	2001	2002
UK females aged 20–60 (m)	15.5	15.5	15.5	15.5	15.5
UK online females aged 20–60 (m)	2.3	3.4	4.5	5.4	6.0
% Online	15%	22%	29%	35%	39%

■ *Our target audience is affluent*: The target audience of A, B and C1's are over-represented within the current female Internet population, representing 72% of the current females online, equal to about 3.2m of the 4.5 m female users between 20–60 years of age anticipated in the year 2000.

■ *Females spend on the Internet*: US experience indicates that the female target audience is attractive as 35% of women shop online versus 28% men, and 47% of women spend over $100 per month versus 23% of men.[21]

■ *Female usage of the Internet is likely to grow quickly*: Currently, women represent 39% of Internet users versus 51% of the population.[22] US experience indicates that this male bias is likely to decline fast as the virtual audience normalises.

Years on the Internet by gender (% US total users)[23]

Gender (% total users)	3+ years	2–3 Years	1–2 years	<1 year	Total US population
Male	67%	59%	54%	51%	49%
Female	33%	41%	46%	49%	51%

(b) Positioning: This will be tested among focus groups of our target audience. The lead concept is:

*Inspiration **and** the ability to recreate it in your home*

Customer insight: To making my house a beautiful home I have to read a lot of magazines for inspiration and then visit many shops to find the right products

Inspiredhome benefit: Inspiredhome is the convenient one stop shop for all the inspiration and products you need to make your house beautiful

Reason to believe: that's because it is full of inspirational ideas and you can buy the products to recreate them in your home with the click of a button.

B. Marketing objectives

We will reach over 0.25% of the online population every month in year 1. For perspective this is very conservative as iVillage reaches over 0.5% of the total US online population every month.

Inspiredhome marketing objectives years 1–5

Marketing objectives	Year 1	Year 2	Year 3	Year 4	Year 5
UK females aged 20–60	15.5	15.5	15.5	15.5	15.5
% Online	28%	34%	38%	42%	45%
UK online females aged 20–60	4.34	5.27	5.89	6.51	3.5
Monthly reach online pop (%)	0.25%	0.40%	0.55%	0.70%	0.90%
Annual reach online female pop (%)	11%	18%	25%	32%	41%
Total reach	0.50	0.98	1.51	2.06	3.72

C. Marketing strategy

We will create a customer-insight led Internet portal providing inspiration and the supporting ability to create beautiful homes. This will be significantly preferred versus bricks and mortar stores:

- *The overriding insight*: is that the portal will satisfy the need to provide a total solution covering

  1. expert content (advice, tips, experience and visuals)

  2. satisfy specific customer-led needs, (for example renovating a Georgian house), supported by the ability to search for and purchase products to create the customer's vision of their home.

- *Customer acquisition*: We will acquire customers through highly targeted mechanics. We will ensure that Inspiredhome meets customer needs by linking to a market leading content provider, and providing a broad product offering.

- *Customer retention*: We will retain through the superior services outlined above.

D. Marketing plans

Overall target: Year 1 marketing plan requires 500,000 first time visitors of which 2% will buy. We plan to over-achieve this conservative plan within the budget, through the use of traditional and innovate online marketing activity, leveraging content provider networks, and creating a superlative brand and service which will drive 'word of mouth' growth.

(a) *Customer insight and relationship management*: Inspiredhome will gain and maintain an in-depth understanding of its target audience. We will leverage content providers' skills and experience to provide Web leading material, and in return be able to provide a value-generating link to the content provider as new understanding of the offline customer base is gained through their online behaviour.

(b) *Branding and corporate identity*: Inspiredhome will build a strong, memorable brand which will become recognised as the category Web reference point. We will test for a consumer preferred name, and the potential to create an umbrella name supported by targeted sub-offers.

Current candidates include; Homemaker, Coordinate, Décor 8, Home Sweet Home, Cre8, Indigo, Façade, Workshop. In addition our brand will be supported by and support content provider brands.

(c) *Advertising*: Inspiredhome will advertise to build the brand, drive traffic and revenue. We intend to leverage the offline publications of the content provider as a significant source of targeted advertising. We will also leverage bounty scheme arrangements or share of revenue arrangements with ISPs/other portals that have like target audiences. Inspiredhome will only accept advertising on-site for products and services that it sells. We will utilise product/service advertising related to our core offer as:

1. a negotiation tool with suppliers/service providers
2. to build our sales on high margin items.

(d) *Public relations*: Will be used to position Inspiredhome as the best site on the Internet for our target audience, particularly management of press, and leveraging 'spokespeople'.

(e) *Grass roots/'guerilla' marketing*: Will deliver creative, low cost, informal marketing that drives traffic. For example, use of low cost labour to monitor and promote Inspiredhome in Internet chat rooms.

(f) *Sales promotion*: Will motivate site visitors to register, increase site usage and spend. Linking to the content provider to leverage offline promotions, and events, as well as stand-alone online based activities such as loyalty programmes and vouchers. We will undertake a series of joint ventures with offline publishers to review home related products and services that available for sale through Inspiredhome.

(g) *Product sourcing and supply*: We will develop and source products from the supply market. We will combine buying/negotiating, product category management and editorial skills to ensure we deliver against consumer needs. Our source of products will vary depending on the category.

(h) *Specific action plans*: We will achieve a duplicated reach of 1.5m female visitors. This is significantly greater than the required 500,000 to achieve business plan. For perspective, if we achieve 1,000,000 visits, we will over-achieve year 1 revenue targets by 80%. The marketing plan will be finalised when major portal deals have been completed during the launch phase. We will review all media on a cost per customer basis and test for effectiveness.

Inspiredhome marketing plan year 1

Marketing action plan	Year 1 female visitors	Expected cost
Online advertising/bounty deals[a]	1,000,000	£400,000
Off-line PR/advertising	100,000	£100,000
Magazine advertising[b]	230,000	N/A
Affiliate programme (house and female sites)	250,000	8% revenue reflected in income statement
Total duplicated visitors	1,580,000	£500,000

Notes:
(a) Assumes major bounty deals at a cost of £15 per buyer
(b) From content deal

- *Customer acquisition through strategic partnerships with a content partner*: We will drive customers to our site through strategic partnerships with a major content company. Specifically, our target audience is likely to read offline magazines based on the home. We are in serious discussion with a major UK content provider to acquire their content and customers.

    - *Offline magazine products can be purchased through Inspiredhome*: Offline magazine content will contain product reviews and reader offers in every publication. These will be for sale through Inspiredhome (versus current situation where telephone numbers of stores are given). The magazine company will take equity (or % of revenue), high on-site branding and links to their Web sites with the ability to purchase their magazines.

- *Customer acquisition through strategic partnerships with online businesses*: We will develop relationships with UK portals. Specifically, we will offer a % margin or bounty deal for all sales through these portals. We have assumed a high average cost of £25 per first time purchaser (versus major UK portal norm of £18), when these come via a portal in the marketing plan. We expect 30% of customers/revenue to come via a portal and have assumed that this costs an additional 8% margin points as they arrive via another site. We judge this to be very conservative and expect to over-achieve. However this will be confirmed in early portal relationship development.

- *Celebrity hosts*: We will leverage celebrities at launch to host the design area. If this achieves significant and low cost reach and awareness we will use other celebrities on each intention. In addition we will have guest hosts within chat rooms, recommending creative tips where appropriate. These could include Jane Churchill, Nina Campbell, David Linley and so on. Other illustrative names are:

Intention	Illustrative Celebrity
DIY	Handy Andy
Decorate	Laurence Llewellyn-Bowen
Furnish	David Linley
Garden	Alan Titchmarsh

IV. Business operating model

A. Key strategic partnerships

Inspiredhome is a collection of major partnerships that will be structured on a win/win, lose/lose basis. These partnerships set Inspiredhome apart from the competition as they rapidly give access to customers and suppliers alike.

Partnership strategy

Partnerships	Basis	They bring	We offer
Content provider	Equity	Rich and dynamic content Access to customers	Sell and continually promote magazines % Revenue on magazine products for sale Equity Customer information
Systems integrator	36-month lease	Technology skills	Pure play reference Fees
Venture capitalist	Equity	Capital Start-up guidance	High returns Major partnerships minimising risk
Best employees	Wage/equity options	Experience Commitment	Win/win – lose/lose options Motivating and dynamic environment
Affinity programme relationships	% Revenue/bounty	Access to customers	8% Revenue
Portals	% Revenue/bounty	Access to customers	Bounty per customer (up to £25)
Major UK celebrity	Fees	Access to customers	Fees Build celebrity brand
Retailer Wholesaler Supplier	% Revenue/equity	Products and services	% Revenue (possible equity if one major retailer) Customer information

B. Customer service and fulfilment: Inspiredhome will deliver exceptional customer service.

■ *Payment by preferred channel*: Inspiredhome will offer credit card payment via telephone and the Internet. The importance of telephone ordering is reflected in ValueAmerica.com who take 40% of electrical product orders over the telephone. In addition, research shows a clear preference for telephone ordering versus Internet ordering among large groups of UK customers. Judgmentally this is particularly important for high value items such as furniture. We plan to outsource call centre operations to ensure they are scalable.

Customer preferred payment methods

Preferred method of payment	% Respondents
Callback feature where the site owner calls you to arrange payment details	38
Enter credit card details online	23
Give credit card details over the phone	22
Send credit card details by email	5
Send cheque through post	5

Base: UK WWW users – last four weeks (746)
Q: If you found something that you wanted to buy on the Internet, what would your preferred method of payment be?[24]

■ *Payment by preferred credit/debit card*: Inspiredhome will accept all forms of credit and debit card payment. Credit cards will include, but not be restricted to, those held by UK online shoppers: Visa (78% held by online shoppers), Mastercard (46%), Amex (10%), Access (8%), Diners (3%).

■ *Fulfilment*: Inspiredhome will offer a home delivery service in line with Direct Mail competition for the majority of products. However we will target superiority on product samples (for example wallpapers, tiles). We will outsource all warehousing, call centre, credit, mail order services, pick and pack/returns and fulfilment.

  ■ *Delivery and fulfilment options*: We will rapidly approach operators to ensure we can deliver superb customer service at a cost effective rate. Options include:

   – *Full service third party fulfilment companies*: These offer call centre capability, credit, mail order processing systems, pick and pack capability with returns handling. Of the four largest companies we believe that Cordena (salestrac) and Prolog offer the best service.

- *Large home shopping companies*: We will target large home shopping firms where we can also structure a buying arrangement to increase speed to market. These firms will offer a similar service to third party fulfilment companies, but will also control parcel carriage. Key players include; Express gifts, Grattan, N Brown, Littlewoods (prefer equity stake), Freemans, and GUS.

- *Call centre services and logistics providers*: We may use a call centre service specialist if we agree a fulfilment service with a major logistics company that does not provide it.

    - *Specialist call centre providers*: these are numerous with many new start-ups. The three that have significant home shopping experience include Mediaphone (clients: JC Penney, Drinks Direct, M&S), SSL (clients: overflow for Littlewoods and N Brown), Brann (client: Sainsbury). Others worth considering are Sitel, Teletech and the Call Centre Service who have significant Web clients.

    - *Logistics providers*: We will only target those warehouse and logistics providers that operate a home delivery service to ensure effective accountability. These include Ryder, Hayes, Tibbett and Britten, TNT, Excel and Wincanton. Of particular interest are Hayes who provide two man delivery (for furniture) and Excel who offer furniture delivery for Argos and M&S.

- *Customer contact and order tracking*: To speed launch we will offer telephone tracking of orders. Specifically, a call centre representative will call to thank the customer for the order and confirm the requested delivery time. They will also call all first-time customers to ensure the product has arrived safely, ensuring they are happy with the service, detailing any future promotional rewards for their custom. We will implement online order tracking within the phased technology implementation plan.

- *The unexpected extra touch*: We aim for all our customers to be delighted with what they receive. We will always have an extra service offering versus bricks and mortar stores. Illustrative examples are:

1. a free paintbrush with sample paint pots
2. larger samples of wallpaper and fabric than they are used to

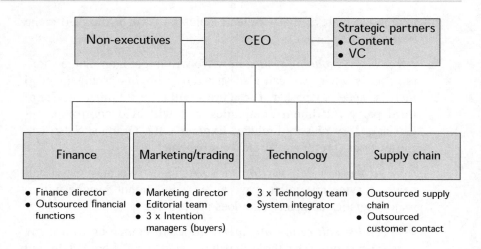

Figure 12.5   The organisation

3. loyalty rewards
4. unprompted returned money where we have found major competitors offering the same product cheaper as a standard price.

C. Organisational plans

The launch organisation will ensure that all key work areas have Board responsibility. We will outsource specialist skills to ensure a flexible and scalable team (see Figure 12.5).

D. Financial processing and the finance function

We will outsource all routine accounting and transaction processing operations to a recognised provider of accounting services such as BDO Stoy Hayward. Such operations will encompass:

- Payroll
- Accounts payable
- Accounts receivable
- Asset and inventory accounting
- Statutory and management reporting.

Initially, cash management and treasury functions will be handled internally by the Finance Director. Note that the financial model estimates the cost based on the expected staff complement required to address the workload, but this cost will be incurred as a monthly outsource charge from the accounting service provider.

V. Proven technical model

A. Guiding principles

Our technological architecture will be proven in the market. Specifically it will be:

- *Full time*: $24 \times 7 \times 365$, with service level contracts with providers.

- *Fast and responsive*: Match usage requirements to customer capability – in 1999/2000, people who use a 28.8kbps modem will be able to download information within 5–15 seconds.

- *Secure and private*: We will use customer-level industry standard security (data encryption and secure sockets layer technology). Additional security and monitoring will be enabled on the site to counter 'extraordinary' activities.

- *Simple to use and navigate*: The novice user will find it easy to use.

- *Scalable*: It will grow with us and be able to handle large fluctuations in demand, particularly around Christmas.

- *Responsive to market*: We will be able to respond quickly to requirements to change content or presentation.

- *Dynamic*: We will utilise technology to allow the site to dynamically reconfigure to meet users needs.

- *Planned commercial roadmap*: We will balance technological capability with commercial gain, and manage this process over time.

- *Cost effective*: We will phase in elements of the technology to manage costs.

- *Personalisation*: Phased introduction of personalisation, as a managed commercial process.

- *Hosting*: We will outsource hosting to proven partner, with a well negotiated service contract.

- *Enable chat*: This can be in house (for example using Microsoft chat) or outsourced to a chat host.

- *Enable advertising*: insertion and affiliate partner display.

- *Innovative technology*: We will develop and introduce new and captivating technologies, including visualisation, decoration tools, and new customer channels. We will leverage appropriate technologies as they reach the market. These will be run as independently costed and managed modules.

- *Reassurance*: We will seek and implement accreditations, registrations and so on that establish a level of trust and comfort with customers, and comply with legislation.

B. Site functions

(a) Site map: The site map (see Figure 12.6) details the required capabilities.

(b) Supporting functions: To make possible the front office capabilities, three supporting functions will be necessary:

- Support customer and content
- Support intentions
- Support enterprise.

Components of each function are: (see Figure 12.7).

- *Support customer and content*

  Order management
  - Fulfilment and shipping
  - Interfaces with suppliers (phased in over time)

  Customer service
  - Return handling, order inquiries, customer comments
  - Customer and supplier support

  Payment processing
  - Handle credit card payments
  - Handle vendor payments
  - Batch mode interfaces to external parties

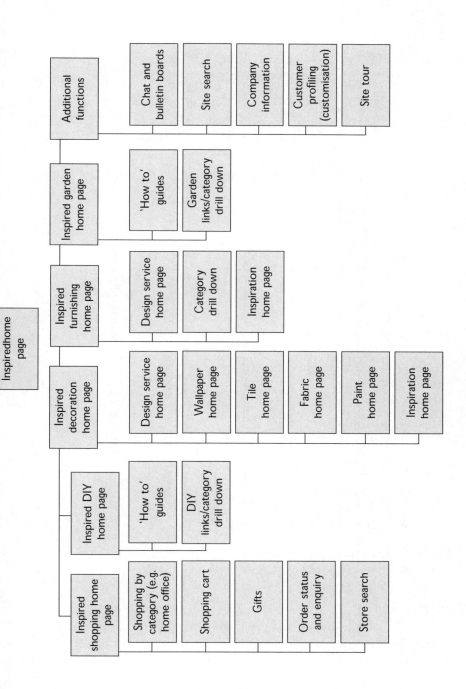

Figure 12.6 Site map

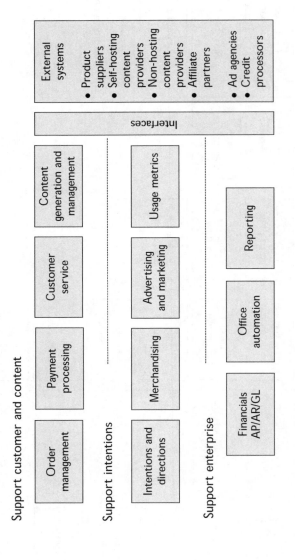

Figure 12.7 Supporting functions

Content generation and management
- Content editing and upload facilities
- Proof and publishing features
- Maintenance and integration of outside content
- Integrated content, template and management tools

- *Support intentions*

Intentions and direction
- Coordination of content and merchandise tie-ins
- Reports of customer profiles, purchasing patterns

Merchandising
- Item selection and maintenance
- Supplier compliance
- Management tools, reports

Advertising and marketing
- Outbound advertising only
- Customer acquisition
- Functions generally supported by office automation tools
- Customer profile aggregation

Usage metrics
- Order reporting.

- *Support enterprise*

Financials
- Accounts payable/receivable, general ledger
- Small business package or outsource

Office automation
- General office services include phone, Internet connectivity, and dial-up support as well as word processing, spreadsheet, and so on.
- Use off the shelf components. Outsource install

Reporting
- Performance reporting.

C. Application architecture blueprint

Based on the definition of the front office and back office components, this details the application architecture blueprint (see Figure 12.8).

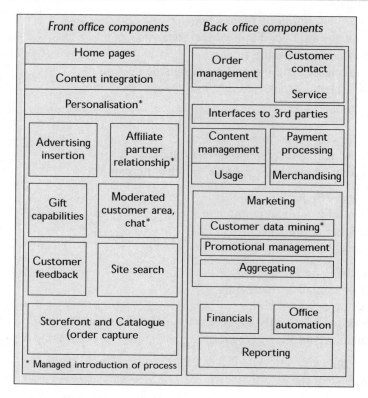

Figure 12.8   Application architecture blueprint

VI. Positive financial model

A. Financial arrangements

Venture capital funds of £4.5m in common stock for a 30% ownership will take the firm from start-up end of year 1.

B. Use proceeds

The money will be used to set up and dominate the UK Internet markets for decoration and furniture products. Specifically:

- £2.0m as technology
- £1.0m as people

- £1.5m as marketing
- £0.5m as inventory.

Financial arrangements

Partners	Investment	Equity
Founder	• £60k excluding loss of earnings of £440k during 3-year period	30%
Angel investors	• Est. £250k	10%
Venture capital	• £4,500k	30%
Content provider	• Access to customers via major home magazines • Content provided	15%
Employees	• Up to £200k and lower salaries	15%

C. Exit strategy for investors

Public offering: We will actively and rapidly seek an Initial Public Offering within 18 months to realise the value of our business and drive it forwards.

Sale: We will be happy to look at a sale where it reflects the true price of the business. This is especially so if the sale brings a strategic asset to the business to fuel its future growth and multiply future returns. Illustrative purchasers are:

- A major portal with access to many customers (for example Freeserve, AOL, Amazon UK deal). This will enable them to:

  1. increase their customer loyalty by offering a leading vertical portal
  2. take a share of future revenues. A recent example is Freeserve's Baby World deal.

- A US site (for example, Good Home, Furniture.com) wishing to globalise its offer by entering the UK market as a foothold to Europe. A recent example is Amazon and its book retailer deal.

- A retailer/A content provider (for example. IPC) may purchase the business to build Internet content scale and leverage their off line assets. A recent example is the Associated Newspaper purchase of 50% of Zoom.co.uk.

D. Financial projections

Income statement

	Launch 6 months	Year 1	Year 2	Year 3	Year 4	Year 5
Revenues						
Product revenue (inc. shipping)	–	1,602,086	9,455,656	29,123,272	66,608,179	92,061,043
Shopping intention – referral fees	–	250,000	375,000	500,000	750,000	1,000,000
	–	1,852,086	9,830,656	29,623,272	67,358,179	93,061,043
Cost of revenues (COGS)						
Product offering	–	1,135,216	6,674,186	20,386,290	46,625,725	64,442,730
Warehousing and eFulfilment (7% revenue)	–	112,146	661,896	2,038,629	4,662,573	6,444,273
	–	1,247,362	7,336,082	22,424,919	51,288,298	70,887,003
Gross profit	–	604,724	2,494,574	7,198,353	16,069,881	22,174,040
Gross profit %		32.7%	25.4%	24.3%	23.9%	23.8%
Product margin %		29.1%	29.4%	30.0%	30.0%	30.0%
Operating expenses						
Marketing costs	–	500,000	750,000	1,000,000	1,000,000	1,000,000
Customer referrals (portals)	–	38,450	226,936	698,959	1,598,596	2,209,465
Credit card fees (2.5% revenues)	–	40,052	236,391	728,082	1,665,204	2,301,526
Marketing and sales	–	578,502	1,213,327	2,427,040	4,263,801	5,510,991
Content staff	39,000	81,900	128,993	135,442	189,619	199,100
Hardware and systems integration	320,167	640,333	640,333	320,167		
Technology staff	39,000	122,850	128,993	225,737	237,024	248,875
Design	50,000	65,000	65,000	65,000	65,000	65,000
Hosting	–	67,000	68,000	68,000	68,000	68,000
Product development	448,167	977,083	1,031,318	814,346	559,643	580,975
Corporate infrastructure	517,650	936,275	1,043,985	1,258,142	1,482,765	1,607,879
Stockholding costs	–	50,056	126,505	193,013	233,129	277,671
Customer service/ order taking	–	114,660	391,277	853,285	1,227,783	836,220
General and administration	517,650	1,100,991	1,561,767	2,304,440	2,943,676	2,721,770
Selling, general and administrative expenses	965,817	2,656,577	3,806,413	5,545,826	7,767,120	8,813,736
EBITDA	(965,817)	(2,051,853)	(1,311,839)	1,652,527	8,302,761	13,360,304
Cumulative EBITDA	(965,817)	(3,017,670)	(4,329,508)	(2,676,982)	5,625,780	18,986,084
Depreciation				333,000	1,000,000	1,666,667
Tax					1,687,734	5,695,825
Net gain (loss)	(965,817)	(2,051,853)	(1,311,839)	1,319,194	5,615,028	5,997,812
Cumulative net gain (loss)	(965,817)	(3,017,670)	(4,329,508)	(3,010,315)	2,604,713	8,602,525

Summary income statement

	Launch 6 months	2000 (£)	2001 (£)	2002 (£)	2003 (£)	2004 (£)
Revenue	0	1,852,086	9,830,656	29,623,272	67,358,179	93,061,043
COGS	0	1,247,362	7,336,082	22,424,919	51,288,298	70,887,003
Gross profit	0	604,724	2,494,574	7,198,353	16,069,881	22,174,040
Operating expenses	965,817	2,656,577	3,806,413	5,545,826	7,767,120	8,813,736
Net operating gain (loss)	(965,817)	(2,051,853)	(1,311,839)	1,652,527	8,302,761	13,360,304

Balance Sheet

Period ending	Launch 6 months	Year 1	Year 2	Year 3	Year 4	Year 5
Assets						
Current assets						
Cash and cash equivalents	500,000	500,000	500,000	845,798	7,515,343	14,127,054
Accounts receivable (1)	–	41,128	120,464	298,249	638,401	878,286
Inventories		500,564	764,486	1,165,643	1,165,643	1,611,068
Total current assets	500,000	1,041,692	1,384,950	2,309,690	9,319,388	16,616,409
Property and equipment, net	–	–	–	1,666,667	2,666,667	3,000,000
Total assets	500,000	1,041,692	1,384,950	3,976,357	11,986,055	19,616,409
Liabilities						
Current liabilities						
Accounts payable (2)	112,042	227,037	759,783	2,019,939	4,403,995	6,038,998
Accrued expenses	13,875	20,213	27,011	39,070	49,684	47,222
Total current liabilities	125,917	247,250	786,795	2,059,009	4,453,679	6,086,221
Term note/subordinated debt	–	–	–	–	–	–
Total long-term liabilities	–	–	–	–	–	–
Equity						
Initial equity investment	450,000	450,000	450,000	450,000	450,000	450,000
Venture capital equity	889,900	3,362,112	4,477,663	4,477,663	4,477,663	4,477,663
Beginning retained earnings	–	(965,817)	(3,017,670)	(4,329,508)	(3,010,315)	2,604,713
– Net income	(965,817)	(2,051,853)	(1,311,839)	1,319,194	5,615,028	5,997,812
Ending retained earnings	(965,817)	(3,017,670)	(4,329,508)	(3,010,315)	2,604,713	8,602,525
Total equity (deficiency)	374,083	794,443	598,155	1,917,349	7,532,376	13,530,188
Total liabilities and stakeholders' equity	500,000	1,041,692	1,384,950	3,976,357	11,986,055	19,616,409

(a) Revenue generation assumptions: We will generate revenue predominantly from sales margin.

- *Products*: We will take a margin on all products sold. We will charge a referral fee or commission on products purchased via an alliance partner. We plan to own 30% of gross revenues in inventory.

- *Network fees*: We will charge alliance partners fees for managing our network.

- *Consumer data*: We will offer alliance partners individual consumer data where customers are happy to enable this to happen. Data will be also be aggregated for sale. We will consider this within year 2, to avoid a diversion of management attention from our core eCommerce offering.

- *Advertising*: We will advertise our own products and services. We will not sell advertising on the web site to third parties. This reflects the fact that:

  1. it is strategically wrong to drive people from your site
  2. it would account for only 1–3% of revenue
  3. it would be a diversion from management attention.

- *Supplier funding*: We will request that suppliers fund the listing of products and services, own inventory until sold and contribute to advertising costs. Our ability to do this will strengthen with a major content provider/retail relationship.

(b) Cost detail:

- *Cost of goods*: the two key elements of cost of goods are the actual cost of the goods supplied (on average 70% of product revenue as discussed in the previous paragraph) and warehousing and fulfilment costs which are estimated at 7% of revenue.

- *Fulfilment and supply chain costs*: cost of goods includes a provision of 7% of product revenue to cover the cost of outsourced warehousing and fulfilment operations. In addition, general and administrative costs include a further provision for stock shrinkage and obsolescence of 10% of average stock balances per annum.

- *Technology costs*: initial establishment of the site and trading environment including hardware, software and systems integration will cost an estimated £1.9m. We will meet this expenditure by means of a three-year lease arrangement (for example, with Hewlett Packard).

In addition to the start-up costs, we will establish a small in-house technology team in support of the technology director responsible for ongoing site design and development. At the end of year 2, we will embark on a major programme of capital expenditure (£6m over three years) to upgrade the site and enhance the Inspiredhome retail experience.

- *Marketing costs*: Marketing costs reflect two key routes to market – external spend of £500k increasing by year 3 to £1,000k (not including advertising provided by content partner) and bounty or referral deals with portal partner referring customers to the Inspired-home site (the assumption here is that 30% of revenue is received by this route and referral deals average 8% of referred revenue).

- *General and administration costs*: Inspiredhome will keep fixed establishment costs to a minimum through creative use of outsourcing arrangements. Thus finance and accounting services, legal and other professional services will be provided by outsource partners. General and Administrative costs also include the costs of the management team and the commercial (and buying) team, limited executive support, a small office and associated office equipment.

(e) Company valuation: High market values are being driven to areas of Internet innovation. The level of valuation multiple is dependent of the type of business. Inspiredhome, as a vertical portal with a retail commerce revenue stream could expect to be valued on a multiple of revenues of between 5 and 100. The valuations in the financial model assume an IPO (or other exit) at the end of year 2 at a prudent multiple of ten times year 2 revenues. Additionally, the valuation takes the net present value of the IPO proceeds (at a discount rate of 15%) and deducts the net cash outflow to that point.

This prudent view gives a net present value of the investment of over £60m (an actual valuation of almost £90m at that point in time). Subject to confirmation of the division of equity, this could represent a return of 11 times the original venture capital investment in just over two years. Even an exceptionally cautious multiple of revenue valuation of five times would yield high returns to the venture capitalist.

If the valuation were to achieve a revenue multiple of 20 (still less than the average for all Internet IPOs today) then the net present value of the investment would be over £100m.

VII. Critical risks and problems

Inspiredhome.com has plans in place to address all key business risks.

(a) Fulfilment arrangements may dramatically change the business model:
Our going-in assumption is that we will own inventory to the value of
30% gross revenue. The accuracy of this assumption will be qualified
early on in our discussions with suppliers. For other items we plan
stock to:

- be shipped to a central distribution point, repackaged and sent on to
the customer
- be sent direct to the customer from the supplier.

Our third party will handle our distribution warehouse and we will
outsource all delivery. We will however hold stock of product where it
offers a significant point of difference in the market.

(b) We are beaten to launch by a major competitor: We are not aware of
any initiative of this nature over and above those described in the
competitive review. To mitigate this risk we will:

- Ensure we take the space first:

  - moving at 'eSpeed' to be first to market in the UK
  - ensuring that our offering is competitive to all US comparables
  - spending a high % of our revenue on marketing spend to ensure
  fast success
  - calling major suppliers to ensure no current movements in the
  market
  - rolling out across Europe as soon as concept is launched in UK.

(c) Dependence on key management: The founder will complete a
corporate will on agreement of financing to clarify what happens in the
event of his death.

(d) Internet stocks decline from current revenue multiples: This has been
taken into account in the Investment returns, exit strategy and business
model approach. Specifically:

- *Investment returns*: are based on a ten times revenue multiple,
which is significantly lower than current market multiples which
range from 5–100 times. For perspective, average retail eCommerce
sites are currently achieving 23 times revenue.[25]

■ *Exit strategies*: IPO is only one exit strategy. Others include purchase by existing bricks and mortar businesses to speed entry into the Internet channel, and purchase by major portals desiring vertically integrated sites such as Inspiredhome.com to build customer loyalty.

■ *Business model*: We will always focus on delivering dramatic revenue growth, to rapidly build the support for future market valuations.

Notes

1. Magazines.co.uk
2. *Mintel, *Home Decoration and Leisure Intelligence*, June 1998
3. Mediametrix.com
4. Redherring.com, July 1999
5. *Yahoo Finance*, 14 May 1999
6. IDC 'Internet Usage and Commerce in Western Europe, 1997–2002,' December 1998
7. ibid.
8. For perspective this figure is conservative, 15%/1.4m people shopped in the last four weeks in the UK (June 1999, *NOP Research*, August 1999)
9. CDB Research and Consulting, August 1998
10. *Yahoo Finance*, 14 May 1999
11. *Internet Overview Update*, Morgan Stanley Dean Witter, 6 May 1999; Worldscope Database, *Global Researcher*, June 1999 (non-Internet companies)
12. Home Decoration, *Leisure Intelligence*, June 1998
13. *Mintel Retail Intelligence, *Furniture Retailing*, February 1999
14. *Mintel Retail Intelligence, *Furniture Retailing*, February 1999
15. BMRB/Mintel*
16. *Mintel Retail Intelligence, *Furniture Retailing*, February 1999
17. ibid.
18. ibid.
19. *Red Herring*, August 1999
20. *NOP Research*, August 1999
21. *CDB Research and Consulting*, August 1998
22. *NOP Research*, August 1999
23. *Goldman Sachs Investment Research*, July 1999, original data from Forrester Research, Inc
24. *NOP Research*, August 1999
25. *Yahoo Finance*, May 1999

* Mintel can be contacted by telephone on 020 7606 4533 or at www.mintel.com

INDEX

liability for content 256–7
links 112
Webvan 281
weddings, websites 63–4, 65, 70
Welles, Terri 243–4
wholesalers/distributors, traditional
  roles 27–8
Wincanton 357
Windows CE 225
Wireless Application Environment
  (WAE) 209
Wireless Application Protocol (WAP)
  206–8
  business roles 214–20
  future 221, 226–9
  geographic snapshot 222–4
  glossary 231–2
  scepticism 225–6
  services 212–14
  site providers 217–18
  standards 208–11
  web sites 230–1
wireless datacommunications 205–6
Wireless Datagram Protocol 211
Wireless Markup Language (WML)
  209, 211, 227
Wireless Session Layer 209
Wireless Transaction Protocol (WTP)
  209

Wireless Transport Layer Security
  (WTLS) 209, 211
WML Script 209, 227
women, target audience 350–1
women.com 325
work permits 11
World Wide Web 163
WorldPay 160

X

XLL 174
XML 172–4, 209, 225
  impact 174–9
XML.org 175, 179
XSL 173, 176

Y

Yahoo! 34, 42, 216
Yahoo.com 109

Z

Zagat Survey 25
Zoom.co.uk 365